STALIN AND THE SOVIET UNION

STEPHEN J. LEE

ROUTLEDGE

London and New York

First published 1999 by Routledge
11 New Fetter Lane, London EC4P 4EE

Simultaneously published in the USA and Canada
by Routledge
29 West 35th Street, New York, NY 10001

Routledge is an imprint of the Taylor & Francis Group

© 1999 Stephen J. Lee

Typeset in Grotesque and Perpetua
by Keystroke, Jacaranda Lodge, Wolverhampton
Printed and bound in Great Britain by Clays Ltd, St Ives plc

British Library Cataloguing in Publication Data
A catalogue record for this book is available from the British Library

Library of Congress Cataloging in Publication Data
Lee, Stephen J.
    Stalin and the Soviet Union / Stephen J. Lee.
        p.   cm.   -- (Questions and analysis in history)
    Includes bibliographical references and index.
    ISBN 0-415-18573-4 (pbk.)
        1. Stalin, Joseph, 1879-1953. 2. Heads of state--Soviet Union--
Biography. 3. Soviet Union--Politics and government--1917-1936.
4. Soviet Union--Politics and government--1936-1953. I. Title.
II. Series.
DK268.S8L37   1999
947.084'2'092--dc21
    [B]   99-11755 CIP

ISBN 0-415-18573-4

CONTENTS

SERIES PREFACE

Most history textbooks now aim to provide the student with interpretation, and many also cover the historiography of a topic. Some include a selection of sources.

So far, however, there have been few attempts to combine *all* the skills needed by the history student. Interpretation is usually found within an overall narrative framework and it is often difficult to separate out the two for essay purposes. Where sources are included, there is rarely any guidance as to how to answer the questions on them.

The Questions and Analysis series is therefore based on the belief that another approach should be added to those which already exist. It has two main aims.

The first is to separate narrative from interpretation so that the latter is no longer diluted by the former. Each chapter starts with a background narrative section containing essential information. This material is then used in a section focusing on analysis through a specific question. The main purpose of this is to help to tighten up essay technique.

The second aim is to provide a comprehensive range of sources for each of the issues covered. The questions are of the type which appear on examination papers, and some have worked answers to demonstrate the techniques required.

The chapters may be approached in different ways. The background narratives can be read first to provide an overall perspective, followed by the analyses and then the sources. The alternative method is to work through all the components of each chapter before going on to the next.

ACKNOWLEDGEMENTS

Author and publisher are grateful to the following for permission to reproduce copyright material.

T.H. Rigby, ed.: *Stalin* (Prentice-Hall, 1966): 1A, 1H, 4B, 7B; L. Fischer: *Men and Politics: An Autobiography* (Jonathan Cape, 1941): 1C; J.V. Stalin: *Works, vol. X* (Progress Publishers, 1955): 1B; D.M. Cole: *Joseph Stalin, Man of Steel* (Rich and Cowan, 1942): 1D; G.F. Alexandrov et al.: *Joseph Stalin: A Short Biography* (Moscow 1947): 1E; L. Trotsky: *Stalin: An Appraisal of the Man and His Influence*, ed. and trans. by C. Malamuth (Hollis and Carter, 1947): 1F; *The Anti-Stalin Campaign and International Communism: A Selection of Documents*, ed. by the Russian Institute, Columbia University (Columbia University Press, 1956): 1G, 2C; R. Wolfson: *Years of Change* (Hodder and Stoughton, 1978): 3A; M. Lynch: *Stalin and Khrushchev: The USSR 1924–1964* (Hodder and Stoughton, 1990): 3B; Sidney and Beatrice Webb: *Soviet Communism: A New Civilisation* (Longman, Green and Co., 1935): 3C, 4D; Sir William Citrine: *I Search for Truth in Russia* (Routledge, 1938): 3E; E. Zaleski: *Stalinist Planning for Economic Growth 1932–1952* (Macmillan, 1960): 3F; Andrew Smith: *I Was a Soviet Worker* (Robert Hale, 1937): 3G; J. Scott: *Behind the Urals* (Secker and Warburg, 1942): 3H; Y. Kukushkin: *History of the USSR* (Progress Publishers, 1981): 3I; R.W. Thurston: *Life and Terror in Stalin's Russia* (Yale University Press, 1996): 2A; A. Rybakov: *Children of the Arbat* (Random Century Group; Little, Brown & Company Publishers, 1989): 2B; J. Arch Getty and Roberta T. Manning (eds): *Stalinist Terror: New Perspectives* (Cambridge University Press, 1993): 2D; Fitzroy MacLean: *Eastern Approaches* (Jonathan Cape Ltd, 1951): 2E; J. Laver (ed.): *Russia 1914–1941* (Hodder and Stoughton, 1991): 2F, 2G, 4A; R.C. Tucker and S.F. Cohen (eds): *The Great Purge Trial* (Grosset & Dunlop, 1965): 2H; N. Mandelstam: *Hope Against Hope* (Collins, Harvill, 1971): 4C; Victor Kravchenko: *I Chose Freedom: The Personal and Political Life of a Soviet Official* (Robert Hale, 1947): 3D; J. Degras (ed.): *Soviet Documents on Foreign Policy*, vol. III (Royal Institute of International Affairs, 1953): 5A, 5B; M. Lynch: *Stalin and Khrushchev: The USSR, 1924–64* (Hodder and Stoughton, 1990): 5C, 5D; G. Roberts: *The Soviet Union and the Origins of the Second World War* (Macmillan, 1995): 6B, 6C, 6D; *Soviet Foreign Policy during the Patriotic War: Documents and Materials*, vol. 1 (Hutchinson, n.d.): 6E; J.V. Stalin: *On the Great Patriotic War of the Soviet Union* (Hutchinson, 1945): 6F; W.L. White: *Report on the Russians* (Harcourt Brace Jovanovich Inc, 1945, 1973): 6H; Heinz Guderian: *Panzer Leader* (Michael Joseph, 1952): 6I; N.A. Voznesensky: *The Economy of the USSR during World War II* (Public Affairs Press, 1948): 7A; J. Laver: *The USSR 1945–1990* (Hodder and Stoughton, 1991): 7C; N. Khrushchev: *Khrushchev Remembers* (André Deutsch, 1971): 7D; H. Commager: *Documents of American History*, 9th edition (Prentice-Hall, 1973): 7E; *A History of Soviet Foreign Policy 1945–70* (Progress Publishing, 1973): 7F.

For illustrations used, acknowledgements are due to the following: *Evening Standard*: 6A; Imperial War Museum: 6G.

1

STALIN'S RISE AND RULE

BACKGROUND NARRATIVE

At the time of Lenin's death in 1924, Stalin was forty-five. He had become a member of the Central Committee of the Bolshevik Party in 1912 and arrived in Petrograd in February 1917 after a period of enforced exile in Siberia. He played only a minor role in the October Revolution and a relatively inconspicuous part in the Civil War. He did, however, spend the period between 1917 and 1924 building up his position within government and the Party. By the time of Lenin's death he had accumulated the posts of People's Commissar for Nationalities in 1917, liaison official between the Politburo and the Orgburo in 1919 and General Secretary of the Party in 1922. These roles gave him a greater overview than was possessed by anyone else: the implications are examined in Analysis (1).

This did not mean that Stalin would automatically become Lenin's successor. Indeed, his ambitions incurred Lenin's distrust to the extent that, in his Political Testament, Lenin warned against Stalin and, in a codicil added in January 1923, recommended his removal from the post of General Secretary. However, Lenin died before any further action could be taken and Stalin was soon able to put himself forward as one of the contenders for the succession.

At first Stalin was seen by other Bolsheviks as less of a threat than Trotsky who, it was thought, might use his influence with the army to introduce a military dictatorship. Hence Kamenev and Zinoviev joined with Stalin in a power-sharing triumvirate. This was committed to pursuing a policy of 'Socialism in One Country', based at this stage on giving priority to the cautious pursuit of economic recovery within Russia through the continuation of the New Economic Policy (NEP), which had been started by Lenin in 1921. Ranged against this approach was the more radical Permanent Revolution favoured by Trotsky. This incorporated proposals for revolution abroad and radicalism at home – including rapid industrialisation and the introduction of collective farming. These views failed to gain widespread acceptance and Trotsky was increasingly marginalised during the course of 1925.

Then, between 1925 and 1927, Stalin became involved in a conflict with Kamenev and Zinoviev, who now considered Trotsky a lesser threat and therefore lined up with him to form the 'Left Opposition'. Stalin promptly aligned with the Party's 'Rightists', especially Bukharin, Rykov and Tomsky. This alliance secured the expulsion of Trotsky, Kamenev and Zinoviev from the Party. During the course of 1929, the Rightists were, in turn, attacked, as Stalin removed Bukharin, Rykov and Tomsky. By the end of 1929 Stalin's position as leader was secure. Bukharin warned that 'Stalin will strangle us. He is an unprincipled intriguer who subordinates everything to his lust for power.'

Meanwhile, Stalin had also changed the emphasis of his policy. Socialism in One Country came to mean the abandonment of the moderate NEP and the pursuit of a more radical programme of collectivisation and rapid industrialisation. In effect Stalin was now implementing ideas similar to those of Trotsky – although without the connection with Permanent Revolution.

Analysis (1) explains the reasons for the rapid shifts and changes that helped place Stalin in power, while Analysis (2) considers what type of rule Stalin actually established.

ANALYSIS (1): WHY DID STALIN SUCCEED LENIN?

Stalin's rise to power between1924, when he appeared to have been ruled out of the succession by Lenin's codicil, and 1929, when he had eliminated all credible alternatives, has inevitably attracted a wide range of explanations. These need not necessarily be exclusive of each other: indeed, a combination is more likely to reflect the complexity of the background and issues involved.

A general starting point is the cyclical pattern that has frequently been applied to revolutions. Between 1793 and 1794, for example, the French Revolution had experienced a radical phase, often known as the Reign of Terror. This had been sharply reversed by the *coup d'état* of Thermidor, in which the policies and leadership swung to the right, eventually to be taken over by the military under Napoleon Bonaparte. By 1802 the French Republic had been converted into the personalised rule of Napoleon.

The Bolsheviks drew lessons from this pattern that helped shape future events. One of the main advantages that Stalin had was that he was seen as a much safer alternative to Trotsky. The latter was associated by many with a possible Bonapartist threat, largely because of the way in which he had built up the Red Army during the Civil War between 1918 and 1921. Because of this deterministic belief that revolutionary patterns might repeat themselves, Trotsky was feared and isolated which, ironically, enabled Stalin to emerge. In exile during the 1930s, Trotsky redefined the lessons of history by associating Stalin with the Thermidorian reaction and with the slide towards Bonapartism – by which time the damage had already been done. The lessons of history differ according to the power of those who interpret them. The Bolsheviks, by trying to avoid repeating one mistake, merely committed another.

What made Stalin appear historically 'safe' to the Bolsheviks was the general perception of him at the time. He was considered pedestrian: Trotsky referred to him as 'the Party's most eminent mediocrity'. He certainly lacked Trotsky's intellectual ability, had no contacts with European culture and spoke no European language apart from Russian. These points, however, worked to Stalin's advantage. He was considered to be safer than Trotsky, who was clearly influenced by contacts with Western Europe. For this reason, Stalin's obvious Slavic influences were advantageous, particularly since the failure of Trotsky's plans for revolution elsewhere in Europe boosted the credibility of Stalin's emphasis on isolationism. Trotsky was condemned in a Party Central Committee Resolution in January 1925 for 'a falsification of communism in the spirit of approximation to "European" patterns of pseudo-Marxism'. (1) Trotsky was also considered to be intolerably arrogant by his colleagues, a perception that blinkered all the other leaders to the even greater dangers of his underestimated rival.

For beneath Stalin's bland and grey exterior was a singularly ruthless and opportunist character. While posing as a moderate, he waited for the opportunity to attack other candidates for the leadership – first Zinoviev and Kamenev, then Bukharin. Historians have remained in agreement about Stalin's attributes here. Martin McCauley's view is typical: 'He was a very skilful politician who had a superb grasp of tactics, could predict behaviour extremely well and had an unerring eye for personal weaknesses.' (2) In particular, he was able to capitalise on Bukharin's inability to convert his plausible economic theory into a credible programme, on Kamenev's lack of vision and on Zinoviev's organisational weakness. Stalin, by contrast, showed consistent skills in grouping around him an alternative set of allies – men like Kalinin, Kuibyshev, Molotov and Voroshilov.

Particularly important in Stalin's rise was his manipulation of the central organs of the Communist Party. The process was mutually reinforcing. As General Secretary in 1922, Stalin controlled the Party organisation and the promotion of its leading members. They, in turn, came to support him against his potential rivals. The Communist Party was officially a democratic institution, in which the local parties elected the central Party Congress which, in turn, produced the membership of the Central Committee. The Central Committee then elected the Politburo, the key decision-making body. The membership of the local parties was determined by the Secretariat, which was, from 1922, under Stalin's control. Over a period of time, therefore, Stalin's supporters gradually moved into the upper levels of the Party. They were given the added incentive of filling the vacancies of those removed above them – who were usually Stalin's main rivals.

This Party base enabled Stalin to outmanoeuvre his rivals at all stages. It also meant that he was consistently more secure than Trotsky. At first sight this seems odd. Trotsky had, after all, had a powerful military base. As Commissar for War, he had developed and expanded the Red Army in defeating the threats from the Whites. He was also renowned for his powers of oratory, for his administrative abilities and for his skill in mobilising the limited resources of Bolshevik Russia at the time of its greatest peril. For these reasons Trotsky has been referred to as 'the dynamo of the militarised Bolshevik state'. (3) But this apparent strength was also a major source of weakness. Trotsky was essentially a man of the state, which had, of course, become subject to the Party – over which Stalin had consolidated his position. Hence Stalin controlled the methods by which Trotsky could be outmanoeuvred. Trotsky, admittedly, had control over the means by which Stalin could be overthrown but, for ideological reasons, this was too strong a measure to use. Yet, because he had this potential power, other Bolshevik leaders were persuaded that Trotsky posed a Bonapartist threat and therefore supported Stalin.

But even this would have had limited effect if he had not been assisted by objective circumstances, the most important of which was the threat of the impending collapse of Bolshevism into chaos, to which two main factors contributed. The first of these was the failure of revolution abroad. Trotsky's reputation had been closely tied to the spread of communism in Europe. But the opportunities for this had all disappeared by 1919. The Spartacists failed to seize power in Germany, while the Bela Kun regime was overthrown in Hungary in under a hundred days. The benefit to Stalin was enormous. According to Colletti, 'The first rung of the ladder which was to carry Stalin to power was supplied by the Social-Democratic leaders who in January 1919 murdered Rosa Luxemburg and Karl Liebknecht . . . The remaining rungs were supplied by the reactionary wave which subsequently swept Europe.' (4) Against this Stalin could project a solid, traditionally Slavic appeal that was more in keeping with his emphasis on Socialism in One Country.

The second factor favouring Stalin was the insecurity of Bolshevik economic policies. The two strategies proposed for the 1920s appeared to be alarmingly antagonistic. On the one hand was the planned retreat of the NEP – what Lenin described as 'one step forward, two steps backward'. Bukharin interpreted this as meaning that the economy should now progress at the pace of 'the peasant's slowest nag'. On the other hand, Trotsky and the Leftists argued for increasing the pace of industrialisation to implement socialism. Russia was therefore caught up in a conflict involving a new peasantry, which benefited from a revived capitalism allowed by the NEP, and the urban workers who had more to gain from accelerated socialism. Stalin was actually one of the few leading Bolsheviks who were able to make the necessary adjustments between these extremes, being adaptable to the conditions of the time. The early 1920s favoured the NEP and the Rightists, whereas the procurement crisis of 1927 demonstrated that the NEP was no longer working and hence needed a radical rethink. His struggle against Bukharin, Rykov and Tomsky was therefore seen by many at the time as a balanced reaction to a policy that had failed by all objective criteria. This may or may not have been true, but the important factor is that the majority of the Party thought this way. They also considered that they had good grounds for supporting the leader to whom many owed their places. Stalin therefore confirmed support for his position by reading correctly the signs of the economic times. A recent view is that 'Machine politics alone did not account for Stalin's triumph'; rather 'the salient political fact' of 1928–9 was 'a growing climate of high party opinion'. (5) Stalin's ability to bend like a reed therefore owed much to the prevailing wind of circumstances.

One final issue needs careful analysis. The rise of Stalin can be seen too much as the calculation of a supremely rational Party machine taking advantage of an efficient dictatorship already established by Lenin. What we have already seen *might* point in this direction. Or the reverse could apply. The revolution had experienced an emergency in the form of the Civil War, which had created widespread chaos. Policies and organisations were thrown into the melting pot. Stalin was an average politician by normal criteria but his rather basic skills were enhanced by these circumstances. He succeeded not in producing order overall but in controlling particular pressure points. Trotsky was right about Stalin's ability but wrong about the situation that allowed the latter to prevail. The situation in Russia favoured the pragmatist, who had built up his base within the Party. This had been made possible by the use of certain skills that had been misinterpreted – part of a more general political enslavement to the 'lessons' of history.

Questions

1. Was Trotsky's description of Stalin as 'the Party's most eminent mediocrity' a true one?
2. Why, against Lenin's express wishes, did Stalin assume the succession?

ANALYSIS (2): WHAT SORT OF DICTATOR WAS STALIN BETWEEN 1929 AND 1941?

Interpretations of Stalin are beginning to change. This is for two main reasons. The first is that historians have already done much to revise earlier views about Hitler and Nazi Germany. It was always likely that Stalin would be next in line for their attention. Second, the collapse of the Soviet Union in 1991 released a considerable amount of material not previously seen and also altered many earlier conceptions about the type of regime Stalin had established. There are now two main images of Stalin and students have never had a greater opportunity to develop their own interpretations of the period – based on either, both or neither.

Traditional views

The traditional view of Stalin is easily recognisable. Once he had established himself in power by 1929, his regime became utterly ruthless and, because of this, was the most efficient of the totalitarian dictatorships. Politically it was more rigidly controlled than Nazi Germany or Fascist Italy. Neither Hitler nor Mussolini swept away the previous political systems of his country; instead, they simply added another layer and created administrative problems. In Russia, by contrast, the Bolsheviks had destroyed the Tsarist political system, rejected the Western democratic alternative to which the Provisional Government might eventually have led, and radically altered Russia's institutions. Lenin had set up a system of soviets that were subordinated to the Bolshevik Party. Stalin took this further: he exerted greater personal control over the Party and therefore headed a fully integrated system of political control. His personalised dictatorship was much more successful than Hitler's or Mussolini's.

To intensify this control and to ensure its permanence, Stalin unleashed a flood of coercion and terror that was unprecedented and unparalleled. The NKVD and the purges were responsible for the deaths of many millions of Soviet people. This was on a scale unequalled by Mussolini's OVRA or Hitler's SS, even if one includes the Nazi policy of genocide against the Jews. The sheer efficiency of this control meant that Stalin was never seriously threatened politically; he could even afford to introduce progressive changes like the 1936 Constitution, knowing that he could easily stamp out any move towards meaningful opposition to him.

Stalin was able to use his political power to introduce a series of economic changes. These were, admittedly, of mixed success. His policy of collectivisation, launched in 1928, was a disaster in terms of agricultural production. It also resulted in widespread peasant opposition. His whole intention, however, was to exploit agriculture as a means of subsidising industrial growth which, in the long term, was a major success. The first three Five-Year Plans succeeded in developing heavy industry to the point where it was ultimately responsible for the survival of the Soviet Union during the Second World War. It managed to do this without having to resort to any sort of dependence on outside investment; success was achieved by exploitation of the Soviet population. Peasants were obliged to subsidise industrial growth through the sacrifice of their profits in agriculture, while peasants and workers alike had to give up any hopes of acquiring consumer goods as heavy industry took priority over light industry. In other words, Stalin's economic policy was ruthless but arrived at an effective industrial outcome.

Stalin was also responsible for some major social and cultural changes, again enhancing his own power. He reversed the radicalism of the Lenin era, which had aimed to achieve greater equality, to weaken the family and to experiment with new approaches to education. Stalin restored differentials, based on economic performance, revived the family as the basic social unit and brought traditional methods back to education. These measures, together with his emphasis on a tradition- ally Russian culture, were all designed to enhance his own image and to ensure that he was able to exert effective control through well-defined social channels.

Even foreign policy was dominated by Stalin. Although there has always been some debate as to what his precise objectives were, he nevertheless determined its overall rationale and dictated what course it should take. He made errors among his successes but was unquestionably one of the most pragmatic of all the statesmen contributing to the international scene between the wars. The Nazi– Soviet Non-Aggression Pact, drawn up with Germany in 1939, was the creation of an adept planner or a supreme opportunist; either way, it was the cynical act of a ruthless dictator at the peak of his power.

Revised views

Such is the traditional view of Stalin, which links his ruthlessness with the overall effectiveness of the Soviet Union as a totalitarian regime. We are now seeing the early stages of an alternative view of Stalin that will inevitably raise some eyebrows and incur some resistance.

It is important to emphasise that one thing has *not* changed. Stalin is still seen by most historians as perhaps the most ruthless dictator of the twentieth century, responsible for the deaths of many millions and prepared to make cynical use of terror on a massive scale. It remains extremely difficult to attempt to justify Stalin's actions, and many historians are still anxious not to be seen to be rehabilitating Stalin as a character. Some, indeed, build this into their otherwise radical reinterpretations almost as an apology. Stalin therefore remains largely condemned for his actions.

What *is* beginning to change is the assumption that ruthlessness of necessity brought efficiency. Instead, Stalinist Russia is now starting to be seen as even more ramshackle than Nazi Germany, with Stalin being pushed by circumstances as much as he controlled them. His effectiveness is therefore being cut down to size so that he has been reduced to the same level as Hitler. The overall argument for this is summarised below.

Stalin achieved power partly through his own abilities, but largely through circumstances that were moving in his favour. Lenin's Bolshevik regime had run into the buffers by 1921 and had had to resort to the New Economic Policy and a general relaxation of the earlier, radical War Communism. By 1927, however, moderation was failing to deliver results, so radicalism was revived with renewed energy. This coincided with Stalin's consolidation of power, so that he was able to take the initiative in launching a series of new programmes such as collectivisation, the Five-Year Plans and political centralisation. In this respect Stalin was reactivating the earlier dynamism of the Bolsheviks and was stealing some of the policies for which he had condemned Trotsky to exile. He was determined to push ahead with this radicalism through economic and social change, making full use of his greatly enhanced political power.

So far, there is much continuity with the traditional line on Stalin. But then comes a major departure. Far from being a model totalitarian dictatorship, the Stalinist political system was remarkably defective. The main problem, as shown in Chapter 2, was that there was less power at the centre than is commonly supposed. The core of both the administration and the Party had enormous difficulty in exerting controls over local officials and institutions. Although Stalin took the *initiative* for most of the policies of the period 1929–41, he frequently lost control over their *implementation*, as here the initiative passed to the localities. Usually what happened was that local officials and groups pressed on too enthusiastically in carrying out their orders, creating widespread chaos that then had to be dealt with by the centre applying the brakes. This, in turn, would transfer to local inertia so that, again, the centre had to recreate the initial momentum. There were therefore violent swings of the pendulum: local interests sought to interpret central policies in the most favourable way, in response to which the centre had to take corrective action. As a general principle, therefore, Stalin's political power was used initially in a *proactive* way, but then became increasingly *reactive*. At times he came dangerously close to losing control altogether. This pattern can be seen in four main areas.

The first is the purges. The traditional assumption is that Stalin was entirely responsible for the terror that swept the country during the 1930s and again after 1945. Certainly he initiated it. But it is highly questionable whether he was able to control it, and it could well have assumed a momentum far beyond what he had intended. Analysis (2) in Chapter 2 shows how the purges were exacerbated by local forces that interpreted Stalin's orders in their own way, whether on collective farms or in factories. The incidence of terror ebbed and flowed as Stalin sought constantly to regain the initiative.

A similar picture emerges with the economy (Chapter 3). Stalin launched a policy of collectivisation in 1928, only to find that it was implemented too rapidly and unsystematically. Local party officials and detachments of the NKVD exceeded their quotas, for which they were rebuked by Stalin in 1930. When the brakes were applied, local interests became more defensive so that a second offensive had to be launched and the whole economy became caught up with the purges. In industry, too, local managers had their own reasons for reinterpreting instructions from the centre. The overall result was that economic changes were defective in their planning and execution.

Stalin's social changes have also been misinterpreted (see Chapter 4). He did not reverse a radical Bolshevik trend: this is too positive a perception. The situation was that the changes made by the Bolsheviks were already beginning to slow down under the impetus of the NEP after 1921. Stalin attempted to revive the radical policies in relation to the family and education – only to find that these added to the chaos of the early 1930s that was apparent in politics and the economy. For this reason there was a swing back to support for traditional social institutions and a revival of conservative educational policies. This has been seen as part of a deliberate effort to underpin Stalin's personal authoritarian status. It could, however, be interpreted as a more instinctive reaction to escape the consequences of a programme that was not working.

Even Stalin's foreign policy had examples of measures to compensate for mistakes and for periodic loss of control over events. Chapter 5 shows how he actively assisted the rise of Hitler up to 1933, only to discover that he had helped create a monster that he could not control. For this reason he sought security in a Franco-Soviet pact in 1935 which, in turn, was wrecked by the Anglo-French policy of appeasement towards Germany. Faced with this situation, Stalin was pushed increasingly towards agreement with Hitler. The Nazi–Soviet Non-Aggression Pact of 1939 was the climax of a series of adjustments and attempts to regain lost initiative.

Of these two broad approaches to Stalin, Chapters 2 to 5 will develop the latter. Chapters 6 and 7 will convey a similarly revisionist interpretation of the period 1941–53.

Questions

1. Why does historical interpretation change?
2. How, in general terms, has the interpretation of Stalin's dictatorship between 1929 and 1941 changed?

SOURCES

1. STALIN'S RISE TO POWER

Source A: extracts from Lenin's Testament (24 December 1922) and the codicil added to it in January 1923.

(24 December 1922)
Comrade Stalin, having become General Secretary, has concentrated limitless power in his hands, and I am not certain that he will always be careful enough in his use of this power.

(4 January 1923)
Stalin is too rough, and this shortcoming, while completely tolerable in relations among us communists, becomes intolerable in the post of General Secretary. Therefore I propose to the comrades to think over the means of transferring Stalin from this post and appointing to it some other person who is superior to Stalin only in one respect, namely, in being more tolerant, more loyal, more polite and more attentive to comrades, less capricious, and so on. This circumstance may seem an insignificant trifle. But I think that, from the point of view of preventing a split and from the point of view of what I have written . . . about the relations between Stalin and Trotsky, it is not a trifle, or it is the kind of trifle that is capable of acquiring decisive significance.

Source B: from a speech by Stalin to the Fifteenth Congress in 1927.

Our Party is a living organism. Like every organism, it undergoes a process of metabolism: the old and obsolete passes away [applause], the new and growing lives and develops. [Applause] Some go away, both at the top and at the bottom. New ones grow, both at the top and at the bottom, and lead the cause forward. That is how our Party grew. That is how it will continue to grow.

The same must be said about the present period of our revolution. We are in the period of a turn from the restoration of industry and agriculture to the reconstruction of the entire national economy, to its reconstruction on a new technical basis, when the building of socialism is no longer merely in prospect, but a living, practical matter, which calls for the surmounting of extremely great difficulties of an internal and external character.

You know that this turn has proved fatal to the leaders of our opposition, who were scared by the new difficulties and intended to turn the Party in the direction of surrender. And if certain leaders, who do not want to sit firmly in the cart, now fall out, it is nothing to be surprised at. It will merely rid the Party of people who are getting in its way and hindering its progress. Evidently, they seriously want to free themselves from our Party cart. Well, if some of the old leaders who are running into trash intend to fall out of the cart – a good riddance to them!

Source C: from an eyewitness report on Stalin by the American journalist Louis Fischer, who accompanied an American labour delegation on a visit to the Soviet Union in 1927.

Trotsky waves the magic wand of a magnetic personality and captures his interlocutor. Stalin does not. But as he talked to us hour after hour my respect for his strength, will, and faith grew. He built up this impression as he built up his political position – slowly, methodically, brick by brick. Nothing Stalin said throughout the interview was brilliant. He was pedestrian, solid and simple. His statements interested professors of economy and would have been intelligible to factory hands. The questions had been submitted to him in advance, and he probably prepared the answers in advance. Sometimes he did not grasp the meaning of the question, and rambled before he reached its pith, but finally he did get to the point. His replies were always long and thorough. His mentality lacked the witty epigram or the remark with insight which can light up a whole field of thought. He ploughed long and deep. His complete composure, the complete absence of nerves, and his calm voice reflected inner power. One could see that he might be a man of iron.

Source D: a later comment by Khrushchev, Stalin's successor, on Lenin's Testament.

Stalin himself has always regarded Lenin's reference to him as more of a compliment than otherwise. In an address to a later Congress he repeated the words, adding, 'Yes, Comrades, I am rude to those who seek to weaken the Party by their activities and I shall continue to be rude to such people.'

Questions

*1. (i) Explain the term 'General Secretary' (Source A). [2]
   (ii) Other than Trotsky, name two of 'the old leaders who are running into trash' (Source B). [2]
2. To what extent is Lenin's view of Stalin, contained in Source A, confirmed by Stalin himself in Sources B and D? [6]
3. How useful and reliable are Sources C and D as assessments of Stalin? [6]
4. 'Stalin's rise to power was due to his own strengths and ruthlessness.' To what extent do Sources A to D, and your own knowledge, confirm this view? [8]

Worked answer

*1. [The first question is a factual one, and the answer should be as short and as precise as possible. Generally, where one mark is allocated, a single word or phrase will do. Where there are two marks, two points, one explaining the other, will be expected.]

(i) The 'General Secretary' was in overall charge of the Bolshevik Party. In this capacity, he controlled the various organs of the Party's Secretariat.

(ii) Kamenev and Zinoviev.

SOURCES

2. STALIN AS LENIN'S SUCCESSOR

Source E: from an official biography of Stalin published in Moscow in 1947.

Stalin's whole career is an example of profound theoretical power combined with an unusual breadth and versatility of practical experience in the revolutionary struggle . . .

Everybody is familiar with the cogent and invincible force of Stalin's logic, the crystal clarity of his mind, his iron will, his devotion to the Party, his ardent faith in the people, and love for the people. Everybody is familiar with his modesty, his simplicity of manner, his consideration for people, and his merciless severity towards enemies of the people . . . Stalin is wise and deliberate in solving complex political questions where a thorough weighing of pros and cons is required. At the same time, he is a supreme master of bold revolutionary decisions and of swift adaptations to changed conditions.

Stalin is the worthy continuer of the cause of Lenin, or, as it is said in the Party: Stalin is the Lenin of today.

Source F: from Trotsky's *Stalin: An Appraisal of the Man and His Influence*, completed in 1940 and published in 1947.

Stalin represents a phenomenon utterly exceptional. He is neither a thinker, a writer nor an orator. He took possession of power before the masses had learned to distinguish his figure from others during the triumphal processions across Red Square. Stalin took possession of power, not with the aid of personal qualities, but with the aid of an impersonal machine. And it was not he who created the machine, but the machine who created him. That machine, with its force and its authority, was the product of the prolonged and heroic struggle of the Bolshevik Party, which itself grew out of ideas. The machine was the bearer of the idea before it became an end in itself. Stalin headed the machine from the moment he cut off the umbilical cord that bound it to the idea and it became a thing unto itself. Lenin created the machine through constant association with the masses ... Stalin did not create the machine but took possession of it.

Source G: from a speech by Khrushchev to the Twentieth Congress of the Communist Party of the Soviet Union (February 1956).

When we analyze the practice of Stalin in regard to the reaction of the Party and of the country, when we pause to consider everything which Stalin perpetrated, we must be convinced that Lenin's fears were justified. The negative characteristics of Stalin, which, in Lenin's time, were only incipient, transformed themselves during the last years into a grave abuse of power by Stalin, which caused untold harm to our Party ...

He discarded the Leninist method of convincing and educating; he abandoned the method of ideological struggle for that of administrative violence, mass repressions, and terror. He acted on an increasingly large scale and more stubbornly through punitive organs, at the same time often violating all existing norms of morality and of Soviet laws ...

Collegiality of leadership flows from the very nature of our Party, a Party built on the principles of democratic centralism ...

Whereas during the first few years after Lenin's death Party Congresses and Central Committee Plenums took place more or less regularly, later, when Stalin began increasingly to abuse his power, these principles were brutally violated ...

Central Committee Plenums were hardly ever called ... In practice Stalin ignored the norms of Party life and trampled on the Leninist principle of collective Party leadership ...

Source H: a decision of the Twenty-second Congress of the Communist Party of the CPSU (1961) on the mausoleum of Lenin.

1. The Mausoleum in Red Square by the Kremlin Wall, created to perpetuate the memory of Vladimir Ilyich Lenin, the immortal founder of the Communist Party and the Soviet state, the leader and teacher of the working people of the whole world, is henceforth to be known as: The Mausoleum of Vladimir Ilyich LENIN.

2. It is acknowledged as inappropriate to retain the sarcophagus containing the coffin of I.V. Stalin in the Mausoleum any longer, since Stalin's serious violations of the behest of Lenin, his abuse of power, his mass repressions against honest Soviet people, and other actions in the period of the cult of personality make it impossible to leave the coffin with his body in the Mausoleum of V.I. Lenin.

Questions

1. Explain the references to
   (i) 'Lenin's fears' (Source G) [2]
   (ii) 'Central Committee' (Source G) [2]
*2. How do Sources E and F differ in their presentation of Stalin's specific strengths? How would you explain these differences? [5]
3. What comments might the historian make on the usefulness of Source G as an overall assessment of Stalin? [4]
4. What does the content and language of Source H show about the attitudes of the Party to the Soviet leadership? [4]
5. 'Stalin was not the natural successor to Lenin.' Do these sources, and your own knowledge, support this view? [8]

Worked answer

*2. [This question requires a combination of material from the sources ('How do Sources E and F differ . . . ?') and inferences and knowledge which go beyond the sources ('How would you explain these differences?'). It would be best to write two separate paragraphs. References should be made to the sources, but any quotations should be kept very short.]

Source E is overwhelmingly positive about Stalin's strengths, while Source F is generally negative. One difference concerns Stalin's intellect: Source E refers to his 'profound theoretical power' and 'the crystal clarity of his mind', while Source F maintains that he was neither 'a thinker' nor 'a writer'. Another difference is the perception of his personal qualities. Source E refers to 'his devotion to the Party' and his 'love for the people', while Source F emphasises that he took over 'before the masses had learned to distinguish his figure from others'. The former allowed him to be a 'worthy continuer of the cause of Lenin', but the latter considers that he merely 'took possession' of the machine created by Lenin.

The basic reason for these differences is that the two sources were produced in different circumstances and served different purposes. Source E was a piece of official propaganda, produced during Stalin's administration and designed to reinforce and legitimise his power. Source F, on the other hand, was written in exile by Stalin's main opponent; it was therefore bound to seek to vilify Stalin while attributing his success to a system that he had not created.

2

STALINIST POLITICS AND TERROR

BACKGROUND NARRATIVE

By the time Stalin had become a member of the leadership triumvirate in 1924, he was already well placed in the Party that Lenin had led to power in 1917. He also inherited the political infrastructure of the Soviet system from the Bolshevik period. This took the form of the 1918 Constitution of the Russian Soviet Federated Socialist Republic (RSFSR), to which Stalin added the 1924 and 1936 Constitutions: these first established and then refined the Union of Soviet Socialist Republics (USSR). Meanwhile, he had also secured his position within the three key components of the Communist Party – the Politburo, the Central Committee and the Orgburo. After 1929 Stalin tried to tighten the Party's grip on the state institutions – the soviets and the Council of People's Commissars, while at the same time increasing his own control over the Party itself. Everything seemed to point to the emergence of a more personalised regime that Stalin intended to use to bring about an economic transformation. Since this would require subordinate institutions and a compliant workforce, the way ahead was through intensification of dictatorship.

The process involved a considerable degree of coercion and the deliberate use of terror. To some extent this had already been applied before 1924. Stalin now reactivated the earlier Cheka in the form of the GPU, OGPU and the NKVD. His ruthlessness had already been shown in his systematic destruction of the alternative leadership between 1924 and 1929. During the period of the first Five-Year Plan and collectivisation the focus was on those who were considered to be resisting economic change, including the kulaks and managers in industry. The assassination of Kirov in 1934 was used by Stalin to sharpen the political focus to the terror, in the form of show trials and extensive activities by the NKVD against the populace at large. The first show trial in 1936 disposed of Kamenev and Zinoviev, the second (1937) of Piatakov and Sokolnikov, and the third, in 1938, of Bukharin, Rykov and Yagoda. The purges also affected the army and the navy (the latter losing all eight of its admirals). By 1939 the terror was reduced, only to be revived after the end of the Second World War.

These developments in the political structure and in the purges have traditionally been used to emphasise the increase in Stalin's power as a direct result of a totalitarian dictatorship. Terror, power and efficiency have therefore been closely associated. Analysis (1) questions the extent of the efficiency of Stalin's political system, while Analyses (2) and (3) consider the implications of this for the effects of the purges.

ANALYSIS (1): HOW POWERFUL WAS STALIN? $\mathcal{IMP}.$

The traditional interpretation of Stalin's power is that he made use of the political institutions established by the Bolsheviks during the period 1918–24 and personalised his control over them to create the most ruthlessly efficient totalitarian regime of the twentieth century. This process is known as the Stalinist Revolution. There are two separate propositions here. One is that such a change did actually take place; the other is that it was effective. The first is easier to substantiate than the second.

There is little disagreement that Stalin used and developed Lenin's power base, in the process adding his own. He converted the Leninist Party into his own natural medium and capitalised on the Bolshevik infiltration of all state institutions, including the soviets, by the various Party committees. He had also benefited from the strengthening of the Party by the elimination of other political groups, such as the Socialist Revolutionaries and Mensheviks, in the purges of 1920 and 1921. To this trend, Stalin added his own emphasis in several ways.

As we have seen in Chapter 1, he consolidated his position within the Party. He also changed the Party's character, converting it into a channel for his personal power. The next stage was to squeeze any form of democracy out of the Party: he was able to operate increasing influence over the Politburo through the Orgburo, which he controlled. He dominated all the overlapping committees at the centre and made regular use of the Orgburo to create a permanent bedrock of personal support. Stalin also ended any duality between the Party and state apparatus. Central decisions fell more to the Politburo, at the core of the Party, and less to Sovnarkom, or the Council of People's Commissars. Stalin clearly regarded this development as crucial, for 'With this combination we will have full unity of the soviet and Party summits that will undoubtedly double our strength.' (1)

Stalin advanced two forms of justification for these changes. One was ideological: he rewrote a basic Marxist principle. Marxism had emphasised that the fundamental entity in any society was the 'infrastructure', or 'base', which comprised the underlying economic system. The political, social and cultural institutions formed the 'superstructure' which always grew out of the base. Orthodox Marxists believed that changes to the superstructure would have to be preceded by the transformation of the base; socialist institutions, for example, could be established only on a socialist economy. Stalin, however, was determined to use the new political superstructure, already set up by the Bolsheviks, to redesign the economic base. He therefore took a more pragmatic view of the underlying theory.

> The basis gives rise to the superstructure, but this does not at all mean that it merely reflects the basis, that it is passive, neutral, is indifferent to the fate of its basis, that it is passive to the character of the system. On the contrary, having made its appearance in the world, it becomes the greatest active force, actively assists its basis to take shape and acquire strength, and makes every effort to help the new order to finish off and liquidate the old basis and the old classes. (2)

Stalin's other justification for greater centralisation was that he was simultaneously extending the range of democracy. In 1936 the Soviet Union adopted a Constitution that remained the basis of the Soviet system until slight amendments were made to it in Brezhnev's Constitution of 1977. The main improvements were universal suffrage at the age of eighteen, the introduction of the secret ballot and the end of voting weighted in favour of the urban workers and against the peasantry. The soviets were also altered: the Supreme Soviet now comprised two chambers, the Soviet of the Union, based on electoral districts, and the Soviet of the Nationalities, reflecting the regional and ethnic composition of the country as a whole. Stalin could therefore claim that he was involving the population more than the previous regime had done. Many intellectuals from the West, including George Bernard Shaw and Sidney and Beatrice Webb, believed that the Soviet system was opening up and becoming more progressive.

The reality, however, was that, in his pursuit of power, legitimacy was always a relative concept. The Constitution was in many respects a façade, designed to justify Stalin's personalisation of power. It was also a gesture that was unimportant in practice since any increase in theoretical democracy within the Constitution was cancelled out by the reduction of democracy within the Party – which, of course, controlled the Constitution. Ultimately, there was nothing to stop the centre from pursuing any policy it considered appropriate. This was done, for example, in the economy through central planning which, from 1929, forced the pace of industrialisation and collective farming (see Chapter 3). It also made possible the terror and purges, sustained throughout Stalin's period in power.

There is no question that all this actually happened. Stalin *did* centralise the administration, establish personal ascendancy over the Party and neutralise any concessions to democracy. But the question that needs to be asked is 'How effective was it in practice?' The totalitarian regimes of the twentieth century have recently undergone extensive re-examination by historians. This applies especially to Nazi Germany, but the process is now also gathering momentum with respect to the Soviet Union. The key point is that although dictatorship may well have been strengthened at the centre, this could not be fully effective unless it was implemented at local level, within both the state apparatus and the Party. Centralised dictatorship had to operate outwards through effective channels or, to use a different image, the influence of the apex had to seep down through all levels of the hierarchy.

In the Soviet Union the link between the central decision-making process and the localities proved to be a particular problem. Evidence for this has recently been produced in a variety of areas: the Party, the administration, the factories, the collective farms and the army. The process can been described as follows. In the first stage, policies were issued by the leadership – but without being sufficiently specific. These were then variously interpreted by officials at different levels within the state and Party, all of whom had their own aims and agendas. Local Party secretaries defended the interests of their particular sector and interpreted orders from the centre as they saw fit. This, in turn, came in for criticism from the centre, which soon realised that policies were not being strictly adhered to. Stalin made frequent accusations that bureaucrats were actually impeding policy; in 1930, for example, he complained that local officials had become 'dizzy with success' in exceeding central quotas for collectivisation. The centre therefore tried to restore discipline over the lower levels of management. Further waves of chaos followed in the localities as rank and file members now attacked their branch leaders or factory managers or collective farm chairmen. The latter retaliated by identifying troublemakers and dealing with them summarily. The whole decision-making structure was therefore riddled with conflict and dissent. In the ensuing chaos the centre sought to restore a semblance of order, by adjusting, intensifying or ending particular campaigns. In these circumstances the centre was often reacting to the local branches.

Overall, the localities had a considerable impact on the centre. According to one recent view, 'Campaigns – including purges – could be stalled, sped up, aborted, or implemented in ways which suited local conditions and interests.' (3) Real power lay in local hands and with local Party and government machinery. 'Even if one assumes Stalin's personality was the only or main factor in the initiation of policies, one must still explain the obvious disparities between central orders and local outcomes.' (4) The situation was given further instability by the constant expansion of local officialdom. This made it increasingly difficult for the centre to control local officials without creating more officials, and hence compounding the problem. Ironically, Stalinism, supposedly confined to the centre, in practice created the ideal conditions for 'little Stalins' in the localities. These were not a threat to the basis of Stalin's power. But they did inhibit the effective enforcement of his policies.

This argument, emphasising the contrast between dictatorship at the centre and still powerful local initiatives, has two overall implications. First, Stalin was less completely in control of policy than is generally supposed. He certainly intended to direct the economy and foreign policy through periodic decisions and adjustments, just as he was determined to remove all opposition and democracy within the Party. But he frequently lost control of what he had started: the complexity of the administration defeated the attempts of the centre to monitor the changes, with the result that there was as much chaos and anarchy as there was order and direction. And second, the impetus, as opposed to the inspiration, for change came as much from below as from above. The result could be violent changes, oscillations and swings as the top tried to correct the bottom's attempts to adapt to the direction imposed from above. Seen in this light, Stalin spent as much of his time adjusting as he did initiating.

These points have a particularly important bearing on the phenomenon with which Stalinism is most commonly associated: terror and
the purges.

Questions

1. Was Stalin in control of his political system?
2. How could the same regime produce the 1936 Constitution
   and the purges?

ANALYSIS (2): WHAT WERE THE REASONS FOR THE STALINIST TERROR?

More than anything else, Stalin's regime is associated with terror. This
existed on a scale unparalleled, in terms of the number of casualties,
in the twentieth century – which is to say, in the whole of human
history. Until very recently the reasons for this terror attracted very
little controversy: the driving force was considered to be, solely and
uniquely, Stalin himself, who created a ruthlessly totalitarian system.
Current historians are not, however, content with stereotypes, even if
they are largely true. The Stalinist terror was too complex to admit a
single explanation. This analysis will attempt to integrate traditional
views and recent research into an overall synthesis. The argument
progresses stage by stage.

All revolutions contain within them the potential for purges. They are
driven by two dynamics – to preserve their power base and to transform their legacy. Both involve radical measures that may well include
calculated violence against a perceived enemy within. Justification is
sought in the form of 'cleansing' or 'purging'; in the process, 'terror' is
invoked as a positive force, as a means of achieving a higher goal. The
Russian Revolution was particularly susceptible to this trend. It involved
an ideology that recognised, as a transitional period, the 'dictatorship of
the proletariat' and it had a blueprint to transform Russia's institutions
and society. The whole situation was radicalised, between 1918 and
1921, by the Civil War. Trotsky's maxim that 'we shall not enter the
kingdom of socialism in white gloves on a polished floor' justified
the establishment, under Dzerzhynski, of the Cheka, as well as
the expulsion of Mensheviks and Socialist Revolutionaries from the
soviets in 1918 and the show trials of political opponents in 1922.
There were also systematic purges of the Bolshevik Party; it has been
estimated that in 1921 about a quarter of the Party was deprived of its

membership cards. Even though the terror was officially ended in 1922, a powerful precedent had been set for the future.

To an extent, therefore, later coercive measures can be seen as a revival of a ruthless trend within an uncompromising ideology. But a powerful personal factor was also involved. Traditionally, the intensification of terror has been attributed to Stalin's own personality. Khrushchev, for example, later referred to Stalin's brutality, vindictiveness, pathological distrust and 'sickly' suspicion. Although there may well be something to this explanation, it is oversimplistic as it stands, and it demonises the subject without properly explaining his objectives.

Assuming that Stalin was driven by personal forces, what were his *reasons* for reintroducing the terror? Clearly the most important was the consolidation of his power. The view of R. Conquest and others is that Stalin accomplished two main objectives: 'A vast number of past or potential "hostile" elements had been destroyed or sent to labour camps, and the rest of the population reduced to the most complete silence and obedience.' (5) R. Tucker endorses this: the Great Purges of the 1930s were an effort 'to achieve an unrestricted personal dictatorship with a totality of power that Stalin did not yet possess in 1934.' (6) Stalin aimed to wipe out the entire generation of Bolsheviks who had been associated with Lenin between 1917 and 1924; this alone would guarantee Stalin as the sole heir to Lenin and would secure his position for his lifetime. Some of the threats were obvious: hence Kamenev and Zinoviev were disposed of in the show trial of 1936, Piatakov and Sokolnikov in 1937 and Bukharin, Rykov and Yagoda in 1938. Many others were, however, added to the list of victims almost on a quota basis. There was, seemingly, no limit to Stalin's fear of future opposition.

A second rationale commonly attributed to Stalin's purges was economic. The forced pace of industrialisation and the implementation of collective farming required a disciplined workforce and a compliant peasantry. Both involved the use of force. Measures had to be taken against reluctant managers in the factories in 1930 and 1931, while the NKVD operated dekulakisation squads to clear the countryside of resistance to collectivisation. As the pace of industrialisation speeded up in the second and third Five-Year Plans, additional labour was provided by the growth of the Gulag system. Convict labour built the Belomor Canal, opened in 1933, and provided the mainstay of mining in Siberia, especially in the inhospitable Kolyma region. Terror was, therefore, inseparable from Stalin's vision of modernisation.

Some historians have attributed to Stalin another motive. He was, above all, afraid that the West would destroy the Soviet Union before he had the chance to complete the process of industrialisation. Stalin's solution, according to Tucker and Conquest, was to engage in temporary co-operation with Germany. This incurred the hostility of many of the older-style Bolsheviks who saw fascism as a deadlier enemy than either Britain or France. Tucker and Conquest therefore argue that Stalin was obliged to remove the anti-Hitler element to make possible the accommodation with Germany that eventually produced the Nazi–Soviet Non-Aggression Pact of August 1939. A different approach to the theme of the external threat is put by I. Deutscher. Stalin was concerned that the regime would be destroyed from within – by internal revolt as a result of external invasion. Stalin therefore had to remove any alternative leaders and to make the population at large accept their removal. Hence 'They had to die as traitors, as perpetrators of crimes beyond the reach of reason . . . Only then could Stalin be sure that their execution would provoke no dangerous revulsion.' (7)

Stalin therefore ruthlessly manipulated an authoritarian system, inherited from the Bolsheviks, into a totalitarian one. He used it to cut huge swathes through the population in the pursuit of his economic and political objectives. This is where most previous analyses have stopped. But, until recently, it has never been fully explained why the purges were so complete and so all-embracing – and why so many of the population played an active part in them. The traditional analysis adopts a monolithic 'top-down' approach and assumes that Stalin remained in control and dictated the momentum of the terror. But did he? Was the Soviet administrative system that efficient? And did the apex of the bureaucracy really succeed in imposing its will on the localities? Some historians now emphasise that there were 'bottom-up' reactions to 'top-down' orders that gave the purges an additional momentum far beyond anything intended by Stalin. In other words, although Stalin introduced the policy centrally, the way in which it was carried out was determined locally.

In the countryside terror was endemic from the beginning of the process of collectivisation. This was largely because the central instructions were actually exceeded and measures had to be taken to try to control the dekulakisation squads. The All-Russian Central Executive Committee, or Council of People's Commissars, issued decrees in 1929 defining precisely who was to be classified as a kulak and warned that dekulakisation should not become an end in itself. This, however, scarcely diminished the wave of terror that followed, so that Stalin had to try to stem the tide in 1930. When the campaign was resumed later that year, and extended between 1932 and 1934, the central government attempted to exert more direct control. In each case L. Viola distinguishes between the repressive policy that the state undoubtedly pursued and the methods used by the cadres in the field to implement the policy. The latter were influenced by a 'general political culture of the early 1930s', which was based on 'a mixture of traditional Russian radical fanaticism' and the 'unleashing of years of pent-up class rage and retribution'. (8) This was intensified by shortages created by collectivisation and by the development of a siege-like mentality. We could go even further. The repression and persecution at local level were manifestations of the breakdown of central control. Peasant resistance, disobedience and defiance were others. The two extremes fed off each other – resistance to the local terror undermining official policy. Or, in the words of J. Arch Getty, 'Stalin had initiated a movement with vague instructions and ambiguous targets. As the process unfolded on the ground, though, it degenerated rapidly into chaotic and violent struggles based on local conditions.' (9)

Industry, too, became affected by endemic terror. There was widespread chaos as managers came into conflict with the Party and the workforce, all in pursuit of different interests. An additional complication was the Stakhanovite movement. R. Thurston argues that this created tension in factories as young Stakhanovites with personal and political ambitions upset the productivity balance that managers tried desperately to maintain. In turn, the latter became subject to accusations of wrecking and sabotage. 'Whatever its scope, as the terror unfolded the resentments and demands fostered by early Stakhanovism heightened tensions in industry.' (10) Much the same applies to the army. R. Reese claims that the Party organisations within the armed forces experienced upheaval that was well beyond the control of the central administration. (11)

At all levels there was a feeling of direct involvement in the purges. People everywhere had a variety of motives. Some used the opportunity of informing on others to settle old scores. Many were genuinely convinced that the economy was riddled with 'wreckers' and saboteurs who had to be brought to book. Here an important part was played by the show trials, which helped whip up suspicion of and resentment against managers. (12) Peasants provided information and they testified at district trials (local counterparts to the show trials). A striking simile has been advanced with 'mice burying the cat'; (13) because of the special conditions interacting with longer-term tensions, this happened all over the country. Paranoia spread through all levels of society, helping to maintain the momentum of terror at the lowest levels. G.T. Rittersporn maintains that the regime's emphasis on the 'subversive' activities of 'conspirators' interacted with traditional prejudices to produce an 'imagery of omnipresent subversion and conspiracy'. (14) According to R.G. Suny, 'The requirement to find enemies, to blame and punish, worked together with self-protection and self-promotion . . . to expand the Purges into a political holocaust.' (15)

Overall, it is right to move away from the limited view of Stalin as the sole driving force behind the terror. Whether he was insane or suffering from paranoia is only partly relevant. He inherited a revolution, revived the terror that had atrophied and renewed the turmoil at all social levels. But the sheer scale of the upheaval can only be understood on a national scale, as the intervention of local factors that distorted the central intention. Until further evidence becomes available, a provisional conclusion might be that, although Stalin initiated and maintained the purges, they assumed a momentum that outpaced even his expectations. This reflects the relative inefficiency of the Soviet system and a loss of control by it. The terror becomes even more terrible, since it can no longer be attributed entirely to one man's paranoia, but also to the multiple manifestations of human nature.

Questions

1. What was the role of terror in the Stalinist system?
2. How valid is the distinction between 'top-down' and 'bottom-up' approaches to terror in Stalinist Russia?

ANALYSIS (3): WHAT WERE THE CONSEQUENCES OF THE STALINIST TERROR?

Analysis (2) showed that the terror was less carefully controlled and centralised than has often been thought. The corollary to this is that the effects are also less clear-cut and need partial reinterpretation.

It has been argued that the terror was the chief method by which the Party machinery of the Bolshevik state was transformed into the personalised totalitarian dictatorship of Stalin. As a result, Stalinism created a regime that was more consistently ruthless and pervasive than even that of Nazi Germany. This is partly, but only partly, true. Any capacity for debate about different strategies was certainly squeezed out of the centre of the Party with the elimination of Kamenev, Zinoviev, Bukharin, Rykov and others. The chances of persuading Stalin to adopt a different course to what he had in mind, whether in economic or foreign policy, could never seriously arise after 1934. It could also be argued that the terror was a necessary complement to the development of the Stalinist personality cult – the obverse of the same coin. The terror also made it possible to experiment with more obvious democratic forms in the 1936 Constitution, since these were neutralised and therefore never amounted to anything in practice.

Terror did all these things. But it has traditionally been seen as working in one way only – as tightening the political system and therefore enhancing the powers of dictatorship. There is, however, another possibility – that it unleashed chaos into the system that actually limited the extent to which dictatorship could operate effectively. Analysis (1) provided examples of how local groups in industry and the countryside interpreted central decisions. Normally such groups would have been cautious but the terror acted as a stimulus for greatly intensified activity, for reasons given in Analysis (2). The result was more often a descent into chaos, with wild oscillations developing as, first, the local groups implemented the instructions of the centre in their own way, then the centre attempted to restore an approved line. Paradoxically, terror was a democratising force, although in a negative sense: it created a tyranny *of* the people quite as much as the traditional image of a tyranny *over* the people.

The economic impact of the terror was also paradoxical. It is normally seen as having provided the impetus for the command economy; and the debate has focused on whether such an economy was preferable to a mixed economy that would have allowed a measure of market consumerism. But it can now be argued that terror confused the command network, thereby undermining the whole Stalinist system. Two examples of this can be given. One was the approach to collectivisation and dekulakisation that, as we have seen, was conducted with excessive zeal by local Party and NKVD officials. The result was one of the greatest mass disobedience campaigns of the twentieth century, aimed not at Stalin but at those who were interpreting his orders more freely than even he wanted. The second example is the impact of the Stakhanovites in industry. Their initiative, which was intended to promote an increase in productivity, actually helped slow it down. In the climate of terror, managers were understandably hostile to anyone who distorted their own implementation of industrial plans. This, in turn, made them a target for denunciation, with the result that the very people most likely to achieve local stability were removed. Far from underpinning the command economy, therefore, terror did much to disrupt its smooth operation.

What of the impact of the Stalinist terror in terms of the amount of suffering caused? No-one doubts that Stalin was directly responsible for the deaths of millions. Accurate estimates have, however, always been open to dispute, and the opening of the Soviet archives since the onset of glasnost has only served to accentuate this. The total number of deaths has been put by Nove and Wheatcroft at between 4 and 11 million, significantly below Conquest's estimates of 20 million and recent Russian textbook figures of 40 million. Estimates of prison populations also vary from Nove and Wheatcroft's peak of 5.5 million in 1953 to S. Rosefielde's 10 million during the late 1930s and Conquest's up to 8 million in 1938 and 12 million in 1952. The main problem is distinguishing between those who died as a direct result of a purge and those whose deaths were caused by famine or diseases associated with Stalin's agricultural policies.

There is also growing doubt about the once-held belief that Stalin was widely hated as well as feared – because he was seen as the instigator of the terror. We have seen, in Analysis (2), that the terror was often sustained and intensified at grass-roots level, which meant that huge numbers of people were directly implicated in actions against colleagues or neighbours. Paradoxically, this meant that Stalin, who may well have been held responsible for starting the process, was also seen as the only person who could genuinely transcend and stop it. The people who were most feared and blamed were those who carried out changes locally. The surprising and unpalatable truth is that Stalin remained popular. The real test came when the Germans invaded the Soviet Union in 1941. Those who collaborated with them had a grievance on traditional grounds, not against Stalin himself. Collaborators were highest among the minority nationalities who aspired to independence, not among repressed Russians who aspired to freedom. Despite years of terror, there was far greater unity and patriotism in the Second World War than there had been in the First.

This brings us to the impact of the terror on the security of the Soviet Union. The purging of the armed forces cannot but have had a negative effect on Soviet defences. Experience was undoubtedly affected by the wholesale deaths and expulsions outlined in Analysis (2). The real loss was of experience at the highest level, surely a crippling blow to any impending war effort. The result, it is generally argued, was a humiliating performance against Finland in the Northern War of 1939–40 and a disastrous collapse when the Germans invaded the Soviet Union in 1941.

Yet, again, the impact of the terror may have been exaggerated. Most of those purged in 1938 were not actually arrested but expelled from the Party. Hence the impact was more limited than once thought. It was originally estimated that the purges had accounted for between 25 per cent and 50 per cent of army officers. Recent estimates have put the figures at somewhere between 3.7 per cent and 7.7 per cent. (16) There are two main reasons for this disparity. One is a previous underestimate of the size of the officer class in the Red Army, the other the rapidity with which many were rehabilitated. Both of these points have the effect of diluting the impact of the terror on the efficiency of the armed forces. In any case, many military expulsions from the army were not accompanied by loss of military rank. It has now been estimated that 30 per cent of army officers discharged between 1937 and 1939 were reinstated. (17) This was part of the policy of the central authorities to reduce the scale of denunciations. At the Eighteenth Party Congress in March 1939, for example, it was said that 'Political organs and Party organizations often expel Party members far too light-heartedly. The Party Commissions of the Political Administration of the Red Army find it necessary to reinstate about 50 per cent of the expelled men because the expulsions were unjustified.' (18) It seems, therefore, that measures were being taken to correct the severity of the purges well before the German invasion.

Overall, we may conclude that the effects of the terror were more blurred than is traditionally supposed – largely because the momentum was less centrally controlled. Effect overlaps into cause, spontaneous momentum into deliberate policy. Hence the state benefited less from the terror because it was unable to control it. Similarly, because of that lack of contol, the terror was much more devastating than even Stalin intended.

Questions

1. Did the use of terror strengthen or weaken the centralisation of the Soviet political and economic structure?
2. Has the damage caused by the terror to the Soviet Union been exaggerated?

SOURCES

1. THE REASONS FOR THE PURGES

Source A: from R.W. Thurston: *Life and Terror in Stalin's Russia* (published in 1996).

This book argues that Stalin was not guilty of mass first-degree murder from 1934 to 1941 and did not plan or carry out a systematic campaign to crush the nation. This view is not one of absolution, however: his policies did help to engender real plots, lies, and threats to his position. Then this fear-ridden man reacted, and over-reacted, to events. All the while, he could not control the flow of people within the country, job turnover, or illegal acts by managers and many others. He was sitting at the peak of a pyramid of lies and incomplete information, and he must have known it. His power was constrained in fundamental ways, which contributed to his anxiety and tendency to govern by hit-and-run methods. His attitudes and deeds must be situated in the context of vast, popular suspicion generated in part by World War I and the Russian Civil War. Several conclusions follow: Stalin becomes more human than others have portrayed him. And his regime becomes less malevolent but possessed of greater public support than is usually argued.

Source B: from *Children of the Arbat* by A. Rybakov (this had been suppressed in the USSR for twenty years before being published in Britain in 1989).

Stalin mused . . . Yes, the history of mankind was the history of class struggle, but the leader emerged as the expression of class, and therefore the history of mankind was the history of its leaders and its rulers. Idealism did not come into it. The spirit of an epoch was determined by the man who made the epoch himself . . .

. . . all opponents, past, present and future, had to be liquidated and would be liquidated. The sole socialist country in the world could survive only if it were unshakably stable, and this would also be seen as a sign of its stability by the outside world. The state must be strong in case of war; the state must be mighty if it wants peace. It must be feared.

In order to turn a peasant society into an industrialised country, countless material and human sacrifices were necessary. The people must accept this. But it would not be achieved by enthusiasm alone. The people would have to be forced to accept the sacrifices, and for this a powerful authority was needed, an authority that inspired fear . . . the theory of undying class war provided for all such possibilities. If a few million people had to perish in the process, history would forgive Comrade Stalin . . . All the great rulers had been harsh.

Source C: from a speech by Khrushchev to the Twentieth Congress of the Communist Party of the Soviet Union (February 1956).

It became apparent that many Party, Soviet and economic activists who were branded in 1937–1938 as 'enemies' were actually never enemies, spies, wreckers, etc., but were always honest Communists . . .

Stalin was a very distrustful man, sickly suspicious; we know this from our work with him. He could look at a man and say: 'Why are your eyes so shifty today?' or 'Why are you turning so much today and avoiding to look me directly in the eyes?' The sickly suspicion created in him a general distrust even toward eminent Party workers whom he had known for years. Everywhere and in everything he saw 'enemies', 'two-facers' and 'spies'.

Possessing unlimited power, he indulged in great wilfulness and choked a person morally and physically. A situation was created where one could not express one's own will.

Source D: from an article by Roberta T. Manning: 'The Soviet economic crisis of 1936–1940 and the Great Purges' (1993).

In this way, the economic problems of 1936–41 and the Great Purges appear to be inexorably linked. The industrial slowdown, which set in at a time when the USSR could least afford it, when a two-front war without allies seemed to be the Soviets' inevitable fate, shaped the course of the Great Purges at least as much, if not more so, as the terror in turn influenced the operation of the economy. In 1936–8, as veteran journalist William Henry Chamberlain has pointed out in regard to Soviet political persecutions of the First Five-Year Plan period, 'When plans went awry, when deprivations, instead of disappearing, became more severe, when promised improvements in food supply did not materialize, the subconscious temptation to seek scapegoats became almost irresistible.'

Questions

1. Explain the references to:
   (i) 'peak of a pyramid of lies and incomplete information' (Source A); [2]
   (ii) 'class war' (Source B). [2]
2. What similarities and differences are there between Sources B and C concerning Stalin's 'responsibility' for the purges? How would you explain the differences? [7]
*3. Assess the value of Source A to the historian studying the Stalinist terror. [6]
4. 'Stalin conceived the purges and dictated every part of their

course.' Discuss this view, using Sources A to D and other information known to you. [8]

Worked answer

*3.   [Occasionally a secondary source may be used as one of the documents. This adds an extra component to the answer – historiography. There is also a chance to consider the merits and defects of secondary sources, although care has to be taken to avoid low-level generalisations about these.]

The value of Source A is potential rather than actual. It provides a summary of an overall argument on Stalin's involvement in the purges, which alerts the reader to the highlights of the more detailed inter- pretation that follows; it does not, therefore, give supporting evidence at this stage. As a secondary source, it is based on a wide variety of other sources, both primary and secondary, and has the advantage of retrospective analysis which, on an issue as complex as the purges, can provide a clearer perspective than contemporary accounts and views. In this case, the emphasis is on confusion and chaos, rather than on Stalin's ruthless manipulation of power, which has characterised past interpretations. The major deficiency of an argument as strong as that in Source A is that it may be overstated, perhaps because it is an initial attempt to show a new perspective. On the other hand, the historian benefits in two ways from revisionist approaches that raise new issues and consider new possibilities. First, revisionism leads to further ideas that can eventually form a synthesis; it may, for example, be appropriate to accept Thurston's arguments for chaos while, at the same time, dis- agreeing with his view that Stalin's 'regime becomes less malevolent'. Second, revisionist arguments like this will be based to an extent on newly discovered primary sources, which can be used in other contexts.

SOURCES

2. THE 1938 SHOW TRIAL

Source E: a description of the 1938 show trial by Fitzroy MacLean, a British diplomat.

It was an impressive list of defendants: Bukharin, . . . Rykov, . . . [and] Yagoda who, until eighteen months ago, had been People's Commissar for Internal Affairs and supreme head of the all-powerful NKVD.

The prisoners were charged, collectively and individually, with every conceivable crime: high treason, murder, espionage and all kinds of sabotage. They had plotted to wreck industry and agriculture, to assassinate Stalin, to dismember the Soviet Union for the benefit of the capitalist allies. They were shown for the most part to have been criminals and traitors to the Soviet cause ever since the Revolution – before it even. The evidence accumulated filled no less than fifty large volumes. One after the other, using the same words, they admitted their guilt: Bukharin, Rykov, Yagoda . . . There was no attempt to evade responsibility. They were men in full possession of their faculties; the statements they made were closely reasoned and delivered with every appearance of spontaneity. And yet what they said, the actual content of their statements, seemed to bear no relation to reality.

Source F: from the confession of Bukharin at the 1938 show trial.

I shall now speak of myself, of the reasons for my repentance . . . For three months I refused to say anything. Then I began to testify. Why? Because while I was in prison I made a re-evaluation of my entire past. For when you ask yourself: 'If you must die, what are you dying for?' – an absolute black emptiness suddenly arises before you with startling vividness. There was nothing to die for, if one wanted to die unrepented. And, on the contrary, everything positive that glistens in the Soviet Union acquires new dimensions in a man's mind. This in the end disarmed me completely and led me to bend my knees before the Party and the country. And when you ask yourself: 'Very well, suppose you do not die; suppose by some miracle you remain alive, again what for? Isolated from everybody, an enemy of the people, in an inhuman position, completely isolated from everything that constitutes the essence of life . . . ' And at once the same reply arises. And at such moments, Citizens Judges, everything personal . . . falls away, disappears . . . But here we have also the internal demolition of the forces of counter-revolution. And one must be a Trotsky not to lay down one's arms.

Source G: from the confession of Yagoda at the 1938 show trial.

I want to correct the Procurator and make an objection on a part of the charges he has made . . . The Procurator is not right in considering me a member of the centre of the bloc . . . I am not a spy and never have been one . . . It is untrue to say that I was an accomplice in the murder of Kirov . . . I have committed heinous crimes. I realise this. It is hard to live after such crimes, it is hard to sit in prisons for tens of years. But it is terrible to die with such a stigma. Even from behind the bars I would like to see the further flourishing of the country which I have betrayed . . .

Source H: the concluding speech of Prosecutor Vyshinski at the show trial of Bukharin and others in 1938.

Time will pass. The graves of the hateful traitors will grow over with weeds and thistle ... But over us, over our happy country, our sun will shine with its luminous rays as bright and joyous as before. Over the road cleared of the last scum and filth of the past, we, our people, with our beloved leader and teacher, the great Stalin, at our head, will march onwards and onwards, towards Communism!

Questions

1. Explain the references to Yagoda (Source E) and to Trotsky (Source F). [4]
2. How far do the arguments used in Sources F and G agree with the overall summary of the trial given in Source E? [5]
*3. How effective are the language and tone in Source F in reinforcing the argument made in Bukharin's confession? [4]
4. What hints are given in Sources F, G and H that the Soviet concept of justice differed from that of the West? [5]
5. 'The purges in Stalin's Russia succeeded only because their victims were prepared to co-operate.' Discuss this view in the light of Sources E to H and your own knowledge. [7]

Worked answer

*3. ['Language' and 'tone' questions are quite common and need to be handled with explicit reference to the source. 'Language' refers to the specific wording within the passage, while 'tone' is more the general, overall impression conveyed by the words. Both need to be covered, in roughly equal proportions. It is also crucial to have a clear picture of Bukharin's overall argument: this could be dealt with first.]

Bukharin's argument in Source F is that he discovered that his own life and death had no real meaning outside the collective context of the Soviet Union: hence he had to repent and testify. The language conveys this very effectively. The prospect of personal 'black emptiness' that contrasted with the positive 'that glistens in the Soviet Union' opened his mind to 'new dimensions' and led him to 'bend my knees'. These are powerful metaphors. The general tone of the passage is similarly striking. We are left with an impression of a deep personal crisis in which Bukharin considered and rejected first dying for, then living with, 'isolation'. The influence of this flows through the whole argument and provides a justification for his decision to confess. Whether the words were entirely premeditated is debatable; if they were not, they acquire the extra dimension of inventiveness.

3

STALIN'S ECONOMIC POLICIES

BACKGROUND NARRATIVE

Immediately after the Bolshevik Revolution (October 1917), the new regime began to take steps to transform the economy. The first changes comprised the transfer of the land from the aristocracy to the peasantry and the nationalisation of key armaments factories and foreign trade. Between 1918 and 1921 the process was accelerated by War Communism, under which the grain produced by the peasantry was requisitioned for the urban workers and the army; at the same time, the remaining industrial enterprises were placed under state control. By 1921 it had become apparent that War Communism was deeply unpopular and that the regime was facing a crisis of confidence. Lenin therefore introduced the New Economic Policy, which restored an element of private enterprise to agriculture and industry. The peasantry were permitted to grow grain for the market, under licence, while most of the smaller industrial enterprises were denationalised. By the time of Lenin's death the NEP had attracted widespread support and its continuation was urged by the Rightists within the Party, including Bukharin, Rykov and Tomsky.

Some, however, considered that a more appropriate strategy would be rapid industrialisation and the introduction of collective farming. Trotsky, in particular, favoured this approach as part of his strategy of Permanent Revolution. At first, Stalin supported the continuation of the NEP, which he associated with 'Socialism in One

Country. By 1928, however, he had reversed the NEP and associated Socialism in One Country with rapid industrialisation – an apparent turnabout in policy. This followed an agricultural crisis in 1926 and 1927, during which only 17 per cent of the grain produced actually reached the cities. Stalin used this as a reason – or possibly a pretext – to introduce a policy of compulsory collectivisation of peasant land in 1928. In the same year he introduced the first Five-Year Plan, which was designed to transform the industrial base of the Soviet Union. The organisation of this was the responsibility of the State Planning Bureau, or Gosplan. The emphasis was placed on heavy industry rather than on consumer goods, and especially on coal, steel, oil, electricity and armaments. The second and third Five-Year Plans followed in 1933 and 1937, the third being interrupted by the German invasion of the Soviet Union in 1941.

The collectivisation of land proceeded very rapidly – indeed, ahead of Stalin's target. The resulting chaos made Stalin call for a period of consolidation, after accusing the enforcers of the programme of being 'dizzy with success'. The process was, however, started up again from 1932, only to overlap a major famine. This was exacerbated by the widespread slaughter of cattle, sheep and goats by peasants resisting the enforcement of the collectivisation decrees. The recovery of agriculture subsequently proved extremely difficult; indeed, the legacy of the 1930s proved a long-term liability for the Soviet economy. The industrialisation programme, meanwhile, involved a huge increase in the workforce, which was swelled by impoverished peasants from the rural areas. New industrial centres developed, such as Magnitogorsk, while Siberia acquired a new industrial infrastructure. The usual interpretation, therefore, is that heavy industry developed within the Soviet Union at the expense of agriculture. Is this true?

ANALYSIS (1): WHAT WERE THE REASONS FOR AND EFFECTS OF STALIN'S AGRICULTURAL POLICIES?

Reasons

Most explanations for Stalin's agricultural changes start with the procurement crisis of 1926–7. The release of only 17 per cent of the total grain harvest to the cities convinced the leadership that it was essential to reintroduce requisitioning, a measure last used during the period of War Communism between 1918 and 1921. This led inexorably to the longer-term policy of collectivisation, which was intended to reverse the whole policy of the NEP and move Russian agriculture into a collectivist phase.

Two main perspectives can be seen here. One is that Stalin used the procurement crisis in a deliberate policy to bring the whole economic system into line with his own preconceptions: in other words, he dictated the trend. The other is that Stalin was pushed by the crisis into a series of reactions over which he had no real control.

By the first argument, Stalin was the prime mover of economic change. He saw two possibilities. 'There is the capitalist way, which is to enlarge the agricultural units by introducing capitalism in agriculture,' but this would ultimately impoverish the peasantry. Alternatively, there was 'the socialist way, which is to set up collective and state farms'. This would provide the means, both technical and organisational, for using agriculture as a means of subsidising industry and developing socialism. These views had already been put forward by Preobrazhensky, but he had not been able to resolve the problem of how to persuade an innately conservative part of society to accept the role of being in the forefront of socialist development. Stalin was able to overcome this problem through the ruthless exercise of his power.

Some historians have gone further. If Stalin had not taken the decision to act, the NEP would have led to a return to a capitalist system. Vladimir Brovkin argues that by the late 1920s Russian society had recovered its equilibrium after the appalling experience of the Civil War, and that the NEP was evolving away from communist dictatorship. The impetus was for the search for fair prices by the peasant producer, the development of free trade unions by the workers and the search for academic freedom in education. Stalin was convinced that all this needed to change. 'From the Bolshevik point of view, it was a society in crisis. Seen from this perspective, Stalin's revolution from above was a move to stop the processes unfolding in NEP Russia. Peasants had to be herded into state-controlled units.' This was all part of a tightening up of discipline from the centre, which affected workers, women, students and teachers. Hence the break with the NEP was 'a preemptive strike of the central party–state apparatus'. By this analysis, Stalin intervened to destroy a system that was working economically in order to recover the control of the centre. It was a deliberate and calculated policy that went against the natural trend that Russia was following. It was part of the conscious construction of dictatorship as 'an admission of the failure to generate voluntary social support'. (1)

An alternative perspective has, however, been suggested. Stalin was by no means in control of the changes in agriculture. Rather than imposing collectivisation as a policy decision, he stumbled into it with neither planning nor forethought. The reason was the opposite to that given by Brovkin. The NEP did *not* work. The very fact that the peasantry were retaining most of their grain indicated that industry was failing to provide the goods for the peasants to buy. The NEP had ceased to function properly because it could not satisfy consumer needs, the oxygen for private enterprise, even in a mixed system. Stalin was forced to react because there was simply no choice. According to M. Lewin, 'The market mechanism of NEP, which had worked wonders at the start simply by following its natural course, had in the end led the regime into an impasse.' Hence, when faced with the procurement, Stalin reacted instinctively by operating 'the lever whose use he best understood; he resorted to force'. It is, however, important to realise that 'When he manipulated this particular lever in January 1928, Stalin did not know where the process set in motion by his "emergency measures" would ultimately lead him.' (2)

Forced collectivisation was therefore a characteristic reaction by Stalin. But it was more of a panic measure than anything else. It did not mean that he had created a policy. Rather, in order to extract Russia from an emergency Stalin had implemented a temporary measure that he had no squeamishness about converting into something more permanent. Some historians go further still, in denying Stalin any of the credit (or blame) for the decision to introduce collectivisation. The main argument here is that Russia was moving in this direction anyway and that Stalin went with the momentum. According to J. Arch Getty, although Stalin was officially responsible for collectivisation, he was strongly influenced by 'the social, economic and political environment that he did not create'. (3)

A possible synthesis would accept Stalin's ruthlessness and willingness to use force while, at the same time, downgrading his understanding of the underlying economic forces. The economy was not within his expertise, whereas the consolidation of personal power was. Hence political criteria dominated the economic. By 1927 there were two examples of this. One was the prospect of political humiliation caused by the procurement crisis. Stalin was faced with the choice of making further concessions or taking a tougher line. The other was the opportunity to cut down his remaining opponents, especially Bukharin, who favoured the continuation of the NEP. Hence he took a strong political decision – which is not the same as merely drifting into it. It was, however, along the lines of a policy towards which Russia might have been moving anyway.

Effects

The impact of Stalin's policies needs to be examined in terms of the speed with which collectivisation was carried through; the effect on productivity; the reaction of the peasantry to their new orders; and the extent of suffering caused by rural disruption. Finally, new light has been shed on the extent to which agriculture actually subsidised industrial growth.

The standard argument is that agriculture was sacrificed to the development of industry. The emphasis was on collectivisation to destroy individual consumerism. Hence, one of the criteria for success was surely the number of units actually collectivised. In this respect the process went ahead with remarkable speed. The proportion of holdings collectivised rose from 23.6 per cent in 1930 to 52.7 per cent in 1931, 61.5 per cent in 1932, 66.4 per cent in 1933, 71.4 per cent in 1934, 83.2 per cent in 1935, 89.6 per cent in 1936 and, finally, 98 per cent by 1941. The problem, however, was that this happened *too* quickly. Far from being in control of the situation, Stalin found that the centre lost the initiative to the localities – to local party officials, to local managers and to local NKVD officials. These forced Stalin to call a halt in 1930–1, accusing the local officials of being 'dizzy with success'. He restarted the process after 1931 and intensified the campaign of dekulakisation. Historians have tended to see this as an excuse used by Stalin to explain collectivisation's unfortunate side-effects before he then started the process up again as a deliberate strategy. But this assumes that he was fully in control. Another emphasis might be that he was struggling to retain control of a situation that was slipping beyond him. The administrative chaos was genuine – and Stalin had good reason to be concerned about excessive zeal, which needed to be checked. Having done this, the local forces again took over and this time increased the pressure on the brakes. Hence, the process needed to be started up again by the centre. These policy reversals were bound to have serious repercussions.

Production figures showed collectivisation to be a disaster. The grain harvest declined from 73.3 million tons in 1928 (itself a problem year) to 71.7 million in 1929. An increase to 83.5 in 1930 was followed by a sharp downturn to 69.5 in 1931 and 69.6 in 1932. The figures for 1934 and 1935 were 67.6 and 75.0, respectively. In the process, collectivisation created great resistance and suffering. Resistance came from all levels of the peasantry, who grew less grain and slaughtered their livestock. This resulted in catastrophic losses in numbers of animals between 1928 and 1932, cattle declining from 70 million to 34 million, sheep and goats from 146 million to 42 million and pigs from 26 million to 9 million.

What were the reasons for these losses? One possibility was that it was deliberate defiance sparked by fear: collective resistance on a massive scale, another indication that Stalin had lost control over the whole process – to the extent that his own position was endangered by the possibility of a spontaneous national revolt. An alternative view is that the whole infrastructure for production collapsed under the pressure of reorganisation and the hunt for kulaks as class enemies. In other words, local conditions were so volatile that it became impossible in some areas to fulfil the normal agricultural processes of sowing, harvesting and breeding. Defiance against the system was less in evidence than bewilderment at its incompetent application.

Either way, the result was misery – although the extent varied. There was an overall decline in food consumption between 1928 and 1932; for example, average per annum bread consumption dropped from 250 kilos per head in 1928 to 215 in 1932 and yearly consumption of potatoes from 141 kilos to 125. But these figures do not show the disproportion between the urban areas and the countryside, the latter being much the worse off. Between 1932 and 1933 large areas, especially the Ukraine, experienced a major famine. The suffering also showed itself in the unprecedented upheavals caused to Russian society. Peasants were turned against each other, layer by layer. The kulak minority was targeted by less affluent peasants everywhere. Smaller-scale producers fell victim to the hysteria and panic that affected the localities (see Chapter 2). There was also a knock-on effect on the urban areas as factories, workshops and munitions works were overwhelmed by the influx of millions of desperate peasants seeking employment and survival. Although this can be seen as part of the larger process of industrialisation and the switch in balance between agriculture and industry, it nevertheless compounded the urban accommodation difficulties.

In one respect Stalin has been given a reprieve by historians. Perhaps he should not have been. He is usually credited with finding the means whereby agriculture was used to subsidise industrial growth, thereby avoiding dependence on loans from the West. But this approach can be challenged on two grounds. One is the sheer administrative difficulty of such a process. There was simply no means of effecting an efficient transfer of resources from one sector to the other. Far from having a beneficial effect, the role of the agricultural changes was actually to impede the rate at which industrial growth could occur. The transfer of population was too rapid for industry to employ effectively; this created huge administrative problems as well as appalling social conditions. The other is the view of some historians that capital *never* flowed from agriculture into industry. Either it stayed in agriculture or there was a reverse flow from industry into agriculture. Any agricultural recovery in the second and third Five-Year Plans depended on restoration of a degree of individual initiative on the one hand and on the growth of the institution of the machine tractor station (MTS) on the other. The former showed capital being retained by agriculture, the latter showed capital being invested in agriculture by industry. Thus, in one respect the flow of investment to industry from agriculture was cut off, in another the flow was reversed.

Overall, it remains difficult to see anything positive in Stalin's agricultural policies. The results were uniformly disastrous and views on this are unlikely to change significantly. The areas where some defence has traditionally been attempted are now also open to doubt, providing even stronger condemnation. Questions have been raised as to the extent of the control shown by the centre in making and implementing decisions, and the effectiveness of agriculture in subsidising industrial growth can no longer be taken for granted. The picture is uniformly bleak.

Questions

1. Why did Stalin reverse the New Economic Policy (NEP)?
2. Why was the enforcement of collectivisation so disruptive?
3. Did Stalin's agricultural policies benefit industry?

ANALYSIS (2): WHAT WERE THE REASONS FOR AND THE EFFECTS OF STALIN'S INDUSTRIAL POLICIES?

Reasons

As in the case of his changes to agriculture, the reasons for Stalin's industrial policies can now be seen in two different ways. Here, again, it is possible to see him in control, directing – even dictating – the process from above. Or, alternatively, he may have been influenced – even pushed – by pressures from below.

The perspective of decision-making from above starts with the consolidation of his own power base against the Left Opposition and the Rightists. This meant that he was actually in a position to make a decision on the economy. His policy of rapidly accelerating industrialisation was based on two main considerations. In the first place, he aimed to create a command economy that was specifically geared to the survival of the Soviet regime against the hostility of the Western powers. This is apparently given full credence by Stalin's uncompromising speech in 1931: 'We are fifty to a hundred years behind the advanced countries. We must make good this distance in ten years. Either we do it or we shall be crushed. That is what our obligations to the workers and peasants of the USSR dictate to us.' (4) Hence it makes sense to many historians to see Stalin moving the Soviet economy on to a war footing. This also explains the emphasis on heavy industry – iron, steel and machinery that could easily be converted to armaments production – at the expense of light or consumer industry. This is a corollary to one of the explanations of Soviet foreign policy considered in Chapter 5. It has also been argued that there was a change in Soviet military strategy during the 1930s. Stalin was influenced by military theorists who believed that the Soviet Union should no longer follow the traditional Russian defensive strategy of allowing an enemy to be swallowed up by the sheer size of the country. Rather, Soviet power should take the offensive. This meant that armaments should be built up rapidly and stockpiled for a massive pre-emptive strike at a time of Stalin's choosing. The Five-Year Plans were, therefore, gearing the Soviet Union to total war. These points are dealt with in further detail in Chapter 6.

The other element of the decision-making process was ideological. Industrialisation was the only fully reliable means of developing a socialist economy. If Stalin made the decision to switch from the NEP in 1928, this was bound to mean a reorientation from agriculture to industry, since the NEP had been geared to the former. Stalin now accepted that Socialism in One Country had to focus on enlarging the urban proletariat and that the socialist way of doing this was through state-controlled industrial enterprises. This meant curbing the consumer sector. Capitalism had to be eradicated from the Soviet Union and since it was most entrenched in the peasantry, Stalin was able to justify using the peasants to subsidise industrial development and to reduce the emphasis on consumerism.

The change-from-above model is very popular but it may attribute rather too much to the decisions of one man. As well as the initiatives from above, which undoubtedly existed, there were pressures from below. Stalin's abandonment of the NEP can be seen as a tectonic decision: he went with the considerable social pressure exerted by an increasingly important part of the population. The argument goes something like this: corresponding to the ideological arguments of the left and right were the underlying influences of the growing industrialised working class and the conservative peasantry. The urban proletariat above all wanted readily available food and greater job security, both of which depended on a compliant peasantry. The peasants, however, wanted higher food prices that would enable them to buy more consumer goods. Unfortunately, consumer goods were not the way to guarantee job security for the workers or state investment in industry. Within the constraints of the Bolshevik system there was therefore a growing clash between the two sectors of agriculture and industry. This tension was bound to well upwards to influence the decisions taken in the name of the various groups. Hence, Stalin was reacting to the perceived needs of the working class in the cities, just as he had to the perceived dangers posed by the peasantry over the procurement crisis.

An overall synthesis is possible. By 1927 Stalin had moved towards taking command of an economy that, through the NEP, had been left to take its own course. In part, this change was due to Stalin's own accumulation of power, in part to problems within the economy that required attention. Stalin developed a series of priorities related to future security, which meant that the emphasis was bound to be on heavy industry and, in particular, on armaments. But the process was not a blueprint and it involved changes in the meaning of Socialism in One Country, together with borrowing elements of Trotskyism. Industrialisation meant a degree of planning – but the influence of sub-groups was considerable. This tension between direction from above and influence from below was bound to affect the development of industrialisation.

Effects

How efficiently was industrialisation implemented?

The traditional view draws two distinctions. One is between industry and agriculture – the former generally well controlled, the latter badly handled. The other is between heavy and light industry, the former accelerated at the expense of the latter. This was a decision taken by Stalin and carried out through a chain of command which enabled Stalin to build on past achievements and to develop the heavy industrial base that saved Russia from defeat by Germany after 1941.

Several major achievements have been attributed to Stalin. The first three Five-Year Plans did much to develop the basic industries. This was not, of course, without precedent in Russian history. The industrial foundations had been laid during the reign of Peter the Great and were later consolidated before the 1905 Revolution, with the development of textiles in the Moscow area, heavy industrial plant around Petrograd, coalfields in the Donets region, iron and steel in the Ukraine and oil at Baku. Stalin, therefore, did not create industry from nothing. But he did enormously enhance the scale of heavy industry. 'Gigantomania' meant the construction of new industrial cities such as Magnitogorsk, with the emphasis on heavy plant and steel production.

The scale of the increase is impressive. Although it is difficult to be precise, production figures, calculated from a variety of sources by E. Zaleski, rose as follows: the first Five-Year Plan (1928–32) increased steel production from 3 million to 6 million tons, coal from 35 million to 64 million and oil from 12 million to 21 million; the second Five-Year Plan (1933–7) raised the figures to 18 million for steel, 128 million for coal and 26 million for oil. The last complete figures for the third Five-Year Plan before it was interrupted by the 1941 German invasion were 18 million, 150 million and 26 million, respectively.

This, in turn, had a positive impact on employment: far higher levels were achieved than had been anticipated at the outset of the first Five-Year Plan. Instead of the 3.9 million expected in state industry by 1932–3, the number reached 6.4 million. The pace then slowed down to 7.9 million by 1937 and 8.3 million by 1940. The bulk of these were peasants leaving the countryside. Urban populations also increased dramatically by something like 200,000 per month, or by a total of 30 million between 1926 and 1930. Unemployment ceased to be a serious factor since the magnet of industrialisation brought in ever increasing numbers from the countryside and enabled more ambitious targets to be established for projects in heavy industry.

In the process, Stalin generated the capital and labour necessary for such developments from within the Soviet Union itself. This was the purpose of subordinating agriculture to industrialisation. Stalin therefore effectively sealed off Russia from the West and enabled her to survive amid its hostility. Ultimately, Stalin's industrialisation assisted the Soviet Union's survival in the Second World War. According to R. Hutchings, 'One can hardly doubt that if there had been a slower build-up of industry, the attack would have been successful and world history would have evolved quite differently.' (5) In a more direct sense, heavy industrialisation had made it possible for the Soviet Union to rearm. The infrastructure expanded. In 1933 defence comprised 4 per cent of the industrial budget; by 1937 it had risen to 17 per cent and by 1940 to 33 per cent. Heavy industrialisation therefore translated into ultimate survival.

Some of this argument can still be supported, but a number of reservations need to be added. It is true that Stalin tried to set an overall agenda and established the priority for accelerating heavy industry. But the effectiveness of the planning mechanism has been increasingly called into question. Indeed, recent research has shown that targets did not in themselves constitute planning. It was one thing for the central administration, including Gosplan, to draw up target figures for the different components of industry, but quite another to develop the mechanism whereby these might be achieved systematically.

Hence, although the Stalinist dictatorship was ruthless, ruthlessness did not necessarily produce efficiency – even in the area of its greatest supposed achievement, heavy industry. There was, for example, little overall consistency in the pace of the Five-Year Plans. This was due largely to the disruption caused by local influences. Local managers had to protect themselves by exaggerating their needs for investment and by hoarding materials to ensure that they had sufficient supplies. This meant shortages elsewhere and a consequent lack of overall balance. (6) In other words, the unrealistic demands from the centre forced the localities into defensive measures that could be obstructive to balanced growth.

Increasing emphasis is now being placed on the complete lack of harmony between the different sectors of the economy. It is instructive to compare Soviet industrial development with that in the United States. The latter benefited from a series of auxiliary developments that enhanced industrialisation. These were the growth of transport and services and the development of managerial and accounting expertise. (7) The American system produced in a series of parallel patterns, all interrelated and all developing their own administrative structures as a result of private enterprise. The Soviet initiative lacked these parallel structures and therefore needed a state initiative to supply them. This involved the sort of administrative complexity that could not be provided centrally and the problem was compounded by Stalin's own unwillingness to consider integrated advice, which resulted in serious distortions.

In effect, argues D.R. Shearer, there was 'a command-administrative economy' but it was 'not a planned one'.

Centralization of administrative mechanisms and the elimination of the commercial economy enabled the Party and government leaders to shift massive resources from one economic sector to another at will. In the absence of market mechanisms or at the very least proper accounting methods, however, centralizing reforms created no systematic administrative process by which to manage those resources. (8)

The problem is that complexity within the process seemed to pass for 'planning', whereas what was actually happening was administrative chaos. This had one particularly serious long-term consequence. When the Germans invaded the Soviet Union in 1941 the whole system was taken completely by surprise. Stalin had prepared the Soviet Union for an offensive war, while the situation in 1941 required a defensive response. All the mechanisms related to the Five-Year Plans were geared to this and therefore reacted badly to the crisis. The result was that the planning mechanism had to be relaxed to achieve the levels of mobilisation required. This contradiction is examined in Chapter 6.

Much less controversial than the question of whether there was a planned economy is the assertion that industrial growth was extremely unbalanced. There is no doubt that Stalin sacrificed light, consumer industries in order to press ahead with a select few heavy industries – coal, steel, oil, farm machinery and armaments. This produced a major social upheaval. The pressure on accommodation was enormous, resulting in extreme overcrowding and extensive squalor as huge dormitories were established for workers. Hence, there was an inherent contradiction in the whole process. Collectivisation and industrial-isation, intended to modernise Russia, actually tore apart its social fabric. The result was the collapse of many accepted codes of behaviour and morality. This made it easier to exploit the population but more difficult to stabilise working patterns. It also meant that there was an undercurrent of fear that contributed enormously to the purges and to political instability.

Effect brings us back to cause. Starving the consumer sector to develop heavy industry can be seen either as a deliberate strategy to create an industrial superpower with a compliant population, or as an example of inefficient planning exacerbated by fluctuating local conditions. If it was the former, then the imbalance was the result of a planned policy and was outweighed by the more positive achievements of industrialisation. If the latter, however, the pattern of industrialisation was almost as badly flawed as that of agricultural change. This is bound to raise fundamental questions about Stalin's industrial, as well as his agricultural, legacy.

Questions

1. Why was Soviet industrialisation made a priority under Stalin?
2. How efficiently was the industrial development conducted under Stalin?

SOURCES

1. SOVIET AGRICULTURE 1928–35

Source A: levels of agricultural production 1928–35 (Soviet figures).

	1928	1929	1930	1931	1932	1933	1934	1935
Grain (million tons)	73.3	71.7	83.5	69.5	69.6	68.6	67.6	75.0
Cattle (million head)	70.5	67.1	52.5	47.9	40.7	38.4	42.4	49.3
Pigs (million head)	26.0	20.4	13.6	14.4	11.6	12.1	17.4	22.6
Sheep and goats (million head)	146.7	147.0	108.8	77.7	52.1	50.2	51.9	61.1

Source B: from a report by a Reuters correspondent, 29 March 1932.

Russia today is in the grip of famine. I walked alone through villages and twelve collective farms. Everywhere was the cry, 'There is no bread; we are dying.' This cry came to me from every part of Russia. In a train a Communist denied to me that there was a famine. I flung into the spittoon a crust of bread I had been eating from my own supply. The peasant, my fellow passenger, fished it out and ravenously ate it. I threw orange peel into the spittoon. The peasant again grabbed it and devoured it. The Communist subsided . . .

The government's policy of collectivisation and the peasants' resistance to it have brought Russia to the worst catastrophe since the famine of 1921 swept away the population of whole districts.

Source C: a description of parts of Russia in 1932 and 1934 by Sidney and Beatrice Webb, prominent members of the British Labour Party. This was published in their book *Soviet Communism: A New Civilisation* (1935).

Without expecting to convince the prejudiced, we give, for what it may be deemed worth, the conclusion to which our visits in 1932 and 1934 and subsequent examination of the available evidence now lead us. That in each of the years 1931 and 1932 there was a partial failure of crops in various parts of the huge area of the USSR is undoubtedly true. It is true, also, of British India and of the United States. It has been true, also, of the USSR and of every other country of comparable size, in each successive year of the present century. In countries of such vast extent, having every kind of climate, there is always a partial failure of crops somewhere. How extensive and how serious was this partial failure of crops in the USSR, in 1931 and 1932, it is impossible to ascertain with any assurance. On the one hand it has been asserted by people who have seldom had any opportunity of going to the suffering districts, that throughout huge provinces there ensued a total absence of foodstuffs, so that . . . literally several millions of people died of starvation. On the other hand, Soviet officials on the spot, in one district after another, informed the present writers that, whilst there was a shortage and hunger, there was at no time a total lack of bread, though its quality was impaired by using other ingredients than wheaten flour; and that any increase in the death-rate due to disease accompanying defective nutrition occurred in only a relatively small number of villages. What may carry more weight than this official testimony was that of various resident British and American journalists who travelled during 1933 and 1934 through the districts reputed to be the worst affected and who declared to the present writers that they had found no reason to suppose that the trouble had been more serious than was officially represented. Our own impression, after considering all the available evidence, is that the partial failure of crops certainly extended to only a fraction of the USSR; possibly to no more than one-tenth of the geographical area. We think it plain that this partial failure was not in itself sufficiently serious to cause actual starvation, except possibly in the worst districts, relatively small in extent.

Source D: a recollection of a conversation with a Russian peasant in 1933 by Victor Kravchenko, published in *I Chose Freedom: The Personal and Political Life of a Soviet Official.*

'I will not tell you about the dead', she said, 'I'm sure you know. The half-dead, the nearly dead are even worse. There are hundreds of people in Petrovo bloated with hunger. I don't know how many die every day. Many are so weak that they no longer come out of their houses. A wagon goes round now and then to pick up the corpses. We've eaten everything we could lay our hands on – cats, dogs, field mice, birds. When it's light tomorrow you will see the trees have been stripped of their bark, for that too has been eaten. And the horse manure has been eaten.' I must have looked startled and unbelieving. 'Yes, the horse manure. We fight over it. Sometimes there are whole grains in it.'

Questions

1. (i) Explain briefly the reason for the fall in livestock figures shown in Source A. [2]
   (ii) What is meant by 'the government's policy of collectivisation', referred to in Source B? [2]
2. What differences are there between the approaches of Sources B and C to the issue of the 'famine'? How would you explain these differences? [7]
3. How much does Source D add to our understanding of conditions in the early 1930s? [6]
*4. 'The events of 1932–4 are sufficient to show that Stalin's agricultural policies of 1928–34 were an unqualified failure.' Comment on this view, in the light of Sources A to D and of your own knowledge. [8]

Worked answer

*4. *[The last of all of the questions on the sources is invariably the longest. It is the closest the student is likely to get to writing an essay, although within a much shorter timescale. The recommended approach is to consider the answer in two roughly equal parts. The first deals with the instruction 'in the light of Sources A to D', the second, in a separate paragraph, with the scope of 'your own knowledge'. Each should be clearly identified as such in the opening sentence of the paragraph.*

Within these paragraphs, an argument should be developed as an essay-type response to the question. Hence, the wording is important; consideration needs to be given to 'sufficient', to the dates '1932–4' and '1928–34' and to 'unqualified failure'. The first sentence or two should, if at all possible, signal the general line of argument to be followed.]

The sources provide some strong evidence for the failure of Stalin's policies between 1932 and 1934. There are, however, limits that prevent the use of the word 'unqualified' and its extension to the period 1928–34. An uncompromising view is taken by Source B. Russia is seen as 'in the grip of famine' and as experiencing the 'worst catastrophe since the famine of 1921'. The disaster was also widespread, affecting 'every part of Russia'. Even more powerful is the evidence of Source D, with its references to 'the dead', the 'half-dead' and the 'nearly dead', the 'wagon . . . to pick up the corpses' and the eating of 'horse manure' for the 'grains' within it. Source A adds statistical evidence with the rapid decline in the number of cattle, pigs, sheep and goats between 1932 and 1934. Two of the sources do, however, take a broader perspective, which dilutes the description 'unqualified failure'. Source A shows that grain is less severely affected throughout the period 1928–32 than livestock and that, despite the trough of 1932–4, the years 1928–31 and 1935 were less disastrously affected. Source C provides a less bleak picture overall. The Webbs maintain that the 'failure of the crops in various parts' is 'partial', and that this needs to be placed within the context of the experience of other countries. They also seem willing to take the word of the 'Soviet officials on the spot' that the problem was less shortage than adulteration of the wheat.

The sources therefore provide a mixed view. The same applies to additional material on Stalin's agricultural policy. If his purpose was to undermine agriculture to boost industry, then his policies did not fail over the period 1928–34. Nor did the speed with which collectivisation was accomplished; indeed, in 1931 Stalin criticised those implementing collectivisation as being 'dizzy with success'. On the other hand, there were serious repercussions that are more appropriately considered a failure. Recent research, especially by J. Arch Getty, has shown that it was very difficult for the central administration, under Stalin himself, to keep control over the application of agricultural policies by local officials. Overall, there was a fundamental imbalance in the economic hierarchy that was bound to increase the levels of inefficiency and to open the way for the type of disaster referred to in the sources. This could be seen as 'relative' rather than 'unqualified' failure.

SOURCES

2. PRIORITIES IN SOVIET INDUSTRIALISATION UNDER STALIN

Source E: from Sir William Citrine: *I Search for Truth in Russia* (1938).

As to the standard of life in Russia, whilst I have repeatedly said it is rising, it is useless for anyone to deny that it is still low, and in some respects deplorably so. So much of the national income is devoted to capital equipment that there is not enough for immediate consumption. The Russian workers evidently feel this represents a sacrifice which is worthwhile. They are buoyed up with confident hope for the future and the knowledge that their standards are progressively improving. The psychological value of this is immense and I believe it represents one of the greatest assets that the Soviet government possesses.

The people see their country being equipped with plant and machinery, which should one day rank it amongst the most efficient in the world. They are desperately anxious to make themselves independent, economically, of the capitalist states and to furnish the means of effective defence should they be attacked.

Source F: official Soviet statistics showing the extent to which the targets of the first and second Five-Year Plans were achieved. Figures are percentages of targets.

	First Five-Year Plan (1928–32)	Second Five-Year Plan (1933–37)
National income	91.5	96.1
Industrial production	100.7	103.0
producer goods	127.6	121.3
consumer goods	80.5	85.4
Agricultural production	57.8	62.6

Source G: a description by Andrew Smith, an American, of a factory barracks in Moscow in 1932. His recollections were published in London in 1937 under the title *I Was a Soviet Worker*.

Kuznetsov lived with about 550 others, men and women, in a wooden structure about 800 feet long and fifteen feet wide. The room contained approximately 500 narrow beds, covered with mattresses filled with straw or dried leaves. There were no pillows, or blankets ... Some of the residents had no beds and slept on the floor or in wooden boxes. In some cases beds were used by one shift during the day and by others at night. There were no screens or walls to give any privacy ... There were no closets or wardrobes, because each one owned only the clothing on his back.

Source H: a description of life in Magnitogorsk by John Scott, an American communist. This was published in his book *Behind the Urals* (1942).

Magnitogorsk was ... built from scratch. Within several years, half a billion cubic feet of excavation was done, forty-two million cubic feet of reinforced concrete poured, five million cubic feet of fire bricks laid, a quarter of a million tons of structured steel erected. This was done without sufficient labour, without necessary quantities of the most elementary materials. Brigades of young enthusiasts from every corner of the Soviet Union arrived in the summer of 1930 and did the groundwork of railroad and dam construction necessary. Later, groups of local peasants and herdsmen came to Magnitogorsk because of bad conditions in the villages, due to collectivisation. Many of the peasants were completely unfamiliar with industrial tools and processes. A colony of several hundred foreign engineers and specialists, some of whom made as high as one hundred dollars a day, arrived to advise and direct the work.

From 1928 until 1932 nearly a quarter of a million people came to Magnitogorsk. About three quarters of these new arrivals came of their own free will seeking work, bread cards, better conditions. The rest came under compulsion.

Source I: a view of Soviet industrial achievements as put forward in 1981 by an official *History of the USSR*.

While the economies of the capitalist countries were sinking ever deeper into recession, the Soviet economy was booming. The laying of a firm foundation for a socialist economy created favourable conditions for the further progress of the country's national economy in the second Five-Year Plan period, 1933–7.

The key economic task of the second Five-Year Plan period – technical re-equipment of the national economy – was fulfilled … During the second Five-Year Plan period, industrial output went up by 120 per cent. The USSR moved into first place in Europe and second in the world in gross industrial output.

Questions

1. Explain the references to
   (i) producer and consumer goods (Source F); [2]
   (ii) Magnitogorsk (Source H). [2]
*2. What does Source I show of the priorities of Soviet industrialisation? [4]
3. Compare Sources E and G as comments on the conditions experienced by Soviet workers in the 1930s. [4]
4. How much reliance can the historian place on Sources H and I as a comment on Soviet industrial progress during the 1930s? [5]
5. 'The first and second Five-Year Plans largely overcame the obstacles in the way of Soviet industrial growth.' Comment on this view, in the light of Sources E to I and of information known to you. [8]

Worked answer

*2. [On the surface, this is a straightforward question, requiring a description of the content of the source. This is, however, an oversimplification, since certain inferences need to be drawn from the content. The answer therefore needs to go to a higher level than mere description. One possibility is to develop the inferences and support these with the specific wording.]

Several priorities can be inferred from the wording of Source I. One is the need to compete aggressively with the capitalist economies, especially while the latter were 'sinking ever deeper into recession'. This would in turn enable the Soviet Union to proceed to the structural alternative to capitalism by laying a 'firm foundation for a socialist economy'. It would, of course, be necessary to work through the earlier stages of consolidation to achieve the 'technical re-equipment of the national economy' but this would then enable rapid growth that could be sustained and become self-generating ('industrial output went up by 120 per cent'). Focusing on 'gross industrial output' would enable the Soviet Union to overtake the West where it mattered most. The lack of any reference to 'consumer industry' shows that the focus is very much on heavy industry, with all the potential this provided for machinery and armaments.

4

SOCIETY AND CULTURE

BACKGROUND NARRATIVE

Stalin sought to personalise the political system and to transform the economy. This had a profound effect on society and culture in the Soviet Union. One practical result was the strengthening of the family as a vehicle for political and ideological control. Hence there were restrictions on divorce from 1935 and a ban was placed on abortion in 1936. Stalin also moved away from an earlier emphasis on social equality; instead, he reintroduced wage differentials and accentuated ranks within the army. Meanwhile, the provision of education was expanded through Narkompros (People's Commissariat for Enlightenment), while traditional forms of discipline were restored in schools – as were formal examinations. All cultural activities were brought within the overall criteria of Socialist Realism. This affected architecture, painting, music and film, and, of course, literature, which was placed under the additional constraints of the Russian Association of Proletarian Writers (RAPP) and the Union of Writers. Attempts were also made to destroy the religious base of the lives of Russians and the ethnic minorities. All forms of Christianity were attacked, along with Islam and Buddhism, and atheist organisations like the League of Godless were actively encouraged.

The usual assumption is that Stalin reversed the earlier and chaotic social experiments of the Bolsheviks and replaced them with a more successful totalitarian structure. Analyses (1) and (2) examine this perspective.

ANALYSIS (1): HOW EXTENSIVELY DID STALIN TRANSFORM SOVIET SOCIETY AND CULTURE?

According to the usual scenario, the Bolsheviks under Lenin introduced radical changes. These were intended to transform all areas of society and culture and to remove bourgeois influences. But this attempted transformation proved far more difficult than Lenin had ever anticipated, with the result that there was a serious backlash. Stalin's role was to reverse the radicalism of the Bolsheviks with a more conservative and traditional social policy.

This view is an oversimplification. The actual pace of the changes is more complex and varied. The relaxation of Bolshevik radicalism began in 1921 at the same time as the NEP. The Stalinist regime at first revived the radical impetus of the Bolsheviks. When this proved impossible to implement it retreated into a more pragmatic and cautious approach.

This pursuit of radicalism, followed by a revival of conservatism, can be explained in two contrasting ways. On the one hand, Stalin himself took the initiative, moving deliberately to the construction of a totalitarian state. This involved, as the first stage, going further than Lenin in proving his Bolshevik credentials and then, after he had achieved uncontested power, developing his personality cult through close association with Russian traditions. Throughout the whole process Stalin was in control. On the other hand, it is claimed that Stalin found the policies he pursued had a habit of recoiling on him so that he was forced to make unplanned adjustments. This does not make his system any less ruthless in its conception or its execution, but it does raise considerable questions about its effectiveness as part of a totalitarian state. His reversal of earlier social and cultural policies can be interpreted as a system out of control: Stalin was trying to dictate from the centre through the pursuit of radicalism. When the centre lost the initiative to local forces, he tried to regain the initiative by more traditional controls. This 'bottom-up' theory works as follows: Stalin found that local officials and educational bodies were over-enthusiastic in their application of radical theories and policies. Their motive, as with economic change and the pursuit of purges, was to survive within an increasingly competitive and hostile environment by trying to exceed central diktats. Any attempt by the centre to restore control increasingly involved the return to more traditional – and authoritarian – influences.

What are we to make of these arguments? The case for fully effective totalitarianism does appear to have been discredited – as can be seen in the case of official attitudes to education, equality, women and the family, religion and culture.

In education, the initial trend was the intensification of the Leninist approach, followed by a more traditionalist backlash. History, in particular, was taken to Marxist extremes during the late 1920s and early 1930s in the books of Pokrovskii, which emphasised the negative heritage of the tsarist and capitalist past. At first this harmonised with the Stalinist prospects of modernisation and socialist acceleration. By 1934, however, Stalin had gone a long way to rehabilitate part of Russia's past and was creating heroic figures out of Ivan the Terrible and Peter the Great. This fitted into his revival of other forms of tradition in education, part of his attempts to wrest the initiative back from the radical dynamic that was out of control by the end of the 1920s. Other examples of revived conservatism were the restoration of school uniforms, including compulsory pigtails for girls, and of formal discipline and corporal punishment.

A similar trend can be seen with egalitarianism. One of the key components of early Bolshevik ideology had been the abolition of all forms of social distinction. This meant the end of wage differentials, to be substituted by the Marxist maxim 'from each according to his ability, to each according to his need'. The Bolsheviks also undermined military ranks and decorations within the army. Again, Stalin initially went along with, and even intensified, this trend. But the crisis caused by the extent of the early radicalism meant that Stalin revived distinctions. This was one of the crucial effects of the Stakhanovite influence, the ethic of which was profoundly against equality. The regime went on to abolish 'wage equalisation' and to devise scales which would 'take into account the difference between skilled and unskilled labour'. The Marxist principle was therefore changed to 'from each according to his ability, to each according to his work'.

Stalin also swung from one extreme to the other in his attitude to women and the family. The Bolshevik era between 1918 and 1924 based its social changes on the Marxist premise that the family was a bourgeois institution that involved the exploitation of both the proletariat as a class and women as individuals. Attempts were therefore made to change the whole system. This was done partly by making the institution of marriage obsolete, and partly by freeing women as individuals through social measures such as readily available divorce, abortion on demand, and economic equality within the labour market. Again, this process was intensified by early radical measures of collectivisation from 1928 onwards. But the social backlash was so serious that Stalin had to institute a reversal of the policy on family and seek refuge in traditionalism. In 1935, for example, divorce became more difficult and expensive for women to obtain and abortion was made illegal the following year. The trend found its way into literature as a ban was placed on any mention of extra-marital love or sex. The emphasis had moved away from Bolshevik amorality to a Stalinist revival of the strictest sexual code. Nowhere are the contradictions of Stalinism greater than with the reluctant acceptance of the family.

The law, too, underwent a change. The West has always seen the law as a means of upholding social cohesion. Individuals have the right to initiate legal proceedings against each other. At first the Bolsheviks considered that such litigation would be unnecessary in a socialist state, while all that was necessary to maintain a socialist system was a set of revolutionary courts to deal with crime – which could be expected to 'wither away' with the end of capitalism. The process was taken further in the early Stalin period. Krylenko, who had organised the revolutionary tribunals during the Civil War period, in 1930 consolidated the legal measures in a new criminal code that incorporated criminal law into measures to deal with all 'class enemies'. Yet this proved too unstable. It was open to wide interpretation and added to the chaos of the purges at grass-roots level. Hence, from the mid-1930s onwards, the legal process became more complex, and attention was once again restored to property, whether state or individual. The motive was clearly to reintroduce social stability. At the same time, the emphasis remained on dealing with class enemies. The Procurator General from 1939, Vyshinskii, maintained that what was being introduced was 'a new, higher type of law', which was the will of the proletariat expressed through the Party.

The developments in religion followed a similar but somewhat more diverse and complex pattern. At first Stalin accelerated the campaign for atheism that had been promoted during the Leninist period. From 1928 onwards League of Godless volunteers and members of OGPU pulled down steeples and church bells; conversions were forbidden; and the purges affected the church hierarchies of the different denominations. Eventually there was a rethink. But in this case it was later and less complete than for education or for the family. It took the emergency of war and the need to appeal to patriotism to change Stalin's policy. During the struggle with Germany the Orthodox Patriarchate, abolished during the radical period, was re-established to provide a focus for Russian patriotism. It is therefore reasonable to assume that any concessions made by Stalin to religious groups were due to expediency. Where he felt that there would be little benefit to the regime the concessions were not forthcoming. Hence, there was no let up for the Jews – who, in the circumstances, were hardly likely to support the German invaders, or the Muslims, most of whom were outside the German invasion path, or the Buddhists, who were considered irrelevant to the war effort. There is also the point that Stalin considered the Islamic areas of the Soviet Union to be fundamentally more unstable than the others. This was largely because they had been nineteenth-century additions and contained largely Turkic populations. Hence, he took the important political measure of breaking the area down into the five Central Asian Soviet Republics – a division that survived the collapse of the Soviet Union itself in 1991.

In culture the Stalinist regime initially sought to continue the early radicalism of the Bolsheviks. Art and literature were mobilised specifically for the Five-Year Plans and collectivisation. 'Artistic brigades' were set up, subordinate to the Russian Association of Proletarian Writers (RAPP). The problem was that works of real merit were excluded, while local judgement, on broadly interpreted political criteria, allowed mediocrity to flourish in an atmosphere of repressive confusion. Clearly something had to be done to instil a greater degree of order so in 1932 RAPP was replaced by the Union of Writers, which redefined cultural criteria in accordance with the precepts of Socialist Realism. Stalin interpreted this as being 'socialist in content' and 'nationalist in form', arguing that writers should essentially be 'engineers of human souls'. The whole expression of culture became caught up in the Stalinist personality cult, which meant that in the long run the criteria for quality were decided by the General Secretary himself. The results of this are discussed in Analysis (2).

Overall, Stalin shifted early continuity with Bolshevik radicalism to a revival of past traditions. This has usually been put down to a deliberate policy on his part. It is, however, more in keeping with the ramshackle nature of his regime to see it as a response to initial failure and as an attempt to restore central control by abandoning radicalism in favour of more tested authoritarianism. This suited the character of his rule, but his changed attitude to society and culture was at least partly due to his failure to be a successful Bolshevik.

Questions

1. How far did Stalin accept previous social and cultural policies?
2. Was there a 'Stalinist revolution' in society and culture?

ANALYSIS (2): DID STALIN'S SOCIAL AND CULTURAL POLICIES BENEFIT THE SOVIET PEOPLE?

We have seen in Analysis (1) that there was a shift from radical to conservative policies over social and cultural issues, which showed that Stalin was not completely in control and that conservatism was an attempt to reverse the chaos caused by radicalism. All this inevitably had a mixed effect on the population.

In education, for example, the 'radical' period, from 1927 to 1931, saw huge increases in institutions and enrolments. Narkompros (People's Commissariat for Enlightenment) focused on creating education for the masses. The number of schools increased from 118,558 in 1927–8 to 166,275 by 1933, with the number of pupils rising from 7.9 million to 9.7 million. But during the radical phase the emphasis was on socialist construction, productive labour within the context of the collectivised farm or factory – which meant that formal teaching was all but abolished. During the same period the number of universities dropped from twenty-one to eleven, while 1,466 specialist institutes and departments came into existence between 1927 and 1934, student numbers increasing from 168,500 to 458,300.Teaching itself was radicalised as 'bourgeois' influences were eradicated.

This momentum did not last and the benefits of a greatly expanded base began to give way to the problems of a serious decline in quality. As in collectivisation, the leadership soon came to realise that changes had come to assume a momentum of their own and that basic educational stability was threatened. In 1931 Narkompros was criticised by the Party for falling short on educational standards, in particular in general knowledge. Between 1932 and 1935 the curriculum was extensively changed. Formal teaching methods were reintroduced, along with formal discipline, grades and examinations. History acquired a new dimension, with the emphasis on heroic figures from Russia's past, such as Ivan the Terrible and Peter the Great. In higher education examinations returned and the theoretical element of the sciences was once again given full emphasis. More significantly, the social intake of students was altered so that members of the proletariat were no longer given automatic preference. Entrance requirements were based on academic success, which once again favoured the more articulate sectors of society. Overall, it seems, greater numbers in education were more obvious as a result of radical influences, improvements in standards as a result of the restoration of traditional influences.

The role of women within the context of the family is problematic in any society. Measures to protect the family may enhance the role of women in one respect while, at the same time, reducing their freedom and options in some others. This was certainly the case in Russia. Bolshevik and early Stalinist policies emphasised the importance of women making their own decisions – and the easy availability of divorce and abortion made this a practicality. In Muslim areas women were also relieved of such customs as polygamy and were able to dispense with the veil.

But the consequences could be socially damaging within a society that had always placed a high value on the family unit. By 1934, 37 per cent of marriages in Moscow ended in divorce, there were 2.7 times as many abortions as live births and there was a massive increase in juvenile crime and social disruption. Particularly worrying to the authorities was the real threat of a long-term population fall. Consequently the restoration of the family took precedence over the more progressive treatment of women, although it has to be said that, with the limitations imposed on the workforce, there was still a greater degree of gender equality in the Soviet Union than in the West.

In the case of religion it is much easier to see the negative than the positive effects of Stalin's dictatorship. On the negative side were the ruthless and relentless persecution of the minority groups. Jews were equated with capitalism and with cliquish opposition to Communist principles; there were even periodic, although not explicit, revivals of the type of anti-Semitism that had been apparent in tsarist Russia. Islam and Buddhism experienced virtually no direct benefits from a regime that was profoundly suspicious of both. The 26,000 mosques that had existed in 1921 had been reduced to only 1,312 by 1942 and all Islamic courts had been abolished. On the other hand, Islam was never seriously weakened. The social influence of Islamic society, along with the minimal destruction caused in Central Asia by the Second World War, meant that the population growth of the Muslim republics of Kazakhstan, Uzbekistan, Kirgizia, Tadzhikistan and Turkestan was more rapid than that of the Slavic population of the Soviet Union. This had enormous implications for the future.

As in all other areas, Stalinism had a mixed impact on culture. On the one hand, Stalin placed firm controls on the experimentation of the 1920s and did whatever possible to reduce all art forms to state subservience. This had obvious implications for quality. On the other hand, the Soviet Union did, in one or two areas, experience something akin to a renaissance. Probably the most productive of the arts between 1924 and 1953 was music. Stalin's own tastes were extremely limited and therefore restricted experiment. He disliked the atonal music that was appearing in the 1920s and, like Hitler, insisted on melodic themes. Yet composers were able to work more successfully under such constraints in the Soviet Union than they were in Nazi Germany. The output of Prokofiev, Khatchaturian, Kabalevsky and, above all, Shostakovich was impressive by any standard. The Soviet Union had a greater musical output than any other dictatorship of the twentieth century. The reason might be the coincidence of four great composers or, alternatively, that Socialist Realism allowed sufficient flexibility for the expression of traditional national influences without becoming as obsessive as the clearly inferior music produced in Nazi Germany.

Artists were less renowned for work of high quality. Painting was more directly exposed to connections with political propaganda. This meant that the majority of pictures were stilted and identified with the official line on collectivisation. The most common themes were therefore contented peasants on collective farms, industrious workers with Stakhanovite aspirations, and the paternalist qualities of Stalin himself. Architecture was even more directly controlled by the state, since plans and designs could rarely be implemented without state funding. Priorities were given to prestige projects, which formed an integral part of the regime's obsession with 'gigantomania'. Also under state control and geared to propaganda purposes was the film industry. But film was used more subtly in Russia than in Germany, producing abiding masterpieces such as *Red October*, *Battleship Potemkin* and *Ivan the Terrible*. The film director Eisenstein ranks as one of the greatest of the century. Stalin was not entirely responsible for these achievements: indeed, he often interfered with Eisenstein's work. His influence was, however, less inhibiting than that of Hitler and Mussolini in Germany and Italy, neither of which produced a single feature film of any quality.

As an overview, Stalin's later social policies were generally, although not entirely, more beneficial, or less harmful, than his earlier ones. The fracturing of society by collectivisation and enforced industrialisation was predominantly negative, while the reassertion of traditional values carried certain benefits, which also provided greater stability for cultural developments. All changes were, however, made to bolster an insecure dictatorship, which resorted to purges and controls as a means of enforcing conformity, as has already been discussed in Chapter 2. The result was that the main casualty of Stalin's policies, whether radical or traditional, was individual identity.

QUESTIONS

1. Which were the most and least beneficial of Stalin's social and cultural policies?
2. Which areas of society and culture were most and least open to Stalin's influence?

SOURCES

THE EFFECTS OF SOCIALIST REALISM

Source A: from a resolution by Lenin, 8 October 1920.

All educational work in the Soviet Republic of workers and peasants, in the field of political education in general and in the field of art in particular, should be imbued with the spirit of the class struggle being waged by the proletariat for the successful achievement of the aims of its dictatorship, i.e. the overthrow of the bourgeoisie, the abolition of classes, and the elimination of all forms of exploitation of man by man.

Source B: from a speech of the writer A.O. Advienko to the Seventh Congress of Soviets, 1935.

Thank you Stalin because I am joyful. Thank you because I am well . . . Centuries will pass, and the generations still to come will regard us as the happiest of mortals, as the most fortunate of men, because we lived in the century of centuries, because we were privileged to see Stalin, our inspired leader. Yes, and we regard ourselves as the happiest of mortals because we are the contemporaries of a man who never had an equal in world history.

The men of all ages will call on thy name, which is strong, beautiful, wise and marvellous. Thy name is engraven on every factory, every machine, every place on earth, and in the hearts of all men . . .

I write books. I am an author. All thanks to thee, O great educator, Stalin. I love a young woman with a renewed love and shall perpetuate myself in my children – all thanks to thee, great educator, Stalin. I shall be eternally happy and joyous, all thanks to thee, great educator, Stalin. Everything belongs to thee, chief of our great country. And when the woman I love presents me with a child the first word it shall utter will be: Stalin.

Source C: from a poem about Stalin by the writer Osip Mandelstam, May 1934.

We live, deaf to the land beneath us,
Ten steps away no one hears our speeches,
All we hear is the Kremlin mountaineer,
The murderer and peasant-slayer.

His fingers are fat as grubs
And the words, final as lead weights, fall from his lips,

His cockroach whiskers leer
and his boot tops gleam.

Around him a rabble of thin-necked leaders –
fawning half-men for him to play with . . .

Source D: from *Soviet Communism: A New Civilisation* by Sidney and Beatrice Webb, prominent members of the British Labour Party, 1935.

There is, it must be candidly admitted, in the USSR of today, little of the sort of culture that used to be recognised as such in the Oxford or Cambridge common rooms, or in the artistic coteries of Bloomsbury or Chelsea; and even less governmental influence of it, or encouragement to it . . .

It is not unfair to say that the British devotees of culture not only accept as inevitable the exclusion of the masses from the 'realms of gold' in which they themselves find so much virtuous enjoyment, but also secretly rejoice at their own exclusive possession of something in which the common lump of men cannot share . . . In the usage of Soviet communism there is, in the conception of culture, no such connotation of inevitable exclusiveness, of a pleasant aloofness, or of a consciousness of superiority. It is, at any rate, definitely the policy of the Soviet Government . . . that the possession of culture shall be made, not necessarily identical or equal, but genuinely universal . . . Soviet Communists actually believe that, by a sustained effort of self-sacrifice on the part of the older people, the entire generation that is growing up in the USSR can be raised to a high level of culture. There will be some who will see in that very belief, and in the strenuous efforts that it inspires, a real evidence of culture in the best sense of the word.

Questions

1. Explain the references to
   (i) 'proletariat' and 'bourgeoisie' (Source A); [2]
   (ii) 'Congress of Soviets' (Source B). [2]

*2. Comment on the two approaches to Stalin's leadership shown in Sources B and C. [6]
3. Comment on the view of Soviet culture in the 1930s contained in Source D. [6]
4. 'Socialist Realism was essentially a sham.' Discuss this view in the light of Sources A to D and of your own knowledge. [8]

Worked answer

*2. ['Comment on' is a general instruction that leaves the criteria for the answer much more to the student. This can be an advantage if clear criteria can be found quickly. Otherwise it might lead to an answer without a proper focus. The criteria are suggested in the answer that follows.]

Both sources are examples of cultural responses to Stalin's leadership. But, although produced within a year of each other, they differ widely in several ways. Source B is an example of a public oration, in which the writer Advienko uses a semi-poetic style in the form of a eulogy. By contrast, Source C uses verse as a more private medium to convey biting satire. The image of Stalin's leadership could not be more differently presented. Source B projects him as an 'inspired leader' without 'an equal in world history', directly responsible for everything of value. Source C, on the other hand, emphasises the negative and deadening effect of Stalin's power. These conceptions are reinforced by the imagery used which, in each case, is extravagant and extreme. Source B considers Stalin's very name to be 'strong, beautiful, wise and marvellous' while, in Source C, there are references to the 'murderer and peasant-slayer' with fingers as 'fat as grubs'. The two sources also have different expectations about the response to Stalin's leadership. In Source B praise is seen to be the natural response for all the benefits received from Stalin. Source C, however, considers that Stalin is surrounded by 'fawning half-men'. Overall, Advienko and Mandelstam are typical of the two extreme responses that are likely to exist within any totalitarian system, the former encouraged and the latter in great peril.

5

STALIN'S FOREIGN POLICY, 1929–41

BACKGROUND NARRATIVE

As a result of the Bolshevik Revolution, Soviet Russia found itself isolated in international diplomacy and excluded from the Paris Peace Conference. Then, in 1922, while Lenin was still, in name at least, in charge of Soviet affairs, Russia and Germany stunned the other powers by drawing up an agreement at Rapallo that conferred mutual diplomatic representation and provided trade and investment links. This was tightened in 1926 by the Treaty of Berlin, which was, in effect, a neutrality pact. Relations between the Soviet Union and other capitalist powers were more problematic. Diplomatic relations were established with Britain in 1924, broken by Britain in 1927 and re-established in 1929. It seemed, therefore, that the most consistent connection before 1931 would be with Germany.

The rise of Hitler threw Soviet policy into the melting pot. Between 1931 and 1933 Stalin was convinced that Hitler in power would be the best option for the Soviet Union, for reasons that are examined below. He certainly saw no immediate reason to seek to replace the Treaty of Berlin. By the mid-1930s, however, Stalin appeared to have made a substantial switch. In 1935 he drew up the Franco-Soviet Pact and, with France, guaranteed the existence of Czechoslovakia by the Treaty of Mutual Assistance. Meanwhile, the Soviet Union had also joined the League of Nations and Foreign Minister Litvinov seemed a keen supporter of the policy of collective security that was designed originally to contain Germany. Stalin's attitude to the Spanish Civil War also indicated strong ideological moves against fascism. The Soviet Union was the only power to give direct assistance to the Republic in its struggle against the Nationalist forces of Franco, which received arms and equipment from Mussolini and Hitler. Stalin also urged the adoption of 'popular front' alignments of all centrist and leftist groups against the fascist right.

The period between September 1938 and August 1939 proved to be another turning point in Stalin's foreign policy. The Soviet Union played no part in the Anglo-French policy over Czechoslovakia and became increasingly concerned about the concessions being given to Germany. Early in 1939 the Soviet Union sought more specific commitments from France and Britain against Germany, but these were not forthcoming. Meanwhile, Litvinov's successor, Molotov, was engaged in secret discussions with his German counterpart, von Ribbentrop. In August 1939 these produced the Nazi–Soviet Pact. On the surface this was a non-aggression agreement but a 'Secret Additional Protocol' made possible the partition of Poland between Germany and Russia. Both Hitler and Stalin proceeded to claim their share in September.

Stalin appeared to have gained the security he had sought, particularly since Hitler now focused the attention of Germany on the West in 1940. Stalin used this period to wrest territory from Finland but the Winter War that followed showed the vulnerability of the Soviet armed forces. Stalin also put increased pressure on Hitler to concede territory to the Soviet Union in the Baltic States and Romania. At the same time, however, he refused to heed warnings from Western countries and his own intelligence services that Hitler was now planning to attack the Soviet Union. Hitler proceeded to do this in June 1941, taking Stalin completely by surprise.

ANALYSIS (1): WHAT WERE THE MOTIVES OF STALIN'S FOREIGN POLICY UP TO AUGUST 1939?

The motivation behind Stalin's foreign policy should be analysed at two levels. First, and fundamentally, what was the underlying objective for the regime of Soviet relations with other powers? Second, and arising from this, why were specific policies pursued at particular stages between 1924 and 1939?

Stalin did appear to have an underlying motive: to provide external security for the internal construction of communism. If successful, this would, in the long term, enable the Soviet Union to turn its power outwards – at a time of its own choosing. In Stalin's own words, 'Our banner remains, as before, the banner of peace. But if war breaks out, we shall not be able to sit with folded hands – we shall have to make a move, but the move will come last. And we shall act so as to throw the decisive weight onto the scales, the weight that should be preponderant.' (1) According to T. Uldricks, Stalin assumed 'hostility from all imperialist powers and, therefore, the need to keep them divided'. (2)

These underlying assumptions resulted logically in three developments. The first was the creation of an industrial superpower as the only means of providing the military base necessary for survival. In justifying his policy of Socialism in One Country and the introduction of the planning system Stalin constantly harped on the theme of Soviet insecurity. (3) The second development was the policy adopted to safeguard the Soviet position while this reconstruction was under way. Stalin had already opted for Socialism in One Country rather than Permanent Revolution, which might well have upset the external situation to Russia's internal disadvantage. The third development was the utilisation of military involvement to ensure Soviet security and to foster Soviet expansion. The period between 1939 and 1941 was to prove that Stalin had an irredentist attitude to the boundaries of tsarist Russia: he intended to reclaim as much as possible of what had been lost in the treaties of Brest Litovsk (1918) and Riga (1921). In this sense war, not revolution, would be the means.

Stalin's overall approach to foreign policy seems therefore to have encompassed rapid internal growth regulated by a planning mechanism, short- or medium-term external security, and long-term military intervention. But how could this best be achieved? Historians have tended to follow one of two lines of argument.

One is the Rapallo approach. The argument here is that Stalin aimed to continue the special relationship established with Germany by the Treaty of Rapallo in 1922. This made sense for a number of reasons. Rapallo and its successor, the Treaty of Berlin (1926), conferred upon the Soviet Union benefits from German investment and a degree of military co-operation. It also had the advantage of putting pressure upon the new Polish state, which had, after all, won the Russo-Polish

War of 1920–1. In addition, it might neutralise the Anglo-French combination. This was an important consideration since Britain and France were likely to be as hostile to the Soviet Union as they were to Germany; they had, of course, played the leading roles in supporting the counter-revolutionary White forces during the Civil War between 1918 and 1921. Sooner or later, the Soviet Union's special relationship with Germany would pay off, especially if Germany could be induced into a conflict with the other capitalist powers, independently of initial Soviet involvement.

The alternative interpretation of Stalin's foreign policy is that he adopted a collective security approach. This involved seeking a more important role in Europe than a mere bilateral relationship with a single power would permit. The Soviet Union would play a pivotal rather than a peripheral part. Since Germany was perceived as the most likely threat to Soviet security, Stalin's foreign policy would have to be directed towards maintaining contacts with Germany's most likely opponents and constraints. This meant increasing Soviet contacts with France, especially during the period between 1933 and 1938.

The Rapallo and collective security approaches may be seen as mutually exclusive of each other. By one analysis, the Nazi–Soviet Non-Aggression Pact of August 1939 was a logical and direct consequence of a long-term strategy. The pact represented 'the fruition of Stalin's whole complex conception of the means of Soviet survival in a hostile world and the emergence into a commanding international position'. (4) There is a certain logic to Tucker's view. The Soviet position would be greatly enhanced as Germany, apparently secure in the guarantee of Soviet neutrality, would be free to turn on the West. The result would be general exhaustion, as had occurred in the First World War, only this time Russia would avoid joining the initial hostilities. Instead, intervention would be at a time of Stalin's choosing, calculated to regain Russia's former frontiers, which would, in turn, provide a base for further territorial expansion.

Why did the emphasis in Stalin's policy change during the 1930s – from supporting the rise of Hitler to power before 1933, to moving towards an agreement with France by 1935, before returning to collaboration with Germany by 1939? The argument is that Hitler was at first seen by Stalin as a temporary phenomenon; while if he survived, he would provide the best prospect of provoking a war between Germany and the West. Between 1933 and 1938, however, Hitler was moving ahead, with his repudiation of the Versailles settlement, more confidently than anyone had expected. Stalin therefore considered it necessary to put pressure on Germany by temporary and outflanking diplomacy involving France and Czechoslovakia. By 1939 Stalin was able to return to his preferred Russo-German co-operation, knowing, from March, that there was a strong prospect of a war between the West and Germany over Poland. The Nazi–Soviet Pact was therefore the pinnacle of Stalin's foreign affairs strategy throughout the 1930s.

There are, however, several problems with this approach. First, it attributes to Stalin the sort of long-term objectives that amount almost to a blueprint. Changes in Stalin's policy are seen as mere tactical deviations in pursuit of a long-term strategy. Might they not actually have been a change of long-term strategy as a result of short-term indecision and uncertainty? After all, this was a common reaction in the 1930s to rapidly changing circumstances. Stalin would have had to transcend not only Chamberlain and Daladier – admittedly not too difficult – but even Hitler, whose forward planning has now been called into question by a battery of historians. Stalin should, perhaps, be seen within this context. In any case, his commitment to foreign policy has been disputed. According to J. Haslam, Stalin 'took only a sporadic interest' in this area; indeed, 'on the whole, Stalin abstained from direct intervention and contented himself with merely reviewing and approving . . . Even the process of review was occasionally delegated to others.' (5) We could go further down the road travelled by Haslam. The swings in policy were attempts to correct previous errors of his own and to re-establish control over those who had not fulfilled the tasks delegated to them. For example, his policy of assisting Hitler into power had clearly backfired by 1934. The Nazi regime was strengthening its position at home and abroad, so that Stalin was obliged to seek, through collective security, to control the monster he had helped create. This explains the Franco-Soviet Pact of 1935 as well as his policy of encouraging broad anti-fascist fronts all over Europe, especially in Spain. He was provided with an apparently rational approach at this stage by Foreign Minister Litvinov, who sought to improve Soviet relations with the West through involvement in the League of Nations. When, by 1938, it had become apparent that collective security had not worked, Stalin switched to another tack. He blamed Litvinov for moving the Soviet Union too closely to France and replaced him with Molotov, who pursued a more pro-German line. In each case Stalin was influenced by his advisers quite as much as he directed them – until things went wrong and he needed a scapegoat.

The violent oscillations in foreign policy were, by this analysis, similar to what happened in domestic policy: far from being in overall control, Stalin had to pull back after an earlier policy had gone *out of* control.

He was fundamentally pragmatic, adjusting his policies according to immediate needs rather than to long-term plans. He had the power and authority to make sudden changes and explain away previous errors of judgement in a way that would have been much more difficult in a democracy. This gives the illusion, rather than the substance, of control.

Questions

1. Was Stalin in control of Soviet foreign policy?
2. Was Stalin's foreign policy consistent?

ANALYSIS (2): WAS THE NAZI–SOVIET NON-AGGRESSION PACT EVIDENCE OF THE SUCCESS OF STALIN'S FOREIGN POLICY?

By far the most important development in Stalin's foreign policy to 1941 was the Nazi–Soviet Non-Aggression Pact, which puts into perspective every other initiative taken after Stalin's assumption of full control in 1929. Not surprisingly, two very different interpretations can be advanced about whether it was a success. These depend on whether the Nazi–Soviet Pact was the outcome of a long-term plan or whether it was put together at the last minute to compensate for all the frustrations and difficulties that had occurred during the 1930s.

If it was always Stalin's long-term intention to come to terms with Germany, then the pact can be seen as the fulfilment of a difficult and, at times, frustrating policy. It was undoubtedly the best means of achieving the objective of promoting discord between Germany and the Western powers. Stalin would have known that Hitler could feel confident in invading Poland, which, in itself, was the most direct way of provoking France and Britain into declaring war on Germany. The Secret Protocol also enabled the Soviet Union to regain the areas lost to Poland in 1921 by the Treaty of Riga. Since these were beyond the original frontier of Poland, set by the Allies at the Curzon Line, it was unlikely that Britain and France would declare war on Russia as well; after all, Stalin could be seen as reoccupying former Soviet territory, while Hitler was clearly violating the Polish state itself. In addition, the pact ensured that the Soviet Union would maintain the economic link with Germany that had been started at Rapallo and then resumed, after interruptions, in 1939. Overall, the agreement was a stunning coup. It ensured that Germany would weaken itself in a war with the West while, at the same time, Russia could strengthen itself by the recovery of lost territory and continue to benefit from German industrial credits. Stalin even retained the option of intervening decisively in the now inevitable European conflict. It was the culmination of everything he had planned.

The alternative perspective is much more negative. If the whole process was not planned, then there must have been a violent swing of the pendulum that Stalin was unable to control. As we have already seen in Analysis (1), the 1930s saw a series of disasters in Soviet policy. This started with Stalin's blunder in helping put Hitler into power. He then had to compensate for this by trying to reactivate collective security in conjunction with France, and by seeking to promote popular fronts throughout Europe against fascism. These were clearly desperate measures, merely reactions to offset an original policy that had gone badly wrong. The trouble was that the attitudes of Britain and France were beyond his control and he found himself buffeted back towards Germany by his disappointment with the Anglo-French policy of appeasement. In this perspective, the Nazi–Soviet Pact was a measure that originated from desperation, not from planning. As in domestic policy, Stalin was rarely in control of the situation and was well aware of the threat of impending chaos. The Non-Aggression Pact was, for him, a possible lifeline that he seized without realising its full implications. Even the Polish dimension has been misinterpreted. The pact did not contain a specific agreement to partition Poland between Germany and Russia. Rather, the Secret Protocol focused more generally on spheres of influence in Eastern Europe. According to G. Roberts, therefore, 'The partition of Poland in September 1939 was the direct result not of the Nazi–Soviet pact but of the unforeseen rapidity of the Polish military collapse.' (6) There is an element of desperation here too: Stalin was forced to occupy eastern Poland to limit the extent of the German advance, the speed of which took him completely by surprise. Hence, any territorial advantages of the pact to Russia were entirely unplanned and were the result of a reaction to events as they occurred.

So far we have assessed the Nazi–Soviet Pact in relation to what Stalin intended. There is, of course, another criterion for success. Irrespective of whether it was the logical outcome of Stalin's earlier policies, was the pact the best course for the Soviet Union in the circumstances? Again, there are two possible approaches.

The first would emphasise the positive effects of the pact in delaying Stalin's involvement in the war, thereby enabling the USSR eventually to crush Germany. Soviet historians, in particular, argued that 'subsequent events revealed that this step was the only correct one under the circumstances. By taking it, the USSR was able to continue peaceful construction for nearly two years and to strengthen its defences.' (7) During the period 1939 to 1941 Stalin was also able to build up a buffer zone in Eastern Europe; Soviet occupation started with eastern Poland in September 1939, followed by the Baltic States in the autumn (sanctioned by a further pact with Germany, the Border and Friendship Treaty) and the extension of a more secure frontier against Finland between 1939 and 1940. The initial impact of the German invasion in 1941, devastating though it was, was to some extent absorbed by this buffer area.

This view is, however, somewhat simplistic. The alternative is that the pact was not actually necessary for Russia. Indeed, W. Laqueur maintains that it gave Stalin a false security and was to the disadvantage of the Soviet Union in two ways. First, Stalin was binding himself to a commitment the Soviet Union did not need. Hitler was far too preoccupied with Britain and France to launch an invasion on the USSR in 1939. But, second, if he had done, the Soviet Union would have been better off than it was in 1941. Between 1939 and 1941 Germany's armaments production increased proportionately more rapidly than that of the Soviet Union, meaning that Hitler could launch the sort of invasion in 1941 that would have been out of the question in 1939. (8) In addition, it could be argued that Russia lost any strategic advantage with the fall of France to Germany in June 1940 and the inability of Britain to launch an attack on the continent. It is true that over the same period Stalin began the process of extending Soviet security by taking over the Baltic States, Bessarabia and Northern Bukovina but this can be seen merely as a means of compensating for the expansion that the pact had made possible for Germany.

If a respite was provided by the Nazi–Soviet Pact (and this is by no means certain), it could further be argued that Stalin failed to make proper use of it. At the end of 1939, for example, he launched an attack on Finland in an attempt to push back the Soviet frontiers near Leningrad and in Karelia. By the time this objective had been achieved in February 1940, the Winter War had produced some humiliating reverses at the hands of the Finnish army, showing up Russia's military deficiencies and bankrupting her diplomatic reputation to the extent that she was thrown out of the League of Nations for aggression. In all probability these failings convinced Hitler that he could afford to attack the Soviet Union sooner rather than later. The way in which Stalin used the respite in effect seriously shortened it.

But the most serious blunder committed between 1939 and 1941 was Stalin's complete failure to anticipate Hitler's intentions.

He assumed that Russia was safe from Germany at least for the foreseeable future and that it was safe to pursue his own agenda. He therefore conducted diplomacy that was based on a fundamental misconception: the assumption that Germany would become increasingly pliable in proportion to the pressure applied by Russia. But, as Roberts points out, 'Moscow's pursuit of this objective resulted not in the further development of the Nazi–Soviet alliance but the beginning of a fateful crisis in Soviet–German relations which was to end in war.' (9) Stalin did not realise that Soviet pressure depended on Germany's tolerance: it was not likely to increase that tolerance. All Stalin was doing in his insistence on further concessions in the Balkans was to increase Hitler's determination to settle the Russian issue once and for all. And, of course, the problems encountered by the Red Army in Finland contracted the timescale envisaged by Hitler to do this.

Worse was to follow. Even when it became clear that Soviet relations with Germany were deteriorating rapidly, Stalin showed little awareness of any imminent threat. Indeed, it could be argued that he lost control over the whole situation. This can be shown in three ways. First, he failed to make any use of possible contacts with Britain. He considered that this might run the risk of diverting the Nazi war machine eastwards, which would play into Churchill's hands by releasing the pressure on Britain. This subsequently proved to be a mistake, since Hitler was planning to throw the weight of the German armies against Russia. Through his inaction here Stalin therefore lost the initiative. Instead – in a second error – Stalin assumed that any war with Germany would be preceded automatically by warning signals from Germany as part of a clearly visible deterioration in relations; Stalin was confident that, in such circumstances, Hitler would issue an ultimatum before hostilities ensued. In that event Russia would have time to respond by making the diplomatic adjustments necessary to prevent the outbreak of war. This meant that Stalin committed a third blunder by ignoring all the warnings he did receive about an impending German invasion. These came from intelligence reports from Soviet agents as well as details about German troop movements provided by the British government. These will be dealt with in detail in Chapter 6. Consequently, according to Churchill, Stalin and his advisers proved at this stage to be 'the most completely outwitted bunglers of the Second World War'.

There is, of course, an alternative explanation to Stalin's strange behaviour in 1941: he was preparing a pre-emptive strike against Germany. This is a strong argument, based on the proposition that the development of heavy industry in the Five-Year Plans had been geared towards equipping the Soviet Union with the military potential for a massive offensive blow. This view, which is also examined in detail in Chapter 6, might appear to restore the initiative to Stalin by enabling him to attack Germany at a time of his own choosing. But that time was not in the summer of 1941. Indeed, there was every reason for avoiding the possibility of a Soviet attack until 1942, when Soviet armaments production was expected to peak. If Stalin was thinking in this way, then he made a fourth mistake: he became all the more anxious to avoid a conflict in 1941. As a result, Soviet defences might actually have been undermined in the immediate term by the feeling of security given by the knowledge of an offensive in the longer term. At all events, the German armed forces achieved a stunning series of victories against Russia in the opening months of their Blitzkrieg.

We might conclude, as in Analysis (1), that Stalin was not in control of developments in Eastern Europe. The Nazi–Soviet Pact was more a response to the specific situation in 1939 than a long-term target and, as it turned out, was less beneficial than has been traditionally argued. This was largely because Stalin misinterpreted Hitler's intentions. It was fortunate for Stalin that Hitler's subsequent errors were even more serious than his own.

Questions

1. What were the advantages and disadvantages of the Nazi–Soviet Non-Aggression Pact for the Soviet Union?
2. On balance, were the advantages greater than the disadvantages?

SOURCES

SOVIET RELATIONS WITH GERMANY, BRITAIN AND FRANCE, 1938–9

Source A: from a speech by Molotov, November 1938.

The Soviet Union did not, and could not, take part in the bargaining of the imperialists, of the fascists and so-called democratic governments at the expense of Czechoslovakia. The Soviet Union did not, and could not, take part in the dismemberment of Czechoslovakia to satisfy the appetites of German fascism and its allies. No doubt can remain about Soviet policy on this point. While the French government renounced its treaty with Czechoslovakia, at the moment of its decisive test, and came to an agreement with England and German fascism, whatever the cost to democratic Czechoslovakia, the Soviet Union showed that its attitude to international agreements is entirely different. It demonstrated to the entire world its fidelity to the treaties it has concluded for fighting the aggressor is unshakeable . . . The French and British governments sacrificed not only Czechoslovakia but their own interests as well, for the sake of an agreement with the aggressors . . . But one thing is clear: the Soviet Union was not intimidated by threats from fascist countries . . .

This fact is of great international importance, not only for the present moment, but for the entire future international struggle against fascism and fascist aggression. Only the Soviet Union, the land of socialism, stood and stands steadily on the basis of struggle against fascist aggression, for the defence of peace and of the freedom and independence of states from fascist attack.

Source B: official Soviet reply to British proposals for an agreement with the Soviet Union, 15 May 1939.

The Soviet Government have given careful consideration to the latest proposals of the British Government, which were communicated to them on May 8, and they have come to the conclusion that these proposals cannot serve as a basis for the organisation of a front of resistance against a further extension of aggression in Europe.

This conclusion is based on the following considerations:

(1) The English proposals do not contain principles of reciprocity with regard to the USSR and place the latter in a position of inequality, inasmuch as they do not contemplate an obligation by Britain and France to guarantee the USSR in the event of a direct attack on the latter by aggressors, whereas England and France, as well as Poland, enjoy such a guarantee as a result of reciprocity which exists between them.

(2) The English proposals only extend a guarantee to Eastern European states bordering on the USSR, to Poland and to Romania, as a consequence of which the North Western frontier of the USSR towards Finland, Estonia and Latvia remains uncovered.

(3) On the one hand, the absence of a guarantee to the USSR on the part of England and France, in the event of a direct attack by an aggressor, and, on the other hand, the fact that the North Western frontier of the USSR remains uncovered, may serve to provoke aggression in the direction of the Soviet Union.

Source C: extracts from the Nazi–Soviet Non-Aggression Pact, August 1939.

The Government of the German Reich and the Government of the USSR, desirous of strengthening the cause of peace between Germany and the USSR, have reached the following agreement.

Article I.   Both High Contracting Parties obligate themselves to desist from any act of violence, any aggressive action, and any attack on each other, either individually or jointly with other powers.

Article II.   Should one of the High Contracting Parties become the object of belligerent action by a third power, the other High Contracting Party shall in no manner lend its support to this third party.

Article III.   The Governments of the two High Contracting Parties shall in the future maintain continual contact with one another for the purpose of consultation in order to exchange information of problems affecting their common interest . . .

Article V.   Should disputes or conflicts arise between the High Contracting Parties, both Parties shall settle these disputes exclusively through friendly exchange of opinion, or, if necessary, through the establishment of arbitration commissions.

Secret Additional Protocol

1.   In the event of a territorial and political arrangement in the areas belonging to the Baltic States, the northern boundary of Lithuania shall represent the boundary of the spheres of influence of Germany and the USSR . . .

2.   The question of whether the interest of both parties makes desirable the maintenance of an independent Polish state and how such a state should be bounded can only be definitely determined in the course of further developments.

Source D: an agreement between Germany and the Soviet Union partitioning Poland, 28 September 1939.

The Government of the German Reich and the Government of the USSR consider it as exclusively their task, after the collapse of the former Polish state, to re-establish peace and order in these territories. To this end they have agreed upon the following:

The Government of the German Reich and the Government of the USSR shall determine the boundary of their respective national interests in the territory of the former Polish state . . . The territory of the Lithuanian state falls into the sphere of the influence of the USSR, while the province of Lublin, and parts of the province of Warsaw fall to the influence of Germany . . . Both Parties will tolerate in their territories no Polish agitation which affects the territories of the other Party. They will suppress in their territories all beginnings of such agitation and inform each other concerning suitable measures.

Questions

1. Explain the references to
    (i) the French government's 'treaty with Czechoslovakia' (Source A). [2]
    (ii) the 'guarantees' to 'Poland and Romania' (Source B). [2]
2. Compare the Soviet attitude shown to Britain and France shown in Sources A and B. How would you explain any differences? [7]
*3. To what extent are the terms in Source D in conformity with those in Source C? [6]
4. 'The Soviet pact with Germany in August 1939 was the result of desperation, not of any long-term policy.' Discuss this view in the light of Sources A to D and of your own knowledge. [8]

Worked answer

3. ['To what extent?' is a phrase that must be dealt with explicitly. The possibilities for the answer are 'completely', 'partially' or 'not at all'. The overall answer is most likely to be 'partially', although within this there may be elements of the other two. Examples need to be precisely located within the two sources.]

Source D seems to be partially in line with Source C, although there are also certain differences between them. In general terms, Source D shows evidence of the fulfilment of the intention in Source C to 'maintain continual contact with one another for the purpose of consultation'. However, since circumstances had changed by the time that Source D was drawn up, the specific agreements were bound to vary. For example, Source C provides for a future decision on whether 'the interest of both parties makes desirable the maintenance of an independent Polish state', whereas Source D acknowledges 'the collapse of the former Polish state'. This affects the questions of boundaries. Source C leaves it open as to 'how such a state should be bounded', whereas Source D refers to the determination of the boundary between Nazi and Soviet 'respective national interests in the territory of the former Polish state'. Source D goes beyond Source C in another way. The former makes no provision for internal controls by Russia and Germany over internal order in Poland, while the latter provides for a mutual agreement between the two countries not to 'tolerate in their territories' any 'Polish agitation which affects the territories of the other Party'. In one respect one of the terms in Source C is revised in Source D. In the former the northern boundary of Lithuania represented 'the boundary of the spheres of influence of Germany and the USSR', whereas in Source D Lithuania fell 'into the sphere of the influence of the USSR'. This was, however, after mutual consultation between the parties.

6

THE SOVIET UNION AT WAR, 1941–5

BACKGROUND NARRATIVE

Stalin had agreed to the Non-Aggression Pact with Germany in August 1939 to prevent – or postpone – the outbreak of war between Germany and Russia. Yet, on 22 June 1941, Hitler invaded the Soviet Union. The result was military collapse of astonishing rapidity with most of the losses of Soviet troops and equipment throughout the Second World War occurring during the first year of Soviet involvement. Stalin had ordered the withdrawal of the Soviet border troops in Soviet-occupied Poland, which meant that the German panzer divisions, now well-drilled in their Blitzkrieg (lightning war) strategy, could slice through the Ukraine to establish, by 1942, a front extending from Leningrad in the north to Moscow in the centre and Stalingrad in the south. Stalin himself withdrew for a while from public life and Hitler confidently predicted the end of the campaign and of the Soviet state.

Yet, from the end of 1942, a remarkable recovery occurred. The first major success of the Soviet forces was the Battle for Moscow, which prevented the capture of the Soviet capital. The Soviet leadership then decided to concentrate the defensive action on the city of Stalingrad, in which the Germans were eventually forced to surrender in 1943. This was followed by the Soviet victory in the tank battle at Kursk. From this stage onwards the Soviet counter-attack gathered momentum. Kiev was recaptured by November 1943 and Leningrad early in 1944. The Red Army then went on to force German troops out of Soviet territory and advanced into the states of Eastern Europe: Poland, followed by Romania and Bulgaria. By February 1945 the Red Army under Zhukov was advancing into Germany itself and, in April, succeeded in capturing Berlin. Total war seemed to have resulted in total victory.

The extents of both the initial catastrophe and the eventual recovery have inevitably invited very diverse historical explanations.

ANALYSIS (1): WHY WAS THE SOVIET UNION INITIALLY DEFEATED BY NAZI GERMANY?

The extent of the initial Soviet collapse was stunning, even to the Nazi invaders, who had been led by Hitler's propaganda to expect another successful Blitzkrieg. Soviet historians have explained this by the numerical superiority of German armaments in 1941. This simply will not suffice as an explanation, as the Soviet forces outnumbered the Germans; by June 1941 the Soviet Union possessed most of the world's tanks – close on 24,000 altogether. Western historians have tended to focus on the element of surprise and Stalin's deficient leadership in the opening months of the invasion. This is nearer the mark, but now needs to be considered within the context of recent research into the specific way in which the Soviet Union had prepared for the war.

The basic argument to be followed here is in four stages. First, during the 1930s the Soviet infrastructure had been prepared for one type of war but, second, because of his inappropriate diplomatic and other decisions between 1939 and 1941, Stalin blundered into an altogether different one. Third, in these circumstances the infrastructure came close to collapse, which meant, fourth, that there was little to stop the already efficient German strategy of Blitzkrieg.

The main aim of the first three Five-Year Plans had been to mobilise the Soviet Union for total war. Stalin's preoccupation with the Western threat has already been analysed in Chapter 3. In this he was partly influenced by a new overall strategy of warfare developed by military theoreticians such as Varfolomeev and Triandafilov. They turned away from the traditional Russian response of protracted defensive war that had, after all, gone badly between 1914 and 1917. Instead, they argued that the Soviet Union should prepare to deliver a swift and crushing blow through 'the conduct of operations of annihilation'. (1) Furthermore, the Soviet Union would need to be able to deploy all its forces as soon as war broke out to deliver a sudden and decisive blow. Hence, the main focus of the Five-Year Plans was heavy industry; the priority was rearmament; and the motive was an offensive war. Tanks, artillery pieces, aircraft and small weapons were produced and stockpiled on a massive scale throughout the 1930s. Mobilisation was no longer geared for defence and, to be fully effective, would need a pre-emptive strike.

This, of course, did not happen. Traditionally, the initial collapse of the Soviet Union has been put down to Stalin's inappropriate response to Hitler. This is quite true, but it should be seen within the context of a military–economic system that was disastrously affected by this response. Stalin's diplomatic errors delivered the war for which the country was not prepared. The timing of the hostilities was chosen by Hitler, not Stalin, although the latter could well have been building up for a pre-emptive strike at a later date. To prevent a conflict that he clearly regarded as premature, Stalin did what he could to appease Hitler.

In the process, Stalin more than misjudged the situation. He committed blunders of colossal proportions. The most basic was a misinterpretation of Hitler's intentions. Stalin had initially assumed that Hitler and Nazism comprised an unstable form of radicalism, which would soon give way to communism. When this failed to happen he attributed to Hitler a large measure of pragmatism. He assumed that Hitler was basically logical in his objectives and that he would not consider the possibility of fighting a war on two fronts. He believed, as we have seen in Chapter 5, that there would be plenty of warning of any impending attack on the Soviet Union. This made Stalin unreceptive to warnings, from British intelligence in April 1941, of German troop concentrations near the Soviet border. Stalin's reasoning – logically – was that Churchill's intention was to try to provoke a conflict between Germany and Russia that would open up a war on two fronts, to the benefit of Britain. But Stalin also ignored intelligence reports from his own agents. For example, both General Golikov and Admiral Kuznetzov quoted Soviet agents to the effect that the concentration of German troops meant that war was imminent. Soviet agents in Japan and Berlin even gave the precise date of the German attack: 22 June 1941. Stalin chose to ignore these because they did not fit into the way in which he had rationalised Hitler's intentions. In trying to keep his diplomatic options open he had therefore closed off his military options and laid his country wide open to a devastating assault of the type that Hitler had already demonstrated in Western Europe in 1940. When German armies moved up to and across the frontier, Stalin even ordered the withdrawal of Soviet units to avoid border provocations and conflict, in the belief that there could still be a negotiated settlement between Germany and Russia. Soviet defences were further hamstrung by orders from Stalin against the mobilisation of reserves or the conduct of normal military manoeuvres in case these should provoke Hitler. Hence the current view is still that 'The causes of this disastrous behaviour lay in Moscow, with Stalin.' (2) No doubt aware of the extent of his errors, Stalin underwent a collapse, akin to a nervous breakdown. There were even plans to take power from him and to confer it on Molotov instead. Generals Konev and Zhukov both reported that Stalin seemed totally depressed and that he was ready to make peace with Germany and to give up huge areas. All this is clear evidence that he had completely lost control over the situation.

Because of these blunders, Stalin forced upon the Soviet Union a situation in which a defensive war was the only option. As we have already seen, this was precisely the course for which the leadership had not prepared. But could the overall strategy not be adjusted from offensive to defensive? The problem was that any such change would have to be orchestrated rapidly. In the circumstances this could not be done in time to stop the German advance. Long-term preparations for offensive war prevented short-term orderly retreat. The result was a rout on all fronts. The main fault was the failure of the leadership to adjust its strategic thinking. Even when the Germans were in sight of Moscow and Leningrad, propaganda maintained the fiction that there had been no reverses – and that any reference to them was blatant 'defeatism'. This delayed the possibility of tactical retreat until it was too late: Budenny was dismissed for recommending this. There were also longer-term reasons for the military paralysis in 1941, going beyond immediate decisions and back into the layers of confusion that had accumulated in the 1930s. The purges had decapitated the leadership, and thereby reduced the amount of practical experience within the Red Army. Even more important was the growth of massive political interference. According to Konstantin Simonov, any 'military illiterate felt free to meddle with the business of the military'. (3) All this was symptomatic of the chaos that had existed within Stalin's dictatorship throughout the 1930s. Stalin had adopted a strategy, which he had implemented in the planning system. But others, usually as 'political illiterates' spawned by the purges, had interpreted this in their own ways and interfered with the military decisions of the army. Beneath Stalin's blunders there were therefore a vast number of lesser incompetents, suddenly exposed by the emergency of the German invasion.

Under such circumstances, the Soviet Union was vulnerable to physical disintegration. In addition to the military and administrative crisis, there was the potential for the eruption of mass discontent. This might occur for two reasons. One was economic and social, the accumulated resentment of millions of peasants subjected to the rigours of enforced collectivisation. Even more serious was the nationalist resistance to Soviet control. The Germans were initially welcomed as liberators by millions of Belarussians, Ukrainians and Georgians, as well as by peoples of the Baltic States. According to G. Fischer, up to 2 million Soviets defected to and fought for the German armies. (4) How could the Soviet state possibly hope to survive such centrifugal forces?

In this situation Hitler held the military initiative and could take full advantage of the negative response of Stalin's leadership and the lethargy created by the Stalinist system. The German strategy of Blitzkrieg was able to make full use of Soviet military indecision. The Wehrmacht attacked in strength at specific points across a broad front. Fully armoured panzer divisions advanced at great speed, as they had already done against Poland in 1939 and against the Low Countries and France in 1940. Hitler's forces, which comprised 5.5 million troops, 4,950 aircraft, 47,260 pieces of artillery and 2,800 tanks, were sufficient to cut through the Soviet forces and to sustain the momentum of the advance in three prongs – against Leningrad in the north, Moscow in the centre and Kiev in the south, and to extend conquests further to the Volga and Stalingrad in 1942. Blitzkrieg made possible the capture of an area that extended 600 kilometres eastwards and 1,500 kilometres from north to south. The element of surprise explains the shattering impact: 56.7 per cent of all Soviet losses in the war were incurred in the initial campaign of 1941–2, and 17,500 of its 24,000 tanks were destroyed. Because of the enormous area occupied by the Germans, the workforce fell from 66 million to 35 million. The German conquests also threatened to wipe out all the major centres of industrial production that had been developed by the Five-Year Plans.

To summarise, although Stalin had been mobilising the Soviet Union for total war to be followed by swift victory, what the country suffered was swift defeat followed by total war. The German invasion came as a profound shock to the whole Soviet military strategy as the diplomacy of Stalin destroyed any initiative that the Soviet Union might have had. The Red Army was forced back into the more traditional expedient of defensive warfare – for which it had not prepared. The situation appeared desperate.

Questions

1. Was the Soviet Union prepared for war in 1941?
2. Was the rapidity of Soviet defeat in 1941 due entirely to errors of judgement made by Stalin?

ANALYSIS (2): WHY WAS THE SOVIET UNION ULTIMATELY VICTORIOUS OVER NAZI GERMANY?

Given the extent of the initial collapse, the outcome of the war with Germany was remarkable. Most explanations have focused on the reversal between 1943 and 1945 of the negative factors that had contributed to the defeat of the Soviet Union in 1941–2. Credit is given to the recovery of Stalin, who was able to co-ordinate a military revival and make full use of the climate and size of Russia. Despite its earlier loss of territory, the Soviet Union also managed to outproduce Germany in war *matériel*, the direct result of the Five-Year Plans of the 1930s. Finally, the Soviet war effort was greatly assisted by the errors made by Hitler during this period.

These explanations are broadly correct but they require some refining in their emphasis; this applies especially to those theories that are related to Soviet productivity. Overall, a combination of factors existed in delicate balance and it would be a mistake to see Soviet recovery as in any sense inevitable.

The recovery of the leadership was, of course, crucial to the implementation of a more appropriate strategy. Stalin probably reached the peak of his administrative efficiency during the war years, before succumbing to deterioration after 1945 (see Chapter 7). This was sufficient to bring about the necessary structural changes that could enable the Soviet Union to take full advantage of other factors. It meant not so much pulling the components of Stalinism back together after the initial impact of Nazism but rather dismantling some of the components in order to meet the emergency. Two new institutions were established specifically for this situation. One was Stavka, the general headquarters, the other the State Defence Committee, or GOKO. The latter, which was given powers to conduct all aspects of the war, comprised Molotov, Voroshilov, Malenkov and Beria. Under the ultimate authority of Stalin as People's Commissar for Defence, it replaced the usual Party channels of communication The emergency of war therefore did much to reduce the administrative confusion that had been seen at all levels during the 1930s (see Chapter 2) and made possible a more rational approach to economic and military planning as well.

This promoted recovery through a more effective adjustment and mobilisation of resources. The usual argument is that the Five-Year Plans of the 1930s had produced an economy geared to total war and which could massively outproduce the more limited German economy in terms of armaments; meanwhile, there had also been a long-term shift of resources into Siberia, meaning that the Soviet Union had a greatly increased industrial capacity to the east of the European centres. By the middle of 1941 some 20 per cent of Soviet heavy-industrial productive capacity was sited in the Volga, the Urals and Siberia. This meant that the Soviet Union could recover from initial defeat by producing more weapons than Germany, even during the bleakest period – the second half of 1941. The transfer of factories eastwards to escape the German invasion completed the process.

All this is perfectly sound. But the usual corollary is not. It has been assumed that the recovery after initial defeat was due to the full implementation of Stalin's command economy: more armaments were produced after 1942 because the planning system was stepped up a gear. Recently, historians have shown that the reverse happened. It is true that the Five-Year Plans had developed a mobilised economy. But, as we have seen in Chapter 3, it was an inefficient one, with considerable tension between central and local decision-making. The emergency of war necessitated a much more efficient approach. This meant reducing the levels of mutual interference between the centre and the local bodies and allowing for more local initiative in meeting central armaments orders. From 1943 onwards, local production was therefore based on individual decisions about supply of raw materials and on the most effective methods of using the labour force. Market forces became more significant than central administrative constraints. This was, of course, highly paradoxical; as Sapir has argued, the earlier '"mobilisation economy" had to be at least partially "demobilised" to achieve war mobilisation'. (5) The result was a considerable increase in efficiency. This was assisted by keeping the weapons and components deliberately unsophisticated; these had the triple advantage of being quick to build, easy to maintain and inexpensive to replace. This was a contrast to the German emphasis on quality and sophisticated parts. The planning system was therefore geared to compensating for the heavy losses incurred in the first year of the war and providing the *matériel* needed to turn defeat into a series of offensives against the Germans.

The extent of the military recovery was remarkable. Several closely related factors were involved here. The first, as we have seen, was the partial demobilisation of the command economy. This delivered overwhelming numbers of tanks, aircraft, artillery pieces and small weapons to wherever on the front they were required. This, in turn, made possible a new strategy that departed from the unqualified emphasis on 'offensive' warfare developed during the 1930s. Instead, it was now considered more appropriate to combine the more traditional defensive approach with a devastating counter-attack whenever this became possible. Zhukov's advice to Stalin in April 1943 showed this line of thought: 'I consider it inadvisable for our forces to go over to the offensive in the very first days of the campaign . . . It would be better to make the enemy first exhaust himself against our defences, and knock out his tanks and then, bringing up fresh reserves, to go over to a general offensive which would finally finish off his main force.' (6)

The result was a close co-ordination between partisan warfare and the massive thrusts of the Soviet forces at Kursk in 1943, followed by the invasion of Poland and the Balkans in 1944. The turning point of the war was the Battle for Stalingrad, which was finally won in 1943. This represented the end of Blitzkrieg for the Germans and the beginning of the type of Soviet offensive that had been anticipated in the 1930s. Clearly, the army had to be given more initiative to implement these military changes. This was another example of the partial reversal of an inter-war policy – in this instance the earlier politicisation of the army was abandoned. After the catastrophe of 1941 and 1942 Stalin allowed a much greater degree of military initiative. He sanctioned the promotion of the most able officers to supreme command: examples included Zhukov, Tolbukhin, Konev, Malinovsky, Vatutin and Rossakovsky. With this came a greater willingness to permit military decisions to be taken by those *in situ* – in contrast to Hitler who allowed the destruction of the German army at Stalingrad because he ignored the request of von Paulus to withdraw.

In both the economic and military instances, assistance was given from outside. This was considered by Stalin and by subsequent Soviet historians as peripheral to the Soviet effort, providing the slightest of contributions to Soviet victory. More recently, external help has come to be seen as crucial, perhaps even tipping the balance or acting as a catalyst for Soviet recovery. The economy, for example, was served by US and British aid under the Lend–Lease programme. This was chiefly in the form of back-up equipment and transport facilities – such as trucks, jeeps and heavy rolling stock – and enabled the Soviet factories and munitions plants to concentrate on producing armaments. By filling gaps in the Soviet infrastructure, the Allies made it possible for the Soviet Union to move more quickly than it could otherwise have done from the defensive to the offensive.

Much the same applies to military developments. Stalin frequently complained that Britain and the United States were using up Russian lives by not opening up a second front in France. In fact the process of diverting Hitler had already started with the British campaigns against Rommel in 1942 and 1943. These drew off Wehrmacht divisions that were essential for the Russian offensive. It is no coincidence that the victory of the Soviet resistance at Stalingrad occurred at the same time as the German defeat at El Alamein. The interaction between events on different fronts is now increasingly recognised by post-Soviet historiography, which has been prepared to place the 'Great Patriotic War' within the broader context of the 'Second World War'. (7)

None of this undermines the importance of the patriotic response. Indeed, this has recently been upgraded as a factor by historians. Increasingly, however, the connection between the 'people's war' and Stalin's policies is being reassessed. To some extent, patriotism was manufactured by the regime as a response to the threat to external invasion. Somehow, Stalin's propaganda had to penetrate all levels of the population and reverse some of the previous inertia. He had to remove pockets of latent opposition that remained after the purges. He had to overcome the centrifugal ethnic forces that might welcome the break up of the Soviet Union. And he had to deal with the local forces that had interrupted the attempted economic and political centralisation of the 1930s. The initial priority was therefore to prevent disintegration. Hence the measures taken by Stavka and GOKO were designed to keep together a population that had been stirred up and confused, first by the traumas of the 1930s, then by the experience of rapid military defeat. They aimed to eliminate as many collaborators as possible through the forcible exile and resettlement of Balkars, Chechens, Karachais, Meskhetians, Crimean Tartars, Balts, Ukrainians and Cossacks. Although huge numbers of non-Russian civilians defected to the Germans, the core that might have organised mass rebellions was removed. In this sense the Germans inherited a population in turmoil. Soviet citizens were also targeted by propaganda that stressed connections with the Russian past – especially the defeat of the French in 1812. The 'Great Patriotic War' against Hitler was characterised as a replica of the 'Great Fatherland War' against Napoleon.

On the other hand, the degree of patriotic support far transcended Stalin's measures. To claim that Stalin's coercion and propaganda – in other words the outward manifestations of his leadership – were mainly responsible for the resurgence of Soviet patriotism would do less than justice to some of the most remarkable instances of mass heroism of the whole of the Second World War. The self-sacrifice of the citizens of Leningrad in the face of the German siege, or of the Soviet troops at Stalingrad and in the Battle of Kursk, or in the resistance of the partisans behind enemy lines – all were unprecedented in their scale, even in Russian history. The extent to which it was spontaneous will no doubt be the subject of future research.

Soviet recovery from defeat occurred in direct proportion to the German collapse from victory. The Nazis contributed greatly to their own demise. Despite its initial success, Hitler's military strategy was actually inappropriate. The impetus of the German attack was sustainable only in the short term on so wide a front. Once the surprise had worn off, the German numerical inferiority began to count, especially in crucial areas such as Moscow in the autumn of 1941 and Stalingrad from the summer of 1942. Hitler was unable to learn from military errors, the worst of which were committed in Russia. He was also unwilling to accept advice from experienced commanders such as Guderian.

Meanwhile, the atrocities committed against the civilian populations of the captured territories undermined any goodwill that the Germans might originally have encountered. Considered to be *Untermenschen*, or subhumans, the Slavs were targeted for slave labour. Other groups, such as the Balts (Latvians, Estonians and Lithuanians), were considered suitable for Germanisation, but policies were still harsh. Indeed, Hitler's measures acted as a catalyst for a Soviet patriotic revival. The form of administration imposed on the conquered territories allowed no possibility for regional autonomy: Hitler therefore missed the opportunity of enlisting a massive wave of anti-Soviet ethnic support. This was the consequence of appalling misrule, born of extreme racial arrogance, that put Stalin's policies and blunders into perspective. Although brutal, Stalinist measures had no equivalent of the deliberate extermination policies of Hitler's SS units and *Einsatzkommandos*. The Germans failed to develop any clear policy about the form to be taken by the Soviet Union in the future. There were schemes – some put forward by Rosenberg in 1941 – for an independent Ukraine, a Baltic protectorate, a Caucasian Federation, a reduced Muscovy and an independent Siberia. But such schemes were soon squashed by the other members of the Nazi establishment who had simpler and more drastic controls for a defeated population.

Above all, the German economy had not been fully attuned to the realities of such a major undertaking as the destruction of Russia. Whereas the Soviet economy had been mobilised for total war in the 1930s, the Nazi economy had been mobilised only for partial war. Hitler's solution was a series of rapid victories followed by the absorption of the vanquished countries' infrastructure. The German Blitzkrieg was as much an economic as a military policy. The problem was that it was difficult to extend it to make it function more completely. By contrast, the Soviet economy could be made more effective through relaxing some of its constraints. Germany moved to a total war economy only in 1943; the Soviet Union, on the other hand, was already there.

Hitler had expected that kicking in the Soviet Union's front door would 'cause the whole rotten structure to collapse'. He was wrong – not because he misjudged the rottenness of the structure but as a result of underestimating its sheer size and its capacity to recover in a dire emergency.

Questions

1. Was the Soviet recovery after 1942 'inevitable'?
2. To what extent was the Soviet military victory by 1945 due to Stalin?

SOURCES

1. STALIN AND THE BACKGROUND TO THE GERMAN INVASION OF THE SOVIET UNION, 1939–41

Source A: 'Rendezvous', a cartoon on the invasion of Poland by Hitler and Stalin in September 1939 by the British cartoonist David Low.

See Figure 1 on page 90.

Source B: Stalin's private view of the danger from Germany, October 1939.

The Germans might attack. For six years German fascists and the communists cursed each other. Now in spite of history there has been an unexpected turn, but one cannot rely upon it. We must be prepared in time. Others, who were not prepared, paid for it.

Hitler **RENDEZVOUS** Stalin

Figure 1

Source C: Molotov's speech to the Supreme Soviet, October 1939.

In the past few months such concepts as 'aggression' and 'aggressor' have acquired new concrete connotation, new meaning. It is not hard to understand that we can no longer employ these concepts in the sense we did, say, three or four months ago. Today, as far as the European powers are concerned, Germany is in the position of a state which is striving for the earliest termination of war and for peace, while Britain and France . . . are in favour of continuing the war and are opposed to the conclusion of peace . . .

Since the conclusion of the Soviet-German Non-Aggression Pact on 23 August an end has been put to the abnormal relations that have existed between the Soviet Union and Germany for a number of years. Instead of the enmity which was fostered in every way by certain European powers, we now have a rapprochement and the establishment of friendly relations . . . This radical change in relations between the Soviet Union and Germany, the two biggest states in Europe, was bound to have its effect on the entire international situation . . . we have consistently striven to improve relations with Germany and have wholeheartedly welcomed similar strivings in Germany herself. Today our relations with the German State are based on friendship, on our readiness to support Germany's efforts for peace, and at the same time the desire to contribute in every way to the development of Soviet-German economic relations to the mutual benefit of both States.

Source D: the conclusions of a secret Soviet intelligence report, submitted to Stalin by Golikov on 20 March 1941.

1. On the basis of the aforesaid ... I consider that the most probable time operations will begin against the USSR is after the victory over England or the conclusion with her of an honourable peace treaty.
2. Rumours and documents to the effect that war against the USSR is inevitable this spring should be regarded as misinformation coming from the English or perhaps even the German intelligence service.

Source E: Stalin's radio speech to the people of the Soviet Union, 3 July 1941.

Comrades, citizens, brothers and sisters, men of our Army and Navy! It is to you I am speaking dear friends!

The perfidious attack by Hitlerite Germany on our Motherland, begun on 22 June, is continuing. In spite of the heroic resistance of the Red Army, and although the enemy's finest divisions and finest air force units have already been smashed and have found their graves on the field of battle, the enemy continues to push forward, hurling fresh forces to the front ... The fascist aircraft are extending the range of their operations ... Grave danger overhangs our country.

The Red Army, Red Navy and all citizens of the Soviet Union must defend every inch of Soviet soil, must fight to the last drop of blood for our towns and villages, must display the daring, initiative and mental alertness characteristic of our people ...

Questions

1. (i) Who were Molotov (Source C) and Golikov (Source D)? [2]
    (ii) Explain the reference to the 'Soviet–German Non-Aggression Pact' (Source C). [2]
2. Comment on the view shown in Source A. How useful is this source to the historian? [5]
3. Contrast the opinions shown by Stalin in Source B and Molotov in Source C. How would you explain this contrast? [5]
*4. What evidence is there of 'propaganda' in Source E? [4]
5. 'Stalin's blunder was not that he failed to see that Germany would attack Russia, but that he could not appreciate that this attack was imminent in 1941.' Comment on this view in the light of Sources A to E and of your own knowledge. [7]

Worked answer

*3. *[The answer to this question needs an initial definition of 'propaganda', followed by specific examples – including brief quotations – from the text. The length of the answer should be in line with the mark allocation.]*

'Propaganda' involves the active dissemination of ideas and news to achieve an intended response. In Source E it consists of three main elements. First, as is normal in wartime, strong terms are used to describe the enemy and home efforts; hence the 'perfidious attack by Hitlerite Germany' is contrasted with the 'heroic resistance of the Red Army'. This is not so much distortion as interpretation. But, second, the facts are twisted to reduce the severity of the Soviet defeat. Thus the 'enemy's finest divisions' had been 'smashed' and had 'found their graves on the field of battle'. This was patently untrue and was intended to divert responsibility for early defeat from the government itself. Finally, the propaganda involved an exhortation to the public to 'defend every inch of Soviet soil' and to 'fight to the last drop of blood'. The earlier statements were clearly made as a preface to this appeal.

SOURCES

2. SOVIET VICTORY IN THE SECOND WORLD WAR

Source F: Stalin's Order of the Day, 23 February 1943.

In the name of the liberation of our country from the hated enemy, in the name of final victory over the German fascist invaders – I order:

(1) Indefatigably to perfect military training and to strengthen discipline, order and organisation throughout the Red Army and Navy.

(2) To deal stronger blows against the enemy troops, to pursue the enemy indefatigably and persistently, without allowing him to consolidate himself on defence lines. To give him no respite by day or night, to cut his communications, to surround his troops and annihilate them, if they refuse to lay down their arms.

(3) To fan brighter the flames of guerrilla warfare in the rear of the enemy, to destroy the enemy's communications, to blow up railway bridges, to frustrate the transport of enemy troops and the supply of arms and ammunition, to blow up and set fire to army stores, to attack enemy garrisons, to prevent

the retreating enemy from burning down our villages, to help the advancing Red Army, heart and soul, and by all possible means.

In this lies the guarantee of our victory.

Source G: a Soviet cartoon showing the impending defeat of Hitler.

Caption: **Napoleon suffered defeat and so will the conceited Hitler!**

Source H: a report by a Western observer on Soviet victory in 1945.

The war's climax came in 1943, with the successful defence of Stalingrad. The Germans had, by this time, been dealt a crippling blow to their airforce in the great battles with the British in North Africa. Russians point out scornfully that this African campaign involved few men; however, it required masses of highly complicated transport and machines.

Furthermore, the RAF and the Eighth Air Force in England were by then pounding German industry, and the Germans had to strip the Russian front of fighters, to defend their home factories, so that for the first time the Russians had superiority in the air. Lend–lease, including thousands of trucks, was now pouring in, the German lines of communication were perilously extended and, for the first time, it was possible for a Russian army to move quickly out to envelop and cut off a German army, as theirs had been enveloped so many times before.

After that, Germany's superiority in weapons was slowly reduced by Allied air poundings, while Russia's supply increased. Her own factories behind the Urals were working; new ones were equipped with American machine tools. By the summer of 1944 at least half the Red Army's total transportation was being supplied by 210,000 American military trucks, 40,000 jeeps and 30,000 other military motor vehicles. She also had 5,600 American tanks and tank destroyers. At last, Russia's crushing superiority in manpower could become effective.

Source I: the views of a German army commander who served in Russia, from his book *Panzer Leader*, published in 1952.

Hitler's unusually vivid powers of imagination led him to underestimate the known strength of the Soviet Union. He maintained that mechanisation on land and in the air offered fresh chances of success, so that comparisons with the campaigns of Charles XII of Sweden [in 1709], or Napoleon [in 1812], were no longer relevant. He maintained that he could rely, with certainty, on the collapse of the Soviet system, as soon as the first blows reached their mark. He believed the Russian populace would embrace his National Socialist ideology. But as soon as the campaign began, almost everything was done to prevent any such thing from taking place. By ill-treating the native populations in the occupied Russian territories that were administered by high Party functionaries, and by reason of his decision to dissolve the Russian state and to incorporate considerable areas into Germany, Hitler succeeded in uniting all Russians under the banner of Stalin. They were now fighting for Holy Mother Russia and against a foreign invader.

Questions

1. (i) Explain the significance of the point that 'Her own factories behind the Urals were working' (Source H). [2]
   (ii) Explain the reference to 'high Party functionaries' (Source I). [2]
2. How effectively are language and tone used in Source F to raise Soviet morale? [4]
*3. How far does Source I reinforce the view expressed in Source G? [4]
4. Consider the possible motives behind the production of Sources H and I. [5]
5. 'Soviet victory over Germany by 1945 was due predominantly to Stalin's policies and leadership.' Do Sources F to I, and your own knowledge, support this view? [8]

Worked answer

*3. ['How far?' needs to be addressed immediately, since it will provide the shape for the whole argument.]

Source I partially reinforces the view in Source G but, in some ways, goes beyond it by offering explanations for Hitler's defeat that Source G does not contain. Guderian's views overlap the Soviet cartoon by referring to the collapse of the 'campaigns of Charles XII of Sweden' and 'Napoleon'. The common theme of both sources is that history was now repeating itself and that the population was 'fighting for Holy Mother Russia and against a foreign invader'. On the other hand, Guderian offers a more complex assessment that would be impossible to illustrate in any cartoon. This includes references to Hitler's military miscalculations, his dependence on 'the collapse of the Soviet system' and his ill-treatment of 'native populations in the occupied Russian territories'. Even so, none of these explanations invalidate the simpler proposition of the cartoon; they offer a multi-causal basis of support.

7

STALIN'S POST-WAR REGIME, 1945–53

BACKGROUND NARRATIVE

The Soviet Union emerged from the Second World War victorious but badly damaged. Over 23 million Soviet civilians and troops had been killed in the struggle, while the Germans had destroyed 1,710 towns, 70,000 villages, 31,850 industrial enterprises and 98,000 collective farms. Stalin decided from the outset that the Soviet economy should once again be insulated from the West. He therefore re-established the planning controls of the 1930s. The fourth Five-Year Plan ran from 1946 to 1950 and the fifth from 1950 to 1955; the latter was interrupted by his death in 1953 but completed by his successors, Malenkov and Khrushchev. The Plans again placed the emphasis on collective farming and the development of heavy industry at the expense of consumer goods. To ensure Soviet self-sufficiency, Stalin refused the offer of economic aid from the Marshall Plan.

Stalin also reactivated the political and cultural controls of the pre-war period. He abolished the wartime State Defence Committee (GOKO) and sought to re-establish his ascendancy within the Party. He rarely summoned the Central Committee and Politburo and completely ignored the Party Congress. He decided to restore the full force of Socialist Realism under the agency of Zhdanov, while the NKVD, now under Beria, once again operated a policy of terror. Purges accounted for a new wave of Party officials, and even affected officers within the victorious Red Army. Stalin seemed in complete control, but was he? Analysis (1) investigates this.

In foreign affairs the period 1945–53 was dominated by the Cold War. The Soviet Union and the West had already experienced differences at the wartime conferences of Yalta and Potsdam (both in 1945) over the question of the future status of Germany and Poland. Stalin insisted on having a major hand in the formation of post-war governments in Eastern Europe, for which he was accused by the Western Allies of breaking the Declaration on Liberated Europe, which had allowed for free elections. Stalin increasingly saw the area of Europe that comprised eastern Germany, Poland, Czechoslovakia, Hungary, Bulgaria and Romania as a glacis, or buffer zone. He therefore proceeded to formalise Soviet controls from 1948 and to establish economic and ideological links in the form of Comecon and Cominform. The West regarded such developments as sinister evidence of the fall of an 'Iron Curtain'. To maintain Soviet ascendancy in the area, Stalin increased the already huge Soviet military presence and, by 1949, was able to add the atomic bomb to his arsenal. The Soviet Union seemed to have achieved a position of strength through its isolation, but had it? This is considered in Analysis (2).

ANALYSIS (1): DID STALIN REACH THE PEAK OF HIS POWER AND INFLUENCE AFTER 1945?

There has always been a tendency to consider 1945–53 as the culmination of the Stalinist dictatorship, the period in which Stalinism reached full maturity. Victory over Nazi Germany in the Second World War greatly strengthened his position at home and abroad, and he was able to introduce further measures to make it unassailable. The war was therefore the means whereby the totalitarian measures of the 1930s reached their logical fulfilment in the late 1940s.

This view is still very widely held. There is, however, a different perspective. The period 1945–53 is not one of fulfilled or refined dictatorship. All the problems that had previously confronted Stalin now returned so that, far from being secure in 'mature dictatorship', he was as insecure as ever. It was therefore a period of attempted renewal – of retrospection rather than fulfilment. Ruthlessness was as much a theme as in the earlier years, but efficiency was no more apparent than before.

Despite its recent experience of military victory and territorial expansion, Stalinist Russia was much more ramshackle than was previously thought. Indeed, victory had accentuated Stalin's difficulties. For one thing, his personal ascendancy – usually considered to have reached its peak after 1945 – was more seriously challenged than at any time since 1929. The paradox, pointed out by Ward, was that 'whilst the Russo-German conflict strengthened the regime and legitimized the Generalissimo as a symbol of the will to victory, Stalin's personal power was threatened.' (1) The success of the Red Army raised the spectre that Stalin had always feared – that the regime would be militarised. It was for this reason that he had considered Trotsky, the organiser of Bolshevik military victory in the Civil War, a powerful opponent who had to be destroyed. After 1945 he had to neutralise the military again, this time by demoting Zhukov. This was a particularly delicate operation since Soviet security remained a constant priority with the onset of the Cold War. But in a way this made the re-establishment of political control essential, since Stalin was now increasingly vulnerable to the possibility of an internal coup generated by an external crisis. This explains why he wound up the State Defence Committee (GOKO), which had played such a vital administrative role during the war. He also reverted to the inter-war policy of rarely consulting the core of the Party, the Politburo and the Central Committee – again from fear that a rival might emerge from within its ranks to challenge his supremacy.

Neutralising the army and the Party in this way might well upset the balance of tensions upon which Stalin relied to maintain his personal power. Hence he was forced into a new round of purges. But these were for defensive reasons – initiated from a position of weakness rather than strength – to recover rather than to sublimate his power. His targets showed the extent of his insecurity. He sought to re-establish his control over the Party in the 'Leningrad Affair'; this resulted in the trial and execution for treason of Party leaders and war heroes, such as Voznesensky, who had done what they could to organise resistance to the German siege. In a wider sense, Stalin tried to restore his grip on society at large through the 1946 Zhdanov decrees that redefined and tightened up working practices and reimposed the full force of Socialist Realism upon the arts. These had been temporarily relaxed during the war. Underlying the whole system was the revival of the terror. The NKVD continued to take its toll, under the direction of Beria. It is also probable that another purge was about to break in 1953 and was prevented only by Stalin's death. In many respects, therefore, Stalin was having to manoeuvre for power and control, as he had done during the 1930s but he experienced even greater difficulty than in the 1930s in retaining the initiative. Certain individuals grew relatively more powerful after the war than before it – especially Beria, who became a candidate for the succession.

Stalin's economic measures are often explained as an intensification of the command economy in order to deal with the most appalling levels of destruction. What is often ignored, however, is that many of Stalin's measures after 1945 were retrograde steps. The inefficiencies of the 1930s were all revived in the formal planning system. The fourth and fifth Five-Year Plans (1946–50 and 1950–5) intensified the policy of collectivisation in agriculture by increasing the size of the *kolkhozy*, or collective farms, and reducing their number from 252,000 to 76,000; they also maintained the emphasis on heavy industry, especially for defence. After the partial demobilisation of the economy during the war, explained in Chapter 6, this was undoubtedly a negative action. In effect, Stalin missed the opportunity to continue the more progressive wartime policies and thereby abandon the more blatant failures of formal central planning. The result was that, although recovery did occur, it was much slower than that accomplished by the West or Japan. In a real sense the infrastructural damage inflicted by the Second World War was permanent because it was dealt with by the inappropriate measures from the 1930s rather than new measures anticipating the 1950s. The emphasis was very much on restoration rather than renewal.

What of the man behind the system? Stalin had always been arbitrary and despotic. The usual picture is that this arbitrariness increased as a direct result of mature dictatorship: Stalin's power was so secure that he could literally do whatever he wanted. This can now be challenged. His increasingly irrational behaviour was the response to threats to his system and a real fear that it might break up. Age and the war had also taken their toll and it was clear that he was now deteriorating physically and mentally. Hence, in Ward's view, 'This was no self-confident tyrant in charge of a smoothly functioning totalitarian machine, but a sickly old man; unpredictable, dangerous, lied to by terrified subordinates, presiding over a ramshackle bureaucracy and raging, like Lear, against failure and mortality.' (2)

By 1953, therefore, Stalinism was crumbling, not thriving. A new perspective might also be given on Stalin by what happened from the time of his death in 1953. The facts are that, after a brief interim of collective leadership, Khrushchev assumed undisputed power by 1955. In the Party Conference of 1956, and again in 1961, Khrushchev openly attacked Stalin for his brutality, his methods of terror, and for his personal defects – especially his psychosis and 'sickly suspicion'. Meanwhile, under Khrushchev and his successor Brezhnev (1964–82) the official *History of the Communist Party of the Soviet Union* literally wrote Stalin out of the period 1924–53. Although he continued to be mentioned in lists of Party officials, Stalin ceased to have any historical validity as an influence on events. The traditional Western perspective is quite clear on this. It maintains that Khrushchev launched his destalinisation campaign to establish his own power base and to try to weaken that of Stalin, who had to be discredited and debunked; and the Soviet achievements during his period in power had to be depersonalised. Khrushchev, who had grown to political maturity in the Stalin era, therefore turned against his political mentor for the sake of developing his own power.

This is certainly credible; any head of state who can write his predecessor out of history must himself have had more than a streak of ruthlessness and opportunism. Yet the presumption here is that Stalin was a posthumous threat because of his strength. An alternative perspective would be that Stalinism's threat to Khrushchev was his weakness. And that weakness was the way in which Stalin had personally distorted the communist system, which had somehow survived in spite of him. Khrushchev removed Stalin from history for two reasons. First, he genuinely believed that Stalin had corrupted rather than strengthened Soviet communism. It was easier to attribute this to Stalin's personal shortcomings than to the deficiencies of the system itself: this explains Khrushchev's emphasis on Stalin's paranoia rather than on any Janus-type qualities of the bureaucracy. Second, Khrushchev identified several major faults that needed to be reformed – especially agriculture. It would be easier for him to take the initiative if he could blame defective leadership rather than attack an entire system; reformers often allow themselves a loophole by attacking their predecessors.

Destalinisation was therefore launched not to destroy an entrenched system but to clear away its wreckage. Perhaps Khrushchev was the first to realise that the Soviet Union had survived in spite of Stalinism, not because of it. As events turned out, the negative legacy of Stalinism proved stronger than the positive. Khrushchev fell in 1964 at least partly because of the failure of his experiments to revitalise agriculture, a problem that also affected Kosygin in the 1970s. Stalinism therefore persisted after 1953 less as a force than as an inertia. But, to end on a controversial note, one could say that that was what it had always been.

Questions

1. Was the period 1945–53 one of 'mature Stalinism'?
2. Why did post-war Stalinism attempt to return to the policies of the 1930s?

ANALYSIS (2): WHAT EXPLANATIONS CAN BE ADVANCED FOR STALIN'S INVOLVEMENT IN THE COLD WAR – AND HOW SUCCESSFUL WAS HE?

Traditionally, the Cold War is seen as the result of Stalin's interaction with two main developments.

In the longer perspective, the rivalry between Russia and the West goes back to 1917. Trotsky, for example, maintained that Lenin and President Wilson were 'the apocalyptic antipodes of our time'. (3) Stalin therefore inherited the confrontation. What he added to it in the 1930s is open to debate. Tucker argues that Stalin went on to develop a long-term strategy to foment conflict between the Western powers so that the Soviet Union could enter such a war at a critical stage to pick up the pieces. (4) An alternative view is that Stalin found himself at the mercy of Anglo-French diplomacy that generated intense Soviet suspicion. Litvinov, for example, believed that the British and French made 'endless concessions' to fascism and Nazism. (5) Whatever the explanation given for Soviet foreign policy, the seeds of the Cold War were already germinating in the 1920s and 1930s.

In the shorter perspective, the conflict between Russia and the West was intensified as a result of the situation developing out of the Second World War. Stalin was deeply suspicious of the West on several counts. One was the Allies' unwillingness to open up a second front against Nazi Germany. 'All is clear,' Stalin said in August 1942. 'They want to bleed us white in order to dictate to us their terms later on.' (6) When Roosevelt announced that the invasion of France could not take place until 1944, Stalin maintained, 'Your decision . . . leaves the Soviet army, which is fighting not only for its own country, but also for its allies, to do the job alone.' In addition to this, specific areas of lasting mistrust had arisen during the course of the war. These surfaced at the wartime conferences, especially those in 1945 at Yalta and Potsdam concerning the redefinition of the Polish frontiers and the future of Germany. Stalin placed particular emphasis on Poland, which Molotov had considered to be the source of so much anti-Soviet activity: 'Poland has become a convenient ground for all sorts of fortuitous and unexpected eventualities that might create a threat to the USSR.' (7) This explains Stalin's insistence on reclaiming all areas to the east of the Curzon Line for the Soviet Union and rolling the Polish state westwards, at the expense of Germany, up to the Oder–Neisse Line. The future of Germany was also problematic. Stalin naturally preferred to keep Soviet control over the eastern zone and in 1948 reacted to British and US proposals to unite the currencies of the four zones by imposing a blockade on West Berlin. The Polish and German problems were reinforced by ideological differences. The Western powers acted in accordance with the principles of freely elected governments, enshrined within the Declaration on Liberated Europe, which had been agreed at Yalta in 1945 and subsequently reinforced in the 1948 Truman Doctrine. Stalin, however, regarded these as means of undermining Soviet influence and destroying Soviet security. Hence, he acted swiftly to convert the early coalition governments of the Eastern European states into communist regimes under direct Soviet control. This gave permanent effect to the Iron Curtain, the existence of which had been announced by Churchill at Fulton in 1946.

Hence the longer-term rivalry between Russia and the West had been brought more sharply into focus as a direct result of the Second World War. This created future battle lines in Europe. But, in the process, Stalin miscalculated the divisions within the West. The Allied powers had emerged greatly strengthened by the defeat of Nazi Germany, The removal of fascism also sharpened the division between capitalism and communism, as did the new territorial proximity brought about by the military process.

This line of argument still holds as a general explanation of the origins of the Cold War. But there is one important omission. The traditional focus is very much on the *external* pressures on the Soviet Union. Of equal importance, however, are the *internal* pressures and the way in which they helped shape Stalin's responses to the West.

Stalin found the Soviet Union affected in two contrasting ways by the Second World War. In one way the war had exerted a centripetal effect. It had pulled the country together, partly through the massive patriotic response to the emergency of the German invasion, and partly because the military success had prevented it from disintegrating again once the emergency was over. On the other hand, there were also centrifugal influences. Military victory had, as we have seen in Analysis (1), threatened Stalin's personal power and created alternative role models that threatened a weakening of central power. Meanwhile, as the impact of the wartime emergency gradually wore off, there was a revived threat of ethnic disintegration.

To maintain the centripetal effect – and offset the centrifugal – Stalin had to restore the full panoply of coercion and the command economy of the 1930s. Fortunately for him, his measures were given a new justification – the perceived menace of the West that was now in a greatly enhanced form. A direct comparison can be made with Stalin's measures in the 1930s. As in 1929 and 1931, he used the threat of the West to justify forced collectivisation and rapid industrialisation. The Cold War situation between 1945 and 1947 could be used to justify the renewal of such measures. He could also reject any assistance from the West, as he did in his response to Marshall Aid, in very much the same terms. The Soviet Union would continue to go its own way, as it had done in the early 1930s.

The obverse of this coin is that Stalin depended on the Cold War to maintain his system internally. This explains why domestic crises were so often related to the external threat and given the language of the Cold War. He could also use the newly conquered glacis of Eastern Europe as an additional form of security. In tightening Soviet control over the satellite states, he could put additional pressure on ethnic groups within the Soviet Union itself. Hence his subjection of Poles, Czechs and Hungarians was an added guarantee of his control over Ukrainians, Belorussians and Tartars.

To what extent did Stalin succeed in his foreign policy and his attempted manipulation of the Cold War? On the positive side, the Soviet Union seemed to have achieved the security that both Lenin and Stalin had sought. After 1945 it was a superpower with the world's largest standing army. It had achieved direct control over East Germany, Poland, Czechoslovakia, Hungary, Bulgaria and Romania, thereby increasing the security of Soviet territorial gains in the Baltic and the Ukraine. The Cold War had also been the means whereby defeating an enemy had been converted into the spread of ideology. Stalin had proved Trotsky wrong: communism was spread not by Soviet-inspired revolution but by direct Soviet conquest. In this respect Stalin's Cold War policies were the logical means of maintaining and extending the fruits of victory of the Great Patriotic War. From 1949 and 1951, with the respective development of the atomic and hydrogen bombs, the extension of Soviet influence was set more permanently by the protection of nuclear weapons. Thus, compared with Soviet insecurity in 1931, huge steps had been taken by the year of Stalin's death in 1953.

Or had they? Stalin's use of the Cold War to increase internal security generated its own problems, which made the Soviet Union more vulnerable to pressures from outside. For example, the spread of

Soviet influence in Eastern Europe provoked a Western response that was far more concerted than anything that had happened in the inter-war period. This included the Truman Doctrine and Marshall Plan and the establishment of NATO in 1949. In addition, Stalin was obliged to back down over the Berlin blockade in 1948–9. As C. Kennedy-Pipe maintains, 'The Cold War was not a competition of equals: rather, it was an unequal struggle between one strong regime, the United States, and one fragile regime, the Soviet Union.' (8) In addition, having to maintain the high levels of defence expenditure necessitated by the Cold War meant that there was never any real possibility of lightening the burden on the Soviet consumer. The contrast in living standards between the Soviet Bloc and the West became even greater than it had been during the 1930s – and would be a huge problem in the future. Finally, the creation of the glacis was to provide a constant concern about the possible impact of protest movements within Eastern Europe upon the Soviet Union itself.

These problems became particularly apparent after Stalin's death. Despite attempted economic reforms, Khrushchev found it virtually impossible to improve the facilities of the long-suffering consumer. Part of the reason was continued expenditure on the Cold War, which experienced its most dangerous phase under Khrushchev. The situation was exacerbated by the Cuban Missile Crisis: Soviet humiliation brought about the fall of Khrushchev and made his successor, Brezhnev, determined to equal and overtake US armaments production. Mean-while, both Khrushchev and Brezhnev found themselves forced to take active measures to prevent any liberalisation within the Soviet satellites, in case this should affect the Soviet Union itself. Khrushchev therefore mobilised the Warsaw Pact to invade Hungary in 1956, while Brezhnev did the same to Czechoslovakia in 1968.

The two trends came together during the 1980s to produce impossible pressures for the Soviet Union. Under Gorbachev the policy of *perestroika* released consumer demands that could not be met by a command economy, even by one that was in the process of being liberalised. Meanwhile, the Soviet Union relaxed its grip on Eastern Europe, which promptly experienced a series of 'people's revolutions' in 1989. The combination proved too great for the Soviet Union, which died – unwanted – at the end of 1991.

Stalin's ultimate Cold War legacy was, therefore, to enlarge and externally strengthen the Soviet system. At the same time, he made it more vulnerable to internal collapse. This explains the irony that the Soviet Union, which had triumphed in war, eventually succumbed to the peace that followed.

Questions

1. To what extent was Soviet involvement in the Cold War due to domestic influences?
2. How far did Stalin shape the development of the Cold War?
3. Had the Soviet Union 'lost' the Cold War by 1953?

SOURCES

1. RECONSTRUCTING THE SOVIET ECONOMY?

Source A: an extract from an official Soviet history, published in 1948.

The Soviet people is reconstructing the national economy of the USSR with its heroic efforts, and will surpass the prewar level of production and overtake economically the main capitalist countries.

Source B: extracts from a speech to the Soviet public by Stalin in 1946.

What material potential did the country dispose of before the Second World War? *[Gives production figures]* ...

What policy enabled the Communist Party to ensure this material potential in such a short time?

First of all the Soviet policy of industrialization of the country ...

Secondly, the policy of collectivization of agriculture ...

Now a few words about the work plans of our Communist Party ...

So far as plans for a longer term are concerned, the party intends to organize a new upsurge of the economy, which will make it possible for us to something like treble the level of our industry compared with the pre-war period ... Only on this condition can we consider that our Motherland will be guaranteed against all accidents. This will require, say, three more Five-Year Plans, if not more. But this thing can be done, and we must do it.

Source C: official Soviet figures for the fourth Five-Year Plan (1945–50). These are based on a 1940 index of 100.

	1940	1945	1950 (Plan)	1950 (Actual)
National income	100	83	138	164
Gross industrial production	100	92	148	173
Producers' goods	100	112	–	205
Consumers' goods	100	59	–	123
Gross agricultural production	100	60	127	99

Source D: Khrushchev's criticism of the fourth Five-Year Plan.

I could already see that our output plan wouldn't be fulfilled. I assigned a group of agricultural experts and economists . . . to make a realistic calculation of how much grain we really could produce. They came up with a figure of somewhere between 100 and 200 million pood. This was very little. Before the war the Ukraine had produced as much as 500 million pood, and the State had already assigned us an output plan of 400 million pood for 1946. I felt it was best to approach the problem honestly. I hoped that if I reported the situation to Stalin candidly and supported my report with facts and figures, he would believe me. I wanted to do everything in my power to make Stalin understand our position.

I hoped I could prove I was right this time too, and that Stalin would understand that my request was not 'sabotage'. This term was always on hand as a justification for the repression and the extortion of products from the collective farms. In this case I would be trying to convince Stalin that we couldn't supply the agricultural products we wanted and needed. Our own country needed them, and Stalin also wanted to send food to the other Socialist countries, especially Poland and Germany, who couldn't survive without our help. Stalin was already building up an alliance and fitting himself with the toga of the leader of future military campaigns. He would be very unhappy to hear that the Ukraine not only couldn't fulfil its assigned quota for delivery to the State, but in fact needed food from the State to feed its own people.

Questions

*1. (i) Explain the difference between 'producers' goods' and 'consumers' goods' (Source C). [2]

(ii) Explain the reference to 'Germany' (Source D). [2]

2. To what extent does Source C show that the objectives stated in Sources A and B were genuinely under way by 1950? [7]

3. What can be deduced from Source D about the problems in designing and implementing the agricultural component of the fourth Five-Year Plan? How reliable is this source? [6]
4. 'More of the same.' 'A new approach.' In the light of Sources A to D, plus further information known to you, which of these is the more accurate description of Stalin's economic policies after 1945? [8]

Worked answer

*1. *[Two marks indicate that an explanation needs to be more than merely a word or phrase. On the other hand, too much time should not be spent on this question at the expense of the others.]*

(i) 'Producers' goods are those that relate to industry, especially to plant, armaments and farming equipment. Consumers' goods are those intended for everyday use by the population, particularly household items and textiles.
(ii) Khrushchev was referring to the Soviet zone of Germany. Even after it had become the German Federal Republic, it was initially heavily dependent on the USSR for its economic validity.

SOURCES

2. ARGUMENTS BEHIND THE COLD WAR

Source E: from the Truman Doctrine, 1948.

One of the primary objectives of the foreign policy of the United States is the creation of conditions in which we and other nations will be able to work out a way of life free from coercion . . .

To ensure the peaceful development of nations, free from coercion, the United States has taken a leading part in establishing the United Nations. The United Nations is designed to make possible lasting freedom and independence for all its members. We shall not realise our objectives, however, unless we are willing to help free peoples to maintain their free institutions and their national integrity against aggressive movements that seek to impose on them totalitarian regimes. This is no more than a frank recognition that totalitarian regimes imposed on free people, by direct or indirect aggression, undermine the foundations of international peace and hence the security of the United States.

The peoples of a number of countries of the world have recently had totalitarian regimes forced upon them against their will. The government of the

United States has made frequent protests against coercion and intimidation, in violation of the Yalta Agreements, in Poland, Romania and Bulgaria. I must also state that in a number of other countries there have been similar developments.

At the present moment in world history nearly every nation must choose between alternative ways of life. The choice is too often not a free one.

One way of life is built upon the will of the majority, and is distinguished by free institutions, representative government, free elections, guarantees of individual liberty, freedom of speech and religion, and freedom from political oppression.

The second way of life is based upon the will of the minority forcibly imposed upon the majority. It relies upon terror and oppression, a controlled press and radio, fixed elections, and the suppression of personal freedoms.

I believe that we must assist free peoples to work out their own destinies in their own way.

I believe our help should be primarily through economic and financial aid which is essential to economic stability and orderly political progress.

Source F: an extract from the official *History of Soviet Foreign Policy 1945–70* (Moscow 1973).

In an address containing venomous slander against the socialist countries, Truman in effect raised the question of the USA undertaking the role of world policeman in order to interfere in the affairs of other countries on the side of reaction and counter-revolution, help strangle the liberation movement in all parts of the world and openly oppose revolution and socialist development . . .

The Soviet Government and press graphically exposed the imperialist character of the Truman Doctrine. *Pravda* wrote that the doctrine signified further interference in the affairs of other countries. The USA's claims to international leadership were growing together with the appetites of the interested American circles. The newspaper pointed out that in the new historical situation the American politicians were ignoring the fact that the old methods of the colonialists and die-hard statesmen were outworn and doomed.

The USSR sharply denounced the Truman Doctrine also in the UN, stressing that the USA's attempts to dictate its will to other independent countries were incompatible with the principles proclaimed by the General Assembly in 1946, one of which was that aid to other countries should not be used as a political weapon.

The USA's aggressive policies in the regions adjoining the Soviet Union and the People's Democracies led to the further unity of these countries, which were vitally interested in safeguarding peace and the sovereign rights of nations against encroachment by imperialists.

Questions

1. Explain the references to
   (i) 'the Yalta Agreements' (Source E); [2]
   (ii) 'People's Democracies' (Source F). [2]
2. What can be inferred from Source E about Stalin's objectives in Europe from 1945? [6]
*3. What similarities can be detected between Sources E and F over their criticism of each other's policies? [4]
4. How would you explain the similarities referred to in Question 3? [3]
5. 'The grounds for Stalin's hostility towards the West were primarily ideological.' Do Sources E and F, and your own knowledge, support this view? [8]

Worked answer

*3. *[This question is best handled by finding several points on which to establish similarities – and then illustrating with precise quotations from the sources.]*

There are several similarities. Sources E and F both refer to the need to defend 'democracy' against the aggression of the other side in the Cold War. The Truman Doctrine points out the threat to 'free peoples' from 'aggressive movements' seeking to impose 'totalitarian regimes'. The official Soviet history, for its part, condemns the 'aggressive policies' of the United States 'in the regions adjoining the Soviet Union'. Second, both sources argue that such interference is dangerous to 'the foundations of international peace' (Source E), or to 'safeguarding peace and the sovereign rights of nations' (Source F). Third, both aim to justify their case by reference to the United Nations. According to Source E, 'the United States has taken a leading part in establishing the United Nations', while Source F asserts that US actions were 'incompatible with the principles proclaimed by the General Assembly'. Each source aims, therefore, to produce the most convincing condemnation possible of an ideological enemy.

8

AN OVERALL SUMMARY

This book has attempted to establish an alternative to the way in which Stalin and Stalinism are usually presented to students. It might be helpful to review the overall perspectives.

THE TRADITIONAL OVERALL INTERPRETATION

Stalin's regime was ruthless and efficient, creating an effective totalitarian state during the 1930s, although with enormous suffering. The result was a form of totalitarianism that was more complete than that of Nazi Germany. Stalin was in control of internal developments and pursued a foreign policy which, with occasional changes in tactics, had a strategy of dividing the Western powers.

Because of these developments, and despite the suffering of its own population, the Soviet Union was able to inflict defeat on Nazi Germany. This followed a disastrous initial response, in which Stalin completely misinterpreted Hitler's intentions. But Stalin's subsequent recovery interacted with long-term economic and military preparation, along with the established centralisation, to overcome the much more limited military and economic base of Nazi Germany.

As a result of eventual victory, Stalin's position was greatly strengthened after 1945. He was therefore able to reimpose the type of constraints that had existed during the 1930s in a new set of purges. He also spread Soviet influence across Eastern Europe and set the pace in the development of the Cold War. In all respects, this was the period of 'mature dictatorship'.

After his death in 1953, Stalin's monolith threatened to leave his successors in its shade. Khrushchev therefore took measures to discredit Stalin's name by focusing on the man's brutality and many personal deficiencies. Even so, the influence of Stalin remained powerful and his system continued to dominate the Soviet body politic until the Gorbachev era.

A REVISED INTERPRETATION

Stalin's regime was ruthless but not consequentially efficient. Totalitarianism was as flawed in Stalinist Russia as it was in Nazi Germany. During the 1930s this was strongly apparent in domestic policy. Stalin sought to centralise a political and economic system that frequently fell to local initiatives. As a result, central correctives had to be applied, which meant that Stalin's policies were as much reactive as they were proactive. Similarly, his foreign policy had to be steered on to corrected courses, partly because of earlier errors of judgement and partly because of circumstances beyond his control.

The war with Germany initially paralysed the whole system. The economic planning of the 1930s had been geared to mobilising Russia for an offensive campaign, whereas Stalin's inappropriate diplomacy necessitated a defensive response that could not immediately be delivered. Major changes were, however, introduced to transform the situation. Soviet production was made more efficient, paradoxically, by partially demobilising the planning structure to enhance military mobilisation. The Soviet Union defeated Germany because it was able to transcend the limits imposed by Stalinism since the 1930s.

After 1945 Stalin's position was vulnerable, not least to the very forces that had been responsible for military victory. He therefore had to reinstitute the sort of controls that had existed during the 1930s but that had been relaxed during the war. But these were an expression of insecurity rather than of 'mature dictatorship'. Expansion in Europe was less controlled and calculated than has been thought. In part, it was a response to circumstances, in part a means of justifying internal policies, a rerun of the interaction between foreign and domestic policy during the early 1930s.

Stalin's system was already in decline when it was taken over by Khrushchev, who did what he could to reform its most depleted part, agriculture. Khrushchev's replacement by Brezhnev led to an attempt to revive Stalinist centralisation but the infrastructure had long since withered to create an excessive vulnerability to Western competition. The result was the decline and collapse of the Soviet state.

NOTES

1. STALIN'S RISE AND RULE

1   E.H. Carr: *Socialism in One Country 1924–1926* (London 1958), Ch. 4.
2   M. McCauley: *Stalin and Stalinism* (Harlow 1983), Ch. 1.
3   N. Krasso: 'Trotsky's Marxism', in *New Left Review*, 44, 1967.
4   L. Colletti: 'The Question of Stalin', in *New Left Review*, 61, 1970.
5   S.F. Cohen: *Bukharin and the Bolshevik Revolution: A Political Biography 1888–1938* (London 1971), pp. 327–8.
Source A: Quoted in T.H. Rigby (ed.): *Stalin* (Englewood Cliffs, N.J., 1966), p. 73.
Source B: J.V. Stalin: *Works*, vol. X (Moscow 1955), p. 382.
Source C: L. Fischer: *Men and Politics: An Autobiography* (London 1941), p. 90.
Source D: D.M. Cole: *Joseph Stalin, Man of Steel* (London 1942), p. 60.
Source E: G.F. Alexandrov *et al.*: *Joseph Stalin: A Short Biography* (Moscow 1947), pp. 198–203.
Source F: L. Trotsky: *Stalin: An Appraisal of the Man and His Influence*, ed. and trans. by C. Malamuth (London 1947).
Source G: *The Anti-Stalin Campaign and International Communism: A Selection of Documents*, ed. by the Russian Institute, Columbia University (New York 1956), pp. 9–85.
Source H: *Pravda*, 31 October 1961, quoted in T.H. Rigby (ed.): op. cit., p. 128.

2. STALINIST POLITICS AND TERROR

1   R.G. Suny: 'Stalin and His Stalinism: Power and Authority in the Soviet Union, 1930–1953', in I. Kershaw and M. Lewin (eds):

Stalinism and Nazism: Dictatorships in Comparison (Cambridge 1997).

2 Quoted in T.H. Rigby: op. cit., p. 55.

3 J. Arch Getty: 'The Politics of Stalinism', in A. Nove (ed.): *The Stalin Phenomenon* (London 1993), p. 128.

4 Ibid., p. 129.

5 R. Conquest: *The Great Terror* (Harmondsworth 1971), p. 639.

6 R.C. Tucker: 'Introduction', in R.C. Tucker and S.F. Cohen (eds): *The Great Purge Trial* (New York 1965), p. xxix.

7 See I. Deutscher: *Stalin: A Political Biography* (London 1966), Ch. 9.

8 L. Viola: 'The Second Coming: Class Enemies in the Soviet Countryside, 1927–1935', in J. Arch Getty and Roberta T. Manning (eds): *Stalinist Terror: New Perspectives* (Cambridge 1993), pp. 69–70.

9 J. Arch Getty: op. cit., p. 132.

10 R. Thurston: 'The Stakhanovite Movement: Background to the Great Terror in the Factories, 1935–1938', in J. Arch Getty and Roberta T. Manning (eds): op. cit., p. 160.

11 See R.R. Reese: 'The Red Army and the Great Purges', in ibid.

12 See S. Fitzpatrick: 'How the Mice Buried the Cat: Scenes from the Great Purges of 1937 in the Russian Provinces', in C. Ward (ed.): *The Stalinist Dictatorship* (London 1998).

13 Ibid.

14 G.T. Rittersporn: 'The Omnipresent Conspiracy: On Soviet Imagery of Politics and Social Relations in the 1930s', in J. Arch Getty and Roberta T. Manning (eds): op. cit., p. 114.

15 R.G. Suny: op. cit., p. 50.

16 R.R. Reese: op. cit., p. 199.

17 Ibid., p. 210.

18 Ibid., p. 213.

Source A: R.W. Thurston: *Life and Terror in Stalin's Russia* (New Haven and London 1996), p. 227.

Source B: A. Rybakov: *Children of the Arbat* (New York 1989).

Source C: *The Anti-Stalin Campaign and International Communism: A Selection of Documents*, ed by the Russian Institute, Columbia University (New York 1956), extracts from pp. 9–85.

Source D: Roberta T. Manning: 'The Soviet Economic Crisis of 1936–1940 and the Great Purges', in J. Arch Getty and Roberta T. Manning (eds): op. cit., pp. 140–1.

Source E: F. MacLean: *Eastern Approaches* (London 1951).

Source F: 'Report of the Court Proceedings in the Case of the Anti-Soviet "Bloc of Rights and Trotskyites", March 1938' in J. Laver (ed.): *Russia 1914–1941* (London 1991).

Source G: Ibid.

Source H: R.C. Tucker and S.F. Cohen (eds): op. cit., p. 586.

3. STALIN'S ECONOMIC POLICIES

1 V. Brovkin: *Russia after Lenin. Politics, Culture and Society, 1921–1929* (London 1998), p. 222.
2 M. Lewin: *Russian Peasants and Soviet Power: A Study of Collectivization* (New York 1968), pp. 516–17.
3 J. Arch Getty: op. cit., p. 140.
4 M. Lynch: *Stalin and Khrushchev: The USSR, 1924–64* (London 1990), p. 30.
5 R. Hutchings: *Soviet Economic Development* (Oxford 1967), Ch. 6.
6 E. Zaleski: *Planning for Economic Growth in the Soviet Union 1918–1932* (Durham, NC, 1971), Chs 6 and 7.
7 See D.R. Shearer: *Industry, State and Society in Stalin's Russia 1926–1934* (Ithaca and London 1996), p. 235.
8 Ibid., p. 236.
Source A: R. Wolfson: *Years of Change* (London 1978), p. 347.
Source B: Quoted in M. Lynch: op. cit., p. 34.
Source C: S. and B. Webb: *Soviet Communism: A New Civilisation* (London 1935), pp. 200–1.
Source D: V. Kravchenko: *I Chose Freedom: The Personal and Political Life of a Soviet Official* (London 1947), p. 113.
Source E: Sir W. Citrine: *I Search for Truth in Russia* (London 1938), p. 377.
Source F: Adapted from E. Zaleski: *Stalinist Planning for Economic Growth 1932–1952* (London 1960), p. 503.
Source G: A. Smith: *I Was a Soviet Worker* (London 1937), p. 43.
Source H: J. Scott: *Behind the Urals* (London 1942).
Source I: Y. Kukushkin: *History of the USSR* (Moscow 1981).

4. SOCIETY AND CULTURE

Source A: Quoted in J. Laver (ed.): *Russia 1914–1941* (London 1991), p. 82.
Source B: *Pravda*, 1 February 1935, quoted in T.H. Rigby: op. cit., p. 111.
Source C: N. Mandelstam: *Hope Against Hope* (London 1971), p. 13.
Source D: S. and B. Webb: op. cit.

5. STALIN'S FOREIGN POLICY, 1929–41

1 Quoted in R.C. Tucker: 'The Emergence of Stalin's Foreign Policy', in *Slavic Review*, xxxvi, 4 December 1977.

2 T.J. Uldricks: 'Soviet Security Policy in the 1930s', in G. Gorodetsky (ed.): *Soviet Foreign Policy 1917–1991* (London 1994), p. 73.

3 See R. Hutchings: *Soviet Economic Development* (Oxford 1967), Ch. 6.

4 R.C. Tucker: 'The Emergence', op. cit.

5 J. Haslam: *The Soviet Union and the Struggle for Collective Security in Europe, 1933–39* (New York 1984), pp. 52–3.

6 G. Roberts: *The Soviet Union and the Origins of the Second World War* (London 1995), p. 97.

7 *A Short History of the Communist Party of the Soviet Union* (Moscow 1970), p. 247.

8 See W. Laqueur: *Russia and Germany: A Century of Conflict* (London 1965), Ch. 12.

9 G. Roberts: op. cit., p. 121.

Source A: J. Degras (ed.): *Soviet Documents on Foreign Policy*, vol. III (London, 1953), p. 360.

Source B: Ibid., p. 320.

Source C: Quoted in M. Lynch: op. cit., pp. 80–1.

Source D: Ibid., p. 81.

6. THE SOVIET UNION AT WAR, 1941–5

1 J. Sapir: 'The Economics of War in the Soviet Union during World War II', in I. Kershaw and M. Lewin (eds): op. cit., p. 210.

2 B. Bonwetsch: 'Stalin, the Red Army and the "Great Patriotic War"', in ibid., p. 196.

3 Quoted in ibid., p. 193.

4 G. Fischer: *Soviet Opposition to Stalin* (Harvard 1952), p. 45.

5 J. Sapir: op. cit., p. 234.

6 V. M. Kulish: 'Russia Strikes Back', in Purnell, *History of the Twentieth Century*, vol. V (London 1968), p. 1936.

7 See M. von Hagen: 'From "Great Fatherland War" to the Second World War: New Perspectives and Future Prospects', in I. Kershaw and M. Lewin (eds): op. cit.

Source A: *Evening Standard*, September 1939.

Source B: G. Roberts: op. cit., p. 104.

Source C: Ibid., p. 104.

Source D: Ibid., p. 142.

Source E: *Soviet Foreign Policy during the Patriotic War: Documents and Materials*, vol. 1, 22 June 1941–31 December 1943 (London n.d.).

Source F: J.V. Stalin: *On the Great Patriotic War of the Soviet Union* (London 1945), p. 6.

Source G: Imperial War Museum.
Source H: In W.L. White: *Report on the Russians* (Harcourt Brace Jovanovich Inc 1945, 1973).
Source I: Heinz Guderian: *Panzer Leader* (London 1952), p. 440.

7. STALIN'S POST-WAR REGIME, 1945–53

1   C. Ward: *Stalin's Russia* (London 1993), p. 187.
2   Ibid., p. 188.
3   A. Fontaine: *A History of the Cold War from the October Revolution to the Korean War 1917–1950*, trans. by D.D. Paige (London 1969–70), Ch. 1.
4   See R.C. Tucker: 'The Emergence', op. cit.
5   G.F. Kennan: *Soviet Foreign Policy 1917–1941* (Princeton, NJ, 1960), Document 29.
6   A. Fontaine: op. cit., Ch. 8.
7   N.V. Sivachev and N.N. Yakovlev: *Russia and the United States* (Chicago 1979), Ch. 5.
8   C. Kennedy-Pipe: *Russia and the World 1917–1991* (London 1998), p. 211.
Source A: N.A. Voznesensky: *The Economy of the USSR during World War II* (Public Affairs Press 1948).
Source B: Quoted in T.H. Rigby: op. cit., p. 53.
Source C: Adapted from J. Laver: *The USSR 1945–1990* (London 1991), p.4.
Source D: N. Khrushchev: *Khrushchev Remembers* (London 1971), p. 252.
Source E: H. Commager: *Documents of American History*, 9th edition (New Jersey 1973), p. 526.
Source F: *A History of Soviet Foreign Policy 1945–70* (Moscow 1973), pp. 46–7.

BIBLIOGRAPHY

PRIMARY SOURCES

Selections of primary sources may be found in: T.H. Rigby: *Stalin (Great Lives Observed)* (Englewood Cliffs, NJ, 1966); M. McCauley: *Stalin and Stalinism* (Harlow 1983); N. Rothnie: *Stalin and Russia 1924–1953* (London 1991); J. Laver: *Russia 1914–1941 (History at Source)* (London 1991); J. Laver: *The USSR 1945–1990 (History at Source)* (London 1991). Foreign policy is comprehensively covered in J. Degras (ed.): *Soviet Documents on Foreign Policy* (London 1953).

Individual works with a personal viewpoint of the Stalinist period include: N. Khrushchev: *Khrushchev Remembers* (London 1971); L. Trotsky: *Stalin: An Appraisal of the Man and His Influence*, ed. and trans. by C. Malamuth (London 1947); N. Mandelstam: *Hope Against Hope* (London 1971); and Victor Kravchenko: *I Chose Freedom: The Personal and Political Life of a Soviet Official* (London 1947). Western attitudes can be seen in Sidney and Beatrice Webb: *Soviet Communism: A New Civilisation* (London 1935); Fitzroy MacLean: *Eastern Approaches* (London 1951); Sir William Citrine: *I Search for Truth in Russia* (London 1938); and Andrew Smith: *I Was a Soviet Worker* (London 1937).

TRADITIONAL WORKS

Useful introductions to the subject are: M. Lynch: *Stalin and Khrushchev, 1924–64* (London 1990); M. McCauley: *Stalin and Stalinism* (Harlow 1983); N. Rothnie: *Stalin and Russia 1924–1953* (London 1991); J. Laver: *Russia 1914–1941* (London 1991); and J. Laver: *The USSR 1945–1990* (London 1991). Among the more detailed and longstanding Western surveys of Stalin and Stalinism are: E.H. Carr: *Socialism in One Country 1924–1926* (London 1958); I. Deutscher: *Stalin* (Harmondsworth 1966); R. Conquest: *The Great Terror* (Harmondsworth 1971); R. Hutchings: *Soviet Economic Development* (Oxford 1967); W. Laqueur: *Russia and Germany: A Century of Conflict* (London 1965); and G.F. Kennan: *Soviet Foreign Policy 1917–1941* (Princeton, NJ, 1960).

NEW INTERPRETATIONS

Although not yet on the same scale as publications on Nazi Germany, there has been an impressive array of recent material on the Soviet Union during the 1990s, with some extensive reinterpretations that I have tried to reflect in this book. Invaluable among the general works are: C. Ward: *Stalin's Russia* (London 1993); A. Nove (ed.): *The Stalin Phenomenon* (London 1993); C. Ward (ed.): *The Stalinist Dictatorship* (London 1998); and I. Kershaw and M. Lewin (eds): *Stalinism and Nazism: Dictatorships in Comparison* (Cambridge 1997).

Recommended for more specific areas are: S. Fitzpatrick: *Stalin's Peasants* (Oxford 1994); D.R. Shearer: *Industry, State, and Society in Stalin's Russia 1926–1934* (Ithaca and London 1996); J. Arch Getty and Roberta T. Manning (eds): *Stalinist Terror: New Perspectives* (Cambridge 1993); R.W. Thurston: *Life and Terror in Stalin's Russia 1934–1941* (New Haven and London 1996); P.H. Solomon: *Soviet Criminal Justice under Stalin* (Cambridge 1996); V. Andrle: *A Social History of Twentieth-century Russia* (London 1994); L.H. Siegelbaum and R.G. Suny (eds): *Making Workers Soviet: Power, Class and Identity* (Ithaca and London 1994); V. Brovkin: *Russia after Lenin: Politics, Culture and Society,*

1921–1929 (London 1998); G. Roberts: *The Soviet Union and the Origins of the Second World War* (London 1995); C. Kennedy-Pipe: *Russia and the World 1917–1991* (London 1998).

These new approaches will doubtless be added to rapidly in the next few years. The reader can therefore expect – and welcome – further reinterpretations on Stalin and Stalinism.

INDEX

NOTE: Page numbers in **Bold** refer to Background Narratives

industrialisation 5, 19, 22, 40, 46, 61; and military readiness 42, 67, 73–4; rapid **2**, **35**, **36**, 103; sources 50–2

industry, effects of Stalin's policies 43–6; heavy 7, **36**, 42, 43, 44, 45, 73, 80, 85, **96**, 99; and the NEP **35**; production figures 44; reasons for Stalin's policies 41–3; use of agriculture to subsidise 37, 39–41, 42; *see also* Stakhanovites

infrastructure 18, 80; damage to 99

intelligence reports re Hitler 81, 91

'Iron Curtain' **97**, 102

Islam **54**, 58, 60

Italy 6

Ivan the Terrible 56, 59

Japan, Soviet agents in 81

Jews, Nazi policy of genocide against 7; Soviet persecution of 58, 60

Kabalevsky, Dmitry 61

Kalinin, Mikhail Ivanovich 4

Kamenev, Lev Borisovich **1**, **2**, 3, 4, 26; show trial (1936) **17**, 22

Karachais, forcible exile and resettlement of 87

Kazakhstan 60

Kennedy-Pipe, C. 104

Khatchaturian, Aram 61

Khrushchev, Nikita 22, **96**, 99–100, 104, 111, 112; criticism of the Fourth Five-Year Plan 106; on Lenin's Testament 12; speech to 20th Congress (1956) 14, 30

Kiev, Battle of **79**, 83

Kirgizia 60

Kirov, Sergei, assassination of (1934) **17**

kolkhozy (collective farms) 99

Kolyma region, Siberia 22

Konev, Ivan Stepanovich 82, 86

Kosygin, Alexei Nikolaevich 100

Kravchenko, Victor, *I Chose Freedom* 48

Krylenko 57

Kuibyshev 4

kulaks **17**, 23–4, 40

Kun, Bela 5

Kursk, Battle of (1943) **79**, 86, 88

Kuznetzov, Admiral 81

land, transfer from aristocracy to peasantry **35**

Laqueur, W. 72

law, change in 57

League of the Godless **54**, 57

League of Nations **65**, 69; Russia expelled from (1940) 72

'Left Opposition' **2**, 5, 41

Lend-Lease Programme 86

Lenin, Vladimir Ilyich **2**, 5, 6, 7, 8, 22, **35**, **65**, 101; and the Bolsheviks 17, 55; death (1924) **1**; on his mausoleum 14; Political Testament (1922) **1**, 11, 12: Codicil (1923) **1**, 2, 11; resolution quoted (1920) 62

Leningrad, Battle of (1941) **79**, 83, 88

'Leningrad Affair' 98

Lewin, M. 38

Liebknecht, Karl 5

literature 57, 58; and Socialist Realism **54**

Litvinov, Maxim **65–6**, 69, 101

living standards, East and West compared 104

local official influences 9, 19–20, 23, 26, 39, 45, 55

Low, David, cartoon of Nazi-Soviet Pact 89, 90

Low Countries, offensive (1940) 83

Luxemburg, Rosa 5

McCauley, Martin 4

machine tractor station (MTS) 41

MacLean, Fitzroy, description of 1938 show trial 31–2

Magnitogorsk **36**, 44, 51–2

Malenkov, Georgi Maximilianovich 84, **96**

Malinovsky, Rodion Yakovlevich 86

managers in industry **17**, 24, 26

Mandelstam, Osip, poem about Stalin 63

Manning, Roberta T., *The Soviet Economic Crisis of 1936–40 and the Great Purges* quoted 30

marriage 56, *see also* divorce

Marshall Aid 103, 104; refusal of **96**

Marxism 18, 56

Mensheviks 17, 21

Meshketians, forcible exile and resettlement of 87

military, neutralisation of the 98; ranks undermined by Bolsheviks 56; recovery in WWII 84–5, 102; strategy (1930s) 42, 67

Molotov, Vyacheslav 4, **66**, 69, 82, 84, 101; speech (1938) 74–5; speech to the Supreme Soviet (1939) 90

Moscow 44, 51; Battle of (1941) **79**, 83, 88

music 60–1

Muslims 58, 60

Mussolini, Benito 6, 7, 61, **66**

Mutual Assistance, Treaty of *see* Franco-Soviet Pact (1935)

Napoleon Bonaparte 3, 87, 93

Narkompros (People's Commissariat for Enlightenment) **54**, 59

nationalism 58, 83

NATO, established (1949) 104

navy, purges of the **17**

Nazi-Soviet Non-Aggression Pact (1939) 8, 10, 23, **66**, **79**; cartoon 89, 90; evaluation of 68–9, 70–4; extract from 76; Secret Additional Protocol **66**, 70, 71, 76

Nazism 7, 81, 84, 88, 101

New Economic Policy (NEP) **2**, 5, 8, 10, **35–6**, 37–8, 42, 55

NKVD 7, 9, **16**, **17**, 22, 26, 39, **96**, 98

Nove, A. 27

nuclear weapons **97**, 103

October Revolution *see* Bolshevik Revolution

Oder-Neisse Line 102

OGPU **16**, 57

Orgburo 1, **16**, 18

Orthodox Patriarchate 57

OVRA 7

Panzer Leader, views of a German army commander 94

Paris Peace Conference **65**

Thurston, R.W. 24; *Life and Terror in Stalin's Russia* quoted 29

Tolbukhin 86

Tomsky **2**, 5, **35**

total war 42, 80–1, **80**, 83, 85, 89

totalitarianism 6–7, 17–21, 23, 25–8, **54**, 55, 97, 110; flawed 8–10, 111–12

Triandafilov 80

Trotsky, Leon **1**, **2**, 3, 4–5, 6, **35**, 98, 101, 103; in exile (1930s) 3, 9; on socialism 21; *Stalin* quoted 13–14

Truman Doctrine (1948) 102, 104; extract from the 107–8

Tsarism 7, 56, 60

Tucker, R. 22, 23, 68, 101

Turkestan 60

Turkic populations 58

Ukraine 40, 44, **79**, 88, 103

Ukrainians 83, 103; forcible exile and resettlement of 87

Uldricks, T. 67

Union of Soviet Socialist Republics (USSR), collapse of (1991) 6, 58, 104, 112; Constitutions (1924, 1936) **16**; defence expenditure 104; losses in WWII 83; victory report by a Western observer (1945) 93–4

Union of Writers **54**, 58

unions, trade 37

United States, economic aid 86–7; Soviet industrial development compared with 45; *see also* Cold War

universities, number of 59

Urals 85

urban areas, influx of peasants to 40–1

Uzbekistan 60

Varfolomeev 80

Vatutin 86

Versailles, Treaty of (1919) 68

Viola, L. 24

Volga 83, 85

Voroshilov, Kliment Efremovid 4, 84

Voznesensky 98

Vyshinski, Andrei Yanuarievich 57; Prosecutor, concluding speech at show trial (1938) 33

wage differentials 7, **54**, 56

war, defensive 80, 82, 83; theories of 80; *see also* total war

War Communism (1918–21) 8, **35**, 37

Ward, C. 98, 99

Warsaw Pact 104

Webb, Sidney and Beatrice 19; *Soviet Communism* 47–8, 63

Wehrmacht 83, 87

Wheatcroft 27

Whites 4, 68

Wilson, Woodrow 101

Winter War (1939–40) 27, **66**, 72, 73

women, Stalin's attitude to 56, 60

workers, urban 5, 7, 18, 42, 43

World War I 68

World War II, Soviet Union in (1941–5) 7, 27, 44, 79–95, **79–80**; after 101; initial defeat **79**, 80–3; ultimate victory 84–9, 92–4, 97

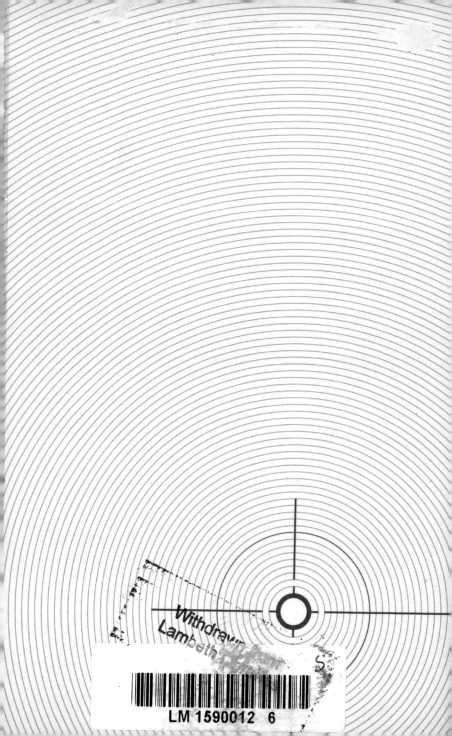

TRUB
REDI
BLINK

BY

Y

FORT

LAUREN CHILD

AND YOU DIE

HarperCollins *Children's Books*

First published in hardback in Great Britain by HarperCollins Children's Books 2016
First published in paperback in Great Britain by HarperCollins Children's Books 2017
HarperCollins Children's Books is a division of HarperCollins Publishers Ltd
1 London Bridge Street, London SE1 9GF

For Ruby Redfort games, puzzles, videos and more, visit:
www.rubyredfort.com

Visit Lauren Child at **www.milkmonitor.com**

1

Copyright © Lauren Child 2016

Illustrations on pages 543-558 © Lauren Child 2016

Series design by David Mackintosh
Illustrations © David Mackintosh 2016

Map layouts by Martin Brown
Map illustrations © Emily Faccini

ISBN: 978-0-00-733429-2

Printed and bound in the UK by
Clays Ltd, St Ives Plc

MIX
Paper from
responsible sources
FSC® C007454

For **Lucy G**

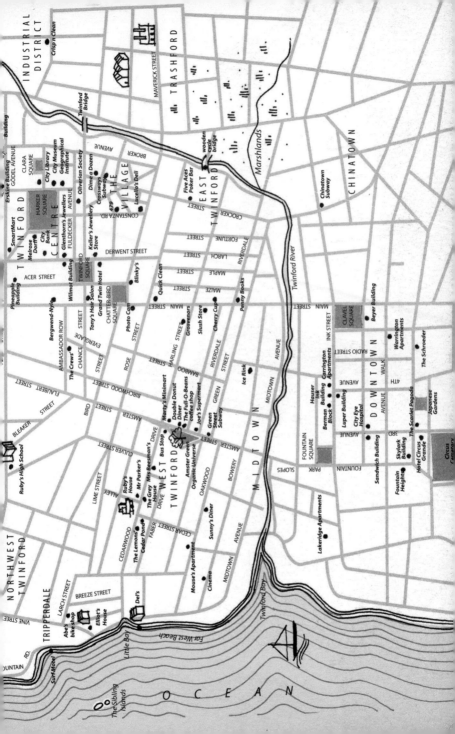

MOUNTAIN RD.

Big Sky Lake

Emerald Lake

Autumn Lake

Mountain Ranch Camp

LAKE RD.

Still Water House

Dry River Canyon

Ruby rock climbs

VINE ST.

DRY RIVER ROAD

GAS

Lucky Eight Gas Station

MOUNTAIN RD.

Red's House

Frederick Lutz's

SILVER HILLS

FLOWER ROAD

Desolate Cove

Meteor Island

DERILLA DRIVE

NORTHWEST TWINFORD

The Mountain Chateau

Boulder Valley

Bike Park

Fir Forest Edge

FLATLANDS

Twinford River

NORTH TWINFORD

City Nurseries

UPTOWN
(UPPER-EAST SIDE

Planetarium

EAST 23RD ST

23rd Street Hotel

The Costume
Museum

FIBONACCI ST.

COLLEGE
TOWN

CENTRAL
CITY PARK

MAIN ST.

UPPER EAST AVE.

Movie Museum

LITTLE SEVEN ST.

Little Seven Grocers

St Angelina
Hospital

STAR
PARK

Cathedral Subway

The Mirror Building

City Pool

Charles
Burger

72ND ST.

Pineapple Building

SmartMart

Music School

Erskine Building

GÖDEL AVE

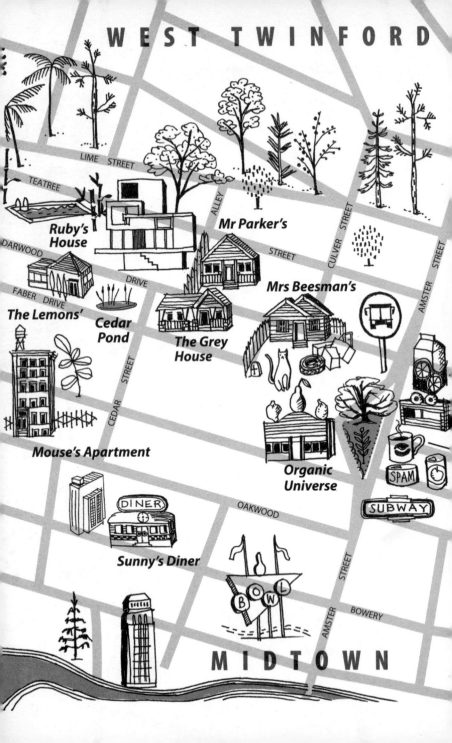

N O R T H
T W I N F O R D

City Pool

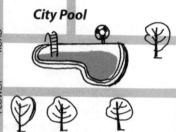

ROAD

FLOWER

St Angelina
Hospital

STREET

CENTRAL
CITY PARK

Pineapple
Building

72ND

STREET

STREET

Bergwend-Nyle

Melros
Dorff

BLEAKER

FLAUBERT

STREET

MAIN

STREET

ACER

Wilmot
Building

AMBASSADOR   ROW

STREET

The Crews'

EVERGLADE

CHANCE   STREET

TWINFORD
SQUARE

BIRD

AMSTER

STREET

Tony's Hair
Salon

ROSE

BIRCHWOOD

STREET

STREET

STREET

CHATTER-BIRD
SQUARE

Grand
Twin
Hotel

Photo Cam

23rd Street Hotel

EAST 23RD STREET

COLLEGE TOWN

UPPER EAST AVE.

FIBONACCI STREET

The Costume Museum

Little Seven Grocers

Movie Museum

LITTLE SEVEN ST.

NUMERAL ST.

Charles Burger

STAR PARK

ADMIT ONE

PYTHAGORAS ST.

SUBWAY

Cathedral Subway

The Mirror Building

ALGEBRA STREET

Music School

72ND STREET

SmartMart

TWINFORD CENTRE

Erskine Building

Old City Bank

HARKER SQUARE

LIBRARY

CLARA SQUARE

City Museum

Glenthorn's Jewellers

FULDECKER AVENUE

Oliverian Society

Geographical Institute

Keller's Jewellery Store

DERWENT ST.

Dime a Dozen

SUPER

479

SUBWAY

Crossways Subway

AVENUE

Twinford Bridge

THE VILLAGE

ROKER

Lucello's Deli

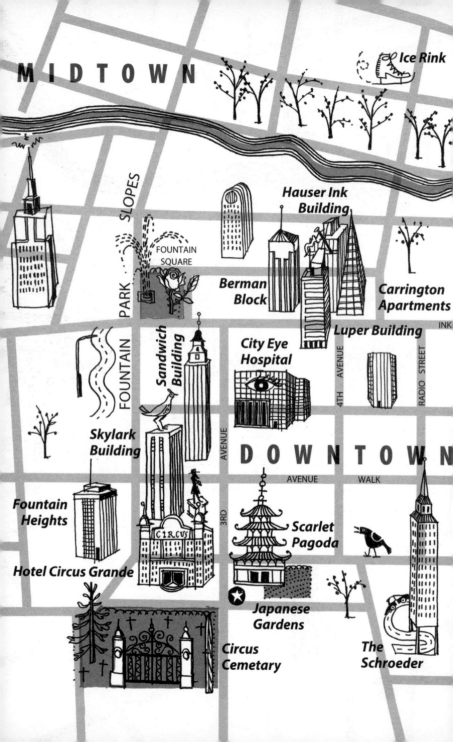

'Close your eyes and see the truth'

Author anonymous,
from the indigo
code-breaker's bible

The buried fear

IT HAPPENED ONE BRIGHT APRIL DAY when the child, then barely five weeks old, was sleeping. The world crashed down and the baby opened its eyes, but there was only darkness to see. The walls were packed around it, almost touching, and the doors and the windows all gone. The baby cried out, but no one came. It screamed and clenched its furious fists, trying in vain to push at the tomb of rubble, but nothing happened. Its little mind began to panic, its eyes closed shut and its heart began to hurt.

She was alone and no one would ever find her.

The baby had been left in the care of the housekeeper, who had just put some cookies to cool on the porch when, without warning, the ground began to shift and the buildings began to shake, trees creaked and then cracked. Some of them – the big oak on Amster Green – stood firm, others – the giant cedar of west Twinford – fell.

Sidewalks buckled and streetlights toppled. The earth tremor lasted just a few seconds and Twinford City escaped by-and-large unscathed – a few buildings needed repair, but remarkably no one, not a soul, lost their life. The townsfolk mourned their fallen trees, but counted their blessings: no one had died. There was only one real casualty; the Fairbank house on Cedarwood was completely destroyed. After 200 years of standing just exactly where it was, looking out across the ever-changing townscape of west Twinford, this historic house was gone.

It was the housekeeper who dug the child out with nothing but 'the hands God gave her'. This woman had endured more than earthquakes in her time and no mere earth tremor was going to have her standing by while an infant lay buried, perhaps dead, perhaps alive. By the time the baby's parents returned to their home, now a wreckage of wood and brick, their daughter was lying in the housekeeper's lap quiet as a lamb and smiling up at them. Everyone was very relieved, their little girl saved, not a scratch to her perfect face, no damage done.

Or so they thought, for in that baby's head a tiny kernel of fear had lodged, a fear which would grow and grow until in her thoughts a monster lurked.

An ordinary kid

WHEN RUBY REDFORT WAS THIRTEEN AND THREE QUARTERS, she found herself confronting the biggest dilemma of her short life. On the desk was an apple split in two. In her hand was a tiny piece of paper.

On the paper were printed two small letters; small letters which spelled something so vast and so terrifying that it made her eyes water.

The letters told of betrayal and murder.

It was the Count who had planted suspicion, posed the grim question and introduced the poisonous thought that the untimely death of Spectrum's most valuable agent, Bradley Baker, might have been 'arranged'.

'The question is,' he'd said, 'who pulled the trigger?'

It was the apple, the messenger of doom, which held the answer.

If Ruby was to believe in its truth then life had suddenly become dramatically more dangerous. She looked down at the paper inscribed with the initials of the woman who called the shots, who held the lives of so many in her hands.

The boss of Spectrum 8.

LB.

Ruby looked into darkness and wondered who she could trust.

Trust no one, she thought.

Some several weeks later...

Chapter 1.
A window on the world

RUBY REDFORT WAS PERCHED ON a stepladder looking out of the high landscape window which ran the length of her room. The window was designed to allow the light in rather than to provide a view of the street below, but today it was the view Ruby was interested in. She was looking down at the network of roads and alleys, contemplating the scene below. Mrs Beesman was wheeling her shopping cart down one of the back alleys which ran between the rows of houses. The cart was filled with several cats and some jars, saucepans and a whole lot of random junk. A few of the cats appeared to have socks wrapped around their middles, presumably to keep them warm. Mrs Beesman herself was wearing several coats and a fur hat with earflaps, ski gloves and an extremely long, moth-eaten scarf. Mrs Beesman tended to wear a coat in all weathers, but today, bundled up as she was, suggested that it was a pretty chilly morning. As the old lady trundled past Mr Parker's yard, so his dog Bubbles began to bark.

On Ruby's lap was a plate of pancakes: her second serving

and it was still only 6.47 am. Ruby had been away from home for the whole of November, and the housekeeper had missed her more than she would ever say. The minute Ruby had walked through the door Mrs Digby had reached for the batter and the skillet and while she flipped pancakes so they chatted. Their conversation had been interrupted by an urgent call from Mrs Digby's cousin Emily and Ruby, knowing the time these phone calls often took, had carried her breakfast on up to her bedroom.

The pancakes were lasting longer than usual because Ruby's eating was interrupted by her neighbourhood observations. Every few minutes she would put down her fork and take the pencil from behind her ear and make a note in the yellow notebook which lay in her lap. It was surprising how much was going on out there given the time of day. Ruby had taken up the yellow notebook habit when she was four years old and she now had 625 notebooks full of the exciting, interesting, ordinary and often dull happenings that had occurred in the world around her. She stored the 624 notebooks under the floor, the 625th she kept hidden inside the door jamb.

Ruby had returned unreasonably early that December morning from what she referred to as the 'dork pound' and what the organisers would call Genius Camp 'for the mathematically gifted'. As far as Ruby was concerned, it was four weeks of her life she would never get back. It had been no walk in the park, not because the work had been particularly hard, but because some of the kids enrolled in the course were, well, *not particularly nice*, and some of them were a whole lot worse than *that*, namely Dakota Lyme. Ruby had run into Dakota not so long ago at the October mathletics meet, one of the less pleasant days of Ruby's (on the whole charmed) life. Ruby had found herself going head to head with the objectionable girl in the final round of the one-day competition, and for all the trouble it had caused her, Ruby would have gladly conceded victory and walked away from the whole stupid circus. However, she won and took the consequences, which were a lot of abuse and a nasty encounter in the mathletics meet parking lot. One of the problems for Ruby was that her brilliant brain brought her a lot of attention, attention she really didn't want, nor, given her status as an undercover agent, *need*.

Mr Parker came out onto the lawn to shout at Bubbles. The sound of his voice was a whole lot more unpleasant than the sound of the dog's barking.

Ruby's life as an agent was no picnic, but then that was hardly a surprise given the kind of people one was inclined to run into during the day-on-day battle of good v evil. *Evil*, a much overused word in Ruby's opinion. Not every person who committed a crime was *evil*, and only rarely (extremely rarely) would one consider them through and through bad with not an iota of goodness in them. But when it came to the Count, Ruby would have to concede that if there *was* any good in him then it was too small to see. Blame it on a bad childhood, a life gone wrong, his ma and pa's genes, blame it on the weather, but whatever the reason, it didn't change the facts – goodness had deserted him utterly, and his soul had gone to rot. Around this monster of a man swirled a murky soup of the vile and the unhinged, all eager to do his dirty work. The plots they hatched and cruelties they inflicted were dark enough to give Wonder Woman herself reason to keep the nightlight lit. So how did a thirteen-year-old school kid from Twinford hold her nerve? Well, no one had promised her it was going to be easy. But what scared Ruby more than the cruel ones, more than the Count even, was the force behind it all, the one who pulled the strings. Because there *was* someone, and according to the Count it was this someone who wanted Ruby dead and caused the Count himself to shudder.

And one should always, in the words of Mrs Digby:

Fear the wolf that other wolves fear.

Ruby watched as a removal van turned the corner and made its way down Cedarwood Drive. It stopped outside the grey clapboard house, the oldest house on the street. It seemed it was about to become vacant once more. As far back as Ruby could remember, no one ever stuck around long enough to make the house a home.

Ruby Redfort was a girl who embraced change and was not fearful of a little adventure, but lately she wouldn't mind if the whole world stood still.

A car drove by. It stopped at the junction; the driver wound down the window and threw a soda can onto the street.

October had been a busy month. Her life as an agent at the most secret of secret agencies – known only to those in the know as Spectrum – had been dominated by the growing sense that somewhere in Spectrum's subterranean corridors there lurked a mole. Ruby had felt the steely looks as the eye of suspicion was trained on her. She had been interviewed by the head of Spectrum 1, Agent Delaware, and it had not been a comfortable experience, particularly when with a steady gaze he had uttered the words, *'I could be staring into the eyes of a traitor right this very moment and not know it.'* But Ruby shouldn't have taken it personally – it was simply protocol. Every agent in Spectrum was under suspicion, every single one of them interviewed, investigated and scrutinised. No one had been identified as the mole, no one had been cleared; the tension in HQ was palpable.

As October brought in the storm winds, so the Spectrum investigation brought an uneasy atmosphere which crept through its halls, seeding suspicion and mistrust. And for Ruby everything was beginning to settle at LB's door.

A builder's truck manoeuvred its way down the street and pulled up outside the Lemons' house, blocking part of Cedarwood Drive. An angry driver began honking his horn, but the truck didn't move. The driver got out of his car, the truck driver out of his truck, and they began shouting at each other. The shouts of the men in the street masked the sound of footsteps on the roof above her. It was only when the hatch opened that Ruby realised that someone was up there.

'Who's there?' cried Ruby, the ladder rocking dangerously as she turned to look.

'Ah,' said Hitch. 'It looks like you're back.'

'Jeepers! Ever think of knocking?' scolded Ruby.

'A bit weird isn't it – knocking on the ceiling?' said Hitch. He had a tool belt around his waist and a reel of cable slung across his shoulder.

'What are you doing up there anyway?'

'It's a long story and I'll fill you in on it when I've got time, but I ought to get going.'

'You don't want to hear the latest?' she asked.

'Itching to hear your news kid, but it's a pleasure I'm going to have to put on hold.' He opened the window and climbed out onto the ledge.

'Doors too good for you, are they?'

'I hadn't realised you were so hung up on the rules,' said Hitch as he disappeared from view. 'Good to see you kid,' he called.

Chapter 2.
Long distance

RUBY HAD BARELY REPOSITIONED HERSELF on the stepladder when there was a knock at her bedroom door. Her husky dog Bug got to his feet and ambled over.

'Is that you?' she called, slipping the notebook under her behind.

'Who else would it be?' came the reply.

'You may enter,' Ruby called.

'One day you'll break your neck,' said the housekeeper walking into the room.

Ruby looked down to see Mrs Digby, holding a tray and scanning the floor for empty mugs and dirty plates.

'That's not a very cheery greeting,' said Ruby.

'It won't be a very cheering sight if it happens,' said the old lady. 'Nor if that butler falls off the house,' she said, peering out of the window at Hitch. 'Is he after squirrels again? Or is it window weevils?'

'Who in only knows?' said Ruby.

'What are you doing up there anyway? Spying on folks, I'll

warrant.'

'Watching,' corrected Ruby.

'Same thing,' sniffed the housekeeper. 'Never was there a child as curious as you.'

'Did my folks have a late night or something?' said Ruby, looking at her watch. It was rare for them to lie in; they were what Mrs Digby called 'early birds'.

'If you want the answer to that question then you're going to have to dial long distance,' said Mrs Digby.

'Huh?' said Ruby.

'Paris, France,' said the housekeeper, 'that's where they are.'

'They are?' said Ruby. '*Why*?'

'That butler friend of yours talked them into it.'

'Hitch?' said Ruby, like the Redforts had a team of butlers.

'He thought they needed a vacation; *why* I don't know since the only vacation they could use is a vacation from vacations.' Mrs Digby tutted. Just thinking about the number of trips that pair made could make her travelsick.

'So when are they home?' asked Ruby.

'Day after tomorrow. They wanted to be back in time for your return, but apparently all the flights were chock-a-block.'

'I'm sure Hitch could get them home. He's pretty good at persuading airline people to do what he wants.'

'Well, he failed this time,' said Mrs Digby, 'but I guess even he doesn't have much hold over the weather.'

'The weather?'

'Blizzards,' said Mrs Digby. 'Paris is under several feet of snow.'

'Is that so?' said Ruby. 'How long are they expected to—' She broke off, her attention caught by something else. 'Mrs Digby,' said Ruby, peering at the old lady, 'something has happened to your face.'

'Well, that doesn't sound quite polite,' said the housekeeper.

'I mean you look different.' Ruby stared hard at her. '*Tanned!*' she said, finally figuring out what had changed.

'Well, since you ask, I've been cruising.'

'What?'

'I've been cruising around the Caribbean.'

Ruby looked stunned.

'On a boat.'

'I know what a cruise is,' said Ruby. 'I'm just interested to understand how *you* got to be on one.'

'I won it fair and square.'

'Won what?'

'A cruise.'

'How?'

'In a competition. I won it and took Cousin Emily along with me.'

'What competition?' asked Ruby.

'Well, that's the curious thing,' said Mrs Digby. 'I don't exactly remember entering one, but I suppose I must have, and you know what they say...'

'What?' said Ruby.

Mrs Digby looked at her conspiratorially and said, 'Don't ask too many questions or they'll find you out.'

Ruby rolled her eyes. 'You mean they might have made a giant mistake and given you a prize you didn't actually win?'

'I'm not saying it's not impossible,' said Mrs Digby.

Mrs Digby's view on keeping one's mouth shut was similar to Spectrum's number one rule: **KEEP IT ZIPPED.** Ruby herself had a little book of rules, 80 of them to be accurate – it was a magenta book with the word 'Rules' printed on it in red. While the housekeeper busied herself collecting the rest of the dirty crockery, Ruby was left to her thoughts and she was surprised that one of her thoughts was, *I wish my folks were home.* Ruby was an independent kid; she didn't *need* people around her all the time for comfort or security. She had what Mrs Digby called *inner reserves,* by which she meant a strong sense of who she was, but for some reason today sitting up there on that stepladder, Ruby just felt a strong need to see her mom and dad. The house felt not so much quiet without them, as actually: empty.

'By the way,' said Mrs Digby, 'I hate to be the one to tell you, but that Archie Lemon busted into your room and ate some of your books.'

'What? You're kidding?' said Ruby.

'Before you get all animated about it, I should just say, it wasn't while I was watching him.'

'So who *was*?' asked Ruby.

'That would be his mother, Elaine. She was over visiting your mom and neither of them realised he had made a crawl for it – up all those stairs too.'

'How did he manage that?'

'They're over-feeding him is my guess,' said Mrs Digby. 'Who would believe such a tiny person could cause such havoc, but don't worry, I cleaned it all up, wiped the dribble off your books and put 'em all back.'

'Gross,' said Ruby.

'I'm not disagreeing with you.' The housekeeper turned to leave. 'Glad to have you back child.'

'Thank you,' said Ruby. 'I've missed you a bunch, you know that.'

Ruby returned to her musings.

As Ruby ran through all the various things that had happened since March, some nine months ago now, she began to see how time was running out and maybe not just for Spectrum – perhaps for her too.

She was beginning to tune into something that was driven neither by fact nor logic, it was more of a Clancy Crew hunch type of a thing. Just a feeling that whatever trouble was out there, it was now headed her way and about to come knocking at her door.

Chapter 3.
Catching up

AT 3 PM RUBY HEARD A SCRATCHING at the door.

'Bug, is that you?'

She was answered by one short bark.

'OK, I'll see you by the back door.'

She pulled on her boots, coat and hat, wound a scarf around her neck, and climbed out of the window.

Bug was waiting patiently outside for her, and together they set off down Cedarwood Drive, turned right on Amster and continued on as far as the Donut Diner. She left the husky by the coat rack and he settled down for a nap.

It was medium busy, not too crowded, but as usual there were plenty of customers. Marla, the owner, waved to Ruby as she walked through the door.

Ruby took up a seat at the counter where Clancy was already waiting: in front of him, two mugs of ginger tea and a couple of apple donuts.

Ruby unzipped her coat, to reveal a T-shirt which read:
happy to be here

'What's with the tea?' asked Ruby.

'My sister Amy has a cold, my sister Lulu has a cold, my sister Nancy has a cold, my sister Minny has a cold, my dad has a cold.'

'Jeepers,' said Ruby, 'sounds bad.'

'Drusilla says due to the high levels of antioxidants in ginger, ginger tea can strengthen your immunity, warding off infection, and I'm trying to remain uninfected,' said Clancy.

'But why do *I* have to drink ginger tea?' asked Ruby. 'It's you Crews who are the ones harbouring the plague.'

'Who knows who it will strike next; you go down sick, there's more of a chance I go down sick, and I don't want to go down sick. Christmas is my favourite time of year.'

Ruby sipped her ginger tea. When Clancy was in this frame of mind it was easier to fall in behind than argue it through.

'By the way, long time no hear,' said Clancy.

'I wrote you: you didn't get my postcards?'

'I got 'em,' said Clancy. He thought for a moment. 'How come you typed them?'

'I didn't want anyone to recognise my handwriting,' said Ruby.

'Is that why you signed them Aunt Mabel?' asked Clancy.

'I was trying to keep incognito.'

'Well, it brought up a few questions with my mom, I can tell you that.'

'What was she doing reading your postcards?' said Ruby.

'People *read* other people's postcards,' said Clancy. 'They're *postcards*, no envelopes, the *mailman* can read them if he chooses to, I mean if he happens to be particularly bored.'

'So,' said Ruby, 'what did she want to know?'

'Why this Aunt Mabel, who she didn't know even *existed*, was recommending thermal socks. I mean if you were planning on using a code then why didn't you use the regular one?'

'Because if I had written a postcard in gobbledegook then that would have looked really suspicious. This way it looks like I am writing to you about normal stuff.'

'Since when is it normal for an aunt who doesn't even exist to write me about thermal socks?'

'OK, you have a point, I went too much into character, but can we get back to the point?'

'Which is?'

'I *did* keep in touch.'

'But you didn't tell me anything, not really, only that *something* had happened and it was hard to explain in writing.'

'Well, it was.'

'In that case, why didn't you call?'

'It wasn't so easy,' said Ruby, biting into one of the donuts. 'They had this whole lockdown thing going.'

'Since when was Genius Camp so high-security?'

'It was more like boot camp, if you really wanna know – anyone caught out of their study area or generally not complying with mathletics rules was threatened with disqualification.'

'Seriously?' asked Clancy.

'You bet seriously,' said Ruby. 'I mean, you had to ask to use the payphone – you know it *actually* had a padlock on it.'

'When did you ever take notice of petty rules? Or locks for that matter... Plus I thought you would have *wanted* to be disqualified and get sent home early.'

'I thought about it, believe me, but then you know I felt bad for my mom and dad. For some reason having a daughter who is a major dork brainiac *means* something to them.'

'*That* was your reason for staying?' said Clancy. 'Since when do you care so much about your parents' dreams of a "show and tell daughter"? Forgive me, but I just don't buy that.'

'OK, so not *just* that. I had my reasons for sticking around, and one of them was the Pink Pixie. I swear I woulda walked had it not been for that *box of crackers.*'

'You mean Dakota Lyme?'

'Yeah, her,' said Ruby. 'Boy, she was so crazy for winning, her eyes almost popped out of her face – you remember how she tried to injure that kid, Ward Partial?'

'Yeah, I read about that,' said Clancy. 'Don't tell me she did it again.'

Ruby nodded her head. 'Only worse this time. That poor Partial kid was at breaking point. You know, for a dweeb he's actually kinda OK, plus he's only eleven. He can't handle the pressure.'

Clancy nodded. 'So what happened?'

'I'll tell you some other time, but suffice to say, I stuck it out.'

'You know what?' said Clancy.

'What?' said Ruby.

'You're all heart.'

Ruby took a big slug of her drink. 'Well, I couldn't abandon him, could I? Let her go ahead and make mincemeat of him while I swanned off back to Twinford. *You know what,* this ginger tea's not *bad.*'

'What *is* bad is the hogwash you're spouting,' said Clancy. 'Would you quit feeding me this garbage and actually tell me *why you left town?*'

Clancy had a way of sniffing out the baloney, and he knew there was more to Ruby's little math vacation than the tale she had been telling him. Since when was it necessary for her, the brightest kid in Twinford Junior High, to go away for a four-week intensive math and science camp?

Ruby looked him dead in the eye, plucked a serviette from the dispenser and carefully wiped her hands.

'You promise not to get all flappy?'

'Why would I get flappy?' replied Clancy.

'OK,' she said, 'if you want to know so bad, I'll tell you.'

Clancy waited.

'It was all down to Hitch. It was him who was keen I should go, it was him who came up with the idea and wanted me to hunker down at geek camp,' said Ruby.

Clancy looked confused. 'Hitch is interested in your mathematical development?'

'Hitch is interested in me continuing to breathe,' said Ruby, 'and I'm kinda interested in the same thing. The geek camp was just a way of getting me away and out of Twinford while he assessed the situation and made things secure back home.'

'Assessed what situation?'

'The situation regarding who might want me dead.'

Clancy let go of his donut and it splashed into his tea.

'Clance, are you OK?'

'Hitch thinks you're on some kinda hit list?' said Clancy, his voice unsteady.

'Well, maybe...' she said.

'That's why you were in the middle of nowhere for four whole weeks.?' He paused. 'But are you sure it's safe for you to be home?'

'Safe as it's *ever* possible to be,' said Ruby. 'So long as I stay inside the house for the rest of my life everything should be fine.'

'It's not funny Rube.'

'I know,' said Ruby. 'I'm not really laughing, you know that, don't you?'

'So is it the Count?' asked Clancy.

'Well, a month ago I would have said yes,' said Ruby. 'But the last thing he told me down in that crypt was that he had decided *not* to kill me.'

'Why?'

'Apparently he changed his mind.'

'He actually said that?' asked Clancy.

'He said it was in his best interests for me to keep on breathing.'

'Well, that's kind of worrying, don't you think?' said Clancy.

'Why?' asked Ruby.

'Because it sounds like there might be some other crazed killer out there.'

'Yeah, well, I think there is,' agreed Ruby.

'Why didn't you tell me?' said Clancy.

'I'm telling you now,' said Ruby.

'So?'

'So what?' said Ruby.

'So the other thing you're not telling me.'

'What thing?' said Ruby.

'I don't know,' said Clancy. 'That's why I'm asking.'

'OK...' she said, 'but don't get all worked up... you gotta...'

'I knew it!' he said. 'Something happened, didn't it? It was just after I got outta hospital, after the Halloween pageant, the day before you went off to camp, am I right, am I, am I right?' *Now* he was beginning to flap.

'Clance, you promised you wouldn't flap.'

Clancy ignored her and continued flapping.

'Look Clance, the thing is...'

But he wasn't finished. 'Something spooked you, *really*

spooked you.' He was getting all dramatic now, Ruby hated when he got all dramatic – at least, hated when he got dramatic about things that were actually already dramatic.

'Then you suddenly took off without a word. I knew there had to be a bigger reason than hanging out with nerds at some crummy nerd camp and I knew there had to be a bigger reason than just the usual Count encounter.'

'Just the usual Count encounter...?' spluttered Ruby. 'The usual—'

'So what was it that spooked you just after Halloween?' interrupted Clancy.

'Well, it wasn't any kids dressed up as ghouls, I can promise you that,' said Ruby.

'That I figured,' said Clancy. 'But why didn't you tell me what happened, you know, after... that night in the crypt –' his voice was a little shaky now – 'with the undead and... and, you know –' he paused, before whispering – 'the psychopath.'

'Just a regular Tuesday night in Twinford.'

But Clancy was in no mood for making light. He was just looking at her, waiting for her to spill the beans.

She breathed in a long slow breath, exhaled and stared back at him.

'Well, I *was* going to tell you, of course I was, but I needed time to think.'

'About what?' asked Clancy.

'Everything,' she replied. 'It's a big deal what I know, and

I haven't told a soul.'

'No one? But you musta told Hitch?'

Ruby shook her head.

'Blacker?' asked Clancy.

'No one,' said Ruby.

'So,' said Clancy, 'what is it?'

'Not here,' said Ruby, looking around. 'Let's move to that booth in the corner. I don't want to risk being overheard – you know, walls have ears and all that.'

They slid off their stools and took their drinks over to the other side of the diner where the lighting was dimmer and the customers fewer.

'So,' said Ruby, 'ever heard the phrase "a bad apple"?'

Chapter 4.
Baby Grim

CLANCY DID NOT HAVE TIME to answer Ruby's question, nor to wonder what apples had to do with anything, because they were interrupted.

'Hey! Ruby!'

The voice came from across the busy diner and belonged to Elliot Finch.

'You're back,' he called.

Ruby peered at her reflection in the chrome serviette dispenser. She nodded. 'It would seem so.'

Elliot tapped his head and said, 'I saw Bug lying by the diner door and I thought to myself, Ruby must be in here somewhere.'

'Quite the little Sherlock Holmes,' said Ruby.

Elliot slid into the seat next to Clancy. 'So how's the fruit baby?'

'What?' said Ruby.

'He's talking about the Lemon,' explained Clancy.

The Lemon was Archie Lemon, one-year-old son of the Redforts' neighbours Niles and Elaine Lemon, and a baby very lucky to be alive. Had it not been for Ruby's decision to use him as a prop in the Halloween parade, Archie Lemon would have been asleep in his bedroom and the Twinford Tornado would have taken him with it when it whirled into the Lemons' home, destroying Archie's room. However, Archie *had* survived and his parents could not thank Ruby enough. In fact, it was getting to be a problem.

'It must be cool,' said Elliot.

'It's not,' said Ruby.

'Being a hero's not cool?' said Elliot.

'I'm not a hero,' said Ruby.

'You saved that kid's life,' said Elliot.

'I borrowed that baby because I needed him to play the part of Baby Grim in the pageant. I needed him because I wanted us to win. If we had won, we would have got prize money. That's not heroic, it's self-serving.'

'But you saved his life,' insisted Elliot.

'Luck,' said Ruby. 'Coulda been the other way around, coulda been the tornado hit the pageant and it would all have been my fault and they woulda hated me for all eternity.'

'Life is fickle,' said Clancy.

'People are fickle,' corrected Ruby.

'Still, it must be great, his parents *thinking* you're a hero, even if you're not... technically, I mean.'

'It's a pain in the butt,' said Ruby. 'Elaine calls round all the time asking me how I am.' She sighed. '*And* she keeps giving me stuff.'

'She's giving you stuff?' Elliot's eyes grew big. 'Like gifts and things?'

'Yeah,' said Ruby.

'Oh boy,' said Elliot, 'I would love that.'

'Would you?' said Ruby. 'Really? Cos I got a whole bunch of super ugly sweaters you can have: pink ones, purple ones, kitten ones...'

'That's what she's giving you? Sweaters? Why sweaters?' asked Clancy.

'Her sister owns an "ugly knitwear" business,' said Ruby.

'Too bad,' said Elliot.

'Look, the point is not *what* she's giving me, but that I don't want her to give me *anything*.'

The bell over the diner door jangled and in walked Mouse Huxtable.

'You're back!' she mouthed.

Ruby nodded. 'So everyone keeps telling me.'

'Well, you've been missed, that's for sure,' said Mouse. 'Mrs Drisco's been real grouchy.'

'Why's that?' said Ruby. 'I would have thought she would be happy to see the back of me.'

'I think she misses the banter,' said Mouse.

'So what's school been like since I left town?' Ruby yawned.

'Well,' said Elliot, 'it's been a real hotbed of finger-pointing since you were cleared of trying to wreck Del's life.'

'I don't think you can say "hotbed of finger-pointing",' said Mouse. 'It doesn't make a lotta sense.'

'No,' agreed Clancy, 'it doesn't sound right somehow.'

'Like *you* can talk,' said Elliot. 'What was it you said the other day...'

Mouse broke in, 'The point is, Elliot, Ruby's off the hook and in the clear, everyone thinks it was someone from the outside, i.e. not a student at Twinford Junior High.' She shook her head and looked at Ruby. 'Boy, I guess someone really hates you out there.'

'My money's on Dakota Lyme,' said Elliot.

'Don't be so sure,' said Ruby, who knew for a certainty that it was not. 'You gotta be careful making allegations against people, however objectionable they might be.' It was actually the vengeful Lorelei von Leyden, mistress of disguise, who had set Ruby up as saboteur. Dakota Lyme was just a fall-guy.

Clancy checked his watch. 'Yikes, I'd better get going. I have to pick up a load of cough syrup for my sisters or I'll never hear the end of it – and I mean literally: cough, cough, cough.' He pulled on his coat. 'That thing we were talking about before, Rube, we'll catch up first thing, OK?' He shot her a look and she nodded.

'OK,' said Ruby.

Ruby hung out for another half hour before she headed off. She didn't feel like going home just yet, so she turned the corner at Green Street and made a left at Main until she reached Ray

Penny's second-hand bookstore.

On a winter's evening, with its cosy lighting and tropical heating (Ray hated to be cold), Penny Books was a pleasant place to kill time. The store was unusually busy today. Perhaps due to the warmth, and the fact that Ray wasn't much bothered by making a sale, a lot of folks used the place like it was a library.

Ruby browsed the graphic novel shelves; apart from shuffling footsteps as customers edged around bookstands, all that could be heard was the classical music playing on Ray's turntable and the sound of turning pages. Ruby stepped past a bearded guy who was sitting on a stool looking at a book with a beige cover. He wasn't browsing, he was most definitely reading. In another corner was a boy flicking through a comic while he snacked on a flapjack.

Ruby herself settled down with a pile of Space Creep novels and began working her way through them. A moment later she was roused from her reading by the sound of falling books. Through a gap in the shelving, she could see part of a face, serious and intense. It belonged to a young woman who was clutching a pile of poetry books, and continuing to browse even though her arms were already full. Too full. Every now and again one of the poetry books would slide out from the pile and hit the floor and she would mutter, 'whoops' or 'darn' or 'for flip's sake!'

After the fifth drop, the guy with the beard looked up and said, 'Here, let me help you with those.' He put his book down on the stool and took the stack of paperbacks to the front desk.

The young woman was very grateful. 'Thanks a lot, that's so kind, thank you, real nice of you, thank you again.'

Ruby was curious to know what had kept the bearded man so enthralled for the past forty-four minutes and sauntered over to take a look. The object of interest turned out to be a book entitled *Fascinating Fungi*.

Ruby didn't doubt that the study of fungi might be fascinating, but this book was not presented in a way that would entice the casual browser. With its old black-and-white photographs and dense text, you really needed to be a total fungus nut to want to pick it up. But as Mrs Digby would say, 'it takes all sorts'. Ruby had never been a big fan of edible fungi, and even when in a survival-type situation hadn't been overjoyed to see one. However, the poisonous kind interested her quite a lot.

Ruby knew a great deal about poison in all its various forms, and her knowledge in this area had grown in recent weeks due to a series of attempts on the life of the Mongolian conservationist Amarjargel Oidov, organised it seemed by the Count and presumably his employer. No one exactly understood why Oidov had become the target of a murderer, but it seemed likely that it was connected to the ancient and previously undiscovered species of snake she was seeking to protect. The reptiles were an incredible yellow and marked with delicate diamonds of colour. The skins would fetch high prices in the fashion trade and the venom might also be of interest to toxicologists.

Coincidentally, one of the unusual things about the snake

was that it feasted on mushrooms. Why the snakes were of interest to the Count, or indeed the Count's boss, was still an unknown.

Ruby checked her watch: it was getting late and probably time to head home. She thanked Ray, who merely raised his hand in a lazy 'bye-bye', and Ruby pushed her way out into the cold night air.

Chapter 5.
Snakes and mushrooms

IT WAS ANOTHER COINCIDENCE that when Ruby returned home that evening it was fungus that was the main topic of conversation.

Mrs Digby was staring hard at a very ancient-looking recipe book and appeared unusually flustered.

'So what are you looking to cook?' asked Ruby, peering over the housekeeper's shoulder.

'Your mother wants me to rustle up this particular stew – she's got her mind set on it, but I'll be darned if I will ever find the ingredients.'

'Maitake,' Ruby read. 'What are maitake?'

'Hen of the woods,' said Mrs Digby.

'Chicken?' said Ruby.

'Mushrooms,' said the housekeeper.

'What's the big deal with mushrooms all of a sudden?' said Ruby. 'They seem to be popping up everywhere.'

'Everyone's gone mushroom crazy, including your mother, and I can't get my hands on a single one of these rarer breeds.'

'Breeds?' said Ruby. 'Do mushrooms breed?'

'My point is, there's been a run on them, and it's all to do with those darned vipers.'

'What vipers?' asked Ruby.

'Those ones that were on the TV.'

'You mean the yellow snakes?' said Ruby. 'The ones that were exhibited at the Geographic Explorer awards?'

'Those are the critters,' said Mrs Digby. 'There's been nothing *but* chatter about them, all the while you've been away – on the radio, on the television networks, in the newspapers.' Mrs Digby reached for the *Twinford Hound* and slid it across the counter. 'I don't mind telling you, I wish those slitherers had never been discovered.'

'I expect Amarjargel Oidov feels the same,' said Ruby, thinking back to the conservationist's almost-murder. Oidov had made a full recovery, but it had been a close call. Now Ruby could see, as she scanned the evening paper, that the prize-winning conservationist Oidov was working alongside the scientific institute, and they were together:

'STUDYING THE YELLOW SNAKES, THEIR DIET AND THEIR ENVIRONMENT, WHICH REMAIN A CLOSELY GUARDED SECRET.'

It was their diet, which included a rare and unnamed mushroom with rumoured life-enhancing powers, that had sparked this fad for unusual fungi.

Ruby read on.

'THE RESEARCH PROGRAMME IS BEING CONDUCTED
IN SECRECY. THE SCIENTISTS ARE WORKING WITH
A HIGHLY QUALIFIED DIETARY EXPERT FROM
SEVILLE, SPAIN.'

Ruby had a pretty good idea who this dietician might be.

Mrs Digby continued to burble on about the snakes. 'They say those reptiles hold a secret, but if you ask me the only secret they hold is how to get you dead lickety split – one bite and you're a goner.'

'Plenty of snakes will get you dead,' said Ruby. 'Though you're right about the venom; it is unusual. The skins are kinda spectacular too. I mean there are plenty of people who might want to bump off Oidov and turn her yellow snakes into handbags.'

'Just the thought of it makes me queasy,' Mrs Digby shivered. 'What I would kill for is a half-pound of these hen of the woods.'

'Have you tried the grocers on Green Street?'

Mrs Digby rolled her eyes. 'You think I was born this morning?' she said. 'If Green's stocked such a thing then I would go to Green's, but these are no ordinary mushrooms.'

'So maybe the farmers' market would have them?' suggested Ruby. 'They have pretty exotic vegetables.'

'These are exoticker,' said Mrs Digby.

'Exoticker?' repeated Ruby.

'More exotic,' said Mrs Digby. 'More exotic than what the farmers' market sell. These you have to forage for and even then you gotta be lucky, and I don't have the time to be lucky nor the inclination to go roaming through the forests of Minnesota trying to spot a hen of the woods.'

Ruby shrugged. 'So substitute.'

'What with, might I ask?'

'I don't know,' said Ruby. 'How about button mushrooms?'

Mrs Digby shook her head. 'What you don't know about cooking is a lot.'

Which was true.

The phone rang and Ruby picked up.

'Pest control, we spray you pay.'

'Hey Ruby, it's us! We're in Paris!'

'Mom?'

'Oui, but of course.'

'Ciao ciao Ruby!'

'Dad?'

'Yes, it's me.'

'How are you?'

'Well, the weather here is très froid you know, and there's neige.'

'What? You mean snow?'

'Uh huh, lots and lots of neige, the airport is still closed.'

'So when are you likely to make it home?'

'Ooh la la – heaven only knows.'

'Would you like to talk to Mrs Digby?'

'Oui, yes, if you please s'il vous plait.'

Ruby handed the phone to the housekeeper and left them to it.

Maybe she'd have a go at solving Mrs Digby's fungus problem.

Ruby might not know a lot about how to get her hands on a hen of the woods, but she knew someone who probably did.

Chapter 6.
Larger fish to fry

IT WOULD BE BETTER NOT TO LET MRS DIGBY know who Ruby was planning to call; it would almost certainly put the housekeeper in a very sour mood.

Ruby climbed the stairs to her room at the top of the house and there used her private telephone line to make the call. She had quite a collection of phones in all shapes and designs. From lobster to squirrel, donut to clam shell.

She picked up the squirrel and dialled.

'Hola,' said the voice at the end of the line.

'Hey there, Consuela, it's Ruby as in Redfort,' said Ruby.

'Don't tell me, you're sick because you're eating all that garbage food. I bet you have pimples.'

'No,' said Ruby, checking her face in the mirror.

'It's your eyesight; you're not eating your kale?' said Consuela.

'Well...' said Ruby.

'You got bad vision because you don't eat your kale,' said Consuela.

'I have bad eyesight because of genetics,' said Ruby. 'I'm all with you on the good diet theory, but eggs is eggs and facts are facts.'

'Facts you *know*, and yet still you eat all that junk,' said Consuela. 'So why *are* you calling?'

'I just wanted to congratulate you on your new job.'

Silence, then, 'What new job is that?'

'I read you are working for the scientific institute, so I guess you're looking at the diet of those snakes.'

Silence.

'What snakes?'

'The yellow snakes.'

'That was not in the paper,' said Consuela. 'This is all on the low down.'

'Downlow,' corrected Ruby.

'Downlow, low down, is no matter, what I am saying is it is not to be chitter-chatted about.'

'I know,' said Ruby, 'I just sort of figured it out.'

'Well, I hope you will figure out how to keep your mouth shut,' said Consuela. 'So why are you calling when I'm all busy and up to my eyes cooking?'

'I thought you might be able to help me with an ingredient.'

Ruby explained and Consuela listened and then thought about it, clucked her tongue and told Ruby to hang on and hung up.

While Ruby waited she took the opportunity to look up in

her encyclopaedia just what might make these mushrooms worth the trouble.

Maitake: *(also known as Hen of the Woods or Ram's Head) a choice delicacy, known to have many health benefits, including boosting the immune system and improving blood pressure. Grows in large circular clusters of spoon-shaped caps at the base of oak trees, grey on top and white beneath. September-November. Spores when magnified are elliptical and smooth.*

Makes a nourishing and meaty mushroom stew.

Twenty minutes later, Consuela called back with a name. 'You have to go to Mo's store, he's... what do you say...'

'A mycologist?'

'A heart pounder.'

'Say again?'

'Que guapo.'

'Really?'

'I asked him out and guess what he says – "maybe". What good is maybe! His store is Daily Supplies in Little Mountain Side,' she said. 'No one else will have them, not late in the year as it is.'

'Where's Little Mountain Side?' said Ruby.

'Look it up,' said Consuela. 'I got larger fish to fry,' and the call was over.

After supper Ruby did just that, first checking the map that covered the walls of the guest bathroom off the downstairs hall – no sign of Little Mountain Side.

Must be out of town, she thought.

She went into her dad's home office and found a map of the surrounding area and spread it out on the desk. It was not, as she had expected, somewhere near Little Bear, nor was it to the north-east in the Wolf Paw range. Little Mountain Side turned out to be quite a way south of Ridgepoint, which was probably why Ruby had never heard of it: to get there meant a detour off the Pine Forest Pass as the town was tucked away on the far side of the second Sequoia Mountain.

Mrs Digby had recently given up 'getting behind the wheel of an automobile' due to the 'volume of numbskulls on the roads', (her words) and so unless she could find someone willing to pick the mushrooms up *for* her, it was going to be a morning's bus ride for the old lady.

Ruby thought for a minute.

Maybe I'll do her a good turn, make that bus trip myself, discover a new part of the world and clock up some girl scout points while I'm at it. To be honest Ruby could use the good press; after she'd been caught up in a street brawl (not her fault) and had been issued with six hours community service, her angel status had waned. The chance saving of Baby Lemon had restored a little of her good-kid status, but topping it up would do no harm.

If she was honest this was only part of the reason for making the trip. There were tales about the Sequoia Mountains which more than piqued her curiosity. Rumours of unidentified flying objects and little green men appealed to Ruby Redfort, and while she doubted any of them were based on fact, she wouldn't mind taking a look for herself.

That decided, Ruby kicked off her shoes, switched on the portable TV and slumped into the beanbag, clicking through the channels until she reached Horror on 44.

A dark-haired girl dressed in a check shirt, jeans, but no shoes, was sitting at home with her dog. She was listening to music on her record player, and the dog was asleep. The girl sipped lemonade while flipping through a comic. Then all of a sudden the hound began to howl.

'Hey there, Rex,' said the girl, 'what are you barking at?' She stared into the dark.

'There's nothing out there.' The dog continued to whimper.

The camera panned out of the window and into the woodland. In the darkness something moved.

Ruby looked over at Bug. He was fast asleep, no howling, no whimpering.

Her thoughts strayed to the strange happenings of recent weeks.

She picked up her pencil.

To date there were three known dangerous criminals wanted by Spectrum 8:

The Count: a psychopath, thief and murderer with no real motivation for his evil deeds, other than the prevention of boredom and the pursuit of pleasure. What Ruby now knew for sure was that he was working *for* someone else, and what he had recently imparted during their crypt encounter was that he wasn't particularly keen on the arrangement any more. However, what wasn't clear was how he had come to be in the power of another, nor who that individual could be.

The Australian: a close acquaintance of the Count and equally ruthless.

Ruby was not sure what drew these two together, but guessed they had known each other for more than a few years. It would seem the Count had requested the Australian's assistance to help tie up *loose ends*; they trusted each other, and from the way the Count had talked, he had great respect for her.

Lorelei: estranged daughter of the Australian and sometime employee of the Count. Lorelei was a law unto herself, that was beyond doubt now. She had gone rogue, betrayed the Count twice (there would be no third chance) and was hell-bent on raining havoc and destruction on those who strayed across her path – which put Ruby well and truly in the firing line.

Then of course there was the mole, the double agent, the traitor, puppet master, bad egg, bad apple... Call them what you liked, *someone* was pulling the strings; the question was, who?

And the Count was scared.

Not exactly a soothing thought. What kind of soul could

make a soulless monster tremble?

The girl on the TV was getting twitchy: she was beginning to feel sure something was lurking out there in the darkness.

Ruby got up and went over to her own window and stood there looking out into the black. Somewhere something evil lurked. It was a big wild world and this dark soul could be a thousand miles away. They could be watching from Mars or they might be just around the next bend in the Dry River Road. However, what seemed most likely of all, was that this enemy was already within and stalking the corridors of Spectrum.

The sixty-four-thousand dollar question was:

This dark soul, could it really be LB?

HQ was on high alert, Spectrum 1 was in charge of the investigating team, security had been ramped up to carmine level, protection at Spectrum 8 had never been higher, but it was hard to feel reassured. After all, how does one protect oneself when the evil lies on the inside? From the safety of Green-Wood House, Ruby considered her options.

When you are written large on a psychopath's hit list, do you:

A: Stay indoors, turn the locks, switch off the lights, hide under the covers and wait for someone else to do something?

B: Brush up on your kung fu moves, wrap up warm, get out there, root out trouble and save yourself?

She tapped her pencil against her head.

The idea of being a sitting duck until another agent pulled

the clues together, identified the mole and rounded up these murderers was not an appealing one.

'Sit tight' was a Spectrum watchword, but as far as Ruby could tell, this was no time to be taking orders from Spectrum.

She smiled sadly.

It could only be option two.

Death or glory, she thought.

**Meanwhile –
some eleven and
a half years ago...**

...the guy lying on the side of the road looked up at the old man and saw the fear in his face.

'Am I... alive?'

The old man nodded. 'It would seem so.'

'You... OK...?' stammered the guy. 'You... look... like you're... gonna... faint.'

The old man was shrugging off his jacket. He pulled a penknife from his pocket and he began cutting at the sleeve of his own shirt, tearing it right off and wrapping it around the bleeding guy's leg.

'My name, should you be wondering, is Lenny Rivers.' He was working quickly but methodically, binding the wound tight, trying to stop all that blood leaking onto the road.

'Pleased to... meet... you... Len...'

'So what hit you friend, a truck?' The poor guy was a real mess, the worst thing Lenny had ever seen, except for that time when he'd found a hunter who'd been attacked by a bear. That fella hadn't made it. 'Was it one of those haulage trucks smashed into you?' he asked.

The guy smiled faintly. 'The fun... the funny thing... is... I... don't re-mem-ber.'

'Musta been going at a fair old lick,' Lenny tutted. 'Either didn't see you or just decided to leave you for dead.'

'I guess,' said the injured guy, his eyes closing slowly.

'Hang in there,' said Lenny, more to himself than to the half-dead fellow lying there on the ground. He'd do what he could, but this poor soul's ticket was punched, Lenny Rivers was sure of that.

'So what do they call you?' Lenny asked.

One thing Lenny Rivers knew for a certainty was, he'd want to hear his name spoken aloud one final time if he was about to float heavenwards. But the wounded man was already slipping away, his focus gone. 'Hey there son, don't leave me, tell me what you go by.' Lenny gently tapped the injured man's bloodstained cheek. 'Stick with me pal, you must have a name, right?'

The guy's eyelids flickered and opened one last time. He was staring beyond Lenny as if his eyes saw some other figure standing behind him. 'Loveday,' he said. 'It was Morgan... Loveday.'

Chapter 7.
One bad apple or two?

THE SOAP RANG IN THE BATHROOM the next morning and Ruby spat out her toothpaste and picked up.

'So what were you going to tell me?' asked Clancy. Ruby could hear his little sister Olive in the background, talking to someone.

'Who's there with you?' asked Ruby.

'Olive,' said Clancy.

'But who's she talking to?' asked Ruby.

'Buttercup,' said Clancy.

Silence.

'Her doll,' said Clancy.

Ruby listened for a moment. 'Jeepers,' she said.

'Exactly,' said Clancy. 'So what were you going to tell me?'

'Well, I'm not going to say it over the phone, am I, buster?'

'Of course you're not, bozo. I was wondering if you'd like the pleasure of my company, plus if I have to listen to more of this dolly talk I'm gonna go crazy.'

'Anyone would,' said Ruby. 'Is she like this most days?'

'Try every day,' said Clancy.

'I'll meet you in a half hour, usual place.'

The usual place was the tree on Amster. They met there when they wanted to be completely alone and out of sight. It was December and the tree's branches were bare and so the oak would not provide any cover, but at least sitting high in its boughs meant they were a long way from eavesdroppers and interrupters. It was as they sat up in the oak that Ruby filled her friend in on everything she had omitted to tell him before.

'LB killed Bradley Baker?' said Clancy.

'That's what the Count told me,' said Ruby.

'Are you actually serious?' asked Clancy.

'Serious as the look on your face,' confirmed Ruby.

'But... I mean, really? I mean... kill him? How?' asked Clancy.

'What you have to ask yourself is why,' said Ruby.

'*Why?*' said Clancy. 'Why is *why* the question I have to ask myself? Why not – *can you get me outta Twinford as quickly as possible?* Followed by, *could you call the sheriff's office right away?* Because those are the questions I would be asking if I just found out that the boss of the secret agency I worked in had murdered her best friend and not *just* some average Joe either, not that that would make it all right or anything, but we *are* talking about Bradley Baker, legendary agent of Spectrum 8. So if LB did that then yes, *can you get me to a safe house* and *could you call the sheriff* would be my first two questions.'

'Well, thank goodness you're *not* me, Clance, because both of those questions are dead ends. For one: who's actually going to believe any of this? And for two: if LB is really his killer then how far am I gonna get before I end up going the same way as Baker? I mean think about it, Clance, she runs a team of highly trained agents, *secret* agents who are capable of –' she drew her finger across her throat, before adding – '*secretly.*'

Clancy opened his mouth to speak, but could not think of anything cheerful to say.

'So what you gotta look at,' said Ruby, 'is the whole big picture. My boss *might* well be a traitorous killer: she has the means, the power, possibly a motive, but before we absolutely totally conclude she *is* a traitorous killer, we need to examine the evidence. For example, what do we know about Bradley Baker?'

Clancy shrugged. 'He was the youngest spy Spectrum ever recruited, *super* respected and well-liked, *and* he was the most talented code breaker and agent they ever had.' He stole a sideways look at Ruby. 'No offence, Rube.'

'Don't sweat it bozo, I hear it all the time.'

'And,' continued Clancy, 'he was killed in a plane crash.'

'Which it seems was no accident,' said Ruby. 'Nor was it at the hand of the enemy, but rather by the hand of his most loyal ally.'

'And let's not forget fiancée,' added Clancy.

'So now what we got to look at is who exactly is feeding us this information,' said Ruby. 'Who is the deliverer of this sad and bad news?'

'The Count,' said Clancy. 'At least, it was *his* apple.'

'Yeah,' said Ruby, 'it was his apple, and he *wanted* me to find the note.'

'So,' said Clancy, 'so you're asking, do you think we should consider him a reliable source? Maybe he just *wants* us to believe LB is a murderer. He could be just making the whole thing up?'

'Yeah, and the truth is, I can't say I know him well enough to know,' said Ruby.

'You do know him well enough,' said Clancy. 'You know him well enough to know that you can never know him.'

'What?'

'I'm saying he likes to move the goal posts, he sorta enjoys playing with people, creeping them out, just for fun and also, you know... killing them.' Clancy shivered.

Ruby stared into the distance. 'Yeah, he *does* like to mess with people's heads; once he's planted an idea, you just can't shake it. He knows how these thoughts grow, how they take off in different directions – you don't exactly know what they mean or even what you're scared *of*, you just keep running with it.'

'So what has he got you thinking?' asked Clancy.

Ruby paused before speaking. 'What he's got me thinking is, what if Bradley was not all that he seemed; what if *he* were the so-called bad apple?'

'You suggesting he wasn't the super talent everyone thought he was?' asked Clancy.

'No, I think we can accept that Baker *was* the super talent that everyone drones on about, but if he was such a talented agent then he may also have had a talent for espionage.'

'Huh?'

'What I'm suggesting here is, was he leading a double life?'

Clancy was looking at her, his expression one of puzzlement.

Ruby spelled it out: 'Do we know which side he was really on?'

'Oh,' said Clancy, 'that... that wasn't something I was even thinking about.'

'So let's just say he was a double agent, LB woulda *had* to kill him for the sake of Spectrum, for the sake of this country –' she stretched her arms out wide – 'the world even.'

Clancy let out a heavy sigh. 'I'd feel a lot better if that's how it was.'

'It could have been that LB knew what *nobody* else knew: that he was a phoney, a fraud, an imposter.'

'Like some kind of mole, you mean?'

'Yeah,' nodded Ruby.

'Boy, it sure makes you think,' said Clancy. 'Imagine finding out that your best friend, most loyal ally, is a total fake, not to mention murderer.' He looked at Ruby. 'Though I have to say, Rube, if you turn out to be an evil genius, I can't see myself killing you. I kinda like your company.'

'I appreciate that Clance, I really do.'

'Still, I think LB had guts to do what she did,' said Clancy. 'If Baker was a bad egg, she did the right thing.'

'Yeah,' said Ruby, contemplating this for a moment, 'but what if he wasn't? What if it was the other way around?'

'Jeepers, I was just beginning to relax,' said Clancy.

'Yeah, well, don't, cos what if it was Bradley Baker who was the good news in this story and LB eliminated him so she could get on with her plot to take over the world or steal the moon or whatever?'

'The moon?' said Clancy. 'Can you even do that?' He was on his feet now, as if he needed to be ready for what might be coming.

'Geez, Clance, it was just an example, how should I know what she's got planned?' Ruby paused, sorting through the thoughts that were flickering in her brain: the cyan, the indigo, the ruby eyes of the Buddha, the 8 key, the yellow snake. 'If I could figure that out, and how it all links together, the thefts and the murders, the mole within Spectrum, well, then I might know what to do.'

'Yeah, right,' said Clancy, 'if you knew all that then you could just amble downtown and knock on Sheriff Bridges' door and hand him the evidence.'

Ruby sighed. 'Like that's gonna happen.'

'But meanwhile, you figure one of them has to be a bad seed?' said Clancy. 'Either it's Baker or it's LB?'

'Or it's neither?' offered Ruby. 'Unless of course,' – she looked at him out of the corner of her eye – 'they were both bad apples.'

Clancy made a face like he wished she wouldn't say these kinds of things.

'Look, could you give me a break here Rube? I can only cope with one double agent at a time.'

She thumped him lightly on the arm. 'Take it easy,' she said. 'Yeah, I think it's probably *either* Baker *or* LB, and let's hope it's Baker, right?'

Clancy nodded. 'Because if it's Baker then LB is on the level.'

'Only thing is,' said Ruby, 'if LB isn't the bad apple then who *is*, who's the one pulling the strings?'

Clancy gave her the pained look again. 'I don't want to think about that right now.'

'Yeah, well, time's running out. Whoever is behind this whole series of events has a master plan and I get the feeling we're heading towards the end game.'

'So what's your next move?' asked Clancy.

'I guess I need to find out more about Bradley Baker. I mean I know precisely zero about him other than *what a great guy, what a smart agent, how we all wish he'd come back,* but if I could dig down to what made him tick, what thoughts were whirling round that super-brain of his, and of course exactly how and why he died, then I might know more about LB.'

'So ask around,' said Clancy.

'What, are you kidding? People don't talk about Bradley

Baker. They sorta mention him, how brilliant he was, but they don't actually really *say* anything.' Ruby shook her head. 'No, if I started in asking a lot of questions then I would have to explain why I wanted to know, and then I would have to get into the whole bit about LB maybe being a murderer and I get the feeling that's not gonna go down too well.'

'You mean it might get you dead. *If* she's a cold-blooded murderer, is that what you're saying?' said Clancy.

'That *is* the worst case scenario,' said Ruby, 'and me dead is something I'm trying to avoid.'

'You could tell Blacker?' suggested Clancy. 'You trust him, right?'

'Sure, but this is not the same, this is *me* telling *him* not to trust his boss, and if you were asking, do I trust him not to go right ahead and speak to LB about my concerns? That would have to be a *no*. Blacker is loyal to Spectrum, loyal to the core, and I would have a pretty hard time convincing him that his boss is a bad egg or apple or whatever. People generally don't like to believe they have been putting their trust in, and generally *assisting*, a dangerous psychopath.'

'But her name was *inside* a bad apple,' Clancy reminded her. 'Blacker can't ignore that.'

'And who put it there?' said Ruby. 'The biggest bad apple of them all. Everyone knows the Count would be happy to see Spectrum destroyed.'

'You have a point,' said Clancy.

'I know,' said Ruby.

'So you need to find someone who will talk.'

'Who exactly?'

'What about Froghorn?'

'What about him?' said Ruby.

'Do you trust *Froghorn*?'

'I trust him not to push me off a cliff or under a bus, but that's about it.'

'But do you trust him to tell the truth?' asked Clancy.

'Froghorn? Oh, he just loves to tell it like it is,' said Ruby. 'He's like a regular truth trumpet.'

'So ask *him*,' said Clancy. 'I bet you he'll talk. He's dying to rub your nose in the whole Bradley Baker legend, I bet you *anything* he'll tell you whatever you wanna know, just to make you feel small.'

'You know what Clance, that's not such a terrible idea.'

He smiled. 'Really?'

She gave him another friendly punch to the arm. 'Nice going, Crew.' She looked at her watch and then began to climb down the oak.

'Where are you going?' he asked.

'Little Mountain Side,' she said.

'*Where*?'

'It's in the Sequoia Mountains, wanna come?'

'Why would I wanna go to the Sequoia Mountains?'

'Are you kidding? The Sequoia Mountains are a UFO hotspot,'

said Ruby. 'I'm hoping to spot one on my way through.'

'You're looking for unidentified flying objects?'

'Mushrooms,' called Ruby.

'Same to you,' shouted Clancy.

Somehow
Lenny Rivers got the dying guy
to the hospital in Ridgepoint before
the dying guy actually died...

...the old man was relieved, not because he thought the fellow had a hope in Christmas of seeing Christmas, but because he didn't want to see it happen. It was too sad, the idea that this Morgan Loveday could just pass away without a friend to hold his hand, die all alone on a deserted road or in the back of some stranger's truck. Well, it was too tragic to contemplate.

It hadn't been straightforward getting to the hospital. There had been some kind of incident on Pine Forest Pass, a cordoned-off road which Lenny had ignored – he'd had no choice.

Drive on, *he thought,* and have a chance of delivering a man with a pulse.

Turn back and he might as well have driven straight to the undertakers.

When Lenny Rivers handed him over to the ER team, Morgan Loveday was still breathing, but who knew for how long? Lenny gave his number to the triage nurse.

'Would you mind calling me?' he asked. 'When he... you know, when... if... well, call me, his folks might want to speak to the guy that found him.'

'Of course,' said the nurse. 'I promise I'll call you when the time comes.'

Chapter 8.
Little green men

DESPITE HIS RESISTANCE, Clancy Crew did join Ruby on her mission to find mushrooms. It took her no more than ten minutes of persuading before he reluctantly agreed. It took a lot longer than that to reach Little Mountain Side, but the journey was not the tedious experience Clancy had expected. As the bus wound up high into the Sequoia Mountains, the scenery became more and more spectacular, the great red trees rising from the rock. As the woodland thinned, they were confronted by staggering views to the south and west and far away in the distance one could just about see the ocean.

When at last the bus pulled up in Little Mountain Side there was no missing the perfect prettiness of the town either, perched high up there on the south side of the mountain, the sun slanting through the trees. As they stepped off the bus, Ruby and Clancy breathed in the mountain air; it was pretty good.

'Sure doesn't smell like Twinford,' said Clancy.

'You can almost taste the trees,' said Ruby.

By the side of the road was a sign that read:

FRIENDLIEST TOWN IN THE NORTH-
WESTERN MOUNTAINS AND 'FREE OF
SERIOUS CRIME' SINCE 1951.

'That's reassuring,' said Ruby.

It didn't take long to find Daily Supplies.

The man behind the counter looked somehow familiar, but Ruby couldn't place him. She decided that he probably just had one of those faces, even-featured, *nice looking,* a friendly kind of appearance (at least what she could see of it under the beard), older than her dad and perhaps a tad taller.

He waved at them as they walked in, but continued chatting to a customer at the counter and ringing up groceries.

Ruby and Clancy checked out the shelves while they waited. They were stocked with a lot of interesting and unusual things. However, they had no luck finding the maitake mushrooms.

The customer finally paid and exited the shop, and Clancy and Ruby walked up to the counter.

She looked at the storekeeper and then figured it out.

'Oh, I got it.'

'Got what?' asked the storekeeper.

'Where I saw you before,' said Ruby.

'You've seen me before?'

'Yeah, in the bookstore.'

'In Mountain Books?' he asked, pointing in the direction of the bookstore across the street.

'Ray Penny's bookstore,' said Ruby, 'in Twinford – you were reading a book on rare fungi. I mean you must have read the entire book while you were there.'

'It was a cold day and I was waiting for my truck to be fixed,' he said.

'You often in Twinford?' asked Ruby.

'Rarely.'

'You ever been to Penny's before?'

'Never,' said the guy. 'At least, not that I recall.' He paused. 'You ask a lot of questions,' he said. He looked at Clancy. 'She always this curious, your friend here?'

'Curious is a nice word for what she is,' said Clancy.

The guy smiled at that.

The bell above the door jangled and a burly man strode in, a shock-haired baby on his back.

'Hey, Mo,' said the man. 'How's the old leg doing?'

'Limping a bit in this cold weather. You know how it is.'

'You got those Brazilian beans in yet?'

The storekeeper reached behind him and took a package from one of the shelves and stood it on the counter top. 'Anything else for you Sven?'

The man took out a newspaper. 'Seven down,' he said. '*Mix cantaloupe citrus.*'

The storekeeper frowned. 'How many letters?'

'Five.'

'I'll give it some thought.'

'Thanks,' said the guy.

'Anything besides the beans?'

The man shook his head. 'Just the coffee, that'll do it.'

'How are you there, Spike?' The storekeeper directed this question at the baby and it gurgled and looked very pleased.

'See you around, Mo,' said the man as he turned to leave.

'See you Sven, see you Spike, don't be strangers.'

When they reached the door the storekeeper shouted, 'Lemon! Anagram of melon, from cantaloupe.'

'Of course! Can't think how I missed it,' called Sven.

The storekeeper turned to Ruby. 'He's a cryptic crossword nut,' he explained. 'So what can I help *you* with?' he asked.

'That's your name?' asked Ruby. 'Mo?'

'It's what everyone calls me.' He looked at her. 'So what do they call *you*?'

'Ruby,' said Ruby.

The storekeeper shrugged. 'I had you down for something more edgy,' he said.

'What, like Spike?' suggested Ruby.

He shrugged again. 'You could carry a name like Spike,' he said.

'I'll take that as a compliment,' said Ruby.

'That's how I meant it,' said Mo.

'So this is my pal Clancy.'

Mo nodded. 'Good to meet you, Clancy – what can I do you two for?'

'Hen of the woods,' said Ruby.

'You've left it a bit late in the season,' said the storekeeper.

'I have?' asked Ruby. 'Are you sure?'

'Pretty sure,' said the guy. 'It's one of the few things I know something about.'

'You seem OK at crosswords,' said Clancy.

He smiled. 'Yeah, that's the other thing...' he said. 'So the maitake season is from late August to late November and I usually order in from my mushroom lady out in Minnesota.'

Ruby looked disappointed enough for the guy to reach for a pen and paper.

'I'll make a note and see what I can do, you might get lucky. It's been a pretty weird season, weather-wise,' he said, turning to the calendar hanging on the wall. 'She won't be around until next week; can you hang on a day or two?'

'I guess,' said Ruby, 'but it's a long way to come for a bunch of fungi. I don't spose you're going to be visiting Twinford this week?'

'Not if I can help it,' said Mo. 'It's noisy and full of people.'

'That's what I like about it.'

'Each to their own,' said Mo. 'A nice quiet life is what suits me.'

Clancy was beginning to think it might *also* suit *him*. He liked it up here with the trees and the condors and the lack of serious crime since 1951.

Ruby sighed. 'I'll do my best to make it back, but could you maybe call me when you're certain you got them?'

'Sure,' said Mo, 'give me your digits.'

Ruby scribbled down her number and the guy pinned it up on the pinboard behind him.

'Is there anything to see in this town?' asked Clancy.

'More than you'd think,' said Mo.

'My friend here is keen on UFOs and little green men from Mars,' said Ruby. 'Anything like that around?'

'Call in at the Little Green Diner. They do a mean Space Burger, ask for a side of Mars fries and tell Silas that Mo sent you and he'll give you a deal.'

As they were going out the door they heard the phone ring; Mo picked up. 'How many letters?' he said.

Ruby could see that for Clancy stepping into the Little Green Diner was pretty special. It had been wallpapered in space pictures: Apollo 13, the space craft which made the ill-fated third manned trip to the surface of moon, took up most of one wall and a possible UFO sighting filled another.

Ruby and Clancy walked up to the counter.

'Mo said to say he sent us,' said Ruby.

'Oh, he did, did he?' said Silas. 'So I guess you'll be getting a deal.'

'Have you ever seen a UFO Rube?' asked Clancy, not waiting for an answer. 'I think I saw one once, took a photograph too, but my sister Lulu says it was actually a Frisbee and to be honest there's no telling.'

'I think you'd know,' said a small, thin guy sitting at the counter. 'When I saw my first UFO, I was in no doubt about what I'd just been witness to.'

'Well, hang on a tiny minute, Walter,' said the enormous man who sat on the stool next to him. 'The thing is, no one exactly knows what they are looking for, so it's easy to get it wrong.'

'I'm not disagreeing with you there, Duke, but when you've seen one, you've seen one, and I've seen two.'

'It's true,' said Duke, 'he's seen a couple.'

Clancy was all ears. 'So what did it look like?' he asked.

'How you'd expect,' said Walter. 'A craft unusual in appearance, moving pretty fast across the night sky, bright lights, no markings.'

'How do you know it had no markings if it was dark and moving at speed?' asked Silas, who had doubtless quizzed Walter about this many times before.

'I know what I saw,' said Walter, crossing his arms.

'Why do you think Little Mountain Side attracted so many UFOs?' asked Ruby.

'Because of the space base,' said Walter.

'Space base?' asked Clancy. 'There was an actual space base here?'

'No,' said Silas.

'Uh-huh,' said Walter, ignoring him. 'It was some kinda space operation? In the Sequoia Mountains.'

'It was an energy plant,' said Silas.

'Oh yeah, so how do you explain all the comings and goings, all the activity?' said Walter.

'There were more than a thousand people working there, what do you expect?' said Silas.

'I'm not talking about any power plant,' said Walter, 'I'm talking about something covert here, you know –' he leant in close – 'to welcome the aliens.'

'Really?' said Clancy.

'That's what they say,' said Duke.

'Who says?' asked Ruby.

'No one,' said Silas. 'This is Walt talking garbage, as usual.'

'He's not a believer,' said Duke, pointing his thumb at Silas, 'that's his trouble.'

'Likes to cash in on it though,' said Walter, holding up a flying saucer serviette.

It was actually all good-natured banter, and clearly had been said a thousand times before.

'So if there was a space base somewhere here on this mountainside, then why doesn't anyone talk about it?' asked Clancy.

'It was all very much on the downlow, if you know what I'm saying,' said Duke. 'Not for civilians to know about.'

Silas shook his head. 'You guys and your conspiracy theories. It's a bunch of hogwash. Sven's father worked at the plant for a whole number of years and he never once mentioned little green men from Mars.'

'Well, he wouldn't, would he,' said Walter.

Duke nodded his head. 'That's right, Walt. Sven's dad would have signed some official secrecy document, everyone who worked there would have.'

Walter nodded gravely and Silas chuckled to himself.

'I promise you this: if a Martian ever walks into this diner, I'll shake him by the tentacle and give him a side order of fries on the house.'

Chapter 9.
Lucite

IT WAS DISAPPOINTING TO RETURN to Cedarwood Drive empty-handed, but Ruby had enjoyed a more than interesting day, and Clancy, with all this new information about space craft and aliens, could not be shut up. They caught the bus just as it was about to pull out of the stop, clambered on, taking seats towards the back away from the other passengers. Not that it was crowded: there were only seven other people taking the Mountain bus back to Maple Falls.

Ruby had a small, spiral-bound notepad and she was staring hard at a list of things set neatly out down the page. On one side:

What I know

And on the other:

What I don't know

Some of the things had been crossed out, and moved from the *don't know* column to the *do know* column.

Why Buzz was called Buzz, for example.

'Why *is* Buzz called Buzz?' asked Clancy.

'It's not as exciting as you think,' said Ruby.

'What, it's some kinda nickname?' asked Clancy.

'Less exciting,' said Ruby.

'It's her actual surname?' said Clancy

'Less interesting than that,' said Ruby.

'I give up,' said Clancy.

'It will disappoint you to know,' said Ruby.

'Try me,' said Clancy.

'They're her initials, Brenda Ulla Zane.'

'Oh, that's kinda disappointing,' said Clancy.

'I told you,' said Ruby.

'It's just totally obvious when you think about it.'

'I know,' said Ruby.

'Mind you, there's only one Z,' said Clancy.

'Yeah, but you would still call her Buzz, one Z or two.'

'I guess.' He looked back at her list.

One object, `the 8 key`, had been crossed out altogether and replaced with:

`The Lucite key-tag.`

'The Lucite key-tag,' read Clancy. '*What* key-tag?'

'The key-tag that was attached to the 8 key,' explained Ruby.

'Why are you suddenly interested in that?' asked Clancy. 'I thought it was all about the Spectrum *security key*?'

'I figured it had to be the key-tag that was of interest. I mean the locks were all changed as soon as the key went missing. Unless the whole point of the theft was about rattling the whole of Spectrum by proving security was so weak that anyone could break their way in, then stealing the key served no purpose whatsoever.'

'So what's the purpose of stealing a Lucite key-tag?' asked Clancy. He frowned before adding, 'By the way, what *is* Lucite exactly?'

'You know, like Perspex or Plexiglas – Lucite is just a trade name. It's acrylic. Or, if you want to get technical, Poly methyl methacrylate, a transparent thermoplastic, shatter-resistant, lightweight alternative to glass.'

CLANCY: *'So it was light?'*

RUBY: *'Well, not light light, but not as heavy as glass.'*

CLANCY: *'Was anything written on it? A number? An image?'*

RUBY: *'Nothing I could see.'*

CLANCY: *'So what makes it interesting?'*

RUBY: *'Nothing.'*

CLANCY: *'Nothing?'*

RUBY: *'Nothing except for who it belonged to.'*

CLANCY: *'So who did it belong to?'*

RUBY: *'Bradley Baker.'*

CLANCY: *'Really? You know this? Like for sure?'*

RUBY: *'Not actually, and not exactly for sure. I guess I'm guessing in a way, but it just stands to reason, cos LB told me it was a memento, that someone gave it to her when she was a child, and I sorta figured the person closest to her was Baker.'*

CLANCY: *'Why not her dad, or her mom or maybe her grandpa? I mean it could even have been her junior karate master, he was important to her, no? Or her trombone teacher, if she ever learned trombone, that is.'*

RUBY: *'I don't imagine she did.'*

CLANCY: *'Whatever, my point is, it doesn't automatically follow that it had to be Bradley Baker who gave her the key-tag. It could have been a person of influence.'*

RUBY: *'OK, you're right, it doesn't, but you see, well, I kinda have this strange feeling that it was.'* She looked at him. *'Do you think I'm losing it?'*

CLANCY: *'Nah, you're listening to your gut feeling and...'*

Pause.

CLANCY: *'I actually think you're right.'*

Another pause.

CLANCY: *'Well, almost right.'*

RUBY: *'Almost?'*

CLANCY: *'You're saying that the boss of Spectrum 8 was* *given this key-tag by her best friend when he was a kid?'*

RUBY: *'Yes, LB said it was sentimental.'*

She stopped talking. And then her eyes widened like she was seeing something.

It was unusual for Ruby Redfort to feel like she was the last one in the room to see the gorilla. It was more unusual still for her to feel like a complete and utter chump, but this was that moment.

RUBY: *'What a bozo! LB wouldn't use some old key-tag given to her years ago to attach something as valuable as the 8 key, a coder key. Spectrum is a professional outfit, LB's a professional agent, she hasn't got time for this stuff.'*

She looked at Clancy.

RUBY: *'That's what you were going to say, right?'*

CLANCY: *'I wouldn't have called you a bozo, but yeah.'*

RUBY: *'How did I swallow that garbage?'*

CLANCY: *'Quit beating yourself up, everyone screws up once in a while – if we're talking about me, that would be most days.'*

RUBY: *'Yeah, well, you saw through LB's lie right away, why didn't I?'*

CLANCY: *'Because why would you? You had no reason to doubt her two months ago. Plus, when LB told you this story you had just survived being dropped from a high building. Your mind was on other things, i.e. wow, I'm not dead.'*

RUBY: *'Life and death – being thrown from high buildings*

– I'm supposed to be able to deal with things like that.'

CLANCY: 'Yeah, I'm sure it's all part of the job, but don't you see, at that moment, right at that particular instance, this whole key-tag tale was just a detail. LB mentions it in passing and why wouldn't you believe her? Like I said, back then you trusted her completely, if she told you the same story today you'd probably question it.'

He was right about that.

'So how do you think she *did* end up with the key-tag?'

'Beats me,' said Ruby.

Silence.

CLANCY: 'Just one thing I don't get: if LB is the overarching villain and she is the one commissioning the Count to acquire all these truth serums and cyan scents and stuff, then explain why she would go to all the trouble of stealing her own key-tag?'

RUBY: 'That's easy. She wants to throw Spectrum off the scent. You see, everyone gets paranoid about moles and double agents. They're all busy wondering who it could be, but no one's gonna point the finger at her.'

CLANCY: 'Seems kinda far-fetched.'

RUBY: 'Everything's far-fetched.'

CLANCY: 'OK, but what if LB isn't the bad guy here, then what?'

RUBY: 'Then I guess I'm right, there is more to that piece of Lucite than meets the eye.'

Clancy took another look at the list of unknowns. 'So what do you think the deal is with the Jade Buddha? I mean the cyan scent and the truth serum make sense. What criminal wouldn't want a scent that can lure anyone anywhere? Or a drug that can make anyone blab the truth. But what does the Buddha have to do with any of it? What's with that?'

'I don't know,' said Ruby, 'but I think that Buddha holds one pretty big secret, and personally I think the eyes have it.'

'Huh?'

'It's in the *eyes* of the Buddha,' said Ruby.

'Isn't that just some old legend?' said Clancy. 'Look into the eyes of the Jade Buddha at midnight and halve your age and double your wisdom... I mean what fool believes in that nonsense apart from your dad... no offence intended.'

'None taken, Clance. What I'm saying is, I have no idea what the Count read when he shone that light into its ruby eyes, but I'm guessing he was able to see something, a symbol, or even a code maybe.'

'So can't you get someone to look into its eyes for you?'

'It's back in Khotan,' said Ruby. 'Who am I going to ask?'

'Can't you phone someone in China?' suggested Clancy.

'What, just telephone China and say, "Please take a look at the eyes of the jade Buddha of Khotan"?'

'Not just anyone,' said Clancy. 'Obviously it will have to be someone working at the Khotan museum.'

'It's not as easy as that. I still got to figure what that laser light device was, the one the Count used to read its eyes, it wasn't any regular flashlight,' said Ruby. 'And then I have to convince someone at the museum to go and do it.'

'Get someone else to phone the Chinese, like Blacker or someone?'

'I'm not authorised to investigate anything,' said Ruby. 'If I ask someone to put a call through to the Chinese then I'm basically involved in an investigation and only senior agents are permitted to access anything.'

'So ask a senior agent?'

'What, like LB?' said Ruby. 'How many ways have I gotta say it, Clance? I don't want LB to know that I might be onto something if it turns out that *she* is the *something I'm onto.*'

'Right,' said Clancy unsteadily, 'I guess not.'

'I need to know what happened between LB and Baker. If she killed him then *why* did she kill him?'

'If only you could trust LB then you could ask her.'

Ruby sighed. 'If I could trust LB then I would feel better about a whole lot of things. I might even be able to sleep at night.'

'So you're going to have to talk to Hitch. You trust him, don't you?'

'A hundred per cent,' said Ruby, 'but I'm not so sure he'd give me the time of day if I asked, *so Hitch, you think LB might be a murderer?* And to be truthful, I'm not sure I even *want* to go asking that particular question, at least not until I have a whole lot more information up my sleeve and possibly a hideout or some sort of weapon.'

'Are you scared?' asked Clancy.

Ruby looked into the darkness. 'You bet I'm scared. If I wasn't, I'd have to be crazy.'

'So what are you gonna do when you next meet her face to face?'

'Hold my nerve, I guess. The thing is not to let on; act normal.'

This was actually a Ruby rule. **RULE 51: WHEN YOU DON'T TRUST THE OTHER PLAYERS, ALWAYS PLAY YOUR CARDS CLOSE TO YOUR CHEST.**

Chapter 10.
The stars above

'THE WANDERER RETURNS,' said Mrs Digby as Ruby walked in through the kitchen door. 'Where have you been?'

'Trying to solve your hen of the woods problem.'

'Well, knock me down with a feather,' said Mrs Digby, who looked genuinely astonished. 'Any luck with that?'

'I got a lead on them,' said Ruby.

'From whom?'

'You gotta understand, I gotta protect my source, but suffice it to say, the wheels are in motion and there's a good chance I can get the mushrooms to you by the end of the week.'

'Nice work,' said Mrs Digby. 'You earned yourself a cookie, cookie.'

'Just one?' complained Ruby.

'Don't want to spoil your supper,' said Mrs Digby.

Ruby looked at the table, set for two.

'Hitch is coming?' Ruby asked.

'He better be, I've made enough stew to feed an army.' She reached for a ladle, but was interrupted by the ring of the telephone. 'Well, howdie, stranger... *What?*... I can't say I approve... it's not good for you to skip meals, did your mother never tell you that? You'll be jumping into an early grave... I'll leave it in the warmer, if the dog doesn't get to it first.' She put down the receiver.

'He's not coming?' asked Ruby.

'He said he had to get off somewhere in a hurry; something about a friend of his with a broken-down car.' The housekeeper sniffed disapprovingly. 'He'll not be long for this world if he doesn't take the time to eat.'

'I didn't know he had any friends,' said Ruby.

'*Too many* friends, if you ask me,' said Mrs Digby. 'He certainly didn't seem one jot put out by my going off on that cruise. He couldn't pack me off quick enough.'

'Yeah, well, at least you wound up in the Caribbean,' said Ruby. 'He packed me off to spend a month in the back end of nowhere.'

The housekeeper picked up the dog bowl and served a generous portion to Bug. 'Anyone would think he wanted rid of us,' she said.

Ruby decided to get an early night: she needed to catch up on her sleep and if she hit the hay early then she might clock up a round ten hours. That would have been nice, but in the end all she managed was an uneven five. First of all came the phone call from Paris.

'Hey, Ruby, it's us!'

'Bonjour, Mom, bonjour, Dad. Quelle heure est-il, by the way?'

'Pardon?'

'What time is it?'

'Almost lunch time, what time is it with you?'

Ruby reached for her watch.

'Three in the am.'

'Oh, Rube, you should really be asleep,' said her mother.

'Yeah, you might want to try calling a little later, six hours maybe, either that or a whole lot earlier, there's a nine-hour time difference – that's nine hours *behind*.'

'Oh, I thought Twinford was nine hours ahead,' said her father.

'Other way around, Dad.'

'In that case, sleep tight!' said her mother.

'Bon appétit,' said Ruby.

An hour later and she was woken again, this time by the sound of a fly. Judging by the insistent racket it was making, it was in its death throes, and was making a noise like it might be buzzing about on its back, legs in the air.

Still caught in sleep, Ruby attempted to bat it away, but her hand hit the edge of something solid and her eyes blinked open to find, not a noisy upside-down insect, but her Spectrum Escape Watch vibrating on the nightstand. Words in green blinked at her from the face on the dial.

A message from Hitch.

City planetarium 04.35 Row F seat 6

It was four am, really not a good time to greet the day. But if Hitch was planning on taking her into HQ to meet with her (possibly) murderous boss, then four am was as good a time as any.

Ruby reached for her glasses, struggled to her feet, fell over, cursed, hobbled to the bathroom, washed her face, brushed her teeth, combed her hair, and peered at herself with bleary eyes.

Redfort, you have to pull it together, she told herself.

Ruby decided the only way she could wake up would be to stand under the shower. This she did, and it did the trick. She peered out of the window into the still-dark morning. *Cold*, she thought, *colder than yesterday*. The temperature was really dropping.

She dug out some thermal leggings and pulled her jeans on over them, found a thermal undershirt, a T-shirt with the words, ***don't wake me*** printed across the front, a black zip top and a snow parka and earmuffs. Snow was not forecast, but the air had turned icy. When she was ready, she picked up her backpack, tiptoed down the stairs and out of the front door. The only people riding the subway from Green Street were nightshift workers and early birds.

She arrived at the planetarium and was surprised to find the doors open and a guy selling tickets. She had been prepared for a little breaking and entering.

She went up to the booth. 'What's the deal?' asked Ruby.

'What do you mean what's the deal?' said the young man in the ticket booth.

'How come you're open? It's four-thirty in the am.'

'It's to celebrate the anniversary of last year's moon landing, you know, Apollo 17?' said the guy.

'I hate to burst your balloon, but you know you're early?' said Ruby. 'The anniversary is December seventh.'

'Yeah, we do know that, but a lot of people want to come so we're doing a whole month of events,' said the guy, pointing at the huge poster framed there on the wall. 'There's a whole deal of stuff going on. You might have heard, the Observatory on Meteor Island is building a new telescope... it's been in the news, you know: Planet Twinford – 1974's City of *Space*?'

'But it isn't 1974,' said Ruby.

'Yeah, but it will be in like four weeks,' said the guy. 'You really haven't heard anything about this?'

Ruby was looking blank. Then, 'Oh yeah, I think maybe my parents were invited to something spacey, what was it?'

'Could it be the Galaxy Concert? Or the Astro Lectures? Or the Deep Space Gala?' suggested the guy, before adding a little sarcastically, 'what planet have you been on, man?'

'Planet Geek,' said Ruby. 'I guess you might have a ticket for me, in the name of Redfort.'

The guy shuffled through his stack of prepaid tickets and handed her an envelope.

'Enjoy!' he said.

Ruby opened the door to the auditorium and tiptoed quietly down the steps. All the seats in the middle section were taken but towards the edges there were plenty of empty seats. She found F and began sidling along the row.

She sat down. All the seats around her were unoccupied and there was no sign of Hitch.

Mr Punctuality appeared to be late.

She began to watch the show and quickly became absorbed by the commentary.

'Hey,' said a voice.

RUBY: *'Jeepers! I didn't hear you arrive.'*

HITCH: *'You seem tense, kid.'*

RUBY: *'Well, now you mention it...'*

HITCH: *'By the way, have you eaten breakfast?'*

RUBY: *'What, are you kidding? It's not even five am.'*

He handed her a paper bag.

'Thanks,' she said. She pulled out a donut.

HITCH: *'From Blacker.'*

RUBY: *'What's he doing up at this hour?'*

HITCH: *'It's all hands on deck while there's a madman at large.'*

Like every other member of the audience his eyes were trained on the ceiling, where the night sky rotated slowly above them.

Hitch pointed up at a cluster of stars. 'That's Hercules, right?'

Ruby tutted. 'Orion,' she said.

'You sure?'

'Course I'm sure,' said Ruby. 'I read up on all that stuff about a billion light years ago when I was five years old. I can draw you every constellation going – blindfolded and with my hands tied behind my back.'

'That sounds like quite a party trick,' said Hitch. 'Who could know when that talent might come in handy.'

'Yeah, right,' said Ruby. 'What are we doing here anyway?'

'Oh, you know,' said Hitch, 'it's very soothing contemplating the stars, don't you think?'

'I guess,' she said, giving him a 'what's got into you?' look.

'So how was geek camp?' he asked.

'Geeky,' replied Ruby. 'So you been busy?'

'Pretty busy, at least up until your parents flew to Paris. Boy, do they have a social life!'

'So what made you think they needed a vacation?'

'What makes you think it was my idea?'

'Mrs Digby told me it was.'

'Well, I have got to admit, they were driving me a little crazy. Do you have any idea how many parties they attend?'

'I've been living with them the past thirteen years – what do you think?'

'So you understand,' said Hitch.

'More than anyone,' said Ruby. 'I also understand Mrs Digby mysteriously won a free cruise round the Caribbean, what I don't understand is how?'

'I know, who would have guessed?'

'Not her, that's for sure,' said Ruby.

'Life is full of surprises,' said Hitch.

'So what, you felt like you wanted the place to yourself?'

'We needed to make some adjustments to the house, add some security features,' said Hitch.

'For my sake?'

'For all your sakes.'

'You think my folks are in danger?' asked Ruby. 'Mrs Digby even?'

'I wouldn't fancy anyone's chances if they were to go after Mrs Digby.' He smiled. 'But yes, I just don't want any of them to become any kind of target.'

'You think that could really happen? Really, I mean?' asked Ruby. 'The Count *knows* that my parents aren't involved in Spectrum; they aren't exactly agent material.'

'You're missing the point, kid. If the Count has a mind to rattle you, or *worse*, destroy your world, he knows how to do it. He knows where you live, he knows what makes you tick,' said Hitch.

'Meaning... he might make an attempt on their lives?'

'Meaning, it's possible.'

'Hence the safety upgrade.'

'Hence the safety upgrade.'

'So what are you going to do when they get back?' asked Ruby, 'I mean you can't stop them going out?'

'I'll do my best, kid, anything I can to ensure their safety and I'll try my darndest to keep them from knowing anything about it.'

'So what *did* you tell them? About the house, I mean?'

'I didn't want to get them all in a stew about it, so I got a friend of mine who happens to be in construction to persuade them that the windows needed replacing. He told them they had a bad case of window weevils.'

'How did he convince them of that?'

'Sprinkled a bit of glass dust around the place and loosened one of the window panes; they got the picture.'

'Glass dust?' said Ruby.

'They were very concerned,' said Hitch.

'I'll bet,' said Ruby. 'Since when was it possible for a weevil to eat through glass?'

'I know,' said Hitch, 'alarming, isn't it?'

'And Mrs Digby?' said Ruby.

'It was a big job and I didn't want her picking up on what was really going on. She has eyes like a hawk. I told her I had changed the locks and upgraded the alarm system because I had mislaid a set of keys but I kept the real reason from her.'

'Well, so far you seem to have succeeded at keeping her in

the dark. Mrs Digby thinks you packed her off because you wanted to have a high old time with your friends.' She looked at him out of the corner of her eye. 'I told her I didn't think you had any friends.'

'One day I'll introduce you to one of them,' said Hitch.

'Mrs Digby probably thinks you sent my folks to Paris because you couldn't handle their crazy social life.'

Hitch winked at her. 'I'm a trained agent, I can handle any party they throw at me.' He paused. 'Speaking of training, right now we have to get our skates on.'

'Why? Where are we going?'

'A date with LB,' he said.

He caught the expression on her face. 'Jeepers, kid, relax a little. Anyone would think you were about to meet with the Grim Reaper.'

Chapter 11.
Act normal

THEY PARKED THE SILVER CAR down a side street and walked perhaps another two hundred yards.

'Here?' asked Ruby.

'Here,' said Hitch.

'So you meant literally,' said Ruby, '*actually* get our skates on?'

They were standing in midtown outside the ice rink on Bowery.

'No, not actually.'

'But this is the way into Spectrum?'

'It is today,' said Hitch.

'So why did you get me crossing town to meet you at the planetarium when you coulda just told me to make my way to the ice rink?'

'I like that place,' said Hitch.

'The planetarium?'

'Yeah, like I said, I find it soothing.'

Ruby rolled her eyes. 'Whatever floats your boat.'

They pushed through the turnstile and headed to the skate room, a labyrinth of shelves and cubbyholes each holding a pair of skates, too many to count. At the far end of this room was a door without a handle, and pinned to it was a poster of a skater mid-twirl. The skater looked happy, unaware that her tooth had been blackened by the casual swatting of a fly now squashed onto her picture-perfect smile. Hitch pressed his thumb into a barely visible identity scanner and the door clicked open. The door led to some stairs, the stairs led to Spectrum.

Once in the atrium they made their way across the vast space to the place where the Spectrum coordinator sat.

Nothing had changed, at least nothing had changed as far as the *eye* could see, but the atmosphere was very different. Breathe deeply and one could practically choke on the tension.

Buzz was where she always was, seated in the middle of the great round desk just off the main hall. Coloured telephones encircled her, and Ruby guessed that a web of wires and cables must trail around her feet. And though the administrator's expression was as blank and unsmiling as always, in some strange way it was a relief to see her. That said, Ruby had no desire to hang out with the woman – she could bore you to death, if nothing else.

There was no 'how are you', no 'we've missed you', not the briefest snip of small talk, all Buzz said was – 'LB will see you now.'

And Ruby felt her limbs become heavy as she walked the

short walk to her boss's door.

This time it wasn't the fear of failure or of getting fired that made Ruby Redfort dread coming face to face with LB – this time it was a fear of getting found out. What if LB knew what she knew?

Ruby was grateful to have Hitch with her, though felt no certainty that he would take her side if he had to choose between *her* truth and his boss's.

LB was looking steelier than she had done five weeks ago. The signs of fatigue and stress were gone and had been replaced by a cold, unwavering determination. Perhaps she was eating an iron-rich diet, as Consuela would no doubt recommend, or perhaps she had been working on her martial arts. Ruby had heard it rumoured that the Spectrum 8 boss was no slouch in this department, having studied karate in Japan under the great master, Funakoshi. It all seemed very unlikely to Ruby, who had never seen LB outside the walls of HQ, let alone out in the field. It might simply be gossip or it might be a very tall tale, but Agent Holbrook had told her that LB was the only Spectrum 8 agent to have mastered the deadly wrist grasp otherwise known as the 'assassin's handshake'.

None of these assertions were exactly comforting at this moment.

LB waved at her to sit down.

'Do you want me to stay?' asked Hitch.

Stay, thought Ruby, *for Pete's sake, stay.*

'No, that won't be necessary,' said LB. 'Would you give me and Redfort five minutes?'

'Of course,' said Hitch, stepping out.

Ruby had a strong desire to jump up and follow him. But she kept her face composed and herself in her seat.

LB waited for the door to close behind Hitch before addressing Ruby.

'So you're back, Redfort,' she said.

'Yes,' said Ruby.

'How was it?'

'It was OK,' said Ruby.

'I hear you kept your head down and your nose clean.'

'Yes,' said Ruby.

LB peered at her from over her glasses.

'What, no smart remark?'

Silence.

'I'm beginning to wonder if they sent you to Swiss finishing school by mistake. I know I should be relieved, but it's making me feel uneasy.'

Redfort, you're acting weird, pull it together!

LB leaned forward. 'Is there something wrong? Something you want to share?'

'I'm not giving you half my donut if that's what you're getting at.'

'That's more like it. I thought for one horrible minute I was speaking with some Ruby Redfort doppelganger – I don't know,

Lorelei von Leyden in disguise, maybe.'

'It would be a tough act to pull off,' said Ruby. 'I like to think that when they made me they broke the mould.'

'So do I,' said LB sourly. She cleared her throat. 'As you might have heard, Spectrum 8 has handed much of its operations activity to Spectrum 1, just while we try to figure how far this contamination has reached, and which agent if any is responsible for leaking information to the Count.'

'Right,' said Ruby.

If LB was bluffing then she was a seriously cool customer. 'A large number of our department have been suspended until we have clarity on this issue. Spectrum 7 agents will replace them until we have located our mole.'

'So am *I* being suspended?' asked Ruby. She paused, thought about where she had been. '*Was* I suspended? What I mean to say is, was geek camp really a way of getting me out of the picture? So you could check me out?'

'Yes, but if it makes you feel better, we were as much concerned for your wellbeing as we were that you might in some way be leaking information.'

'You thought I might be leaking information?'

'You can see our point of view here, I'm sure. On the one hand, we were suspicious that the Count would keep you alive – we had to ask ourselves why –but on the other, we were concerned that he might change his mind. He doesn't always abide by logic. And besides, his employer presumably still wants you dead, assuming *that* story is true, though when it comes to the Count one should never *assume* anything. Whatever else he is, he is predictably unpredictable.'

'So now what?' asked Ruby carefully. 'Am I trusted employee or traitor?'

'Quit being so dramatic, Redfort, you're neither; no one ever thought you were a traitor – a blabbermouth perhaps, there was always a chance of that.'

Ruby opened her mouth to object, but LB raised her hand.

'I never said you *were*, Redfort, I said there was a chance that you had brought this whole craziness to our door, but I concede that's unlikely. There's no evidence for it.'

Well, that was a relief.

Though what followed was not.

'You, like every other agent in Spectrum 8, will be taken off duty. Eight is effectively closed to all lower-level agents. For all but vital access to our departments, permission must be given by a senior agent. My feeling was that your training should also be suspended until we have this security mess under control.

'However,' she paused and sighed, like what she was about to say was a great effort to her, 'Hitch has persuaded HQ that it might be wise to keep up the survival skills. He seems to think you need all the protection you can get, and though you are no longer a functioning field agent or coding agent, after much consideration, I am persuaded he is right. We have a duty of care and I have to concede that it is our responsibility to protect you.

As such, you will remain in Spectrum as a trainee agent. Under our careful supervision.'

Ruby tried to smile. 'That's good to know,' she said.

A month ago, she'd have felt that LB's office was the safest place on this earth. Now she couldn't help feeling she was a fly, about to be swatted.

Problem was, she had no idea who was holding the swatter.

Chapter 12.
Ghost Files

RUBY WAS JUST TRYING to figure out where Hitch might have got to when she spotted a note on the table in the waiting area.

> *Meet me in Froghorn's coding room –*
> *he will be expecting you.*

She was surprised that he had arranged for them to meet there, and it was odd that Froghorn had agreed to it – with the exception of Blacker, Froghorn generally made it clear that *no one* was welcome in his coding room. Seeing him so soon after she had stepped back into Spectrum was an unpalatable idea, but then she remembered Clancy's words – '*talk to Froghorn, I bet you anything he'll tell you* whatever *you wanna know, just to make you feel small.*' It was true, Froghorn couldn't resist bragging about all the secrets he knew, *and let's face it*, she thought, *he loves nothing better than to drone on about the late great Bradley Baker.*

All I gotta do is get him talking, that's not so difficult.

Knowledge was her only weapon, the only superpower she

really had. And if she was going to find out the truth about how Spectrum's most revered agent met his end then Froghorn was her only option.

The door to his coding room was unlocked, so she was puzzled when she discovered it empty of people. Miles Froghorn was usually very careful about security. Ruby took the opportunity to have a snoop around and she found a lot of interesting things.

There were numerous files stacked neatly on tables, and code books marked with post-its and bookmarks, and notes carefully written in ink. There were several books on data transmission, particularly error-correcting codes that allowed computers to know whether there were mistakes in information they received. It was a subject that fascinated Ruby.

She flipped open a book.

Parity bits are one of the simplest systems for ensuring error-free transmission of binary data. Note though that as they indicate only whether the information contains an even or odd number of 1s or 0s, they are vulnerable to bits in the chain being swapped rather than lost, which is something they cannot...

She stopped reading when she heard footsteps coming down the corridor. She moved away from the table and listened, but whoever it was walked right on by. She continued to peruse Froghorn's papers. There was a whole hand-written list of what must be ideas for locking devices: swipe card, iris lock, thumbprint, keypad, image lock, bolt key, 5 key, pressure key, voice key.

It rather looked like he had been working on some sort of multi-coded security system, because there was a diagram which was basically three squares arranged like an upside-down L, with letters and numbers marked at particular intervals, and to the side of each of the blocks: E1 E2 E3. In the middle of the third square he had written FC1 FC2 FC3. Next to these were six small pieces of coloured paper; each one was labelled with one of the sets of letters on the diagram, E1, E2, E3 etc., and on each paper was written a word or words, some crossed out, some replaced. E1, for example, said: **MUSCA**. E2: **SWAT**; E3: **TRANSMISSION**, F1: **THE SPECTRUM**. FC2 said: **ROTOR MACHINE** and then this was crossed out and had been replaced with **CHROMATIC.** FC3 was just a **?**

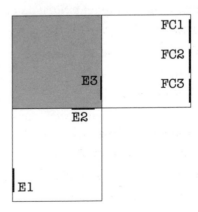

It looked as if he had been trying to figure out the best method of securing each part of a building, or series of rooms.

There was a beep on Ruby's watch and she very nearly jumped out of her skin. A YELLOW FLY, meaning ATTENTION! A message flashed across the screen.

HUGE MISTAKE, I MEANT TO SAY MEET ME IN FROGHORN'S OFFICE! IF YOU HAPPEN TO HAVE MADE IT INTO HIS CODING ROOM THEN GET OUT!
PS MEETING CANCELLED.

Ruby did as instructed and got out of there quick, just in time as it turned out, because as she speed-walked along the corridor she ran into Froghorn coming the other way.

'Oh, you're back,' he said slowly, drawing the words out as if he'd just found something unpleasant on the underside of his shoe.

'Hey, Froghorn,' she said, deliberately ignoring the silent G so the word 'Frog' sounded out very clearly. His irritation could not be missed.

'What a shame, did kiddie camp not work out for you?'

'Genius Camp, you mean?' said Ruby. 'Yes, that *was* fun, but you know what they say, too much fun can get you bored, so I guess it's good to run into *you*.'

'I thought it was going to be a bad day,' said Froghorn. 'Viridian days are always a total drag.'

'What are you bleating on about – viridian days? Jeepers, Froghorn, maybe you need to leave the building for an hour or two.'

'I would if there was anyone who could possibly handle my job, but since we lost Lopez we've had a tough job recruiting anyone with half a brain.'

'I'm surprised you didn't bring up Bradley Baker again, you guys seem to think the sun shone out of him.'

'The sun *did* shine out of him,' said Froghorn. 'That's exactly it, he was a sun ray. And even though he's dead and gone to grey he never was and never will be some pale imitation of an agent, some little girl living a little pastel-pink life.'

'Boy, Froghorn, that's a very colourful picture you paint. So if you're saying Baker was sunshine yellow and I'm insipid pink – which, by the way, I take great exception to – then what are *you*? Potato-head beige?'

'*I'm* someone authorised to be here, what are you? Some little girl who needs to go back to school?' He checked his watch theatrically.

'No one said that about Bradley Baker and wasn't he just some little kid when *he* started out?' said Ruby. Her comment had the desired effect.

'Bradley Baker was *never just some little kid*. He was extraordinary, a talent the like of which we will never see again.'

'What is it with you guys and Bradley Baker? I've yet to

hear one actual thing which makes this bozo so different from anyone else.'

Froghorn stepped back like he'd been slapped. 'What?' he said.

RUBY: *'You people talk about him like he's some kinda super-agent, but he took orders same as you, same as me, same as every agent in this building.'*

FROGHORN: *'Baker took orders because it was his job to take orders. It didn't mean that he wasn't capable of making his own decisions.'*

RUBY: *'So you're saying he did make his own decisions?'*

FROGHORN: *'Of course he did, he was highly qualified, lived by his own rules.'*

RUBY: *'So he was a maverick, a renegade... took authority into his own hands, that sorta thing?'*

FROGHORN: *'No! That's not what I'm saying, not at all! He never did anything to undermine the agency.'*

RUBY: *'I don't get it, now you're telling me he was a zip-it and toe-the-line type of a guy? Make your mind up, Froghorn, either he had guts and initiative or he was just another listen-up-and-do-as-you're-told team player.'*

FROGHORN: *'The sheer magnitude of what you don't know about Agent Baker's guts and heroism would fill this atrium. Baker was an agent in a million.'*

RUBY (YAWNING): *'Yeah, right, so everyone keeps telling me, but it all sounds like a lot of hot air if you want my* *opinion.'*

FROGHORN: 'No one *wants your opinion.'*

RUBY: '*Yeah, and why* is *that? I'm guessing because no one is tough enough to hear the truth.'*

FROGHORN: *'And what is that "truth"?'*

RUBY: '*Simply that there are* other *agents just as talented as him.'*

Froghorn narrowed his eyes. 'Are you actually suggesting that you are even close to being in the same league as Agent Baker?'

Ruby made a face to suggest, maybe she was. Froghorn's reaction was as she'd hoped – very gabby. 'Come with me,' he said.

'Where are we going?' They were heading in the opposite direction now and Ruby had a job to keep pace with him. When he reached his office he opened the door and waved her in with an irritated gesture.

Her visits to this room were rare and usually very brief, so it wasn't perhaps so surprising that she had never before noticed how everything was colour-coded, and not just in a Spectrum way, but in a Froghorn way. His calendar for instance: Mondays green, viridian green, Tuesdays yellow. December dark blue.

Froghorn looked like he was wearing a brand-new suit. It was ever so slightly shiny and he had a new shiny steel pen to match; it was attached to a silver cord which hung around his neck. *Who does that?* she thought. *Who actually* wears *a pen? OK,*

Mrs Drisco does, but she's Mrs Drisco, what else would you expect?
But this guy should know better. Boy, is he ever a potato head.

FROGHORN: *'You think that cracking a five-way-thought code which led us to prevent the leaking of secret government dossiers isn't of value?'*

RUBY: *'Of course it's of value, I'm just saying, is it remarkable? I mean he was a code cracker, right, so wouldn't that be all in a day's work to someone of his agent rank?'*

FROGHORN: *'So how about confronting the Count when he was a junior agent, getting up close and personal with this monster and living to tell the tale? He was the first Spectrum agent to walk away with his life.'*

RUBY: *'What, you mean like I did?'* She studied her nails. *'More than once actually.'*

FROGHORN: *'You got lucky, little girl, hardly heroic. Baker was captured by the Count and rescued by the Spectrum special agent squad.'*

RUBY: *'I rescued* myself, *surely that counts for something.'*

FROGHORN: *'State of the art Spectrum gadgets are what allowed you to escape.'*

RUBY: *'Isn't that how Baker got himself out of trouble a whole bunch of times? I'm sure he would have been toast without the Escape Watch.'*

FROGHORN: *'He was issued with them; you took them without permission.'*

RUBY: *'So that's the difference between being a hero and not* *being a hero – a signature on a slip of paper?'*

FROGHORN: *'If you want to be a Spectrum agent then you have to behave like one.'*

Ruby had quite a few things she wouldn't have minded saying in reply to this patronising remark, but was aware that it might not serve her well to get Froghorn so mad that he slammed the door in her face.

RUBY: *'So name an occasion where Baker actually went above and beyond his job description.'*

FROGHORN: *'You think that leaping from an aircraft without a Spectrum aero-pack in order to save a fellow agent from certain death doesn't make him a hero?'*

RUBY: *'Can I ask, was the plane moving at the time?'*

FROGHORN: *'Try fourteen thousand feet. And it wasn't a regular plane.'*

Ruby shrugged. 'I don't know, Froghorn, I mean, is jumping without a parachute really such a big deal?'

FROGHORN: *'You should try it sometime.'*

RUBY: *'Maybe I will.'*

FROGHORN: *'I'd be thrilled to arrange it.'*

RUBY: *'If there was actually any evidence that Baker had actually done it then I would be only too happy to give it a try.'*

FROGHORN: *'You should read the files; what's contained in them would make your head spin.'*

RUBY: *'Oh, so there are files?'*

FROGHORN: *'Of course there are files!'*

RUBY: *'OK, so I'll read them.'*

FROGHORN: *'You don't have authority to read files, least of all the Ghost Files.'*

RUBY: *'Ghost Files?'*

Silence.

RUBY: *'Oh, come on, Froghorn, you're making this up. Ghost Files? I mean Spectrum's not gonna use a dumb name like that.'*

FROGHORN: *'You know so little of Spectrum. You arrive here thinking you're some kind of wonder-child, but you're not even a shadow of Agent Baker.'*

RUBY: *'Show me the files and I'll devote some minutes to reading them.'*

FROGHORN: *'It would take you more than a few hours to read a list of his achievements.'*

RUBY: *'So point me in the right direction and I'll get started.'*

FROGHORN: *'Why would I ever tell you where the Prism Vault is?'*

RUBY: *'Why would you, when you don't know?'*

FROGHORN: *'Of course I know. I've just this week completed the task of updating the code lock system.'*

So that's what he's up to.

But what she said was, 'So where is it?'

FROGHORN: *'Like I'd ever tell you.'*

RUBY: *'You should, it might help me understand this little love-in Spectrum has with old Bradley.'*

FROGHORN: *'If you ever see the inside of that place then I'll eat my hat.'*

RUBY: *'Really? I'll work on it then, I've always wanted to see someone eat their hat.'*

FROGHORN: *'I'm sure one of your kindergarten friends would oblige – little kids are always eating things they shouldn't.'*

RUBY: *'You not concerned that someone might crack your new vault codes?'*

'No, little girl.'

'No, and why's that?'

'Because first you'd have to understand what code you are dealing with and that's something you aren't ever going to know.'

'Even if you made it there,' continued Froghorn. 'Even if you figured out the location, you would still require *permission* to get inside, and we both know that's never going to happen, *or* you would need to get hold of a Superskin.'

'What's a Superskin?' asked Ruby.

'Exactly,' said Froghorn. 'Then you would need to hold your breath for at least three minutes and we both know you have no talent for that, am I right?'

Boy, is this guy's colour potato-head beige.

'Even if you punched in the correct door code and got inside the vault, even if you did all that, just how many layers of files could you reach? One? Two?'

'Um,' said Ruby, 'is there a three?'

'Layer three you might as well dream about because there's not a chance you'd make it into that.' As he said 'three' he gripped the steel pen and turned it round and round in his hand.

'Careful with that,' said Ruby. 'You don't want to strangle yourself with that little necklace of yours.'

He suddenly looked awkward, self-conscious even, and he barked at her, saying, 'All file layers are code-protected. I set them myself... think about it, little girl.'

'Oh, believe me I am,' said Ruby. 'So you say breath-holding's involved; is this vault underwater or something?'

Froghorn's mouth snapped shut. He had said too much. He began fiddling with his stupid neck pen, nervously wrapping his tie round and round as he tried to backtrack. 'Dream on, you'll never lay eyes on the Ghost Files, let alone read them.' He was confident about that, Ruby could see it: the look on his face said *the Prism Vault is nowhere you'll ever go.*

'You sound very certain,' said Ruby.

'I am,' said Froghorn. 'I spent a lot of time coding those files and I did an excellent job.'

'I'm sure you did your best, Froghorn, but remember what they say: pride comes before a fall, or wait a minute, is it once a potato head always a potato head? I can never remember.'

Chapter 13.
Sprayed and delivered

AS RUBY WAS EXITING FROGHORN'S OFFICE, an announcement sounded over the tannoy:

RUBY REDFORT, REPORT TO RECEPTION.

When she reached Buzz's desk, she was told in a bored tone to report to the gadget room.

When she got there, she found Hal standing next to a bicycle.

'So here you go,' said Hal, stepping aside. 'I've been working on it for a while.'

'For me?' asked Ruby.

'No one else in Spectrum rides a bike,' said Hal.

Ruby smiled. 'Well, thanks.'

'It's got a few features you won't be used to,' said Hal. 'The tyres are of course unpuncturable, and the frame super-reinforced, but it's the bike's ability to grip the road surface which is what makes it special.'

'Meaning?'

'It's very hard to fall off. As with a motorcycle, you can lean pretty low to the ground and so long as the wheels keep turning, the tyres grip the road and you stay on the bike.'

'Well, that sounds cool,' said Ruby.

'It is,' said Hal. 'Spectrum gadgets are 99.999 per cent reliable and this bike is no exception.'

'So what about speed?'

'It has speed, that goes without saying,' he said. 'You just have to decide when you're going to use it. It won't be continuous, but you might get ten minutes of hyper-speed every forty.'

'So what's this?' asked Ruby.

'That's a bell,' said Hal.

'And what does it actually *do*?' asked Ruby.

'It rings,' said Hal. He demonstrated.

'Oh,' said Ruby.

'That's not one of its special features,' said Hal.

'I guess not,' said Ruby.

'Obviously we'll give it a finish, make it some pretty colour.'

'Green,' said Ruby.

'Pardon me?' There was a deafening grinding sound coming from the workshop at the back. 'That doesn't sound good,' said Hal. 'I better go check out what's happening in there. Look, we'll have the bike sprayed and delivered,' he said.

When he was gone, Ruby found herself alone in the gadget room. Of course, she took the opportunity to have a look around.

There was something very particular which she hoped she might find, something which would be invaluable to a person seeking to break into, say, a file room.

As luck would have it, she spotted it almost immediately.

THE MICRO-READER: Hold device five inches from document and press red button. Up to 1500 images can be stored. The device doubles as a projector: press the green button to view your images on a screen or any suitably smooth wall or pale surface.

Checking first that Hal was still otherwise engaged, she pocketed the small object, no bigger really than a large pencil sharpener.

She was just thinking of reaching into one of the other low glass drawers when she heard someone cough. She stood up quickly, which caused her to bump her head.

Ouch.

'Hey, Ruby,' said Blacker, 'are you OK? I didn't mean to alarm you.'

'Oh... no, you didn't,' she said. 'I mean sort of, but hey, yes, I mean hello.'

For a second she was afraid he'd seen what she'd done, but he smiled. 'Nice to have you back, Ruby, though actually it's my job to wave you bye-bye, I'm afraid.'

'What?'

'There's to be no wandering the corridors unaccompanied, so Buzz sent me to escort you on your way out.'

'You're serious? You actually are kicking me out?'

He shrugged and smiled again. 'Not me – a Spectrum command from the top.'

Ruby gave him a puzzled look.

'LB,' he explained.

'OK,' said Ruby. 'I'll go quietly.'

Despite the fact that he was there to march her from the premises, Ruby was glad to see Agent Blacker: he was a reassuring presence, and there weren't so many living creatures you could say that about these days.

As she and Blacker walked to the exit, Ruby struck up a conversation about the Prism Vault.

'Have you ever read the Ghost Files?' asked Ruby.

He stopped for a moment and looked at her. 'Who told you about the Ghost Files?' he asked.

'Froghorn,' said Ruby.

Blacker frowned. 'He's getting blabby.'

'What I'm wondering,' continued Ruby, 'is if Spectrum don't want anyone to read these files, as in *ever*, then why not just erase them?'

'I'm surprised Froghorn didn't tell you,' said Blacker. 'Ghost Files *can't* be erased; they are triple secured and locked so far down in the Prism Vault that you may need a password from

God himself. But they cannot be deleted. Spectrum files are created that way.'

'But they can be read?'

'They can be read if you are *authorised* to read them and if you have code clearance to enter the Prism Vault. Of course, if you had code clearance they'd fly you there in the Spectrum helicopter.'

Why does one need a helicopter to get there? wondered Ruby. 'What if you don't have code clearance?' was what she asked.

'Then you'd be needing flippers or some kind of submersible.'

'It's located in water?' said Ruby.

'It's no secret that the vault's in a watery location,' said Blacker.

'Would that be in a lake? Or in the sea?' asked Ruby.

Blacker cocked his head to one side and looked at her like he was trying to gauge where this conversation was going.

'So how does one go about getting hold of a helicopter?' asked Ruby.

'You're kidding, right?' said Blacker. He was laughing, but he wasn't entirely sure she was joking.

'Of course I'm *kidding*,' said Ruby, flashing him the Ruby Redfort *I'm just a kid* smile. 'Has anyone ever helicoptered *you* in there?' she asked.

'No, mam,' said Blacker. 'Don't like helicopters. And there's no way I'm putting a Superskin on, not unless I have to.'

'They make you feel claustrophobic?'

'No, they're just a heck of a struggle to get in and out of.'

'So what exactly *is* a Superskin?'

He smiled again and shook his head. 'If you're lucky you'll never need to know.'

When Ruby stepped out of Spectrum headquarters it was into an entirely different landscape. No more grey – this one was bright white, the sidewalks already an inch deep in soft snow. She pulled her hood up, zipping the snow parka so her face was framed by its fur. She looked towards the sky, mouth open, and felt the snowflakes melt on her tongue. By the time she reached home the snow was already an inch deeper.

As she crunched up the path to her house she thought about what she had learned.

It seemed she had two unknowns, two problems.

The first: *where* was the Prism Vault?

The second: how to get inside it?

And what in tarnation was a Superskin?

The things she did know were that water was involved and holding your breath seemed to have something to do with it. This second thing was *not* a reassuring prospect, for, just as Miles Froghorn had pointed out, Ruby had never been very good at holding her breath.

Chapter 14.
The wrong kind of snow

RUBY WAS CATCHING UP on some of the homework her homeroom teacher, Mrs Drisco, had thoughtfully sent over while she was at camp. If Mrs Drisco's intention was to overwhelm Ruby with school work then she was to be disappointed. Ruby had worked her way through about a quarter of it and she hadn't yet finished breakfast. If she continued at this rate, she should have the rest finished up by the middle of the week, easy.

Hitch offered to drive her into school, but she said she could just as well take the bus.

'By the way, what was that all about, sending me in to talk to Froghorn and then not showing up?'

'Sorry kid, I had a plan to bring about world peace starting with you two, but I got into an argument with Agent Lunberg and time got away from me.'

'So much for world peace,' said Ruby.

'It's a harder prospect than you might imagine,' he said. 'Have a good day and give Mrs Drisco a run for her money,' he said as he walked out of the room.

'You can count on it!' called Ruby.

She glugged down her juice and stared at the cereal box in front of her. There were some brainteaser puzzles printed on the back and as she figured them out (which took her under a minute) so she thought back to that day when she had found the code on the back of the Choco Puffles packet. At first glance it had appeared to be just some competition aimed at little kids, but if you knew more than a lot about coding and code-breaking you could see what it really was. Ruby had been just four when she'd noticed it. She'd filled in the form, addressed and stamped the envelope and passed it to her father to mail, but he had forgotten and that was that. Now sitting here, some nine years later, she wondered if perhaps this code might have been set by Spectrum recruiters – it wasn't impossible, she thought. *Her* route to this underground agency had been by invitation – a phone call from the boss. Not a straightforward 'would you like a career in code-breaking' phone call, but then nothing about Spectrum was ever straightforward.

Ruby was so lost in thought that she didn't hear the back door open.

'Didn't I tell you there'd likely be snow?' said Mrs Digby as she stamped her boots on the step. 'I can't say I'm surprised these so-called weather fellas missed it. They don't know how to read a sky the way my old pa taught me.' She unwound her scarf. 'It won't settle though.'

'It won't?' said Ruby.

'Mark my words, it will be gone before noon.'

Ruby looked out at the yard with its pristine white blanket. It was impossible to make out the path or the lawn or the patio.

'Looks like it's settled,' said Ruby.

'Wrong sort of snow,' said Mrs Digby. 'It can't last. I'm telling you, by the time the school bell strikes twelve it will have all but disappeared.'

'The school bell doesn't strike, it kinda clangs,' said Ruby.

The first thing Del said when Ruby climbed aboard the school bus was, 'You know you missed Thanksgiving.'

'I didn't miss Thanksgiving,' said Ruby. 'I *had* Thanksgiving, just not with anyone I felt very *thankful* to be with.'

'Why didn't your mom and dad come visit?' asked Mouse.

'They were in Paris,' said Ruby. 'Not that I was allowed any visitors anyway.'

'So who *did* you spend Thanksgiving with?'

'A few of the mathletics guys.'

'Sounds super dull,' said Del.

'Yes and no,' said Ruby.

Del gave her the Del Lasco look of *you must truly have lost your brain.* 'You're actually saying you *enjoyed* hanging out with those geeks?'

'Not all geeks are boring,' said Mouse, reasonably. 'I mean if you define a geek as someone who's good at school stuff and knows all about movies and comics then *Ruby's* a geek right?

No offence, Rube.'

'None taken, but actually this is not the point,' said Ruby.

'What *is*?' said Del.

'I'm saying, if you go into something looking for boredom then more than likely you're gonna be bored; it's about attitude.'

'So I've got a bad attitude – is that what you're saying?'

'No, not *bad*, just you're going into it all wrong. I'm arguing that there's no *need* to be bored, *ever*, not if you've got inner resources, an upbeat way of looking at things.'

Del wasn't buying it and probably never would. Del was like that, once she'd decided something, it could be near-impossible to get her round to your way of thinking, and it was usually a thankless task to try.

RULE 42: DON'T WASTE TIME ARGUING WITH SOMEONE WHO WON'T IN A MILLION YEARS CHANGE HIS OR HER MIND.

Though that said, there was always **RULE 45: NEVER STOP CHALLENGING SMALL-MINDEDNESS.**

Del Lasco was almost back to being her old self except for one thing: she had learned a lesson about evidence and how sure one should be of it before accusing a loyal ally and close friend.

Who to trust when the chips were down?

For Del Lasco now that was a no-brainer. As far as Del was concerned, Ruby Redfort was the only person you could one hundred per cent count on, no questions asked – beyond that, how to know?

When they arrived at school and Ruby walked into her form room, Mrs Drisco did not look especially happy to see her.

Ruby Redfort and Mrs Drisco were never going to see eye to eye on anything. Mrs Drisco did not like Ruby's smart-mouthed attitude and Ruby was not a fan of Mrs Drisco's pettiness.

'Just because you have been away at "camp",' began Mrs Drisco, 'does not mean I won't expect your school work to be in on time.'

'I didn't expect you wouldn't,' said Ruby.

'Good,' said Mrs Drisco, 'so I will expect it before the end of term.'

'If you want to, you can expect it by Wednesday,' said Ruby.

The promise of getting Ruby's homework three weeks early did not, as one might logically expect, make Mrs Drisco happy. In fact, it had precisely the opposite effect. She felt undermined by Ruby's ability to actually succeed in the task set.

The task was meant to be impossible, and here was Ruby once again challenging her authority by succeeding.

'Well,' said Mrs Drisco, 'it sounds like maybe you need stretching.'

'Sounds painful,' said Ruby.

Mrs Drisco's eyes narrowed. 'I will sign you up for the school Christmas show. I'm sure we would all adore to have you entertain us.'

The school Christmas show was Ruby's idea of extreme humiliation. There was no way she was going to embarrass herself by stepping up on that stage and tap-dancing or performing some lame magic trick. But her reply was restrained.

'Mrs Drisco, I would like nothing better than to be a performing monkey, but I'm afraid my optometrist simply won't allow it.'

'Really?' said her teacher. 'And why would that be?'

'I have this condition,' explained Ruby. 'I'm sure you understand.'

'And I'm sure you'll understand that without a note explaining your condition it will be impossible for me to take your word for it.' Mrs Drisco flashed a tight smile.

'He thought you might say that,' said Ruby, rummaging in her satchel, 'which is why I took the precaution of bringing this with me.' She handed a piece of white letter-headed paper to Mrs Drisco, who reluctantly took it.

DEAR MRS DRISCO,

I AM WRITING TO INFORM YOU THAT MS RUBY REDFORT SUFFERS FROM A CONDITION KNOWN AS THE OPHTHALMIC JOGGLE. THIS CONDITION PREVENTS HER FROM DANCING (PARTICULARLY TAP), SINGING, RECITING, JUGGLING, OR INDEED STANDING ON STAGE IN FRONT OF ANY LARGE, MEDIUM OR SMALL GATHERING OF PEOPLE WHILE LIGHTS ARE TRAINED ON HER.

I TRUST, NAY, INSIST, THAT SHE SHOULD NOT BE EXPOSED TO ANY OF THE ABOVE ACTIVITIES. I AM SURE I NEED NOT EXPLAIN THE CONSEQUENCES TO A PERSON OF YOUR STATURE AND INTELLECT, NOR

SHOULD I WANT TO MAKE REFERENCE TO THE LIABILITY ISSUES YOUR
SCHOOL WOULD BE SUBJECT TO.

YOURS SINCERELY,

E.F.P. TOZLPED

Mrs Drisco had never heard of ophthalmic joggle and she felt
she'd been in the teaching profession long enough to have heard
pretty much every classroom excuse and medical condition.
There was something about the name of this optometrist that
made her uneasy but she could not put her finger on what it was.
So Mrs Drisco gave another tight smile and said, 'fine,' in a tone
which suggested things were not fine.

En route to class, Mouse and Ruby passed Vapona Begwell
coming the other way. Mouse was surprised when Vapona and
Ruby did not exchange their usual insults of *bozo* and *dork-squirt*,
but instead sort of nodded at each other. It was the nod of mutual
respect – grudging, but respect nonetheless.

Mouse looked at her friend. 'How did you two end up so
close?'

'We came to an understanding,' said Ruby, without
elaborating further.

Only *Clancy* knew the *whole* story. It all had to do with Ruby
keeping her mouth shut when it really counted, and Vapona
repaying the favour by stepping in on Ruby's behalf and holding
the baby, quite literally as it happened. It did not make these old
enemies friends, but for now at least they were not looking to

trip each other up – a truce of sorts.

At recess Del was looking pretty excited.

'Are you coming snurfing?'* she asked.

'You mean strap a wooden board to my feet and head on down a snow-covered mountain? You have to be kidding,' said Clancy.

'You *skateboard*,' argued Del. 'What's the big difference?'

'What, are you nuts?' said Clancy. 'Skateboarding takes place on a sidewalk. Snurfing is about throwing yourself down a perilous incline, feet tied to a plank of wood, no sticks, no nothing.'

'Suit yourself,' said Del. 'But I tell you, this is gonna become a thing.'

'It *is* a thing,' said Clancy.

'Yeah, but I'm telling you it's gonna become a *big* thing,' said Del.

'I don't doubt it,' agreed Clancy. 'There's no end to what dumb things people will decide to do, but it doesn't mean I wanna join in.'

'Your sister Minny's got a snurferboard,' said Del.

'A perfect example to illustrate my point,' said Clancy. 'Just because Minny is willing to throw herself from a cliff with some plank tied to her shoes, doesn't make it a good idea. Most things Minny recommends are *not* great ideas and should on the whole be avoided.'

'You need to lighten up,' said Del.

'I also need my head to remain attached to my body,' said Clancy, 'which is why you are not getting me snurfing.'

'You can quit discussing it because no one's going snurfing anyway,' said Ruby.

'Whaddaya mean?' said Del. 'I'm going even if that chicken liver doesn't have the guts for it.'

'Not without any snow you're not,' said Ruby.

'Well, duh,' said Del.

'So you're not going today is what I'm saying.'

'You're crazy,' said Del, 'it's four inches deep already.'

But sure enough, by the time the clock struck noon it was all gone, barely a flake on the ground.

'How did you know that was going to happen?' asked Del.

'I have my sources,' said Ruby.

Chapter 15.
Thirty Minutes of Murder

RUBY ARRIVED HOME THAT AFTERNOON to find a pale pink bike to the right of the front steps next to the bamboo. She didn't touch it, she just looked at it.

'Pink?' she said out loud. 'Pastel pink? Why in darn it did he make it pink?'

She typed a message into the Escape Watch; a very short message for Hal:

PINK?!

Ruby went into the house, slammed the front door and started up the stairs.

'Where are *you* off to at such a lick?' called Mrs Digby.

'My room!' shouted Ruby.

'If you're planning to watch TV then make it Channel 44 or Channel 17.'

'Why?' said Ruby.

'You need to swot up on horror,' said Mrs Digby.

'Swot up on what?' asked Ruby.

'Or crime,' said Mrs Digby.

'Again, why?' said Ruby. She turned, walked back down the stairs and stood in the kitchen doorway.

'We got a date,' said the housekeeper, pulling an envelope from her apron pocket and handing it to Ruby.

'What's this?' asked Ruby.

Mrs Digby looked heavenwards. 'Well, you're not going to know unless you open it, child.'

Ruby pulled out a letter. On it was typed the following,

Dear MRS MYRTLE DIGBY,

It is our great pleasure to inform you that you have been successful in your application to appear on the Crime Time quiz show, THIRTY MINUTES OF MURDER. We look forward to seeing you and your nominated TMOM partner, MISS R REDFORT in JANUARY 1974 (exact date to be confirmed). Recording will take place at 11 AM. Please arrive four hours before to ensure enough time for hair and make-up.

Yours sincerely,
PERRY FARRELL,
PRODUCTION CO-ORDINATOR.

Coffee and light lunch will be provided. Please state any scalp and skin product allergies and food intolerances if relevant.

Thirty Minutes of Murder was a film general knowledge show aimed at the older television viewer. All the questions related to the movies of yesteryear, all in the horror, thriller or crime genre.

Ruby looked up at Mrs Digby. 'So you have basically signed me up for a quiz show.'

'That's about the size of it.'

'They need *four hours* to do our hair and make-up? *Four hours!*'

'Is that all you have to say? I thought you'd be tickled,' said Mrs Digby.

'Tickled' was not the word Ruby would have used, but she didn't want to rain on the old lady's parade so instead just said, 'OK, I'll go watch something horrifying.'

Before Ruby had reached the stairs, the telephone began to ring. She picked up.

'Redfort mad house, if we seem sane to you then you're probably crazy!'

'Ahh... Ruby?'

'Hey, Dad.'

'Guten abend.'

'Are you sure about that?'

'What are you saying?'

'My point exactly.'

'You've lost me.'

'Dad, you're speaking German.'

'Oh yes, that's right,' came her mother's voice. 'Brant, wrong lingo, we're in France.'

'Bonne nuit,' said her father.

'Close enough,' said Ruby.

'We're just about to hit la ville,' said her mother.

'When are you coming home?' asked Ruby.

'Tout alors!' said her mother.

'What's that supposed to mean? You're not making any sense,' said Ruby.

'It's your father's translation guide; it doesn't work.'

'I think you must be on the wrong page,' said Ruby.

'We'll call back when we have more vocab,' said her mother. 'Bye, bye, bye.'

Ten minutes later, Ruby set down her glass of banana milk, plonked herself in the beanbag and flicked on the little TV that sat there on the shelf in between her general knowledge books and the lobster phone.

Channel 16 was showing a re-run of a not so funny sit-com. And on Channel 17 *What's Your Poison?* was playing. She watched for a minute.

Greg Valence, the quiz master, asked: 'What venom will cause the victim to repeatedly convulse?'

RUBY: *'Tityus serrulatus scorpion.'*

GREG VALENCE: *'Which animal is widely considered the most dangerous animal in the world?'*

RUBY: *'The golden poison dart frog.'*

GREG VALENCE: *'There's a bonus point if you can tell me under what circumstances a poison dart frog can be handled without using gloves.'*

RUBY: *'When it's in captivity.'*

The contestant did not know this unusual and interesting fact – that the frog's toxicity came from its natural diet of insects. Once out of the wild it no longer posed a threat. *If that's what a change of diet can do to you, maybe I should consider it,* thought Ruby.

She picked up the remote and clicked on, leaving the quiz master to his unchallenging quiz questions. She kept clicking until she came to Channel 44. Currently playing was a movie she didn't recognise. She was fairly certain that it was not one she had watched before. She had entered the story as it was reaching its final scenes; a young woman was tiptoeing down a very grand stone staircase. In the hallway was a shadow of a hand, the fingers long and bony; the shadow reached out to touch the woman's shadow.

The woman, unaware that she had company, walked into a dimly lit drawing room and began frantically searching the desk for something, pulling open drawers and rifling through the contents as if her life depended on it. And maybe it did, because when she found a little box with an amulet in it she sank to her knees and sobbed theatrical sobs. The actress had real screen presence and though the film was on the hammy side, Ruby found herself gripped. However, it was only when the woman caught sight of the figure, an elderly vampire, and the camera zoomed in close on her terror-stricken face that Ruby knew that she had seen her somewhere before. The film reached its inevitable conclusion, and as was the custom with old movies, there was no credit roll, just two words: *The End.*

Before Ruby could begin to wonder *how* she knew this woman, so appeared the smiling face of another, this one elbow-deep in dishes and very happy about the washing-up liquid she had chosen to scrub them with.

Ruby took a look down the periscope, something she had constructed a long time ago so she could check out the to-ings and fro-ings in the kitchen. Mrs Digby wasn't there. So Ruby rang down to the housekeeper's apartment.

'Can't an old lady expect a little peace and quiet?' she complained.

'Are you watching TV?'

'Why shouldn't I be?'

'No reason, which channel?'

'Thirteen.'

'Oh.'

'Why?'

'I wanted to know what movie I just watched – you know, on Channel 44?'

'Ah, glad to hear you're studying. I'll look it up in the *Hound.*'

There was a lot of rustling of paper and then... '*The Shadow's*

Touch,' said Mrs Digby.

'Who was the actress?' asked Ruby.

'It's pitiful you don't know,' said the housekeeper. 'It's a fearful gap in your movie knowledge. I thought you took an interest in horror. You're going to have to pull your socks up or we'll never win the big cheque.'

'*So* I'm taking an interest; just give me her name and I'll look her up.'

'Marnie Novak,' said Mrs Digby. 'Now I gotta go cos the commercials are over and the TV bingo is just about to start again.'

If Ruby had taken anything on board during her thirteen years of life, it was *never interrupt Mrs Digby if she was watching TV bingo.*

Ruby went over to her bookshelves and pulled out the volumes relating to film. She had around forty, and they covered various genres of movie, some dedicated to particular directors or studios, others to actors and movie stars, and quite a lot of them were technical: books on props, sets, make-up and cinematography. It was in one rather dense book titled *Stars of the B Screen* that Ruby came face to face with the woman who had caused her so many sleepless nights.

Marnie Novak *(formerly, Gretchen Ehrling).*

The name was familiar – horribly so. For though Ruby

had never actually *knowingly* crossed paths with the woman who called herself 'Madame Ehrling', she knew someone who had, a person who hadn't lived to tell the tale. Agent Lopez had followed the woman to the Fountain Hotel in Everly, a town south of Twinford. There she had witnessed a meeting of sorts and managed to intercept a message intended for Ehrling's cohort. Unfortunately Lopez had been spotted – for that mistake she'd paid with her life.

The FBI had found no recent picture of Ehrling, unless one counted the image caught on the Twinford City Bank security camera, her face obscured by a veiled hat. When they'd tried to trace her, they discovered that she had been dead for a number of years. So who was she and *why*, thought Ruby, *do I feel so sure I know her?*

As she stared at the film-still of the young movie actress, the answer came to her, the answer to the question: *where have I seen her before?*

Answer: *On Wolf Paw Mountain.* It was the eyes Ruby recognised; cold steel blue, the eyes of the Australian.

So Gretchen Ehrling reinvented herself as Novak, and Novak had gone to the City Bank playing the part of a Madame Ehrling. It seemed likely that Madame Ehrling had been an old relative, now conveniently deceased.

Things were beginning to join up.

There was a brief paragraph on Marnie Novak; a few facts about her short-lived career and a list of some of the films she'd appeared in, most of them thrillers and horror movies.

Marnie Novak had been set for stardom. Regarded as a great talent, she was the protégée of notorious film director...

And then nothing. The following page was missing.

Ruby leafed through the book. *Where is it?*

And then she remembered what Mrs Digby had said about Baby Lemon.

'Darn that baby,' she muttered.

The page had been torn out and very possibly *eaten* so if Ruby wanted to discover anything further about this killer actress then she was going to need to pop to the library.

Chapter 16.
Look under V

RUBY WAS JUST PULLING ON HER COAT, having decided to try Penny Books rather than head across town to the City Library, when she received a phone call from Red.

'Rube, I'm really sorry to do this, but I've got a bit of an emergency here... you see, my laces were undone and I kinda tripped and sorta sat on my brother's guitar and he needs it tonight, but you know I sorta feel I should fix the situation before I tell him and that's why I wondered, kinda hoped you wouldn't mind if I told him he could borrow yours? It's a lot to ask, I know... oh, by the way it's me, Red.'

'Hey, Red.'

'I feel really bad about asking you, you can say no, I mean I haven't forgotten what happened to your violin – I mean I realise I owe you a new one and believe me, I *am* saving.'

'Don't give it a second thought,' said Ruby. 'Who hasn't sat on a violin or a guitar at some point in their life?'

'Thanks Ruby, you're a lifesaver. I'll come and pick it up,' said Red.

It was just at that moment that Ruby was sure she heard a click on the line, like someone was listening to her call – not someone *in* the house, Ruby had her own phone line so that wasn't possible. No: if she was right, then she was being bugged.

'You know what, I'll bring it over,' said Ruby, and two minutes later she was out the door.

Ruby decided, seeing as how it was dark and no one would see the colour, this would be the perfect opportunity to try out the pink bike. Plus the hyper-speed booster would allow her to stay ahead of any danger she might encounter.

The bike, despite its pinkness, was very impressive. It took little effort to cycle up to Red's place in Silver Hills and Ruby arrived in no time.

'Boy, you were quick,' Red said, as she opened the door.

'Yeah, turns out my new bike is kinda speedy,' said Ruby. She looked around. 'So, your mom not home?'

'She's working late, she has this big movie – lots of costumes to design.'

'What kind of movie? Is it fantasy?'

'I'll say,' said Red. 'It's about these kids who morph into crocodiles. But it's the make-up artist who's got the real headache. I mean what does a croc-kid look like?'

Ruby shrugged. 'My guess would be: Archie Lemon.'

It was nice to have the chance to catch up with Red, for despite her proclivity for accidents and her unusual talent for flattening musical instruments, Red was a person who exuded calm. And right now calmness was something Ruby truly appreciated.

Jem, Red's brother, was grateful for the guitar.

'I owe you, Ruby,' he said.

'It's not an owing type of a thing,' said Ruby. 'You're welcome to hang on to it until you get a new one. I don't see myself strumming for the next few weeks.'

The three of them hung out for a while, talking about school and the upcoming holidays, who might be having a New Year's party, would Mrs Drisco ever think of retiring? That type of thing.

'She used to be *my* homeroom teacher,' said Jem, 'so you have my deepest sympathy – I spent a lot of time in detention.'

Finally, they came back to the subject of what on earth a croc-kid would look like.

'My mom told the make-up artist to go talk to Frederick,' said Red. 'If anyone's going to know how you make a kid look like a crocodile, it's going to be him.'

This immediately pinged an idea into Ruby's head. If anyone was going to have the skinny on Marnie Novak, it would be Frederick Lutz.

Frederick Lutz was a Hollywood make-up artist and a nice old man. He had fixed Ruby's face after she'd smashed it up when she and her skateboard had parted company – the resulting black eye had almost ruined her mother's dreams of a picture-perfect photo portrait. Frederick had saved the day with his make-up skills, and no one would ever have guessed that the girl in the picture had collided with a cop car not twenty-four hours earlier.

'Red, do you mind if I make a phone call?'

'Sure,' said Red. 'Why?'

'I'm thinking I might call in on Frederick Lutz,' said Ruby.

Red looked puzzled. 'Why, do *you* need to know what a croc-kid looks like?'

It wasn't much of a detour to get to Frederick Lutz's house. He lived on the edge of Silver Hills, at 119 Derilla Drive, and it was pretty much downhill all the way.

Ruby arrived as evening turned to night.

She rang the bell and when there was no answer she tried the door. It was open.

'Hello?' she called.

'Ruby! Is that you? Come on in.'

She found him sitting in his sunroom looking up through the glass at the stars, his dachshund Paullie on his lap.

'I could look at them forever,' said Frederick, still gazing up at the twinkling night.

'I don't think much of your security system,' said Ruby.

'What does an old guy like me need with a security system? Robbers have got no interest in me,' said Frederick. 'Besides, I got Paullie here.'

He stroked the dog's ears and the dachshund yawned.

Ruby doubted that Paullie was much of a deterrent to robbers, but then again she supposed Frederick was probably right, robbers *were* unlikely to give him the time of day.

'Want an old-fashioned lemon soda?' said Frederick, taking a can from his cooler box.

'Sure,' said Ruby.

He handed it to her.

'So,' said Lutz, 'what is it I can help you with?'

'I was wondering if you'd ever met an actress named Marnie Novak?' asked Ruby.

'Marnie Novak,' mused Frederick. 'Now that's a name I haven't heard in a long while.'

'You knew her?' asked Ruby.

'Oh yes, I knew her,' said Frederick. 'She was a good actress. On the brink of a glittering career, they said.'

'So... did she *not* have a glittering career?' asked Ruby.

'Can *you* name five films you've seen her in?' said Lutz.

Ruby shook her head. 'Actually, I've only seen *one* and I didn't even know her name until about two hours ago.'

'Which movie was it?' asked Frederick.

'*The Shadow's Touch*,' said Ruby, taking a big gulp of soda.

'Oh, that's a good one,' said Lutz. 'No one did horror like the Count.'

The next thing Ruby felt was soda shooting out of her nose.

'Are you OK, Ruby?' said Lutz.

It took Ruby a few seconds to get any words out.

'It sorta went down the wrong way,' she squeaked.

'You're telling me,' said Lutz.

Ruby mopped at her face with her sleeve. 'This Count, who, I mean... you did say Count, right?'

'Yes,' said Frederick. 'He was the director of *The Shadow's Touch*. Boy, was he a talent.'

'*Really*?' said Ruby. 'He was good?'

'Better than good, he was an artist,' said Lutz. He got to his feet. 'Wait there,' he said. He came back five minutes later with a large book, a sort of encyclopaedia of movie directors. 'Here,' he passed it to Ruby, 'you'll find him in that.'

Ruby began flipping through the pages, scanning the Cs.

Clooning...

Coburn...

Coswell...

'He doesn't seem to be here,' said Ruby.

'Of course he's there,' said Lutz, leaning in. 'Well, you're looking under C, that's your problem. What you need to do is look under V.'

'V?'

'V for Von Leyden,' said Lutz. 'Victor von Leyden.'

Pause.

'What? You look like you've seen a ghost.'

'Not a ghost exactly,' said Ruby. 'More of a psycho.'

Chapter 17.
Evil all around

FREDERICK LUTZ WAS LOOKING AT RUBY with a concerned expression.

'Are you quite all right there?' he asked. 'You've gone pale.'

'Too many late nights,' said Ruby.

'Maybe you should ease up on the horror movies,' suggested Frederick. 'They're probably giving you nightmares.'

'It's real life that gives me the nightmares,' said Ruby.

Frederick nodded. 'I know what you mean,' he said. 'There's been a lot of bad things in the news. That poor snake lady for one – imagine getting poisoned by a bouquet of flowers.'

'Yeah, that was creepy,' said Ruby. They were both silent for a moment and then she asked, 'So why *didn't* Marnie Novak go on to have a glittering career?'

'She got in the family way,' said Lutz. 'You know, pregnant.'

'So, what, she couldn't work?' asked Ruby.

'Wasn't allowed to work,' said Frederick. 'You got to remember these were old-fashioned times; people weren't very understanding when it came to unmarried mothers. The father was a big-shot movie producer, and a royal pain in the neck if you were unlucky enough to cross his path.'

'Who?' asked Ruby.

'George Katz,' said Frederick. 'Remember him?'

Ruby certainly did. George Katz had caused an awful lot of grief during his prosperous and happy life, mainly for the women he had dated.

'Why didn't he marry her?' asked Ruby. 'Didn't he love her?'

'Oh, love wasn't the problem,' said Lutz. 'The fact that he was already married was the problem. He didn't want his wife to get wind of what was going on because her daddy was a big-time studio exec, so it was all hushed up, Miss Novak lost her starlet status, and never worked again.'

'So the baby was nothing to do with Victor von Leyden? I mean there's no way it was his child?'

'No, that's a certainty,' said Frederick. 'Lorelei was not his daughter.'

'Then why did he give her his name?'

'That was a kindness to Marnie. He was very fond of Miss Novak: she had been his protégée. He tried to help, but it was too late, the cat was out of the bag, the studio didn't want a scandal. George Katz and his wife were a popular couple so they wanted Marnie out of the limelight and out of the movies.'

'So that was the end of her career?'

'As good as,' said Frederick. 'Victor remained close to Marnie, but no one would offer her work and so in the end she headed off to Australia in search of a new life.'

'With the baby?' asked Ruby.

'She took her along, but it didn't work out,' said Frederick. 'From what I heard Marnie became cruel, resentful of her. She told someone I used to work with back in the day that she blamed the child for the ruination of her life, said she couldn't abide to look at the girl.'

The story was getting more tragic by the minute and had one not known the awful deeds, the terrible crimes and cruelties, perpetrated by Marnie Novak and her daughter Lorelei, one might have felt great sympathy for them both.

'So what happened to her, the girl?' asked Ruby.

'Who really knows – my friend Reggie used to say that the only thing *that* little girl was interested in was greasepaint. Victor tried to make an actress of her, but she had zero talent for it.'

'But she liked getting herself made-up – like a theatre star?' asked Ruby.

'More than that. What she was really passionate about was special effects make-up,' said Frederick. 'She liked inventing characters and disguising herself, playing tricks on people, pretty mean tricks too.' He shook his head. 'But she wasn't an actress, more likely to become a con-woman than an actress.'

'Who taught her to do that? The disguises, I mean.'

'Victor, of course,' said Lutz. 'No one did theatrical disguise like "Count von Viscount". He was famous for it. Always had kids hanging around wanting to learn how to transform themselves.'

'Where did he get the nickname from?' asked Ruby.

'Oh, *that*, that came from all these gothic horror movies he made – and the fact that he dressed a bit like Dracula, elegant style but creepy, all black with cravat and handkerchiefs, an old-fashioned pocket watch and if you ever heard him speak, well, he kinda sounded a lot like Dracula too.'

Ruby did not need reminding of the quality of the voice that whispered to her from her nightmares.

'I'm telling you,' said Frederick, 'fit him with a pair of fangs and you'd believe in vampires for sure. So they called him the Count von Leyden then Count von Victor and later the Count von Viscount and finally just the Count – none of it was meant kindly.'

'So that was his thing, creating characters?'

'He was one of the best, I have to admit. He pioneered a way of changing faces and voices like I have never seen from that day to this. He kept his secret – never told another person in the industry just how he did it – but everyone suspected it was really down to Homer. It was likely him who came up with it.'

'Who was Homer?' asked Ruby.

'A clever fellow Victor worked with in the early days. They were a team: Homer the illusionist and inventor, and Victor the creative – quite a duo.'

'So you admired them?'

Frederick's expression turned serious. 'I admired Homer – he was always a good man. He became nervous when he saw how a couple of Victor's protégés were using their skill in an ugly way; disguising themselves, conning people – Lorelei was the worst – anyway, it became nasty. So he ended up breaking their association.'

'What about you?' asked Ruby. 'What did you think?'

'I admired Victor's talent, but I had no liking for the man he became,' said Frederick. 'He began his career a reasonable enough fellow, but somewhere down the line things changed. He was shot through with something cruel.'

'So he gave up directing?' asked Ruby, though she knew the answer all too well.

'After Marnie, he lost heart they say, and with his protégée gone, he turned bitter, then he fell out with Homer, and there were rumours he left the country, went abroad somewhere.'

If only, thought Ruby.

'Here, take the book,' said Frederick. 'You can bring it back when you're done.'

She thanked him, clipped it onto her bike rack and rode off into the dark.

Ruby was free-wheeling slowly down Derilla Drive when she thought she heard the sound of ringing. Quiet at first, but getting louder. There wasn't a lot of activity in Derilla Drive, not a soul around on this chilly evening, but somewhere a telephone was ringing.

She slowed.

A blue metal payphone.

She rested her bike on the lamppost and walked over to the phone, waited a second or two before picking up.

'Hello?' she said.

'Been doing your homework, Ms Redfort?'

A chill spread through Ruby that had nothing to do with the light snow that was falling, or the north wind that was blowing.

It had everything to do with the voice in her ear.

She looked around – she was utterly alone, a girl illuminated by a single street lamp.

'How did you... how do you...' she stammered, 'how...'

'How do I know where you are? Is that what you want to know? I know lots of things you don't know,' said the voice, '*things* you need to know if you are planning on making it past New Year.'

'What are you say—' began Ruby.

'You're tangled in a web, Ms Redfort, and the spider's watching you, waiting... ready to wind you in.'

'So why don't you just come out and meet me face to face?'.

'Oh, I don't mean *me*,' said the Count. 'I'm not the spider, I'm a pussycat compared to this individual.' He paused before adding, 'A word of advice from one adversary to another – watch your back, Ms Redfort, there's evil all around.'

Ruby felt her legs buckle under her and the receiver slip from her grasp. She lay there watching as it swung back and forth, the sound as it knocked against the phone box like some dull bell of doom.

**Lenny Rivers
was surprised...**

... when the hospital called to tell him that the guy he had found lying next to the road, the guy he had thought was just a few breaths away from his last, was now conscious and breathing unassisted.

'He's out of danger?' asked Lenny. It was kind of hard to believe, this man he had seen lying there bleeding on the tarmac, this man who looked like his final minutes were ticking past, was off the critical list?

'He's actually walking,' said the nurse. 'A little unsteady, but he's on the move.'

'Can I pay him a visit?' asked Lenny. 'I'd like to shake the hand of a guy who returned from the dead.'

'We'd be glad if you would; no one else has been in to see him and he can't remember a thing before the accident.'

Lenny grabbed his coat and hopped into his truck. He was curious to talk to this miracle guy, this Morgan Loveday.

But it wasn't to be. When he arrived at Morgan's room he found the bed empty and no sign of the man who had lain in it.

Chapter 18.
Location unknown

RUBY AND CLANCY WERE SITTING IN THEIR FORM ROOM, waiting for Mrs Drisco to return from the principal's office. She had felt it necessary to escort Dillon Flannigan to Principal Levine that morning because she'd had it 'up to here' with his 'utter disregard for school rules'. No one was sure what the misdemeanour was, but it had certainly riled Mrs Drisco, who was very keen on rules.

'So how come you were visiting Frederick Lutz?' asked Clancy.

'Well, it all has to do with Mrs Digby. You see, I was watching TV last night when onto the screen walks someone I know.'

'Really? What kinda someone? Someone like a friend? Or someone like an acquaintance?'

'Neither,' said Ruby. 'It concerns a someone I've met, but not a someone I particularly want to meet again, though knowing my luck I bet you anything I'm going to run into her at any minute.'

'If you're talking about Vapona Begwell then I can tell you with a total certainty you're going to see her today; she's put her name down for the carolling.'

Ruby made a face. 'Jeepers,' she said, 'what's *that* gonna sound like?'

'She's trying to get out of litter-picking duty – it's the carol thing or a lot of garbage.'

'Oh.'

'So I take it, it wasn't Bugwart you saw on TV?'

'No, not her.'

'So who?'

'You don't want to guess?'

Clancy made a face. 'Could you just *tell* me before I fall asleep? I mean the suspense is just about killing me?'

'Well, *there's* a coincidence,' said Ruby. 'Cos this is the sort of lady who might just be able to arrange a killing.'

'Who?' asked Clancy.

'The Australian,' said Ruby.

The blood instantly drained from Clancy's face. 'Why did you have to mention her?' he said.

'You *asked*,' said Ruby.

'Yeah, but I didn't think you were going to actually say *her*.' He gulped. 'I don't like thinking about that evil-doer. What was she doing on the news anyhow?'

'I didn't say she was on the news,' said Ruby. 'It's a lot more interesting than the *news*.'

Ruby filled Clancy in on everything she'd learned about Marnie Novak and her association with the Count.

'The studio fired her when they discovered she was in the family way.'

Clancy looked blank.

'Having a b-a-b-y.'

'Oh,' said Clancy. 'What's the deal with that? Why wasn't she allowed to have a child?'

'Wasn't married, but it seems the father was – it could have been quite the scandal if it hadn't been hushed up. These were old-fashioned times, my friend – a baby with a married man was not good for her box-office ratings. Plus she wasn't the right shape for the part – a pregnant vampire wasn't what the studio was after.'

'Don't tell me, this baby turns out to be Lorelei?'

'Ping! Give that kid a prize.'

Mrs Drisco walked in. 'Pop quiz, everyone,' she said. 'Pens out, please. I'll be handing out a test.'

'So I haven't told you the creepiest bit,' whispered Ruby as Mrs Drisco walked round the class giving out papers, her tone anxious.

'What creepiest bit?' asked Clancy. He looked like he might be on the verge of flapping.

'I don't want any conferring,' said Mrs Drisco, shooting a look at Clancy.

'The phone call,' whispered Ruby. 'I had a phone call from the Count.'

Clancy began to flap. 'He called you at home?' he said.

'No, on a payphone,' said Ruby.

'What payphone?' asked Clancy.

'The one on Derilla,' said Ruby. 'I was freewheeling down the hill when this payphone began to ring and when I picked up guess who was on the end of the line.'

'But that's worse than him calling you from home,' said Clancy. 'That means he's been watching you.'

Ruby shivered. 'That's what I thought.'

'Ruby Redfort!' said Mrs Drisco. 'I said no conferring! I've got my beady eyes on you.'

You're not the only one, thought Ruby.

When Ruby and Clancy walked up the steps to her house, she noticed that the pastel-pink bike had gone. Had Hal taken it? He hadn't said anything about picking it up. Had someone else come into the Redfort drive and made off with it? *Unlikely – who would want a pastel-pink bike?* she thought.

After a brief chat with Mrs Digby, they went on up to the top of the house carrying a tray laden with two Digby club sandwiches, a half-dozen cookies and a carton of banana milk. Mrs Digby was a big believer in keeping one's strength up.

'You need brain food,' she said. Clancy wasn't sure any of the food on the tray was 'brain food', but he wasn't complaining.

Clancy was struggling with his French homework, and Ruby, she was trying to figure out exactly where the Prism Vault might be.

She had a map spread out on the floor and she was peering at it through a large magnifying glass.

'What are you doing?' asked Clancy.

'Looking for water,' replied Ruby.

'Excuse me?' said Clancy.

'I'm trying to figure out where the Prism Vault is located.'

'Did you say prison vault?'

'Prism,' said Ruby, 'as in light refractor.'

Clancy was still looking confused.

'Look, all you gotta know is that there is this big vault which holds all the archive files relating to Spectrum missions. I want to get in to learn what I can about Bradley Baker and LB. It's called the Prism Vault, I guess, because Spectrum is all about colour, which is made of light, and a prism is something that breaks light into its different colours, or bends its path.'

'What, like the new telescope?' asked Clancy.

'What did you say?'

'The space telescope,' said Clancy. 'They had it on the news last night – you didn't catch it?'

'I was all tied up talking to psychopaths on payphones.'

'Oh yeah,' said Clancy, 'I forgot. Anyway, this guy was explaining how a telescope is basically like this giant prism made of all these folding mirrors that focus light onto a receiver. It was actually kind of interesting.'

Ruby was looking at Clancy with that expression that always made him mad.

'What?' he said.

'So where is this telescope?' she asked.

'Meteor Island,' said Clancy. 'At the Observatory.'

'Oh yeah, that's right.' She remembered now. 'The kid at the planetarium mentioned it.'

'Do you mind letting me in on whatever it is you have just decided you know?'

She chewed her pencil. She was thinking. What she was thinking was, could this be the place Blacker was talking about?

The Observatory was on a small island, more like a large rock really, so you'd need flippers and a wet suit to get there. A helicopter was out of the question and a boat probably not a good idea. Ruby figured Spectrum would be watching the sea and would intercept any vessel coming that way.

Clancy clicked his fingers in front of her face.

'Hey! Earth to Mars, come in Mars.'

'Clance, I think you just solved it.'

'I did?' said Clancy. He looked pleased.

'I think that's where it could be,' she said, thumping him on the arm.

'Oh great,' said Clancy. 'What exactly are we talking about?'

'The Prism Vault. I think it could be on Meteor Island underneath the Observatory.'

'Oh,' said Clancy, 'so now what?'

'I'm going to check it out, of course.'

'Of course you are – and do you have clearance to do that?'

She rolled her eyes. 'It's the place Spectrum keep all the most secret of secret documents, the highly restricted files. The ones no one is meant to see, so that would be "no".'

'So you're going to break in?'

'That's my plan.'

Clancy looked at her. 'Now that is a truly bad idea.'

'Well,' said Ruby, 'that's tough because it's the only one I got.'

'What about the codes? There's no point breaking into a restricted file vault if you can't open the files.'

'True.' She sighed, paused and said, 'I'm pretty sure I know a couple of them; it's the entry code I'm truly stuck on, but I guess I'll just have to figure it out.'

Clancy looked at her. 'Don't take this the wrong way, but I'm praying you don't.'

Meanwhile,
some thirty-five
years earlier...

...the kid was eight years old and living in the suburbs of Colwin City when, while breakfasting on cereal, they noticed an unusual advert on the back of the milk carton. It seemed to be a competition with big prize money; reading between the lines, very big prize money – this was no simple brainteaser.

The kid from Colwin City continued to scoop cereal loops while studying the carton. There was definitely something odd about this particular competition; for one thing, it didn't seem like it was really a competition and for another it didn't seem like it was aimed at the average child. You would have to be some kind of genius to see that this was not so much a word search puzzle as it was a code, and an even bigger genius to figure how to crack it. But that was OK, because the Colwin City kid was both of those things.

Once solved, it was plain to see that it was actually an application form for what seemed like a very exciting future. However, there was a problem. Casey was not eligible for a place on this programme, that was stated clearly in **bold**. That seemed wrong to Casey, unfair and stupid. When were things ever going to change? It was 1938, for goodness' sake!

Then an idea grew: break the rules.

The kid emptied the milk carton, washed it, cut out the coupon, filled in the blanks. The small print made clear that a birth certificate was required, so the kid fetched it from the large oak desk that stood in the study. Before sliding this into an envelope along with the coupon, the Colwin City kid made one very simple alteration to the document. That done, the envelope was addressed and mailed.

Chapter 19.
Minus 10

RUBY LOOKED AT THE CLOCK: it was 2.57am and she was still wide awake, or at least her brain was. Her body felt like it could do with a whole lot more lying down. But by the time the clock ticked round to 3.33am, Ruby gave up arguing with herself and crawled out of bed. She figured she might as well get dressed since there was little likelihood of sleep coming her way. Once clothed, she tiptoed downstairs to the kitchen, turning on the low light which hung over the table so that it was bathed in a warm orange glow. She took a glass from the cupboard, walked to the refrigerator and searched around before pulling out a carton of banana milk. She poured herself a glass, took a swig, sat back in one of the kitchen chairs, and stared out at the snow flurry on the other side of the window.

How to get hold of the Prism Vault entry code? She was still sitting there when a slice of toast popped up from the toaster. Sort of surprising, since she hadn't actually dropped any bread into the little silver kitchen appliance.

She retrieved the slice and read it:

Picking you up in 20.
Hitch

Ruby climbed into the silver convertible at precisely 4am and they drove at great speed north out of town.

'Is it really necessary to leave so early?' yawned Ruby.

'Is it early, or is it just very late?' said Hitch.

'It's early,' said Ruby. 'I know it's early because I was in my pyjamas twenty minutes ago, the sun hasn't come up and the hands on that clock of yours haven't crawled past the six.'

'There's breakfast in the glove compartment, if that helps,' said Hitch.

Ruby shook her head. 'I'm not sure I can eat. My teeth are still asleep.'

When Hitch and Ruby arrived, they were greeted by two familiar faces, Sam Colt and Agent Kekoa. Ruby's heart sank, not because she had anything against these two individuals, in fact she liked them a lot; it was what they represented that was the problem. Sam Colt was a survivalist and survival trainer, and Kekoa was the Spectrum dive instructor. This meant that today was going to be wet and very cold.

'Welcome to extreme elements survival,' said Sam.

'Boy, do I not like the sound of that,' said Ruby.

'That's kind of the point, no one does,' said Sam. 'But with the weather and the storms coming, Hitch here thought it would be a good idea if you took part.'

'Gee, thanks Hitch,' said Ruby.

'Don't mention it,' said Hitch.

There were seven other trainees there, and Ruby was glad to see Kip Holbrook was one of them. The location was up at Big Sky Lake, which was frozen solid.

'Are you thinking what I'm thinking?' muttered Holbrook.

'Not unless you're thinking about finding the first bus out of here,' hissed Ruby.

The first part of the training was easy. Sam Colt taught them some key cold-weather concepts and none of them involved taking a dip in an icy lake. But quite a lot of what he said involved making sure to keep dry.

'Hypothermia is the number one killer of people in the outdoors,' said Colt. 'As the old saying goes, "Stay Dry and Stay Alive". So seeing as how I'm urging you to keep dry, you're probably wondering where the lake comes in, right?'

Ruby wasn't actually wondering this; she was pretty sure she knew how the lake was going to fit into this scenario.

'Well, let's go take a look,' he said, and the eight trainees all followed him out onto the ice.

Two twenty-four-inch holes had been cut in the lake's surface, approximately twelve yards apart.

'First of all, we're going to practise getting a feel for the temperature of the water.'

'I don't like where this is going,' whispered Kip Holbrook.

'To begin with,' said Sam, 'you're all going to have a go at swimming from point A to B, under the ice, but with a line secured around you so there's no chance of you losing your way.'

Ruby was faintly reassured by this news. She might end up frozen to death, but at least they would find her body.

'When you hit cold water, your body's going to do something very unhelpful,' continued Colt. 'It's called the "torso reflex". Basically, the shock of the cold is going to make you breathe in. That's bad. That will get you drowned. So brace, and hold your chest still.'

He went through the rest of the principles of surviving a fall through the ice:

'RELAX your body. Conserve energy. Cold shock will set in quicker if you move around too much.

'FOCUS on getting out as quickly as possible without too much splashing around. The longer you stay in the water, the more likely you are to die.'

It was as unpleasant as Ruby had feared, but she did it and that was something. The next exercise made the previous one seem easy. This time it was all about finding one's way out of the ice without there being any pre-cut hole.

'OK, so the ideal thing to do if you fall through ice is to look for the hole that landed you in this situation. If you can climb out of the same hole you originally fell in through, you can be reasonably sure that the edges are likely to support your weight while you climb on out. But what I am going to teach you is how to find your way out of an ice-covered lake or river if you *cannot* find your original entry point. LOOK for changes of colour in the ice to find a weaker point. These will show up as lighter in colour. When you find one, you need to smash through it. If you're lucky, you'll have a suitable tool provided by Spectrum, but if not, you'll need to use your initiative. Once you have broken through the surface, you need to GET HORIZONTAL: slide your arms full length onto the ice then kick your legs like a seal to propel yourself out. Then you need to ROLL until you get to firmer ice or ground. The key is to get out of the water ASAP.'

Ruby was relieved to see both Hitch and Kekoa clad in wetsuits and in the water.

'At least there's some chance I might get out of this lake alive,' she muttered.

She let her body sink in through the hole.

The cold felt like a punch to the chest.

Relax, she thought.

She swam away from the entry point and began searching for a place to break through.

Focus, she thought.

Around her was all blue and white, and for a moment she had no idea where was up and where was down.

Don't panic, she thought. **RULE 19: PANIC WILL FREEZE YOUR BRAIN.**

Holding her breath, she turned in the water, and saw a

rounder, lighter patch to the left and above. Amazed by how hard it was to move with her clothes soaked and the cold in her bones, she made it through and without help from Hitch or Kekoa.

There was a welcome interval where the recruits dried off and warmed up and every single one of them hoped that that would be it as far as cold water survival was concerned. But as it turned out they were just getting started.

The second half of the training took place at the aptly named Desolate Cove, a windy curve of grey pebble beach.

Here they were faced with a whole new set of problems.

Survival in the ocean was a very different challenge: a vast expanse of moving water, crashing waves, currents and rip tides.

As the day was coming to a close, Ruby saw a figure picking his way across the beach. It was Froghorn. He didn't look too happy to be there. He was trundling a small cart about the size of a wheelbarrow. He was wrapped up warm against the chill; he had really gone to town on the cold weather gear.

'What a drip,' muttered Ruby.

'Hey kid,' called Hitch. 'I have to get back to HQ. So when training's over you can get a lift back with the other trainees. Can I trust you to do the right thing and get home safe?'

'Of course,' said Ruby.

'See you later then,' he said. She watched as Hitch walked over to speak to Froghorn. They talked together for a few minutes, all perfectly fine until Hitch appeared to notice something – perhaps it was to do with Froghorn's attire, it was hard to say from this distance but Ruby recognised the subtle change in Hitch's body language and knew he was not happy, not happy at all. He walked off to the Spectrum tailer while Kekoa briefed the trainees on the equipment they were about to be issued.

Froghorn's job was to sign out the kit to each of the trainees.

Today's items came in a neat little bag, light in weight.

The first was a breathing band, not unlike the breathing buckle Ruby had once acquired from the gadget room, though this device looked a little more up-to-date than that one. It was worn around the wrist and when one needed air it could be pressed to the mouth so you could draw in oxygen. It was intended for emergencies – the hope was that it would buy you just enough time to get you out of a bad situation.

'Use it only when you really, really have to,' warned Kekoa. 'Once the five minutes are through, that's it.'

The second item got *everyone* talking.

'What's this?' asked Lowe.

'That,' said Kekoa, 'is a Superskin. It keeps you warm in cold water and aids swimming. You'll find you move significantly faster, particularly under the surface. The suit will keep you totally dry, but the truly remarkable thing about it is that once you step from the water it will shed every drop within a matter of seconds. You need to take it back home with you and practise getting into it – it's not easy.'

Ruby looked inside the little zip-lock bag. 'So *that's* a Superskin.'

As they trooped back up the beach a quarter-mile on from Desolate Cove, Ruby noticed something written there in the sand. Four words:

L O O K   T O   T H E   S T A R S

The stars were indeed beginning to twinkle and as she gazed on them so she caught sight of the Observatory, perched as it was on Meteor Island. Stars were so often used to point the way, to navigate. *Could it be*, thought Ruby, *that the stars hold an even bigger secret? Musca*, she thought, *the fly constellation.*

If she looked for *those* stars then would she find her way?

**Two months after the
letter was mailed...**

...the kid from Colwin City received a reply in the form of a single line of gibberish. Once deciphered it told of a location. So, wasting no time, a ticket was purchased for the nine hundred and twenty mile bus ride to reach not an address, but a manhole cover. One thing this kid knew for a definite was that even crawling down a drain was preferable to living one more day in the suburbs of Colwin City, and so down the kid went.

The ninety-nine-second test completed, the kid from Colwin City was inducted into the Spectrum 8 JSRP.

No one doubted this kid's brain. 'A phenomenal mind,' they all agreed. 'Aced every one of the junior agent tests.' 'The smartest of them all.' Well, almost.

They said, 'You pass the big one and there's no looking back – make the top eight and your future's Spectrum.'

That sounded good. The life of a secret agent made sense like no other life could.

The Colwin City kid felt good, good enough to raise a smile, a rare occurrence indeed.

'You know,' said the test agent, 'I think one day you might even be up there with Bradley Baker.'

The kid from Colwin City felt a sudden jolt, an inexplicable pain.

Who was Bradley Baker?

The training officer continued to drone on about this agent rival.

'Baker was our first junior recruit, joined when he was just seven, *but now look at him, thirteen and going places. If you get close to being as good as him, we'll give you a medal.'*

Mirror, mirror on the wall, who's the smartest of them all?

Not you, not the kid from Colwin City, some other kid's got that badge.

So how to wipe the smile off this Bradley Baker kid's face?

Chapter 20.
Hold your breath

SHE DIDN'T EXACTLY WANT TO HANG AROUND out there once everyone had gone home – she wasn't even sure that she was right about all this, she could have got the whole thing back to front and the wrong way up – but the way Ruby saw it, if there was a chance she was right, then it was a chance worth taking.

Getting herself into the Superskin was no small challenge. Neither Blacker nor Kekoa had been exaggerating: it was near impossible to put on and uncomfortable to wear. It sort of suckered to the skin, covering fingers, toes, neck and head. Only a small oval of the face was visible.

'Weird,' said Ruby, as she looked down at her feet, 'very weird.'

To make the vision stranger, the material the Superskin was made from resembled fish scales and the effect was not unlike a costume from the well-known B movie, *Return of the Fish-people*.

She hid her snow parka, boots and other clothing, concealing them behind a large rock. The water was black and uninviting, there was no moon tonight and all in all the cove was living up to its name.

Ruby walked to the water's edge and let the waves lap over her feet, and was surprised when she felt no chill at all. She stepped in farther – no, not cold.

'Pretty super,' she said, pulling down her facemask and diving into the slick black water. The Superskin seemed to aid swimming too, and she cut through the water with ease.

When she arrived at Meteor Island, she dived down under the water and searched for the hidden door. She was looking for a series of marks, or points, which might represent the constellation Musca – the sign of the fly.

It took her a few dives to spot it because she had been looking for something tiny, but the fly constellation was marked in fossils and spanned four feet across.

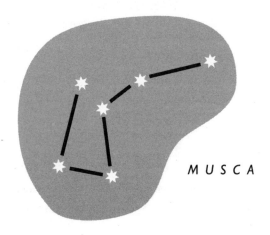

MUSCA

Now it was just a matter of getting in. She felt around, moving her palms along the rock.

At last she found what she was looking for: a panel of glass. When she put her hand on it, a word flashed up: Capricorn. Ruby pressed in the star points.

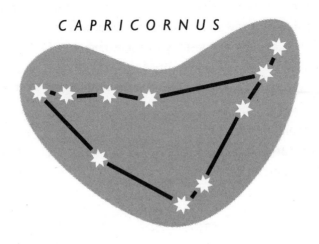

CAPRICORNUS

The screen flashed violet and a new message appeared:

ACCESS APPROVED.

The door slid open and in she swam. Now she found herself in a sort of twelve foot by twelve foot indoor pool, only it wasn't a pool, because pools don't have lids. What this was, was a cube full of water, and as she watched the door to the ocean slide shut, she realised she wasn't entirely sure how she was meant to get out. She swam carefully round and round the cube, searching for a clue which might lead to her release.

Previously, Ruby had only been able to hold her breath for just a second over one minute. Now she was able to do three times that – it wasn't exactly outstanding but it was enough. She found it just in time – a tiny, tiny image of a fly. Once it felt the pressure of her fingertip, the water drained out of the cube and a hatch in the lid slid open, allowing Ruby to climb up a metal ladder and out of the tank into another chamber. By the time she did so the Superskin had shed every drop of water and she was completely dry.

The space she was now in was not so different from the one she had just emerged from. It was the same shape, same size, same colour, but this time the door was *in front* of her, with an entry panel to one side.

HIGHLY SENSITIVE, RESTRICTED AUTHORITY.

There was one violet button next to it. This she pressed and up came a grid. She pictured the books on Froghorn's desk, the ones about error-correcting codes and data transmission.

What she was looking at was an error-correcting code, she could see that. But what kind? Ruby peered more closely at the black and white dots, counting them.

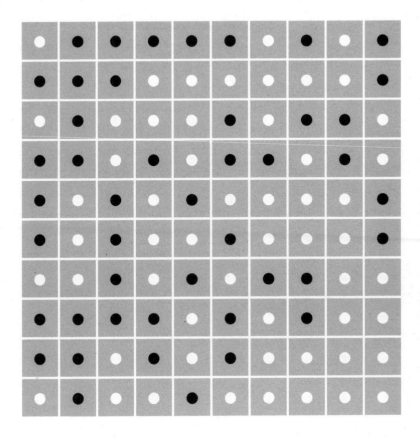

It didn't take her long to realise: it was a parity bit system and the final row and final column of each grid held the parity bits relating to the black dots, saying whether there was an even or odd number in the row or column.

But how to get a code from that...?

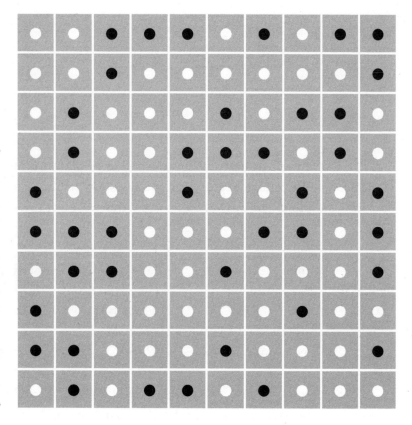

Then she saw it: one row and one column in each grid had the *wrong* parity bit. The fourth row and ninth column in the first, and in the second...

She typed four numbers into the keypad:

4912

A green light came on. And with a hiss, the door opened...

ACCESS APPROVED.
33 MINUTES GRANTED.

The whole room at first glance appeared to be plain white, white floor, white ceiling, white walls; another shiny white cube containing nothing. She ran her hand across the wall and as she did so the wall became colour.

Lots of colours, each one a narrow vertical oblong.

She held her hand on one – a dark red. There was a pneumatic hiss and the red oblong slid out from the wall. The file was labelled: THE NEW DELHI AFFAIR. She tried another, an olive green: THE ITALIAN CONUNDRUM.

Ruby looked around the room. *So where to find information on Baker?*

There were no letters, no numbers. She trailed her hand along part of the wall and watched the files turn from shades of green through yellow, through orange, and to red. They glowed for a few seconds before fading back to white wall.

A colour code?

On Froghorn's diagram was written FC1 = the spectrum.

File Code One is *the colour spectrum.*

So how did this colour code work?

Froghorn had said something about Mondays not being good because they were 'viridian days'. So viridian was a bad thing. The question was, did Miles Froghorn see everything in terms of colour?

Ruby knew that certain people mixed their senses up: the composer Messiaen perceived musical notes as different colours, and the author Nabokov saw letters as colours.

What if Froghorn is one of those people? she thought. *A synaesthete? What if he associates colours with ideas? Like days, or people?*

It would be another layer of code, and a clever one: anyone wanting to find a particular file would either need to have Froghorn with them, or to know what colour he had assigned to a file... The trick, Ruby realised, was to figure out which colour applied to which mission, or which agent: in this case, Baker. Or LB.

The files on Bradley Baker would be... where? What colour would be associated with him? First of all, one had to think what he was. Dead, yes, but then no doubt a lot of people in these files had long since slipped away, so looking for colours associated with death or deadness was probably the wrong way to go.

To Ruby his name suggested brown – it was probably something to do with his name 'Baker' conjuring up bread. *Dumb, Redfort, super dumb.* This felt like entirely the wrong avenue to explore – after all, she wasn't the code maker here, was she... Froghorn was. *So think like Froghorn.*

She thought about Baker. Froghorn had said he was like a 'sun ray'. So it was just possible that to Froghorn, Baker would be represented by gold or sunshine yellow. It took her a few goes to find the right shade, but it seemed she was correct in her thinking – Baker was filed under a golden yellow.

When she opened it she saw there was a pattern of dots next to his name – a logo perhaps?

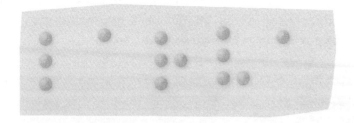

She took out the mini copier and snapped a picture of it.

Then she leafed through the file.

Everything in it seemed to relate to Baker's last flight. It seemed he was in training for some particular mission, though it was unclear exactly what that was. Most of the content was encrypted, and if she wanted to read it she would need to decode it and that could take hours.

She looked at the clock. *Twenty-nine and counting...* no time.

She would have to copy the file so she could come back to this later.

Baker had been returning from ████████ when his craft

had got into 'difficulty' – it said nothing about his being shot down by friendly fire.

Come on, thought Ruby, *someone had to know about it.* She read on and saw that the destination Baker was flying to was also blanked.

There were some details about the crash; not a huge amount. It covered the weather conditions that night; it was October, cold but not stormy. It seemed Bradley Baker had been alone when his craft experienced what was thought to be a malfunction. This was the way it was written up anyway.

```
the pilot died when his craft experienced mechanical
problems resulting in an engine fire and subsequent
explosion. The pilot, though highly experienced,
was unable to save himself due to the speed of the
unfolding calamity. Due to the magnitude of the
explosion and force of the impact, there was little
wreckage that could be retrieved from the crash site.
No sign that the ejector seat had been deployed and
no possibility that the pilot could have survived the
consequent inferno.
```

There were several pictures of the crash site, all taken at night. Ruby was not surprised that Baker's body had not been recovered – the craft was just a mangled heap of steel, the fire had consumed everything it could.

It seemed there were layers of truths, or if you looked at it all another way: untruths. There was something cloak-and-dagger about the incident from the outset. On the very last page of the file was typed:

`Last known contact: Professor Homer Pinkerton.`
`Reason for communication unknown.`

Professor Pinkerton? thought Ruby. Some blurry memory lit up and immediately faded. She shut her eyes to let her mind carry her to it, but all she could see was grey, the colour grey.

She closed Baker's file and began to search for Pinkerton's. She hoped that Froghorn would be predictable enough to file it under the colour pink. She wasn't far off with this guess. It took her just a few attempts to find the exact shade, a sort of chemistry lab pink, the colour of manganese (II).

When she opened the file, her attention was caught by the photograph of the man pictured in black and white.

Professor Homer Pinkerton.

He looked young in the photograph, though of course there was no knowing when the picture had actually been taken and how long it had been buried deep in the Prism Vault.

Professor Pinkerton, it seemed, was not a full-time employee of Spectrum. He was a consultant and special scientific advisor. There was a whole lot of text detailing some of the projects he had contributed to, both before and after joining Spectrum as a consultant. There was more than she could easily read in a day, let alone six minutes.

She flipped through the pages until something caught her eye. This had to do with a discovery Pinkerton had made regarding what seemed from the un-redacted text to be some kind of species of plant-life, which appeared to hold amazing life-giving properties, increasing healthy life expectancy by a great number of years. The professor claimed that 'the body's ageing process is greatly slowed, so that a person of seventy would have the genetic age of a forty year old'. He also asserted that 'the brain's ability to store and process information is also improved by approximately double'.

She scanned the following pages in an attempt to discover what this plant was, but she was soon distracted by another interesting thing. Pinkerton had been doing a great deal of research into memory erasure, primarily how it might one day be possible to extract uncomfortable, painful and harmful memories from the human brain.

Pinkerton's research had been focused on patients who found themselves plagued and tormented by traumatic memories. The patients he'd studied were often the victims of terrible near-death experiences which had resulted in post-traumatic stress disorder. The professor had discovered a way of plucking out and permanently removing memories that tortured the mind. He called this SME or Specific Memory Extraction.

There was an intriguing line about this:

but the rest was blacked out. Ruby turned the page, but the majority of what was written here was also blacked out and stamped across the page in large letters were the words:

RESTRICTED ACCESS LEVEL TWO SECURITY REQUIRED.

It was at that exact moment that Ruby caught sight of a clock, the flashing numerals silently counting down towards zero. It was reading 124 seconds now.

Ruby, you bozo!

No matter how interesting this professor's memory research was, she was forgetting her whole reason for being in this forsaken vault, namely to find out if LB was a cold-blooded murderer.

She had broken one of her rules:

RULE 48: DON'T GET DISTRACTED – FOCUS ON WHAT YOU GOTTA FOCUS ON.

She had a little over two minutes to copy as much of the Baker file and the Pinkerton file as she could and hightail it out of there. This she achieved with about 1.4 seconds to spare.

Scrabbling to her feet, she pushed the files back into their slots, slipped out of the vault and leaned against the heavy door, relieved to hear the loud *thunk* as it sealed itself shut.

Getting *out* of Meteor Island was a lot less complicated than getting in. She climbed back down into the cube, which began to fill with water, and then she searched for the fly, put her finger over it and the underwater door slid open and she was back in the ocean.

It was during her swim back to shore that her brain flashed up the fragment of memory once more: *the grey clapboard house on Cedarwood Drive.*

She muttered to herself as she heaved herself out of the chilly water.

Why? she wondered.

Ruby by now was about as tired as she felt it was possible to get and her limbs felt very heavy, she wished she still had the stupid pink bike. She wished she had any bike. Here she was, walking alone along the deserted coast road in the dark with a madman on the loose. Correction, a madman, *two* crazy ladies and a traiterous mole, who probably wanted her dead. The worst thing was she had the weirdest feeling as if someone was watching her.

Watch your back, Ruby, she thought.

Chapter 21.
C.O.L.D.

UNSURPRISINGLY RUBY WAS FEELING LESS THAN PERKY the next morning. Her legs ached and so did her arms, in fact the *whole* of her ached.

She was grateful to have the note from Hitch which stated that Ruby had been battling a cold and had spent the previous day propped up in bed sipping ginger tea while trying to study. He wrote how Ruby had insisted on coming to class today because she had promised to hand Mrs Drisco the work set for her.

No one, not even Mrs Drisco, could argue with that.

Ruby spent the day waiting for the school bell to clang so she could hurry home and take a look at what she had managed to glean from her thirty-three minutes inside the Prism Vault.

It was unfortunate therefore to find Mrs Digby in a very chatty mood and quite determined to talk about Cousin Emily, who it seemed had both a bluebottle infestation and a mould problem in her apartment. *You wouldn't believe the smell!* And she was being moved to a new place because *it is just not possible to pay that kind of sky-high rent and live with those low-down creatures, to say nothing of the fungus.*

Ordinarily, Ruby would have been only too happy to discuss the ins and outs of pest control and listen to Mrs Digby's lurid descriptions of just how bad they smelt – *they would have a skunk holding his nose* – but not tonight. Right now, all Ruby wanted to do was to open up the copied Ghost Files and discover what secret they held.

'Those creatures get everywhere,' said Mrs Digby. 'You don't always spot them, but they're tiptoeing about all over the place.' She shook her head. 'And the damp and the rot.' She made a face to show her displeasure. 'There's no missing that.'

They chatted for around twenty-five minutes, by which time Mrs Digby insisted it was time for Ruby to eat supper, which Ruby duly did.

At 7.30pm the doorbell sounded and Mrs Digby began telling Lou Patchett, who had come to clip Bug's claws, the whole story of the bluebottles and mould right from the beginning and Ruby was able to excuse herself and slip up to her room. She was careful to lock the door, not that Mrs Digby ever came in unannounced, but if there was one thing Ruby had learned in recent months, it was that you can't be too careful. She had a rule about it, and these days it seemed more fitting than ever:

RULE 9: THERE IS ALWAYS A CHANCE THAT SOMEONE, SOMEWHERE IS WATCHING YOU.

She took down her posters and the cards and the pinning board and then trained the micro-projector at the expanse of now-blank wall.

But when she pressed the reveal switch on the tiny gadget, what was projected was nothing but blurred text, overlapping letters and numbers in dense lines. The files were scrambled, designed to be copy-proof.

Ruby cursed several times and kicked at a volleyball which happened to be sitting in the middle of the room. It bounced off the door and smacked Ruby in the face, which hurt quite a bit, and she cursed again.

The commotion brought Mrs Digby upstairs.

'What in tarnation is going on, child?'

'Nothing,' said Ruby.

'That's a lot of ugly words coming from your mouth all for the sake of nothing,' said Mrs Digby. 'Heaven knows what Lou thought.' She peered at Ruby. 'What happened to your face?'

'I got hit by a ball,' said Ruby.

'I'll keep my thoughts to myself,' said the housekeeper.

'I appreciate that, Mrs Digby.'

'Cursing at your age,' muttered the housekeeper. 'What will people think?'

'That I learned it from you?' said Ruby.

'An old lady's allowed to swear; folks expect it when one gets as aged as I am.'

'You know that's not true, don't you?'

Mrs Digby collected up a few dirty plates and cups and walked towards the door. 'By the way,' she said, 'I'm dropping

Bug round at the Crews' in the morning because I won't have a minute to walk him tomorrow. You can pick him up on your way home.'

'Sure,' said Ruby.

'Oh, and you'll be needing your thermals tomorrow. I predict a freeze.'

Once the housekeeper had gone, Ruby sat at her desk and wrote down everything she could remember reading in the Ghost Files.

Pinkerton and his life-prolonging plant discovery.

His development of a Specific Memory Extractor.

She knew Baker was on a training mission, but had no idea for what.

But she felt none the wiser about his crash – *had* LB actually been the one to pull the trigger?

And what was the meaning of those dots?

Next time she would be sure to take a notebook.

RULE 11: BE PREPARED.

How had she managed to forget that one? Even the boy scouts had *that* rule down.

Despite a pretty good night's sleep, Ruby Redfort, aspiring field agent and avid seeker of action, would have much preferred to stay in bed the next morning. Given the choice, she would have chosen to stay in bed the whole day long. She would *even* have chosen to be infected with the Crew family flu rather than endure another day of Spectrum cold-weather survival training. In fact, she was pretty sure the Spectrum cold-weather survival training would lead to her being infected with the Crew family flu.

But, as any spy recruiter will tell you, you do not get to pick and choose your fate when you enrol as a secret agent; you take it on the chin and suffer the consequences.

Ruby had already been plunged into ice water. Today she would be helicoptered up to the mountains in order to be plunged into snow.

'Kid, you're going to love it,' said Hitch, 'think of it as a snow day, no school just eight hours of horsing around.'

'Horsing around?' said Ruby. 'Since when does Sam Colt let anyone horse around?'

'You have a point,' conceded Hitch. 'It's going be misery but just focus on how you'll feel when it's over?'

Apparently, it was a *good* thing to know how it would feel to be buried alive in snow. 'If it happens you need to know how you are going to react,' said Colt.

Probably by passing out, thought Ruby.

Froghorn was with them again, and Ruby gathered his presence was due to the reduced number of agent personnel in Spectrum 8 – it was all hands on deck as far as cover was concerned.

It was clear from his expression that he found being in charge of handing out kit rather demeaning. It didn't escape

Ruby's notice that he was no longer wearing that dumb pen round his neck. Was that what Hitch had told him at Desolate Cove – take it off – leave it back at HQ? Hitch being Hitch was bound to see it as some kind of safety hazard. *Probably worried the potato head was going to strangle himself*, she thought.

Sam Colt taught the trainees a few of the basics:

C **Keep Clothing Clean**: clothes encrusted with dirt and grease lose some of their insulating power.

O **Avoid Overheating.** 'Might sound crazy when you're hunkering down in a snow shelter, but too much heat can be a problem,' said Colt. 'When you sweat you make your clothes damp, which stops them insulating you properly. And when the sweat evaporates, it drains heat from your body. Try to keep some air circulating.'

L **Wear Loose and Wear Layers.** Tight clothing restricts circulation and increases the risk of frostbite. Layers create pockets of air for insulation.

D **Keep Clothing Dry.** Wet clothes can be the death of you – literally. Make sure to brush yourself down before entering a shelter, as any snow left on your clothes will melt and make you wet, which will make you dead.

'One small but vital piece of equipment is a sun visor,' said the survival trainer. 'If you don't happen to have one with you, you can make your own from a piece of bark.' This was apparently the first thing to do if one found oneself suddenly in a snowy cold environment: otherwise, the light bouncing off all the white would quickly blind you.

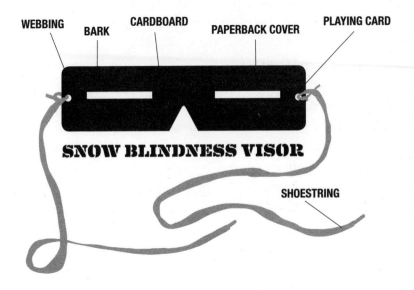

WEBBING BARK CARDBOARD PAPERBACK COVER PLAYING CARD

SNOW BLINDNESS VISOR

SHOESTRING

After that, Ruby and the other trainees learned how to make a snow shelter. If you were lucky you might find a cave; if not, you might want to look for a fallen branch and build your shelter against it.

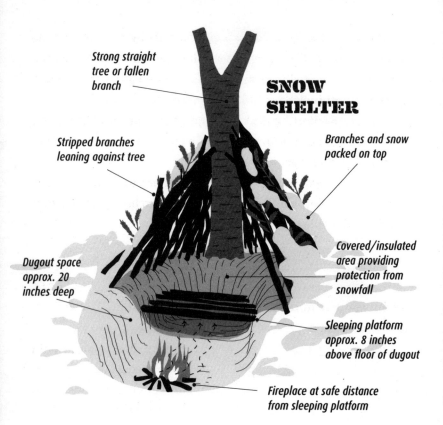

SNOW SHELTER

Strong straight tree or fallen branch

Stripped branches leaning against tree

Branches and snow packed on top

Dugout space approx. 20 inches deep

Covered/insulated area providing protection from snowfall

Sleeping platform approx. 8 inches above floor of dugout

Fireplace at safe distance from sleeping platform

'If you're out in the snow wilderness for a lengthy time,' Samuel Colt began, 'then you might want to make yourself a fur coat – some of you might find this unpalatable, but you have to keep warm if you want to walk out of there alive. It's just the law of survival.'

But the most unpalatable part for Ruby was the whole avalanche thing. She stepped into the hole all right, but as the snow was shovelled in over her head, she began to panic and there was nothing she could do to control it.

'It's OK, Redfort,' said Colt, gripping her hand and lifting her out. 'This is just something we're going to have to work on. Mind over matter; you'll get there.'

Ruby nodded, but she didn't think there was ever going to be a day when being buried alive was going to be something that she would be able to overcome.

Ruby had asked to be dropped on West 72nd Street. Despite the cold and the fact that her brain had almost frozen over, it had not slipped her mind that she needed to pick up her dog from the Crew residence.

She was looking forward to getting back. Mrs Digby would prepare Ruby one of her Mrs Digby hot chocolate drinks, and she would once again be able to feel her feet or at least her legs.

Just make it to Clancy's, pick up Bug and get home, Ruby.

She pictured herself crawling up the front steps, a heartbeat away from hypothermia. Perhaps Hitch would be there to carry her near-lifeless body into the house... no, not Hitch, she didn't want to see *him*, he would probably send her back out again for more of this insane training. What was he trying to do to her, kill her?

She was making her way through the back alley between

72nd Street and Flaubert, mumbling these grumbled thoughts, the alley being the quickest route to Clancy's and getting to Clancy's was all Ruby could focus on. So lost in thought was she that she almost didn't hear the faint hiss from the shadows.

She stopped – was it something or was it nothing?

Silence.

Nothing, she concluded.

She told herself to get it together, or as her **RULE 8** had it: **DON'T LET YOUR IMAGINATION RUN AWAY WITH YOU OR YOU MIGHT WELL LOSE THE PLOT.**

She walked on past the trashcans and dumpsters, keeping her eyes trained on the street ahead; there was nothing to worry about... And then came the sound of a bottle smashing on the cobbles. Her heartbeat quickened.

'Anyone there?' she called.

A cat ran out of the darkness and leapt onto the wall.

She closed her eyes. *Get a grip, Redfort.* She really shouldn't be walking down dark alleys if it was going to get her freaking out like this. But then came that whispered sound again. It definitely seemed human.

She tapped the Escape Watch, which triggered a bright beam of light to shine from it. She directed it into the shadows and over the stacked-up crates and piles of garbage. She heard a noise behind her and turned to see a figure trundling a shopping cart across the top of the alley. *Mrs Beesman?* she wondered. But in the dark one old lady pushing a shopping cart looked very much like another.

She was about to move on, using her watch flashlight to make one more sweep of the alley, when she saw it. It was chalked on the ground, freshly written she guessed, because the chalk was only just beginning to bleed into the damp surface of the alleyway. It was hard to make it out in the dark, but when she did she saw it was a message and she could be in no doubt that the message was for her and her alone:

Beware the child who yearned to be Larva, disguised as a fly, but emerged a spider

Ruby had no intention of hanging around, but her legs had become sort of rubbery and she tripped and went sprawling forward, her coat now tangled in a section of chain-link fence that ran down one side of the alleyway.

She tried to yank herself free, but couldn't.

She pulled at the zip, slid herself out of the parka and left it where it lay ensnared.

Then she ran and ran and she didn't look back.

Chapter 22.
Something remembered

RUBY ARRIVED AT THE CREWS' PLACE, teeth chattering and unable to feel her feet.

The door was opened by eleven-year-old Nancy.

'Hey, Ruby, I guess you've come to pick up Bug?'

Ruby nodded, almost too cold to speak.

'Clance!' she yelled. 'Ruby's here. By the way, where's your coat? It's cold out, you know.'

'Yeah, Nancy, I noticed that too.'

Clancy appeared, followed by Bug, and the Crews' own little dog Dolly, who trotted along behind. Ruby reached out to pat the husky, but her hands were so numb she could not feel the dog's fur.

'Are you OK? You've gone sorta blue,' said Clancy.

'Where's your coat?' said Olive, skipping across the hall.

'*Oh*, am I *not* wearing one?' said Ruby, her tone sarcastic, though Olive seemed unaware of this.

'No,' said Olive. 'My mom says it's stupid to go outside in winter without a coat.'

'*You* should talk,' said Nancy. 'You are always doing *stupid* things.'

'Get inside, Rube,' said Clancy, pulling her into the house and slamming the door shut.

'My fingers are actual icicles,' said Ruby.

'You want a ginger tea?' asked Clancy. 'It might thaw you out.'

'Sure,' said Ruby. 'Right now I'll take anything.'

'Did something happen?' asked Clancy.

'You could say that,' said Ruby. 'Though where to start?'

They sat up in Clancy's room drinking tea. With a woollen blanket wrapped around her and two hot water bottles under her feet, Ruby was slowly beginning to thaw.

She told Clancy about the survival training and her failure to complete the avalanche task.

'Give yourself a break, Ruby. I mean it is actually your deepest most profoundest fear,' said Clancy.

'The point is, that doesn't matter an iota, fear – whether deep, profound or just regular – has to be handled. What if I end up buried alive somewhere and I find I just can't cope?' She looked at him, her expression deadly serious. 'I mean I'd be a goner, right?'

'You'd handle it, Rube, I know you would.'

'Thanks,' she said, 'but I think I'd rather come face to face with a bear than be buried alive.'

'Did they teach you that?' asked Clancy.

'What's to teach?' said Ruby.

This was a running thing between the two of them. Ruby had compiled a lot of rules, 80 in all, and **RULE 79** was the rule for bears. It was more of a joke than a rule really, one that she and Clancy shared: **WHAT TO DO IF YOU MEET A BEAR – WISH YOU HADN'T!** The reason being that if you met a bear there were a number of ways you might persuade it to back off, but only the bear knew which of these approaches was going to work.

'I've been thinking about that whole bear problem actually,' said Clancy.

'Oh yeah?'

'Yeah,' said Clancy. 'What you have to do is go on instinct; you have to use your sixth sense – if you don't, you're dead.'

'And what if you don't have a sixth sense?' asked Ruby. 'What then?'

'Everyone has a sixth sense,' said Clancy, 'it's just most people have forgotten how to tune in to it.'

'OK, so suppose I tune in and I go with my gut and I'm wrong because I just feel it wrong.'

Clancy shrugged. 'Then I guess you're dead, but at least you can die reassured that you'd be dead anyway. Tuning into your sixth sense just gives you a better chance; I can't promise you that it will save your life.'

'Great,' said Ruby, 'truly terrific. Personally, I think what you gotta do is read the signs.'

'*The signs*?' spluttered Clancy.

'Check out the bear's behaviour, what signals he's giving you.'

'You read bear signals now?' said Clancy.

Ruby ignored the ridicule in his question. 'You just gotta react to what he's giving you. Is it curiosity? Is it fear? Or is it simply that there might be something on your person that he wants to eat?'

'What, like your head?' suggested Clancy.

What they did both agree on is who would be the person most likely to save you if you were unfortunate enough to find yourself in this bear clinch situation.

'Mrs Digby,' said Clancy.

'Without a doubt,' said Ruby.

The bear problem didn't only apply to bears. It applied to all people or problems that were unpredictable. *It's something of a bear problem,* Ruby would say when she just couldn't figure out how things might go.

Some problems started off as bears and then given time one could see how they might be tackled, but others remained unpredictable and unsolvable. The Count was perhaps the biggest bear problem of them all.

'If there's bears around, maybe you should be wearing that barrette of yours,' suggested Clancy. 'You might need rescuing.'

'What do you mean?' said Ruby. 'I always wear the fly-barrette – see!' She went to pat it with her hand, but it wasn't there.

'Oh jeepers, I lost it!'

'No, no, it's there,' said Clancy. 'It's caught in your sweater.'

'Boy, that's a relief,' said Ruby. 'I thought maybe it had fallen out when I tripped and got tangled in that fence.'

'You got tangled in a fence?' said Clancy.

'Actually yeah,' said Ruby. 'My coat got caught up in it and I just sorta left it there.'

'Why?' said Clancy. 'Why would you just leave your coat?'

'I got spooked by something,' said Ruby.

'What kinda something?' said Clancy.

'Something a bit like a bear,' said Ruby.

Clancy looked at her, his eyes round as saucers.

'He left a message for me,' said Ruby.

'He? You mean the Count?' said Clancy.

Ruby nodded. 'Uh huh.'

'You're sure?' asked Clancy

'I smelt his cologne.'

'So what was the message?'

'It said: *Beware the child who yearned to be Larva, disguised as a fly, but emerged a spider.*'

'Creepy,' shivered Clancy. 'What does it mean?'

'I have no idea, except for the fly bit, which stands for agent, and I guess spider could be fly killer.'

'Where was it, the message?' said Clancy.

'In that back alley that joins Flaubert.'

'You walked down that alley at *night*? When it's *dark*?' said

Clancy. 'What are you, on some mission to be murdered?'

'It's not that bad,' said Ruby, 'it's just a back alley full of trashcans and garbage.'

'And, it would seem, murderers,' added Clancy.

'OK,' said Ruby. 'Maybe it was a little dumb.'

'What you have got to ask him,' said Clancy, 'if you ever get the chance to speak to him, that is, is: who *is* this boss of his?'

'I'll be sure to ask him next time I run into him.'

'I'm not kidding,' said Clancy. 'You need to know.'

'Seriously?' said Ruby. 'Shouldn't you be saying, *whatever you do, don't run into this guy again*?'

'Ordinarily yes, but I have a feeling that's no longer an option. I have a hunch you have to face facts here – you figure this out or you move to a secret bunker somewhere.'

'I hate to say it, Clance, but I know you're right.'

It was as she was walking home, hands pushed deep into the pockets of Clancy's snow jacket, that she felt something dig into her palm.

'Ow,' she squealed.

The dog looked alarmed, alert for danger.

'It's OK, Bug.'

Ruby pulled out her hand; a tiny bead of blood there in her palm.

What?

She fumbled in the pocket and out fell the badge.

A small circle of white, barely visible against the snow that had recently fallen.

Her badge.

Looking at it lying there next to the kerb shook up another memory from the depths of her brain. This time she saw a yellow leaf flutter through the air. She stood stock-still, trying hard to join the image of the yellow leaf to something else and anchor it to something real. She had found the badge a long time ago on the street near her house. She had kept it pinned to the inside of her coat, a habit she had not let go of.

It had begun, this habit of secrecy, because she had not wanted her parents to take away this 'found thing'. She, being an intelligent child although not yet three, knew that once her parents saw its sharp spike of a pin they would most certainly confiscate it and no doubt bury it deep in the trash bin.

Later on, as Ruby got older, the badge had become a sort of charm, something she liked to have with her. And then in June, she had lent it to Clancy when he'd had to take part in the spring swimathon. She had persuaded him that it was some kind of talisman, and would protect him from sharks and seamonsters, and generally ward off nibblers. He had believed her. It worked.

She had all but forgotten it, the badge, replaced now by *actual* lucky charms in the form of high-tech Spectrum gadgets: the voice thrower, the Escape Watch, the fly-barrette and a whole lot more.

Now she looked at the metal badge with renewed interest, a white circle embossed with random bumps. Her dog was still looking at her, waiting to know what was next.

Something lost, something found.

'Come on, Bug,' she said, 'let's go.'

When she reached Cedarwood Drive, Ruby did not make straight for Green-Wood House. Instead she walked the whole length of the street, up one side and then down the other. She concentrated hard, trying to remember the place she had found this circle of tin. She walked up the road and down the sidewalk until she arrived just outside the grey clapboard house with its white picket fence, and flash went that memory.

Grey house, yellow leaf, white circle of badge.

Slowly, she turned and crossed to her house and began walking up the steps. Bug began to bark and Ruby slowed as she saw something lying by the front door. She could not make out what the thing was. She got closer. Not a living creature. Stranger than that. A shiver went down her spine as she realised that: it was in fact her *coat.*

Chapter 23.
A man's best friend

MRS DIGBY'S VOICE GREETED RUBY as she stepped into the hall. 'Child? Is that you?'

'Uh huh, yeah,' called Ruby.

She hung her coat on the peg and went upstairs to the kitchen where she found Mrs Digby dicing apples.

'Did you happen to notice anyone outside?' asked Ruby. 'Earlier, I mean – like an hour ago?'

Mrs Digby shook her head. 'I don't spend my time standing on the stoop looking out into the darkness,' she said. 'I keep the door shut in winter, and the lights lit. Best not ponder on what lurks out in the gloom.'

Ruby went to the window and peered into the dark. A few houses were lit up brightly, but most people had their curtains drawn against the chill. From here she could see the little grey clapboard house.

'Who used to live there?' she asked.

'Where?' said Mrs Digby

'In the grey house just down the street, where the Joneses

were living until about a week ago.'

'Why, the Hendons,' said Mrs Digby. 'Remember they had that awful parrot? Mr Parker threatened to strangle it and plenty would have been grateful to him.'

'No, before the Hendons, I mean, a long time ago.'

The housekeeper gave her a suspicious look. 'What's got you asking that?' she said.

Ruby shrugged. 'I don't know, just wondered is all. Maybe because I was thinking about the tornado and how that little house was lucky not to be whirled away.'

Mrs Digby nodded. 'That house is lucky all right: survived earthquake *and* tornado.'

'Have you ever been inside?' asked Ruby.

'Oh yes,' said Mrs Digby. 'Often times back when it belonged to the old gentleman – I spent many a sweltering day sitting on that porch getting a little shade.'

'Who was he, the old gentleman?'

'His name was Mr Pinkerton,' said Mrs Digby.

'P i n k e r t o n?' said Ruby, slowly, letting the name tumble around her brain.

'Pinkerton, that's right. He was a nice old fellow. We saw eye to eye on things.'

'Was he a professor?' asked Ruby.

'Why would you ask me that?' she said. 'No, he was just plain old regular Mr Pinkerton, though I'll admit he was as *smart* as any professor I ever met – not that I'm sure I've met a whole clutch of them. Educated is what you'd call him, travelled the world, so he told me. He seemed to know everything, memory like an elephant.'

'How come *I* don't remember him?' asked Ruby.

'I don't see how you could,' said the housekeeper. 'You weren't much more than the size of a turnip when you first met him. It was the day the old Fairbank house was turned into matchsticks during the earthquake of 1960. Mr Pinkerton took us in for a few nights. We became firm friends after that.' She shook her head. 'It's a real shame he left, quite sudden it was, a few days before your first chess tournament: you were not even three. He'd promised he'd come along because he'd been coaching you.'

'He had?'

'Yes,' she nodded. 'He said you had an aptitude for it, he said you had brains. Said you were the most interesting infant he had ever studied – *met*, I think is what he meant, he always talked peculiar.'

'So where did he go?' asked Ruby.

Mrs Digby stood, hands on hips, gazing out of the window at the moonless sky. 'Now you got me there,' she said. 'I really don't know – all I heard was, he was dead.'

'Who told you that?'

'The sheriff,' said Mrs Digby. 'The police investigated his disappearance and one day they turned up evidence that suggested poor old Mr Pinkerton was no more. I wasn't so surprised.'

'Why not?' asked Ruby.

'He was a broken man,' said Mrs Digby. 'After... what was it called... what was its name?'

'What was whose name?' asked Ruby.

'That dog of his, name something like *Nemosign*, I never could say it right...'

'Mnemosyne?' asked Ruby.

'That was it!' said Mrs Digby. 'How did you know?'

'I sort of guessed,' said Ruby.

Mrs Digby tutted. 'Why people insist on calling animals stupid names is beyond me.'

'She was the Greek goddess of memory,' said Ruby.

'Who was?' asked Mrs Digby.

'Mnemosyne,' said Ruby.

'If you say so,' said the old lady. 'But all I know is, when that mutt disappeared, that was that.' She sighed. 'The heart and soul went out of him – never saw a person more chewed-up about an animal, a small one at that.'

'It ran off? Was lost?'

'That dog was too loyal to leave, and too smart to get itself lost; smartest dog I ever met. My old pa used to say, the only dog worth its keep is a smart dog.'

'Like Bug,' said Ruby.

'Smarter,' said Mrs Digby. 'You know, I taught it that trick, the one my pa taught my hound and I taught Bug.'

'The go find trick?' said Ruby.

'Yes,' said Mrs Digby. 'I'll tell you what, that mutt learned it in one day flat.'

'What type of dog was it?'

'The small and pointless kind, looked funny, like a cat – fluffy thing, big bulgy eyes, black nose.' Mrs Digby made a face.

'Pekinese?' guessed Ruby.

'Pekinese.' Mrs Digby tutted. 'He always did keep that breed – photographs everywhere of Pinkerton and those darned Pekineses, decades worth of them and each one looked the spit of the one before. If an uglier breed of dog exists then I've not seen it and nor would I want to.'

'So what do you think happened to Mnemosyne?'

The housekeeper sighed. 'Well, the reason it hit the old fellow so hard was because the dog wasn't *lost*, she was stolen, dognapped while Mr Pinkerton was helping some truck driver with directions.'

In the far reaches of Ruby's mind, a memory was stirring.

She saw again the yellow leaf whirling through a cold blue sky. 'When was this?' asked Ruby. 'What time of year?'

Mrs Digby looked up and tapped her head. 'There you got me.' The old lady thought for a moment. 'November, I think – no, it was October, I know that because I was preparing pumpkins for Halloween.'

'Was it windy that day?' Ruby asked.

'How should I ever remember that?' said the housekeeper, looking at the girl like she was an egg short of a dozen. 'But what

I do know is that it wasn't any wind that stole that dog away, it was a removals truck.'

'That's kinda *weird*, isn't it?' said Ruby. 'Stealing a dog, I mean, unless it was some sort of pedigree pooch.'

'The only reason to steal it,' said Mrs Digby, 'was to make that poor man suffer.'

'Suffer how?' asked Ruby.

'By taking what was most precious to him. It was all he had.'

'No family?' asked Ruby.

'Not a one, but he was a good, kind soul, that man, the only person who ever managed to befriend Mrs Beesman.'

'Mrs Beesman?' spluttered Ruby. 'How did he manage that?' Ruby had never managed to get much more than a grunt out of the woman.

'Charm,' said Mrs Digby. 'He had a lot of charm. And I'm not talking about a superficial meaningless sort of charm, I'm saying he was through and through a good sort.'

Ruby thought about Mr Pinkerton and imagined the grief he must have suffered at the loss of Mnemosyne – how *she* would cope if she ever lost Bug. Bug who was more than just the family pet. A more loyal soul would be hard to find, a hound who would risk his life for hers, *had* risked his life for hers.

Mrs Digby, once again picking up her chopping knife: 'I can't say I don't miss him. He was *the* most interesting fellow, smart as anything and twice as amiable, that Homer Pinkerton.'

'Did you say "Homer"?' said Ruby.

'Well, that was his name,' said Mrs Digby. 'Homer Pinkerton – unusual name, I'll grant you.'

Mrs Digby was still talking when Ruby was halfway up the stairs.

There was the connection. The chances of this Homer Pinkerton not being the Spectrum Homer Pinkerton she'd read about in the Ghost Files seemed very remote.

Ruby sat at her desk at the top of the house, took out her notebook and added Homer Pinkerton and his dog Mnemosyne to her map of names.

```
Homer Pinkerton: discovered a plant
which enhances the memory and prolongs
healthy life.

While working at Spectrum he developed a
device which allows single memories to be
extracted from the brain without harm to
the patient.

Question:
Who had sought to make this man suffer?
```

She pondered this before writing:

Could the Count somehow be part of
this?

As she stared at her notes her mind cast back to her
conversation with Frederick Lutz. Hadn't he mentioned a man
called Homer? An inventor who had worked alongside the Count
back in the early days when Count von Leyden had sought only
to thrill with horror rather than kill.

She found the movie encyclopaedia that Frederick had lent
her and, lifting it onto her desk, she thumbed through it until
she reached the index. Then she searched the names, 'N, O, P...
P... P!'

And there it was:

*Homer Pinkerton, props and special effects. Worked on a
number of films alongside Victor von Leyden.*

Everything was connected.

It wasn't that junior agent
Baker wasn't friendly.
He was, he was more than nice,
he was super nice...

...it wasn't that he wasn't generous or helpful or skilled at working as part of a team, because he was all these things. In fact, he seemed to have no flaws, not one. He was perfect, horribly perfect, and the kid from Colwin City found it was impossible not to be eaten up with a desire to see him fail, and the nicer junior agent Baker was, the more the kid hated him.

It was during the final field test that the kid had a vision of how things could be, would be, if only the boy, Bradley Baker, were out of the picture; if only Bradley Baker was wiped out, and wiped out permanently.

An accident, a stupid mistake, dumb luck, a regrettable but very fatal incident.

Chapter 24.
Hypocrea asteroidi

THE VERY LAST THING RUBY WANTED TO DO at 4am that Saturday morning, aside from run into the Count again and perhaps be buried alive, was to get back into the freezing cold ocean and swim across to the Observatory on Meteor Island. However, if she was going to find out more about LB and Baker, and what the link was between them and whatever was going down between Pinkerton, Spectrum and the Count, then she didn't have a whole lot of choice.

This time she had brought with her a pencil and a notebook, which she zipped inside her Superskin.

She took the bus to Desolate Cove, swam the short distance to the rock, dived down to the underwater door, and held her breath while she waited for the question to pop up on the code panel.

CASSIOPEIA.

She tapped in the constellation and the door slid open.

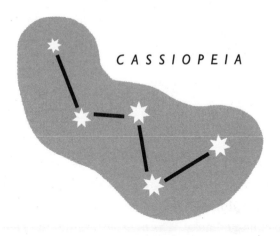

CASSIOPEIA

Once she was in the water chamber she set about searching for the tiny fly image. When found, the chamber emptied and Ruby climbed the ladder to the vault room.

Ruby was faced with another error-correcting code – she wasted no time in figuring out which rows and columns had the wrong parity bits, and punched in the resulting four-digit number. The door swung open and she was in.

Ruby decided to return to the Pinkerton file first. She wanted to read the information she had failed to copy on her last visit. She thought perhaps if she read this, she might discover the connection between the professor and Baker. *Actually,* what she discovered was the name of the life-prolonging plant Homer Pinkerton had discovered. It was a fungus called *Hypocrea asteroidi,* something he had dubbed the Mars Mushroom or the memory mushroom.

She took out her book ready to make some notes, but when she pressed the pencil to the paper nothing happened. Somehow the pencil had become useless, unable to make even a mark. *Not an accident*, thought Ruby – this was by design.

OK, don't get side-tracked, just get on with it, she told herself.

Ruby set down the pencil and notepad and instead drew on her memory skills.

She would have to absorb as much information as she possibly could and get out of there in the thirty-three minutes the clock had allowed her.

Why? thought Ruby. *Why the Mars Mushroom? Did Pinkerton believe this plant had actually arrived on Earth from Mars?* She read on and it seemed, *yes, he did.* She considered this for a moment. It wasn't so far-fetched; a lot of scientists believed that the Earth was seeded by organic matter from outer space. Pinkerton was convinced that the fungus arrived stored in an ancient meteorite which had hit Earth many hundreds of thousands or even hundreds of millions of years ago.

If Ruby allowed herself to think like Clancy, or rather to feel for answers like Clancy, then she would have to say there was something about Pinkerton's file that made her uneasy.

Was *he* troubled by Spectrum, or was it the other way around? Either way, there was something about the tone and wording that suggested there might have been some kind of rift or perhaps even a fervent disagreement between them.

But about what? Ruby wondered. She read on, and as she

digested what the file contained, it became apparent that part of the falling-out seemed to be to do with the lack of information on where this Mars Mushroom grew. Spectrum wanted to know; Pinkerton wouldn't say.

Why? thought Ruby. Why would this professor not want to share such a valuable discovery? A plant which could not only halve one's seeming biological age but also double the amount of memory and information one's brain could hold...

Could it be that Pinkerton wanted to protect humanity from this miraculous plant? Had he perhaps agonised about what might happen if the privileged few were able to purchase long life and heightened intelligence in exchange for thousands of dollars, perhaps even hundreds of thousands of dollars, so allowing society's luckiest to reap the benefits?

And what about his other breakthrough, his pioneering research into the erasure of traumatic memory? A power for good, but in the wrong hands a power for evil. Did he wonder what might happen should either of these discoveries – the life-giver and the memory-taker – leak out into the wider world?

Or was it he who was the dark force here, seeking to wield power by holding onto his secrets and selling to the highest bidder?

Ruby considered this version, but it just didn't fit with Mrs Digby's description of the nice old gentleman sitting on the porch; the charming fellow who was kind to everyone.

Mrs Digby had rated him highly and Mrs Digby was a good

judge of character.

This was as much as this file was going to tell her... Except no, there was one other piece of information. That logo again, the same as the one stamped in Baker's file, and some letters this time too: JSRP, printed in a sky blue:

JSRP

Underneath it said:

PARTICIPATED IN THE JSRP CLEAN-UP OPERATION.

She ran her hands along the file wall until she found a file of the exact same colour, but when she tried to pull it from the wall a message flashed up on the control panel to the left of the door, declaring it was level two access. She pressed the violet button and the panel revealed a keyboard.

File Code Two – Chromatic.

The keys for one chromatic scale were numbered.

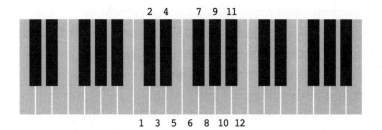

Below this was a button simply saying: ACCESS.

So Ruby pressed it.

A tune played. Then a robotic voice said, 'Enter code now.'

Ruby frowned. *Some kind of missing-note sequence?*

She pressed ACCESS again.

Another tune played. 'Enter code now,' said the voice. 'One attempt remaining.'

Ruby didn't need another attempt – she'd been listening carefully. Not for the first time, she was grateful to have perfect pitch, and she knew both the notes she had heard and the sequence they were following: the Mongian shuffle.*

Quickly, she pressed the keys for the notes she *hadn't* heard, the final four notes in the sequence: 2, 11, 1, 12.

A beep, a hiss and the file was released. She pulled it from the wall.

'JSRP' was printed on the cover, and underneath the letters was that pattern of dots again, this time embossed on the paper. *Not a logo,* thought Ruby, *a language. Braille.*

She read each letter: together they spelled: LARVAE.

* FOR AN EXPLANATION OF WHAT RUBY WORKED OUT HERE, SEE THE AFTERWORD ON PAGE 540

Larvae were undeveloped flies. Spectrum used the fly as its symbol for active agents. So was the word 'larvae' being used here as the collective term for junior spies?

Could this be what the 'JS' in 'JSRP' stood for? And what was the 'RP' – a recruitment programme, perhaps?

Then she thought back to the chalk message: *beware the child who yearned to be Larva.* Did something go wrong with one of these junior spies?

Though much of the file was encrypted, it *was* possible to conclude that Spectrum had indeed once upon a time recruited children, intending to train them up as agents, she supposed. The only child agent Ruby had *ever* heard anyone talk about was Bradley Baker. She had not been aware that there was a whole troupe of these spy kids – why had no one ever told her? But it seemed that Bradley's successful transition from tiny recruit to teenage fully-fledged agent had made an impression. And so six years after Baker's recruitment, Spectrum had decided to roll out the programme. They had found their recruits by printing what appeared to be kids' quizzes and puzzles on the back of cereal boxes and milk cartons. However, to the genius child it was only too obvious what they were looking at. These were no ordinary puzzles, but in fact highly-sophisticated, highly-secret application forms.

The next surprise was that this exciting-sounding programme was abandoned only months after it had been set up. This was due to a near-tragic incident which had taken place during an overseas training exercise. There was a report on this drama that had led to the dissolving of the JSRP.

It detailed a story of attempted murder, of how one agent had tried to murder another. It would have been an unpleasant enough tale had these agents been beyond school age, but the fact that they were both still children added an extra twist to the gruesome story.

It had happened in the northern territories of Australia, crocodile country. It had been set up to look like an accident. The recruits were striking camp and planning to paddle upriver. The victim had been busy loading up his raft with his camping gear when somehow the rope that moored it became untied. When he reached for his paddle, he found it wasn't there. Not only was he now heading for the rapids, but his raft was taking on water – someone had scuttled it. Had he not been rescued, his raft would have sailed him over the waterfall where he would surely have drowned, or perhaps worse still, his sinking raft would have landed him in the river where the crocodiles swam.

While this drama was unfolding, so another was taking place – the screams of a boy who had apparently fallen into the shallows, but managed somehow to scrabble onto one of the rafts. He had incurred a life-threatening injury from a fifteen-foot crocodile, but he was lucky – his cries had alerted rescue and he was dragged from the river before he could be taken by the reptile. The boy suffered severe shock and could not be questioned about the incident.

One of the strange things about this report was the lack of information when it came to those individuals involved.

Only two of the junior agents were named.

The first was the victim of the sabotage, thirteen-year-old Bradley Baker. The second, the boy who was almost swallowed by the crocodile, was named as Art Hitchen Zachery.

Ruby paused when she read this. *Could it be...?* she wondered. It seemed unlikely, but it could be, couldn't it? The name was so similar. *It* could *be Hitch?* But then why wouldn't he have told her? What was really interesting about the report was how Bradley Baker had been saved. It was not down to his skill or experience as a field agent, nor to some lucky river current carrying him to shore. It had been an incredible fluke.

A local kid had been camping out on the riverbank, fishing or some such. This kid had seen it all and raised the alarm; not only that, but had bravely climbed across the rocks and caught hold of Baker's raft and dragged the unconscious boy up and out of the water.

Question: who *were* these kids?

Who had sought to kill, and who to save?

Beware the child who yearned to be Larva,
disguised as a fly, but emerged a spider.

Ruby searched the rest of the JSRP files hoping to find a name, a clue to who might be responsible for the attempted murder of Bradley Baker.

By the time she was two-thirds through, it occurred to her that she had yet to see the face of a girl staring back from one of those inch-sized squares of photographic paper. Had yet to read a name that clearly belonged to someone who was not male.

All these Larvae recruits had been taken on twenty years before Ruby was born. *A sign of the times*, she thought. Not such a great time to be a girl if you were the sort of girl who liked action, adventure or even the chance of a challenging job.

Ruby's eye caught sight of the clock on the wall.

Ten.

Geez gotta fly.

Nine.

She grabbed the file up.

Eight.

Pushed it into the slot.

Seven.

Snatched up her notebook from the floor.

Six.

Where is the door's release switch??

Five.

Don't panic.

Four.

Switch found, door opening triggered...

Three.

Tripping, almost falling...

Two.

Pushing through the vault door, door closure triggered...

One.

Thunk.

Sinking to floor breathing heavily.

'I'm outta here.'

Chapter 25.
Mushrooms from Mars

IT WAS APPROXIMATELY 6AM when Ruby returned home. She fixed the **DO NOT DISTURB** sign to her door and had barely crawled into bed when the lobster phone began to ring.

'Rube, it's us, your mère and père.'

'Bonjour, c'est moi, vôtre fille Ruby.'

'Hello?'

'Howdie.'

'We're coming home!'

'Quand?'

'Bless you.'

'No, when are you coming home?'

'Mardi.'

'Tuesday?'

'No, Sunday.'

'You mean Dimanche?'

'I thought that meant dinner.'

'No, it means Sunday.'

'Oh.'

'C'est merveilleux nouvelles.'

Silence.

'This is wonderful news!'

'Oui, we agree! Can't wait to see you, bye bye bye.'

'Au revoir au revoir au revoir.'

Ruby found herself unable to drift back to sleep because she was going over and over what she knew about Bradley Baker. It seemed to her that the two most significant things that had happened during his life were the way he had died and the way he had almost died. Of course, he had also had that nasty near-death encounter with the Count, but this, though traumatic and certainly terrifying, was not nearly as sinister as being killed by one of your own. So if LB had been the woman responsible for ending his days by destroying his aircraft, then who was responsible for *attempting* to end his days at the crocodile rapids? Why would a kid want another kid dead? Jealousy, envy, ambition? Could it be that simple?

And why might LB have decided to terminate Baker's life? She shuddered; the phrase 'terminate his life' gave her the chills. How much easier, how much more palatable to consider this agent's life being *terminated*, like a machine being switched off; *much more* palatable, say, than issuing orders to have him killed in cold blood. Either way, the question still remained: why?

And then there was the question of what linked Baker to Pinkerton. And what Pinkerton's involvement had been in this 'JSRP clean-up operation'. If she wanted to know then she was going to have to go back.

Oh geez! she thought.

The one thing she *could* do without having to swim back to Meteor Island was to see if she could find something out on these memory mushrooms from Mars, and she knew just who to ask. She decided it could wait a day: Saturday she would devote to sleeping.

When she arrived at Little Mountain Side the following morning, there was something of a commotion just up the hill from the grocer's store. A whole crowd of people had gathered there and they were all looking up as if searching the sky. Curious, Ruby wandered along to see what the attraction was. What she saw was a man climbing what looked to be a pretty unclimbable tree. He was perhaps seventy or eighty feet off the ground.

'He's got it!' shouted a man.

Got what? thought Ruby.

It was only when the climber got a whole lot closer that Ruby saw he was clutching some kind of animal.

'Is that a cat?' said Ruby.

'Uh huh,' said the woman next to her, 'that's Ginger, all right.'

'Who's that with him?' asked Ruby.

'Why, that's Mo from Daily's,' said the woman. 'Isn't he magnificent?'

'That's one word for it, I guess,' said Ruby.

Applause broke out as Mo reached earth, and people walked over to shake his hand and slap him on the back. Ruby waited until the fuss had died down and then followed him back to the store.

'Quite the action hero, aren't we?' said Ruby.

'It's been mewing all night,' said Mo. 'Someone had to get that fur-ball down.'

He passed the cat to Ruby. 'Here, take it, would you? I'm not a cat person. Too much hair, too many claws.'

'Yet you can climb seventy feet up a two hundred foot Sequoia,' said Ruby.

'Trees never bothered me,' said Mo, plucking the orange cat hairs from his jacket.

'So what, you used to be a construction worker, a lumberjack, a high-wire walker?' said Ruby.

Mo shrugged. 'In a past life maybe.'

'With skills like that you might want to join the circus or the fire department,' said Ruby.

'Nah,' said Mo, 'I like an uneventful life.'

'Uneventful? Are you kidding?' said Ruby. 'You think grabbing cats from crazily tall trees is uneventful.'

'So what are you doing up here, anyway?' asked Mo. 'I told you, the maitake won't be in for a couple of days.'

'I know, but I wanted to ask you about *another* kind of mushroom,' said Ruby, 'seeing as how you're such a mushroom expert and everything.'

'Mycologist,' said Mo.

'Exactly,' said Ruby.

'So try me,' he said.

'Have you heard of a Mars Mushroom?'

'Sounds like a question for Walt,' said Mo.

'I'm serious,' said Ruby.

'Are we talking mushrooms from Mars or mushrooms which look like alien things?'

'Don't all mushrooms look like alien things?'

Mo shrugged. 'Does it have a proper name, this Mars Mushroom?'

'*Hypocrea asteroidi,*' said Ruby.

'That sounds kinda familiar,' said Mo. 'I feel like I must have read about that somewhere. I can have a look through some of my journals and specialist books if you'd like me to?'

'I'd appreciate that,' said Ruby, although she didn't hold out much hope that he would find anything. If Pinkerton was trying to keep it secret then it seemed unlikely that there was going to be anything in print.

As soon as Ruby stepped out of the store, it dawned on her just how hungry she was; she hadn't eaten a bite all morning.

She crossed the road to the diner and ordered herself the Pluto Plate, which was basically pancakes with all the extras.

Walter and Duke were sitting at the counter in the same seats, eating the same food they had been eating when she'd first met them that previous Sunday.

They were talking about UFOs and it made entertaining listening. She looked up when the bell on the door jangled and in came another familiar character. It was the cryptic crossword guy, Sven. She watched him lift Spike from the baby chair thing which he had on his back. He looked around, trying to figure out where to perch the baby, then he saw Ruby.

'Would you mind grabbing him a second while I get my coat off?' he asked.

Ruby grudgingly obliged. 'Boy, this kid weighs a ton,' she said. 'He's like some thirty-pound sausage.'

Sven smiled like he was pleased with that assessment of his kid. 'Spike's a big eater,' he said.

He unwound his scarf and shrugged off his coat and hung it on one of the hooks by the door. It was as he turned back towards her that Ruby saw the image printed on his sweatshirt: a sequence of interlocking triangles.

'Cool sweatshirt,' said Ruby. 'Where'd you get it?'

'This?' he said, pointing at it. 'From my old man. He used to work at the power plant over the mountain.'

'So it definitely wasn't a space base?' said Ruby. 'I heard those guys say it *was*.'

'No,' said Sven, 'I can tell you that for nothing – Walter and Duke would like to believe it is, but it ain't.'

'No Mars missions, no alien communications,' said Ruby.

'Just good old electricity,' said Sven.

She shrugged. 'That's a shame,' she said.

When she had finished eating, she caught the bus back down the mountain. She was pretty tired and it didn't take more than a few minutes before she had fallen asleep.

What woke her was a sudden jolt as the driver swerved across the road. He cursed loudly before calling out, 'Boy, that was close!'

'What happened?' asked Ruby.

'Bambi just got lucky,' said the driver.

'Huh?'

'We nearly hit a deer,' explained the woman sitting in the seat across from hers.

Ruby's backpack had catapulted off the seat and some of her things were now rolling around on the floor. She reached to gather them up, but when she checked to make sure everything was now back in the bag, she realised her pencil was missing. It wasn't under the seat; it wasn't anywhere.

So where was it?

Where it was, was safely locked away in the most secure vault in Twinford.

Redfort, you're a duh brain, she cursed, *and you're probably gonna be fired from Spectrum, but not before you're murdered by your boss, who probably is a bona fide agent-killer and knows that you know it!*

Chapter 26.
The trolley problem

WHEN RUBY GOT BACK TO TWINFORD, she felt her watch vibrate as a message came in.

It was from Hal in Gadgets.

```
IF YOU GO TO THE PARKING LOT UNDER THE
ICE RINK YOU'LL FIND A BIG SURPRISE.
```

The parking lot under the ice rink was also the parking lot above Spectrum. *So why does he need to leave whatever he is leaving me in the parking lot?* she wondered. *Why not just tell me to pick it up from the gadget room?* For some reason the whole mystery of it irritated her. There were too many mysteries and she was beginning to crave clarity; clarity on anything would be nice.

She messaged him back.

```
WHY CAN'T I JUST COME DOWN AND
PICK IT UP?
```

she asked.

BETTER THIS WAY, he wrote. BAY D 57

'Have it your way,' she muttered.

Ruby made her way to Bowery Street and on towards the ice rink. She had never actually been in the underground parking lot before; she had never needed to, the elevator took her to Spectrum direct. She walked down the stairwell into the lot and felt glad that this was not a regular thing. The place was creepy; it also smelt bad. She looked around her, searching for the D zone.

Bay 57 was almost at the end, but she didn't need to get close to make out what it was.

'You gotta be kidding me – red?' she muttered. 'I wouldn't be seen dead on a *red* bike.'

She was going to have to do something about this. Red was *worse* than pink, well almost. It was so 'jolly'; so 'my first bike'. Why didn't Hal just go the whole mile and stick a basket on front and attach one of those little colourful whirling windmills to the handlebars?

She didn't register the footsteps behind her – maybe because the woman moved almost without sound.

Ruby kicked at the wheel. There was no way she was taking that thing home with her. *He's torturing me.*

There was a cough and then a gravelly voice spoke. 'A little ungrateful, aren't we?'

Ruby spun around to see a woman dressed entirely in white, her face without expression. Ruby had never once seen her boss outside the confines of Spectrum. If LB had a life beyond the agency then Ruby couldn't imagine it.

'Is this how you treat state-of-the-art Spectrum technology?'

Ruby began to speak, but found herself stammering; no words were forming.

'You seem... what's the word...' LB paused as she searched for the precise adjective. '*Edgy.*' She stared hard at Ruby, and Ruby looked away. It wasn't a comfortable experience to be trapped in this place with an agent-killer.

'I'm concerned, Redfort, I really am. Your behaviour has been a little –' again, she seemed to be groping for the word – '...off.'

'I'm just tired,' said Ruby.

'Tired? And what exactly is making you tired?'

'Oh, I don't know, maybe it's –' her mind had gone blank – 'school...'

'School?' repeated LB. 'School is making you tired?'

Ruby bit her lip. 'No, I guess it's more likely to be the training – not that I'm complaining or anything, it's nothing I can't handle.'

LB just stared at her, an unblinking stare. 'Maybe I can drive you somewhere?'

'Well, I should probably, you know, unlock my bike and, you know, *ride* it home, I mean, since Spectrum went to all the trouble of getting me this machine and...'

'Except you can't possibly do that, Redfort.'

To Ruby's ears that sounded like a threat. And what LB said next sounded a whole lot worse.

'I mean who *would* be seen dead on a *red* bike? Certainly not *you*. So on what colour bike would you be prepared to be seen *dead*?' She put such emphasis on the word 'dead' that a shiver ran right down Ruby's spine.

LB was beginning to remind her of someone; the someone who wore the Italian shoes and the old-fashioned suit.

'I don't mind the colour, not at all actually, I mean, red's so jolly, so like...' What was it like? She couldn't think of a thing other than, well, blood.

'Santa? Is that the word you're searching for?'

'Yes, that's it exactly, so I might just jump right on and get back, get back home or not home, but somewhere... somewhere else.'

'You're acting peculiar, Redfort. Something on your mind?'

The way she said it, the words almost sounded like a challenge.

'I'm cold,' said Ruby. 'Just need to warm up, it's hard to think straight.'

'So your survival training has been a waste of Spectrum resources, is that what you're saying?'

'No, not at all, I'm just...'

'Just what?'

The light overhead went out and Ruby jumped.

'Relax,' said LB. 'They do that.' She waved her hand and they came back on. 'They're motion-sensitive.'

Ruby was looking around her now. Which way should she sprint? She must be able to outrun LB. She knew she couldn't out-fight her, but outrun her, surely.

'You found something out, didn't you?' LB didn't step closer, didn't move an inch, but it felt like she had. 'Why don't you just spit it out, Redfort? There's something you know that you don't want to tell me.'

This was it, this was the moment when the Spectrum 8 boss would pull out some agent-terminator weapon and that would be that.

She might just as well say her piece.

'You killed Bradley Baker.' The words echoed around them. Silence.

LB paused before saying, 'The Count told you?'

'So you're not denying it?'

'No.'

'You murdered him.'

'In a manner of speaking.'

'How could you do that? He was your friend, more than that, he was...'

'It sounds to me like you're passing judgement here?' LB stared hard at Ruby, her eyes unblinking. 'Yet what do you really know? You have a few facts and the word of a psychopath, and yet you feel equipped to condemn me?'

Silence.

'Imagine this, Ruby Redfort. Imagine you have just seconds to make the biggest decision you will *ever* make, imagine that whatever you decide will be wrong. There is no right in this, don't fool yourself into thinking that.'

Silence.

'There's a thought experiment in ethics,' said LB. 'It's called the Trolley Problem. You may have heard of it?'

Ruby shook her head.

'No? Well, lucky you. You see, it's a question of life and death. When I joined Spectrum, part of the training was to consider what you might do if faced with the gritty question: in whose direction do you point the Grim Reaper's scythe?' She smiled a cold smile. 'No, it's worse than that. You *become* the Grim Reaper, *you* decide: is one life worth more than five? Is the life of someone you *value* worth *more* than two that you don't? Is the life of a child worth more than that of an adult? These are the unpleasant issues you have to consider when you become a person who deals in life and death for a living – you become the man with the scythe.'

Ruby said nothing.

'So imagine a trolley car is hurtling down a rail track and it's going to hit five innocent people. You can save them *if* you pull the points lever, so diverting the trolley car onto the parallel track. On this track there is just one person who will die. One life for five?

What do you do?'

Ruby said nothing.

'In my case, the situation was a little more dramatic. A package was delivered anonymously to me at home and when I opened it I found a detonator and instructions to turn on my TV set. Every channel was tuned to the same broadcast, a live countdown, a ticking bomb counting inevitably towards zero.

'A scrambled voice told me what I already knew: a whole site would be destroyed and along with it every one of its one thousand and twenty-seven staff. However, I was offered an alternative outcome: I could save them, every one of them. All I had to do was to press the yellow button there on the detonator. There was a catch, though – there always is in situations like this, always a price to pay.

'"We can trade." That's what the voice said. "One thousand and twenty-seven lives for one." And then the TV flashed up another image: a tiny silver-white craft moving across a blue sky. And it looked so safe somehow, so small in this enormous ocean of sky, and I let my eyes follow it and I knew it was Baker.'

She turned to look at Ruby, eyes unblinking. 'And that was my choice.'

'I...' said Ruby. But she could think of nothing to say. She could see the truth in LB's eyes.

'So do I do nothing?' continued LB. 'In which case, Baker, the person I regard more highly than any other being on this planet, goes merrily on his way, or do I choose to save one thousand and twenty-seven people that I have never met, probably *will never* meet and until now have never thought about.'

She paused, staring Ruby hard in the eye. 'But are they not equally deserving of my protection? Would it not be monstrous to sign the death warrant of so many?' She pondered the question, and then said in a distant voice, 'I will never forget the final question he hissed into my ear. "The clock is ticking, dear LB, what price love, what price life; are the heartbeats of many worth more than your heart's one true desire?"' Her voice was almost inaudible now. 'Ninety-nine seconds is all it took to drain all colour from my life.'

Ruby still could find no words.

'So before you judge me, think about what you would do,' said LB. 'One thousand and twenty-seven people who mean nothing to you, or Clancy Crew?'

'I...' began Ruby, 'I mean it's not possible... to make the right decision, how could one, how could *I* ...'

'As I said, there *is* no right decision,' said LB. 'It's all about your gut instinct. I chose to *save* one thousand and twenty-seven people, but no matter how one tries to square it, it doesn't change the fact that I killed *someone*, my *friend*, *my* choice, no one made me pick *him*. *I* pushed a button which caused the death of the person I happened to like –' her voice cracked – 'to love, more than any other living soul on this sad planet.'

LB turned, strode to her car, climbed in and drove off.

**Casey Morgan
heard the shouting...**

...people were running to the river's edge. Casey saw the boy get pulled out of the rapids: he wasn't moving. There was more shouting, more attempts to resuscitate.

'I think he's dead,' cried a voice. Silence fell.

Samuel Colt didn't give up, wouldn't give up. 'Come on, kid, you need to breathe.'

A cry: 'He's alive, the kid's alive!'

Casey turned and ran, and never looked back.

Chapter 27.
À la mode

RUBY HAD ONLY JUST MADE IT HOME from midtown when she heard the sound of a key in the front door.

'Bonsoir!' called Sabina. 'There's something wrong with my key, could someone let us in?'

Mrs Digby went down to open the door. 'Well, howdie there travellers,' she said, wiping her hands on her apron.

'I thought perhaps we'd been away so long you had decided to change the locks,' laughed Sabina.

'We have,' said Mrs Digby.

'You did?' she said.

'Only because Hitch mislaid his keys,' explained the housekeeper, 'it wasn't personal.'

'Well, that's a relief!' said Brant. 'When a man isn't welcome in his own home, where is he to go!'

'Hey Mom, hey Dad, you actually made it home,' called Ruby as she ran down to greet them.

'Je suis désolée,' said Ruby's mother, giving her daughter a dozen kisses. 'We just got utterly stuck in Paris.'

This was followed by more apologies and a twirling embrace from her father.

'I'm glad you're home,' said Ruby in a strangled voice.

'Good to see you back where you belong,' said the housekeeper.

'Good to see you too, Mrs Digby,' said Brant Redfort, giving the old lady a hearty hug.

'Darling Mrs Digby,' said Sabina Redfort, kissing her on each cheek (a new habit she'd picked up), 'it's so *très bien* to be back, I can't tell you the ways we've missed you.'

'I can believe it,' said Mrs Digby. 'Starting with the need for a decent home-cooked meal, no doubt.'

Brant Redfort smiled, remembering the many *more* than decent home-cooked meals he and his wife had devoured during their stay with the Minister for Culture, whose kitchen was under the command of celebrated chef Antoine Moreau. However, not wanting to disappoint, he nodded and said, 'You can say that again, Mrs D.'

'Boy, am I tuckered out,' said Sabina Redfort.

'I'll get you a nice cup of English tea,' said Mrs Digby, reaching for the kettle. 'You put your feet up.'

'Oh, make mine a large café au lait, s'il vous plait.'

'Coffee? At this time of day? I thought that bad habit belonged to Hitch alone.'

'It's morning in Paris,' said Sabina, yawning.

'Well, I never did,' said Mrs Digby, turning to Mr Redfort.

'So will you be wanting coffee too?'

'Sure, why not,' said Brant. 'When in Paris.'

'We're *not* in Paris,' said Mrs Digby.

'I'll take mine in a bowl,' said Sabina.

The housekeeper looked at her like she hadn't heard right.

'Why ever would you drink coffee from a bowl?'

'It's à la mode,' said Sabina.

'Pardon me?' said Mrs Digby.

'It's what the French do,' said Brant.

'I'm sure there are plenty of bizarre things the French do, but it doesn't mean we should get in on the act.'

'You should try it Mrs D. There's nothing like drinking coffee from a bowl.'

Mrs Digby sniffed. 'I'll stick with my cup, if you don't mind. I've always felt handles were there for a reason.'

'I'll take *my* coffee any way it's going,' said Hitch, walking into the room.

Sabina clapped her hands. 'How merveilleux to see you! We've missed you to distraction.'

There followed a whole lot more kissing on two cheeks and general fussing and then cocktails. Beautifully wrapped gifts were distributed to all and everyone was very pleased.

'Eiffel Tower cufflinks!' said Hitch. 'Just what I need, I mislaid a cufflink a few weeks back and there's not a chance I'll find it.'

'Ironically I lost one of mine at the top of the Eiffel Tower,' said Brant. 'They're such fiddly things, a total liability.'

'Well, I'll do my best to hang on to these ones,' said Hitch.

'You must join us for supper,' said Brant.

'I'm afraid I'm expected elsewhere,' said Hitch, glancing anxiously at his watch.

'Oh no, *really*?' exclaimed Sabina.

She looked so forlorn that Hitch found himself saying, 'You know what, how about I stay for the starter – it really looks too good to miss.'

But unfortunately, just as he raised his fork to his mouth an urgent message flashed up on his watch. No one saw it, no one noticed him read it – no one but Ruby. Hitch made his excuses – an elegant lie – and he promised to make it up to them, and left.

It was a shame, because it was a sumptuous meal Mrs Digby served that night, and although there was some disappointment on the old lady's part that she had not been able to rustle up the hen of the woods stew, no one else minded a bit.

Ruby was relieved to have her parents back, relieved to discover her boss was not a ruthless killer, and happy to have everyone together again under this one safe roof. So merry was the mood that the four of them all stayed up late into the evening playing cards and chatting, and Ruby only went upstairs when she saw that both her mother and her father had fallen asleep right there on the couch in front of her – Mrs Digby having already crept away to her bed an hour earlier.

The first voice Ruby heard the next morning was down the telephone line. The call came through as she was about to leave the house.

'Twinford complaints and moans, what's your grumble?'

'Kid?'

'Go ahead, caller.'

'You want me to list my grumbles?' said Hitch. 'Well, one of them would be that the coffee where I am stinks and the cooking is pretty despicable too. You can tell your folks that I can't wait to make it home tonight.'

'Is that why you're calling?' asked Ruby.

'Just checking in. Is everything AOK?' he asked.

'I guess,' said Ruby. She couldn't exactly discuss the chalk message over the phone. She couldn't discuss *anything* important. He knew that, didn't he?

'How's the bike working out for you?' he asked.

'It's red,' she said.

'That's a problem?'

'Would you ride a red bike?' she asked.

'Depends on the circumstances – now could you pass me on to that wonderful woman who attends to your every need?'

Ruby put Hitch through to the housekeeper's apartment and then set off for Twinford Junior High.

The first voice Ruby heard when she cycled through the school gates was Del Lasco's.

'Redfort, why are you riding that red bike?' she shouted.

'Cos it's the only one I got,' said Ruby.

'I saw you on a pink one the other day,' said Mouse.

'It wasn't jolly enough,' said Ruby.

'It doesn't look right,' said Del. '*You* don't look right.'

'Yeah, well too bad cos it's either this bike or no bike.'

'Yeah, but... *red?*' said Del.

'I'm getting it resprayed, OK?' said Ruby. Until that moment she hadn't considered that option, but now she thought about it, it seemed like a very good idea. Maybe she could do it herself.

Ruby was disappointed to find no Clancy in her form room. She could really do with talking to him.

'Where is he?' she asked Elliot.

'Off sick, I heard,' said Elliot. 'That's what Nancy told Red.'

'He's probably gone down with Crew flu,' said Mouse.

'That or French flu,' said Ruby, who was well aware of the upcoming French exam.

'I wouldn't mind catching it myself,' said Mouse.

'Catching what?' asked Ruby.

'Crew flu, *any* flu.'

'Why d'ya wanna catch the flu?' asked Ruby.

'To get out of this table tennis tournament,' said Mouse. 'I know I'm gonna get destroyed,' she said. 'It's gonna be awful.'

'You're crazy to say that Mouse, you're the best player we have, you're gonna win, I know it,' said Ruby.

'How? Just thinking about it makes me drop my bat.'

Chapter 28.
Nothing but glamour

AFTER SCHOOL, RUBY RODE OVER TO AMBASSADOR ROW. The door was opened by a perfectly healthy-looking Clancy.

'I thought you were supposed to be sick?' said Ruby.

'I am,' said Clancy. 'Come on in.'

'Are you contagious?' asked Ruby.

'Only if my mom gets home early, then you better make a swift exit.'

'I knew you were faking it.'

They went and sat in the lounge with some popcorn and a couple of sodas. The house was quiet; all the other Crews were out.

'You know, you look a bit shaken up,' said Clancy, 'not quite your usual self.'

'Why do you say that?' said Ruby.

Clancy shrugged. 'I don't know, something about your eyes. They seem twitchy.'

'They do?' she said.

'Yeah, it's either something to do with that new red bike, or maybe your contact lenses are bothering you or... it's something else,' said Clancy.

'That's very perceptive of you, and as it happens I *am* a little freaked,' said Ruby. 'It's because...' She paused. 'It's because I ran into LB last night.'

Clancy's eyes immediately became wide. 'Were you alone?'

'You could say that. I was in the underground parking lot.'

'No way,' said Clancy, who was beginning to flap his arms. 'How did you get outta there? I mean did she try to kill you?'

'No,' replied Ruby.

'Well, that's something,' said Clancy.

'Yeah, I was kinda relieved,' said Ruby. 'I thought my number was up for sure. I mean there I am in a deserted parking lot with the woman who killed Bradley Baker.'

'So it's true!' said Clancy, his voice a sort of whispered shriek. 'She really did murder him.'

'It's more complicated than that,' said Ruby.

'More complicated than her murdering her best friend?'

Ruby nodded and then she gave him a word-for-word account of what had happened.

'Jeepers,' said Clancy, 'that's one of the most tragic stories I ever heard.'

'It's beyond tragic,' said Ruby. 'I don't know how she can handle the guilt. She basically had to kill her best friend to save a thousand strangers.'

'Makes you think,' said Clancy. 'I mean you gotta say, she is quite an agent. She sacrificed him and her happiness, *everything*, because it was the lesser of two evils.'

'She's brave, that's for sure,' said Ruby. They sat for a while not talking, just contemplating the magnitude of what LB had done.

After a minute or more Ruby said, 'The thing that gets me is now I'm feeling sorry for the guy.'

'Who?' asked Clancy.

'Bradley Baker,' said Ruby. 'He's always been this massive pain in the butt and now I'm having a hard time hating him and I wanna hate him.'

'Why?' asked Clancy.

'Because... I'm fed up with being told how great he is. You should hear that potato head Froghorn – he literally thinks Baker *is* the sun.'

'He probably *was* a really nice guy,' said Clancy. 'I mean you don't get that many people saying how *nice* you are if you're *not nice*.'

'Well... I mean it *does* happen,' said Ruby. 'Sometimes people feel they should speak well of the dead. It's a kind of an unwritten law.'

'You don't want to like him because he was smarter— because some people *say* he was... more... you know, more experienced than you,' said Clancy.

'You were probably right the first time, he probably was

smarter than me,' said Ruby. 'It's just, do you know how hard it is to be continually compared to someone who happens to be a deal smarter than you?'

Clancy looked at her like she had said something really dumb. 'Yeah, Rube, as a matter of fact I do.'

'OK, sorry, I just mean, working in Spectrum, I get it all the time. They're crazy about this guy.'

'You're just not used to it,' said Clancy. 'I have a lot of practice in this area so I have learned the art of humility.'

'What?'

'I'm not so full of myself.'

'Do you want me to help you with your French or *not*?' said Ruby.

Clancy gave her a panicked look and she punched him lightly on the arm. 'You do know my homework assistance is unconditional?'

'I appreciate that,' said Clancy. 'So,' he said, changing the subject, 'at least you're done with the Prism Vault. I mean now you know the truth about LB you never have to go back *there* again.'

'Are you kidding?' said Ruby. 'Now I absolutely *have* to go back.'

'Why?' spluttered Clancy. 'Why do you have to go back?' He was flapping his arms again.

'Because I need to get into the file which tells me who tried to kill Baker first time around.'

'What?' said Clancy.

'There was this kid who tried to kill him a long time ago, a kid who ran from the scene. I discovered this when I read a file on this Junior Spy Programme Spectrum used to run, and the thing is, if I were you, which I'm sorta trying to be – you know, go with my gut and all – then I would say I have a *hunch* that there's something weird about the way a lot of the important information isn't there any more.'

'You mean you have a hunch someone's tampered with the file?' said Clancy.

'That's exactly what I mean,' said Ruby. 'Blacker told me it's impossible to erase or remove the Ghost Files, but I guess it *is* possible to *move* something from one file to another and hide it – so I have to go back and try to find it.'

'Tonight?' said Clancy. He looked alarmed.

'No,' said Ruby. 'First I have to figure out the final file code. Froghorn had it written up as a question mark which I guess leaves me guessing.'

'Not a clue?' asked Clancy.

'Not a clue,' said Ruby.

Ruby was careful to ride home along the most brightly lit streets, with the most traffic and most restaurant-goers, but still she felt an uneasiness, as if someone was watching. Though she was tempted, she did not activate the hyper-speed booster – she was trying to keep a low profile, and a kid riding a bicycle along Amster at an implausible speed was likely to raise a few eyebrows.

It was as Ruby passed the turning into Lime that she noticed a parked car pull slowly away from the curb. Rather than overtake, it began to crawl behind. She sped up and though she couldn't be sure it seemed as if the car began to move faster. When she reached Oakwood she turned right expecting the car to drive on but it didn't, it followed. Now she *was* spooked. She swept on past her turning and then suddenly squeezed hard on the brakes, causing the bike to skid around so she was pointing in the direction of Cedar Street, she pedalled hard, turned into Cedarwood Drive and ten seconds later was home. The car did not follow.

She ran up the front steps, fumbled for her key, dropped it, picked it up, found the keyhole, opened the door and was in. She made sure to slam it behind her, listening for the reassuring clunk of the lock.

'Ruby, is that you?' called her mother.

'Uh huh,' replied Ruby, panting as she climbed the stairs. She walked into the living room, where she found her mother at her desk.

'Are you all right, honey?' Sabina asked. 'You look a bit flushed.'

'I've been cycling,' said Ruby.

Her mother looked at her sternly. 'You be careful out there in the dark, Ruby, always remember to keep your lights on and your wits about you.'

'I'll remember that,' said Ruby; it actually sounded like good advice.

'Your father won't be home until late as Mr Cleethorp is having a company dinner. I managed to wriggle out of it; it sounded rather tedious,' said her mother. She held something up, a square of card. 'Good news, though! We received our invitation to the Eye Ball.'

'The Eye Ball?' repeated Ruby.

'You haven't heard about it?' asked Sabina. ' *We* heard about it and we were in Paris. The New Year's Eve party at the old Eye Hospital. It's been renovated up to the eyeball – literally.'

What Ruby's mother meant was that every floor of the old thirty-four-storey building had been renovated apart from the top storey, where the giant neon blinking eye was fixed to the outside of the building.

'They've even got that big old eye sign blinking again,' said Sabina. 'Actually, they still have work to do on the east wing of the thirty-third floor, so unless the construction team pull their fingers out the grand dining room won't be ready.'

'That's very disappointing,' yawned Ruby, who was keen to cut this conversation short.

'I know,' sighed Sabina, 'it means no second buffet area.'

'Tragic,' said Ruby.

'And there was going to be a catering lift too, you know, like a dumbwaiter, carrying food up and down from the kitchen –

goodness knows what Consuela will do without it. She's catering the event of course.'

'Cool,' said Ruby, who was by now on autopilot.

Even Sabina could sense her daughter's lack of interest in the behind-the-scenes details of the Eye Ball, and changed tack.

'The party is space themed, you know,' she announced. 'Space is so hot at the moment, with the new observatory and the launch of the space station.'

'Sounds out of this world,' said Ruby.

Her mother did not pick up on her tone.

'It's the must-have ticket this season. It's going to be nothing but glamour,' said Sabina, enthusiasm bubbling out of her. 'And you're coming too, so get excited.'

'I feared as much,' muttered Ruby.

'Pardon?' said her mother.

'I can hardly wait,' said Ruby.

'That's the spirit, honey, talking like a Redfort!' said her mother proudly. 'So what will you wear?'

'I need to decide *now*?' said Ruby, who was hoping to concentrate on more important matters, like how to get a hold of her lost pencil.

'Well, you can't wear just *anything*,' said Sabina. 'No jeans and no T-shirts.'

Ruby looked down at her T-shirt. 'Actually, this one *is* space themed.'

It read: ***space cadet***

'I hope you're kidding,' said her mother.

'I think it would be perfect,' said Ruby.

'So long as you don't wear that black jumpsuit,' said Sabina.

'It's very fashionable,' said Ruby.

'But it's not *right* for a party like this,' said her mother. 'I mean I doubt if you would team it with heels, am I right or am I right?'

'Sneakers,' said Ruby.

'Give me strength,' said Sabina. 'Or better still, a martini. Hitch!'

'He's out for the night,' called Mrs Digby.

'Why?' called Sabina.

'How should I know?' came Mrs Digby's reply. 'Perhaps he's meeting up with an old friend.'

'I didn't know he had any,' said Ruby.

'Of course he has friends,' said her mother. 'Look at him, he's everything a friend could want.'

'Well, he's out,' said Mrs Digby, 'and that's a fact.'

'He called this morning,' said Ruby. 'Said he was coming home.'

'This entire household is falling apart,' said Sabina, sinking down onto the settee.

'You can't rely on anyone these days,' said Ruby.

Mrs Digby appeared, carrying a martini on a tray.

'Mrs D,' sighed Sabina, 'you spoil me to pieces.'

'Tell me something I *don't* know,' said the housekeeper. She walked over to the window and glanced into the darkness.

'I wouldn't be knocked down with surprise if we saw the first real snow tonight,' she said.

'Do you think?' said Sabina. 'It would be better for me if it happened next week. My good warm coat is still at the drycleaner, and I really don't have a nice alternative.'

'What about that one hanging in your closet?' said Mrs Digby.

'The pink one? I never think of pink as a winter colour, do you?'

'What does pink have to do with it? It's fur-lined,' said Mrs Digby. 'If it's warm, it's warm.' She remembered being caught in a freak blizzard when she was barely five and she would have been glad of a pink coat, any coat – she often told the story. '*If my pa hadn't heard the wolves howling and come out looking for me, I would have died of cold as sure as toadstools attract flies.*'

Chapter 29.
Yellow notebooks

RUBY WENT UPSTAIRS. She stood gazing out of the window, watching to see if Mrs Digby's snow premonition was right, but there was not a single snowflake, not yet anyway. What she could see was the grey clapboard house, silent and empty, the new occupants still not moved in. Her mind wandered back to Homer Pinkerton.

If Pinkerton's death is connected to Bradley Baker's, she thought, *then this all began many years ago, long before you stepped a tiny toe on the planet.*

So what important thing connected Pinkerton to Bradley Baker? What had happened to his dog, where had he disappeared to? This thought set her wondering what answers she might have, what everyday observations might hold a truth?

Start at the beginning, Rube. You saw Mr Pinkerton's dog kidnapped, though you don't remember it. What else might you have observed?

She got down on her knees and began rolling back the small geometric-patterned rug which covered one portion of the wooden floor. Then she took a screwdriver from her drawer, pushed it between two of the boards and neatly lifted up a single short plank. In the cavity between the joists were her 624 yellow notebooks.

Ruby had spent more than a lot of hours making notes in these little books, recording the everyday goings on, to-ings and fro-ings, snippets of conversation, strange occurrences, blandly dull incidents. Because as Ruby would say, **EVEN THE MUNDANE CAN TELL A STORY**. It was her **RULE 16**. And though each notebook was not many pages long, and though Ruby was an exceptionally fast reader, there was still no way she was going to manage to read each one cover to cover that evening. It was hard to know where to start, so she began at the beginning.

It was when she was halfway through notebook **46** that she realised one of the occurrences she had noted down was very similar to something which had taken place one previous July in notebook **22**.

Notebook 22

```
My grandmother almost swallowed my mother's
diamond earrings. She found them at the
bottom of her teacup.
She said, 'Is this expensive tea or what?'
```

Notebook 46

```
My grandmother swallowed a pair of my
```

mother's emerald earrings and we spent most of Saturday sitting in the emergency room. The doc said, 'it shouldn't prove fatal and probably will cause you very little discomfort.'

My grandmother wanted to know how the doc proposed she got them out of her system.

And the doc said, 'in the usual way.'

My grandmother said, 'the experience had really put her off tea even if she was thirty thousand dollars more valuable than she had been eight hours earlier.'

My mom said, 'she would never be able to look at those emerald earrings without imagining the journey they had been on.'

She has given them to my grandmother.

My grandmother said, 'It wasn't compensation enough for what she was about to endure.'

Both these jewellery mishaps reminded Ruby of something she had written down in her more recent list titled:

THINGS I KNOW AND THINGS I DON'T KNOW.

Things I don't know

Where my mom's snake earrings are.

And now she was pretty sure she did. They would no doubt be in a teacup somewhere in her grandmother's New York apartment. She hoped the old lady was sticking to coffee as she had vowed.

Ruby made a note to telephone her grandmother. Not now though. Suddenly overwhelmed with tiredness, she put back the notebooks, slotted the floorboard into its gap and replaced the rug. Then she got changed and climbed into bed.

School was pretty dull the next day. The only thing that happened which might be considered of interest was down to Del Lasco. Mrs Drisco had caught her roller-skating down the main corridor. It was a long passage and the floors, being newly surfaced, made for excellent skating.

Mrs Drisco had given Del three hours litter-picking and confiscated the skates. Del had not taken this lying down, she had argued that there was 'nothing in the school rules that said one couldn't roller-skate down the corridor.'

Mrs Drisco argued that, 'since running was not allowed it was hardly appropriate to skate'.

Del said this was 'not the point', since skating was *not mentioned* in the 'long list of activities' one was 'not allowed' to perform in the corridor. And had she known this was a rule then 'of course' she 'would *never* have done it'.

Mrs Drisco said she 'found this very hard to believe'.

Del said she felt 'very undermined by that statement'.

Mrs Drisco said 'rules were rules'.

Del said she 'didn't have a problem with the rules', she said she 'only had a problem with the things which weren't rules but were being bandied around as if they were rules in order to get innocent parties onto litter-picking duty'.

Del spent the rest of the morning in Principal Levine's office.

When she came out she said she was going to take this 'all the way'.

Knowing Del, Ruby felt it was likely she would win; either that or get expelled.

When school was out Ruby rode the bus to the Cherry Cup and while she travelled she pondered the File Code Three conundrum. How to figure out a code when you didn't even know what type of code you were trying to figure out?

Ruby had arranged to meet Mouse after her dental check-up. Mouse was feeling increasingly wobbly about the Twinford Table Tennis Championships and the prospect of fillings had only served to make her more jumpy still.

As Ruby walked in to the Cherry Cup, a young woman attempted to hand her a flyer advertising the upcoming ice-capade.

'I'm not interested,' said Ruby.

'It's going to be space-themed,' said the woman.

'Isn't everything?' said Ruby. She took the flyer without

enthusiasm and pushed open the door to Cherry's.

Ruby found her friend doing a word search puzzle.

'Hey Mouse, that looks boring.'

Mouse made a face. 'It is,' she said. 'I was just trying to keep focused.'

'Focused on what?' asked Ruby.

'Focused on not thinking about the match,' said Mouse.

'What's the deal with the match?' asked Ruby.

'I'm going to have to beat Penelope Fingelhorn.'

'So?' said Ruby. 'You can smash her, no problem.'

'I know,' said Mouse. 'And then I'm going have to beat Kitty Kuramara.'

'So you'll smash her too,' said Ruby.

'I just don't know, Rube, I sorta think this girl's got me beat, you know what I'm saying?'

'It's all in your mind, Mouse,' assured Ruby. 'You can do it, you know you can, you've won a zillion games more difficult than this one. Kitty Kuramara isn't such a big deal.' As she talked, Ruby noticed every time the name Kitty Kuramara was mentioned, Mouse would start winding the ice-capade flyer round and round a drinking straw. It was as Ruby watched her do this for the fourth time that two thoughts dawned.

The pen on the cord, the one Froghorn had looped around his neck like he really, really didn't want to let it out of his sight, that was the first thing that came to mind. The pen was a new addition: until this last week, Ruby had never seen it before.

Then there was Froghorn's new assignment – as coder of the Prism Vault. He was pleased about that, keen to let Ruby know that he was the coding agent tasked with creating all the code levels.

She had noticed without really being conscious of it that when she brought up the subject of the Ghost File codes he had begun twisting the pen in his hand, and later when he was really flustered he had begun rolling it into his tie, just as Mouse was doing with the straw and the flyer.

Ruby was so preoccupied with this thought that she almost lost the thread of her Mouse pep talk.

'So what would *you* do Ruby, if *you* were faced with Kitty Kuramara?'

'Um... you know what I'd do? I'd just forget it's Kitty Kuramara. I mean pretend she's Elliot, or some other kid you know you can slam, you gotta adjust your thinking Mouse, it's all in your mind,' assured Ruby. 'The thing is you're thinking defeat and you should go in there meaning to win.' It was Ruby's **RULE 12: ADJUST YOUR THINKING AND YOUR CHANCES IMPROVE.**

'That's easy for you to say, Ruby,' said Mouse. 'You're not easily intimidated.'

Ruby thought for a moment, and then said, 'So I heard this woman talking on the TV, about how if you adopt a strong pose like, say, Wonder Woman – you know how she stands – feet apart, hands on hips, defiant expression? Well, it does something to your brain's chemistry, it has an actual physical effect; in an interview situation it makes people want to offer you the job, listen to your point of view, so in a tournament situation it's gonna have the same result, it's gonna make you a winner.'

'Are you sure about that?' said Mouse.

'Sure I'm sure,' said Ruby. 'All you have to do is take a few minutes in the restroom, adopt the Wonder Woman pose and when you face Kuramara you're gonna smash her game.'

'I just hope no one comes into the bathroom while I'm doing it,' said Mouse.

By the time Ruby left the diner, Mouse was looking a lot happier, and Ruby was feeling like she might be onto something.

When she arrived home she went straight to her room and scanned the bookshelves until she found the little indigo code book, author unknown.

She leafed quickly through it, stopping when she reached page 101: transposition ciphers. There were a number of these, but the one she was interested in was the scytale, used in particular by the Ancient Greeks and Spartans to communicate orders in military campaigns. Random-seeming letters or numbers were written on a strip of leather. To form the plain text, the leather was wrapped around a cylinder of a specific size and shape, and then the correct symbols would line up.

The cylinder could be a pen, couldn't it? Or something which looked like a pen. *A pen on a cord?*

The strip of cipher text, she figured, would be at the vault location. The cylinder would have to be *brought* there by whoever wanted to gain access to one of the level three security files.

OK, thought Ruby. *All you gotta do is get hold of Froghorn's pen – how difficult can it be?*

Chapter 30.
A stroke of luck

RUBY SLEPT SOUNDLY FOR ALL OF THIRTY MINUTES until she was woken by a buzzing. Her watch flashed, and there was a message:

    HQ ASAP.

Ruby reported to reception, but before she could open her mouth, Buzz raised a hand to say, *wait there*.

Ruby sat and waited.

And waited.

After ten minutes she began to get restless.

After twenty minutes she started to get annoyed.

'So why am I here?' asked Ruby. 'I'm guessing you didn't drag me all the way into HQ just to have me sit on a bench, though then again...'

'I didn't drag you in anywhere, I just made the phone call as instructed.' Buzz was nothing if not literal.

'So Buzz, do you ever feel like a mushroom sitting there in

the middle of that desk?'

'Why would I feel like a mushroom?' asked the administrator.

'It's just something about the way you're sticking up through that hole in the table like you're growing out of it,' said Ruby. 'And, you know, mushrooms grow in the dark and this place is underground.'

'But it's *not* dark,' said Buzz, blinking up at her. 'Spectrum is very well lit.'

'Buzz, do you ever see the funny side to anything?'

'Were you being humorous?' said Buzz.

'I guess not,' said Ruby.

There was zero point trying to engage the administrator in any further conversation, so she sat back down, took out her indigo code book and began reading. She might just as well use her time and learn a little. Finally Buzz beckoned her over. Ruby picked up her coat and went to find out where she was meant to be and who she was meant to see. But a strange thing happened as she approached the desk. The administrator seemed to change colour, from pale to even paler.

'What?' said Ruby. 'What happened? You kinda look like you just saw a ghost.'

But Buzz seemed unable to speak. Ruby followed her gaze and saw what she was looking at – it was the little white badge pinned to the inside of her parka.

'Is it this?' said Ruby, but Buzz did not answer, instead she said, 'LB is expecting you,' then she picked up the green telephone which had begun to ring and said, 'Spectrum 8, declarar sua divisao.'

The atmosphere was chilly when she walked into LB's starkly white office. This time when Ruby looked around at the colour-free space she saw meaning in its whiteness. This interior was not *coloured* white; it was white because it was *without* colour. And in Ruby's head she heard her boss's words, *'Ninety-nine seconds is all it took to drain all colour from my life.'*

'Sit,' ordered LB.

Ruby sat.

'What we discussed the other night,' said LB. 'I trust it will not go any further: the last thing I want is rumours and half-truths spreading through Spectrum 8.'

'Of course,' said Ruby.

'It was decided to keep what happened confidential because it was thought it would harm morale if the truth got out.'

'I understand,' said Ruby, 'and I'm sorry.'

'Sorry?' said LB.

'Sorry for what happened,' said Ruby, 'sorry for my lack of judgement. I wasn't thinking. It's this whole business with the Spectrum mole.'

'Double agent,' corrected LB. 'Never underestimate the power of paranoia.' She looked down at the stack of files in front of her and then looked up at Ruby. 'When we are aware that *one* of us cannot be trusted, it means *none* of us can be trusted.'

Ruby shifted in her seat: the statement made her uneasy.

'So we are clear on this?' asked LB.

'Yes,' said Ruby.

'So keep it zipped,' said LB.

'You can count on it,' said Ruby.

There was a knock at the door and Hitch entered the room. 'You need to get going – the helicopter's waiting for you,' he said to LB.

The Spectrum 8 boss was about to dismiss Ruby with a wave of her hand when Ruby found herself saying, without really meaning to...

'Buzz looked at me funny just now when I came in.'

'Excuse me?' said LB.

'I wouldn't mention it ordinarily, but she's never done that before,' said Ruby.

'I'm not following,' said LB. 'Is this a complaint or an observation? Has she offended you in some way? Because if she has then could you take it up with the human resources team or just better still, get over it.'

'It was when she saw *this*,' said Ruby, holding up her coat and the little white badge which could be seen pinned to its lining.

The atmosphere changed quite suddenly. It was like a spectre had just entered the room.

'Where did you get that?' said LB.

Hitch reached for the coat. 'Kid, did you find this or was it given to you?'

'I found it,' said Ruby, her voice uncertain, 'a long time ago. I found it not far from my house on Cedarwood Drive.'

Hitch was inspecting the circle of tin.

'Is it...?' asked LB.

He nodded. 'Yes,' he said, 'it has the mark.'

'What mark?' asked Ruby.

'The Larva mark,' said Hitch, running his fingers over the Braille bumps.

How did I miss that? thought Ruby, but she said nothing.

'How did it get to be *there*?' said LB. 'It went missing more than thirty years back.'

'What is it?' asked Ruby. 'Who did it belong to?'

Without another word, LB opened the door to the hidden room which adjoined her office, a room Ruby had been in only once before and much to the fury of her Spectrum 8 boss. It was a room lined with photographs, pictures of locations, pictures of agents, some formal photographs: some casual. Some showed dramatic scenes of agents leaping across gullies or climbing up cliff faces, others were off-duty pictures like the one of Hitch eyeballing a huge crocodile, Hitch pulling a stupid face, his eyes crossed. But the photograph LB was pointing to was in black and white and of a smiling boy sitting in the cockpit of a plane. Hitch reached up, took it from the wall and handed it to Ruby.

She recognised the photograph; she had noticed it just minutes before LB had discovered her snooping in her private gallery. Back then Ruby had believed she was looking at some agent's son who had been allowed to sit in the pilot's seat and pretend to be flying the plane. Now she knew she was looking at the pilot.

'Is that who I think it is?' asked Ruby.

'I don't know,' said LB. 'Are you thinking, is that Bradley Baker?'

'That's what I'm thinking,' said Ruby.

'Then yes, that's Bradley Baker.'

The boy was eight, perhaps nine, but that wasn't the interesting thing about the picture. What was catching Ruby's attention was the little circle of white pinned to his T-shirt.

'This was his badge?' asked Ruby.

'He was given it when he made it through the JSRP training – he was the only one to graduate – the whole "kid recruitment" was given up as a bad idea.'

Ruby kept her expression closed, giving no sign that might betray her knowledge of all this.

'This was the only Larva badge issued?' she asked.

'The only one ever made,' said LB.

'So it is *definitely* his?' said Ruby.

'Without a doubt,' said Hitch.

'So how did it end up a few yards from my house?' pondered Ruby.

'How indeed,' said Hitch.

LB's watch beeped loudly and she strode towards the door.

'Lock up here, would you Hitch?' She left the room, taking the Larva badge with her, and the little circle of tin, so long a part of Ruby's psychological armour, would now be locked away in some drawer, and she wondered if she would ever lay eyes on it again. She supposed not.

As they turned to leave, Ruby caught sight of a series of photographs capturing a young woman falling through the air. She looked dazzling because she was clad in a skin of gold which flashed and gleamed as the sun hit it. Around her shoulders was a little white fur-hooded cape and in the final three pictures one could see her hand reach across her chest as she deployed a parachute, the next showed the chute emerging like a puff of gold and in the final frame the woman sailing down to earth, a perfect golden canopy floating high above her head.

'Who is that?' asked Ruby.

'That's your boss,' said Hitch.

'You have to be kidding,' said Ruby. 'You're telling me LB did stuff like that?'

'Sure she did, she was Spectrum's first female field agent and she was one of the best too.'

'That's some suit,' said Ruby.

'Yeah,' said Hitch, 'it's a cold climate skydive suit, it will keep you alive in pretty extreme temperatures.'

'Any chance Spectrum might issue me with that parachute cape?' said Ruby, her gaze trained on the cloud of gold. 'It's the coolest outfit I've ever seen.'

'I think you'd have to do something pretty remarkable before LB let you get your hands on her parachute cape.'

'Remarkable like, keep my mouth shut? Cos I can do that.'

'No, I think it would have to be remarkable like finding lost gold.'

'I'll do my best,' said Ruby.

'No one can stop you from dreaming, kid.'

Hitch and Ruby stepped out into the atrium.

'So I was wondering,' she said, 'were you ever in the JSRP, you know, alongside Bradley Baker?'

'What?' said Hitch.

'Did you train with him, you know, back when you were a boy?'

'Just how old do you think I am?'

'I don't know,' said Ruby, 'fifty-five... fifty-seven.'

'Kid, I'm forty-two.' He shook his head. 'Boy, never ask a child to guess your age; they'll always have you pegged at just shy of decrepit.'

'Didn't mean to offend,' said Ruby.

'Don't mind me, I got skin thicker than a crocodile's,' said Hitch. 'But no, I wasn't in the JSRP.'

She looked at him – if he was lying then he was the best in the business – *he's telling the truth,* she thought.

'Talking of crocodiles,' she said, 'what's with that photograph?'

'What photograph?' asked Hitch.

'The one of you looking into the eyes of that old croc.'

'Oh, so you spotted that? I look good, don't you think?'

'It made me wonder.'

'Made you wonder what?'

'How you with your big fear of crocodiles could get up close and personal with such a huge reptile.'

'Are you kidding?' He began to laugh, really laugh. In fact, he laughed so hard that he didn't look like he was ever going to stop.

'*What*?' she asked, annoyed that she wasn't in on the joke.

'That picture was taken at *Disneyland*,' he wheezed. 'He was made of rubber. Kid, you might want to get a new pair of spectacles.' He stepped into the elevator.

'Where are you off to? I thought maybe we could get a donut or something?' said Ruby.

'I'd love to, kid, but I've just got places to be.' As the doors closed shut, he called, 'See you later alligator!'

'Funny,' muttered Ruby, 'real funny.'

She pulled on her parka, zipping it up ready for the cold

she was about to step into, but just as she reached the door, she bumped into Hal coming the other way.

'Thanks for the red bike,' she said.

HAL: *'I thought it was green.'*

RUBY: *'It's red.'*

HAL: *'Ah.'*

Pause.

RUBY: *'You're colour blind?'*

HAL: *'Yep.'*

RUBY: *'Priceless.'*

HAL: *'So you happy?'*

RUBY: *'Do I look happy?'*

HAL: *'I don't know, do you? We're not that well acquainted. Happy for you might be a whole different deal than for most kids.'*

RUBY: *'I'm not most kids, and I'm not looking happy.'*

HAL: *'Why not?'*

RUBY: *'Why would I want a red bike?'*

HAL: *'Because it's jolly?'*

RUBY: *'I'm not a jolly type of person.'*

HAL: *'Because your name's Ruby?'*

RUBY: *'Man, that's lame. I would like the bike to be green. My bikes are always green.'*

HAL: *'You do realise the colour of the bike doesn't affect your ability to ride it?'*

RUBY: *'In my case it does, in my case it has a pretty big effect* *on my ability to ride it.'*

'Leave it with me,' said Hal, 'I'll have it resprayed.'

'You know what, I think I'll just do it myself,' said Ruby. 'I got a feeling if I leave it with you it might just end up purple, and then I really will be distressed.'

'You not a fan of purple?'

'What do you think?' she said.

Ruby's worry ran deeper than purple, of course. The real reason she wasn't about to hand over her new and improved bicycle was because if one was in the business of needing some kind of getaway vehicle then a Spectrum bike fitted with hyper speed booster was a pretty good option.

'Come with me,' sighed Hal, 'I'll get you a can of green spray.'

She followed him down to the gadget room and waited while he got someone to fetch her exactly the right shade of green.

'You'll find it goes on really easily, no drips, dries instantly.'

Ruby thanked him a little grudgingly and turned to leave.

'I'm meant to walk you to the exit,' said Hal.

'Oh come on, man, I can see myself out and you've got a ton of work to do, right?'

'I got plenty,' agreed Hal.

'So I'll skip along outta here and save you the trouble.'

'OK,' he said, 'but no funny business.'

'I can assure you of that,' said Ruby, her expression angelic.

And off she went down the corridor, just like she should –

only once she rounded the corner, she doubled-back, turned left instead of right, and sprinted along until she reached the violet door of room 324, the 'Frog Pod' as Blacker liked to call it – Froghorn's office. She knocked, but there was no reply. She tried the door – it was locked, hardly a surprise – but Ruby had no difficulty getting past that little problem. She knew Miles Froghorn's code because she'd had to figure it out not so long ago: it was pretty straightforward.

What she was looking for would surely not be on his desk. It would be locked away in his little safe underneath. She walked quickly around to the other side but her bag caught the pen-tidy on top of the table and its contents scattered across the surface and one by one each pen rolled off the desk and onto the floor.

'Darn it!' cursed Ruby, grabbing up the pens as they fell.

And there it was in her hand: the scytale cylinder pen. Froghorn had hidden it in plain sight right there in his neat little pen-pot. Ruby hesitated only for a second before snatching it up and slipping it into her pocket. Then she got out of there fast, aware that she needed to make it to the Prism Vault before Froghorn discovered that the decoder was gone.

The man looked down
at the bedraggled child and
wondered how the creature
had found him...

...'so what do you imagine I can do for you?' he asked. 'Other than have you rounded up by the child-catcher... if only.'

'I want to become your apprentice.'

He laughed at that. 'I don't take on worker bees.'

'You should, I'm smart.'

'I'm smarter than you and me put together,' said the tall thin man. 'Besides, I like to keep my own company. I have no trouble recruiting helpers when I require help. You'd be surprised how many upstanding citizens are prepared to sully their souls for the promise of a little money.'

'I don't want money.'

'Everyone wants money.'

'Not me.'

'I'm intrigued by your naivety,' said the Count. 'Don't tell me you are prepared to become my dogsbody and yet want nothing for your trouble.'

'I don't want nothing.'

'I thought not. We all have our price – what's yours?'

'I want to know what you know.'

'You want me to teach you the ways of the underworld? And what can you possibly give me in return?'

'I know things you want to know.'

'A wretch like you? I doubt that. Name a subject you might possibly know more about than I.'

'Spectrum.'

He was silent for a moment.

Then:

'So tell me, what's your name?'

'I have no name. I'm going to shed my past like a snake sheds its skin.'

'How very poetic,' said the Count.

Chapter 31.
Place of death

THIRTY-TWO MINUTES LATER and Ruby was standing inside
the Prism Vault. She had expected to see her pencil lying there
on the floor, but it had gone. Clearly someone had found it.

Question: if some other Spectrum agent authorised to visit
the Prism Vault had found her pencil then why had they not
notified security? Why had they not at the very least checked to
see who had Ghost File clearance?

*Don't think about that now, just find what you need and get out
of here.*

She tapped in the level two security code and wasted no time
finding the Larvae files. What she hoped to find was the name of
Bradley Baker's would-be assassin. She wanted to know if it was
possible that this young recruit had not let go of his murderous
intention to rid the world of Spectrum's brightest recruit.

The writing in the alley had implied this could be so.

Beware the child who yearned to be Larva,
disguised as a fly, but emerged a spider.

Perhaps this kid had bided his time and waited patiently for the perfect moment to bring his plan to fruition.

She read through the pages at speed, searching for information about the rapids incident and for the names of those there that day, but still she found nothing useful – only pages of encrypted text and blanked-out words with meaningless sections in between. She shook the file in frustration and then slammed it shut, and it was this action which seemed to dislodge a loose paper which had been tucked under the file sleeve.

It was a report of what had occurred that day at the rapids, and in it appeared two names which until then had been missing.

The first was the name of the child thought to be responsible for the attempted murder of Bradley Baker. A kid named Casey Morgan. Nothing could be proved – there seemed to be no witness to the incident – and if Art Hitchen Zachery had observed anything then he was possibly too traumatised to recall it. As for Morgan, he had run from the scene and had never been found, so his guilt was naturally assumed.

The second name in the report was of the child who had pulled Baker from the rapids, a kid named Loveday, that was it, nothing more.

Ruby had spent so long looking for this information that she was fast running out of time to search for the other thing she needed to know: why had Baker's last radio contact been with Pinkerton? Pinkerton, an old man, retired and living quietly in leafy West Twinford? She had not a clue where to look for this information, and in any case she doubted what she hoped to find would be written in one of these files. She suspected that Baker and Pinkerton had communicated in secret. Perhaps they were aware of the presence of a mole even back then? As a last resort she decided to try the black files. *Might they represent the dead?* Was there some miniscule chance that one of these black files might contain information about Baker and Pinkerton, two Spectrum employees whose deaths were somehow intertwined?

It was a long shot, but long shots were all she had.

The black file was level three security and it directed her to the panel on the right-hand side of the door. She clicked it open and there found a narrow strip of paper which was printed with a long series of seemingly random letters. Next she took the cylinder pen from where it was tucked into her Superskin and wrapped the paper so the letters lined up. It said: cjk6xAsihX.

'That can't be right,' she muttered.

She tried again, the letters made a word: Archilocus. The Greek poet who first mentioned Scytales.

Totally Froghorn, she thought.

She tapped the letters into the keypad and this time when she went to withdraw the file, it was released without problem.

What she found there nearly knocked her off her feet.

Black stood for space, not death, and what she read in this file filled in a lot of gaps.

Baker was part of the Spectrum Space Encounter programme.

Space Encounter had top secret status, it said so all over the file and the main body of the document was still encrypted. She had heard not so much as a rumour about it within Spectrum's walls; it was obviously a very well-kept secret.

The Spectrum Space Encounter programme had officially begun in 1961, the year President Kennedy had authorised the US space programme and its ambition to get to the moon.

She thought of Froghorn's strange line, about Baker jumping from 14,000 feet: *'It wasn't a regular plane.'*

Had it been a space craft of some kind? A shuttle?

She glanced at the clock.

Three minutes and counting.

Reading around the encrypted content, it seemed this ambition to conquer space had been in the planning for a number of years, tens of years in fact.

2

Spectrum had been selecting recruits for years, young recruits, very young... kids, in fact.

She turned the page: JSRP, the J the R and the P all pale blue, the S was black.

What does this mean? It means something, but what? Tick tock, tick tock, *think Ruby think.*

Pale blue was Froghorn's code for kid, black was his code for space.

1

Got it!

JSRP did not stand for Junior Spy Recruitment Programme; it stood for Junior *Space* Recruitment Programme.

So where was this Spectrum space base?

She leafed through the pages as quickly as she could; the minutes were already gone, now it was the seconds that were ticking by.

51

50

49

48

Place of death:

en route in Delta V DSO

to base at

No kidding.

44

43

42

Instead of a name, there was just that symbol. Three triangles interlocking. A skyline of mountains, the moon above.

Just like on Sven's sweatshirt.

Bradley Baker had been flying somewhere in the Sequoia

Mountains when someone had forced LB to choose between shooting down his craft or destroying, not a power plant... but the Spectrum space base.

10

9

8

7

6

5

4

She had left it too late. There was a beeping and then the door began to close.

3

She scrabbled to her feet, pushing the file into place...

2

she ran for the exit,

1

threw herself through the gap, and

0

the door *thunked* shut.

She lay there for a minute, her heart racing, grateful to have made it out of the vault in time. She got to her feet and pressed the exit button, the door in the floor slid open and she climbed down into the tank. This time it was already full of water. That didn't seem right.

The opening closed overhead and she began searching for

the fly on the wall. She saw it and swam towards it but as she reached out her hand to touch it, so it moved. She tried again but again it got away from her, over and over she attempted to catch it but found it impossible. She was running out of air, she could hold her breath no longer.

Don't panic. Think!

She felt for the breathing band. Five minutes of air, five precious minutes to figure this out.

She watched the fly as it moved from wall to wall, ceiling to floor, and figured there was a pattern to it. If she predicted its move before it landed, swatted it before it had settled, she would get it.

On the third attempt she did it, her hand slapped at the wall and the exit slid open, and Ruby kicked out into the ocean and up to where she could breathe. She swam slowly to shore and emerged from the black, dragging herself out of the water like some strange and half-dead sea creature. She lay there for a minute or two and when she looked up she spied a figure sitting on the rocks.

Her pulse quickened.

Not him, she thought, *please not him.*

She froze, wondering if it might not be best to head back out to Meteor Island. She was so exhausted she wasn't sure she could make it that far, but she would prefer to drown than face whatever the Count might have in store for her.

The figure stood up and the silhouette alone told her it was not him. The Count would not be dressed in a modern puffa jacket and ear-flapped hat.

Darn it, Froghorn! Does it have to be you?

She had thought she might just be in the clear, that perhaps she had escaped undetected.

There was no point running, certainly not while she was wearing the Superskin – so perfect for swimming, but useless for sprinting. So she got to her feet and trudged up the beach to face what was no doubt going to be a very uncomfortable barrage of righteousness.

But as she got closer she saw she was mistaken: not Froghorn but...

'Clancy?' she said.

Chapter 32.
Hit and run

'HEY RUBE,' SAID CLANCY. He sounded cold, his teeth chattering.

'What are you doing here?' she asked.

'Waiting for you.' He shivered.

'But how did you know I would be here?'

He shrugged. 'A hunch, I guess. You *did* say you would be coming back and I tried to phone you a few times earlier and when you didn't pick up I sort of supposed you would be swimming out to Meteor Island. I mean what else would you be doing at 5am?'

They rode their bikes back along the coast road and stopped in at Green-Wood House, so Ruby could change and pick up her school books. It was still early and the household was not yet awake, so the two of them slipped back out and made their way to the diner on Amster. Ruby ordered a double breakfast and Clancy listened while she described all that had happened.

And finally she told him of her mistake at having imagined

Hitch could have been a junior recruit.

'I think I might have offended him,' said Ruby.

'How?' asked Clancy.

'He asked me how old I thought he was.'

'What did you say?'

'Fifty-two.'

'If you said that to my mom,' said Clancy, 'she would have you on double chores for the rest of the decade.'

School dragged a bit but it couldn't be helped. Had she skipped another day's schooling, Mrs Drisco would be well and truly on the warpath – it was becoming a challenge to think up reasonable excuses.

When the bell clanged, Ruby knew exactly where she was headed.

She found the City Library busy, but she bagged a place at one of the smaller tables towards the back of the hall. Dumping her coat, she walked up the steps to the newspaper archive room and started to go through the store of local news microfiche.

What she knew now was that Walter and Duke were right: there *was* a secret space base somewhere in the Sequoia Mountains and not so far from Little Mountain Side. She *also* knew that Bradley Baker had been flying there in some kind of space craft when he got shot down.

What she wanted to know was: had his crash been reported in the local news?

She had a pretty good idea of what she was looking for and

a pretty good idea of what she was expecting to find.

However, after a few hours of peering through the microfiche viewer at archived newspaper reports Ruby had come up with absolutely nothing regarding a western mountain plane crash in the fall of 1962.

There was no mention of it in the national papers, but perhaps she shouldn't be surprised – a small aircraft crashing would hardly be of great interest to the nation at large, especially since the guy piloting the plane was no one of note. To the wider world Bradley Baker was a nobody.

Ruby didn't give up there, instead she began working her way through the *local* papers, the *West Mountain Tribune* and the *Ridgepoint Gazette*. In this second paper she found a report of a bright light followed by a thunderous noise somewhere just off the mountain road known as the Pine Forest Pass. A small area of woodland had been destroyed and a crater formed, but nothing else: no debris, no human remains. There was speculation as to whether the cause was a meteorite re-entering the Earth's atmosphere.

Only one newspaper, the *Sequoia Herald*, raised the possibility of a plane or other aircraft exploding mid-air, though this idea was quickly rejected by one witness:

'if it was a plane then it must have vaporised, as there was no sign of any wreckage whatsoever.'

The witness was a member of the Sequoia Mountain forestry team and though he had not been present on the night of the explosion, he *did* visit the site the following day and found nothing to lead him to believe that the cause of the explosion could have been an aircraft. All the local articles reported pretty much the same inconclusive findings, with no explanation or useful detail.

However, things got a little more interesting and a little weirder when Ruby picked up Little Mountain Side's UFO quarterly journal, titled *Unidentified*. It was an amateur publication, put together by enthusiastic UFO watchers.

Most of the magazine was taken up with blurry photographs of bright lights in the sky, which, due to the poor quality of the images, could be anything from helicopters to streetlights. There were also articles about little green men, things that went bump in the night and alien encounters, but it was when Ruby turned to page seventeen and found the interview with local man Lenny Rivers that her interest was piqued.

Lenny had been driving back home along Pine Forest Pass in the direction of Ridgepoint when he had spotted an injured man lying on the tarmac.

'a hit and run, probably a logging truck I reckon, poor soul had been left for dead. I half-lifted, half-dragged the fella, and eventually got him into my truck with the intention of driving him on to Ridgepoint hospital, they got a pretty well-equipped emergency unit there. I hadn't gone more than a quarter-mile when I find the road cordoned off, diversion it says, maybe a fallen tree I'm thinking, but I'm in my truck, got my chainsaw with me, and I figure I can deal with that, and heck I don't have much choice here, the guy's dying, I gotta get him some medical attention and quick. I don't have the time to drive fifty miles in the other direction.'

It was en route to Ridgepoint that Mr Rivers witnessed his second dramatic happening of the night:

'It was 1am or thereabouts and pitch dark and then all of a sudden I start to see lights in the trees, all these flashlights and something glowing. Then I begin to make out figures; as I got nearer it was possible to see that these figures were official-looking fellows, black suits, that kind of caper, and all talking on walkie-talkie devices – like FBI agents maybe. I slowed down to ask if they might be able to give my passenger some medical help, but I was waved back, quicker than you can spit, told me the road was closed, like they couldn't get me outta there fast enough. Had to find another route to the hospital which lord knows wasn't easy.' Mr Rivers drove out there the next morning, but found, 'there wasn't a darned thing to see other than a pretty big dent in the ground.'

When *Unidentified* asked Mr Rivers what he believed was the cause of all this 'official' attention, he said:

'Folks in town were talking about a meteorite, but if you want to know what I think, it was a UFO, some kinda spaceship had come down.'

Ruby sat back in her chair. Lenny Rivers wasn't wrong. A meteorite wouldn't have FBI-types closing off roads. If it had been a plane that had crashed, a regular plane, there would have been no reason to keep it hush-hush.

A spaceship full of Martians? Hard to believe.

A space craft, not alien but part of the Spectrum Space Programme? Possibly.

When Ruby had finished reading every single article, paragraph and sentence relating to the Pine Forest Pass incident, she sat back in her chair and wondered what might be her next move.

Go find Lenny Rivers, she thought.

Finding Lenny Rivers' address was the easy part; he was in the phone book.

No time like right now, she thought, as she picked up her satchel and headed off towards the bus depot.

When Ruby arrived at Lenny Rivers' house, the door was answered by an elderly woman.

'I'm sorry to bother you,' said Ruby, 'but I was wondering if I could speak to Mr Lenny Rivers?'

The woman looked puzzled. 'My husband passed on eight years ago now.'

'Oh,' said Ruby. 'I didn't know, I mean I wasn't thinking... geez, I'm sorry.'

'Quite all right, dear,' said the woman. 'Is there something *I* can help you with?'

'Maybe,' said Ruby. 'That is, if you don't mind.'

Once Ruby had properly introduced herself and explained what had brought her to Ridgepoint, and more specifically, why she was standing there on the stoop, they went inside. 'If it's unidentified flying objects you're looking to discuss then I'll be needing tea – you want a cup?'

Dora Rivers was a nice woman – in her eighties now, but still what Mrs Digby would describe as 'with it' in the brain department.

'Oh, Lenny was pretty convinced about those UFOs. Every once in a while he would spot one – or at least imagine he had.'

'You don't believe in them?' asked Ruby.

'I've seen some weird things, believe me,' said Dora, 'but my view is, there's always a reasonable explanation for everything.

A bright light in the sky doesn't make it a flying saucer.'

'What about the weird activity Lenny saw in the fall of 1962? Do you know anything about that?'

Dora scratched her head. 'As I recall it, Lenny was always seeing weird things.'

'This was probably weirder than most,' said Ruby. She opened her satchel and took out the copy she had made of the *Unidentified* article. 'It was out at Pine Forest Pass,' she said. She handed the piece to Dora, who reached for her glasses and looked at it a while.

'Oh yes,' she said, 'I *do* remember this one, I remember it *very well*, because Lenny came home all animated. It was late, maybe 3am.'

'So what did he tell you?' asked Ruby.

'He told me he had found a fella on the road, knocked down by a truck and left for dead.'

'Yeah, but what did he say about the *UFO*?' asked Ruby.

'Oh, he was very exercised about that, all these men in black suits he said, all on walkie-talkies. He was very suspicious, thought they were the FBI.'

'Was he right?' asked Ruby.

Dora shrugged. 'How to know? No one was interested in Lenny's theories, I'm afraid me included. I was much more concerned about the poor soul he took to Ridgepoint Hospital. Lenny didn't expect him to see the night through.'

'But he did?' asked Ruby.

'Yes,' said Mrs Rivers, 'confounded all the doctors.' She paused, musing on the memory. 'Then the fellow disappeared into thin air. According to what the nurse said, he was there one minute and gone the next, never seen again. Of course, that made Lenny think that perhaps the fella was actually some sort of Martian and he'd been beamed back up into his spaceship.' She began to laugh at that.

Ruby smiled. 'But the FBI guys, or at least the men Lenny took for FBI guys, did they ever come *back*?' she asked.

'No,' said Mrs Rivers.

'And the explosion,' asked Ruby, 'I mean did your husband ever change his mind about that, ever think that maybe it was something other than a UFO?'

Mrs Rivers shook her head. 'He was sure as eggs that something fishy was going on. He said, if it was a meteorite then why the fuss? If it was a plane crash then it was some special sort of plane because they cleared that crash site pretty good and quick.'

Ruby sighed. It was all interesting stuff, but this conversation wasn't taking her anywhere she hadn't already been.

'Say,' said Dora, getting to her feet, 'why don't you take this with you?' She went over to the desk by the fireplace and opened a drawer – out of it she pulled a little beige notebook.

'It's Lenny's UFO sightings diary. He wrote up every weird and peculiar happening in that book, a kinda hobby of his.' She handed it to Ruby. 'You've got more use for it than I have,' she said. 'That I can promise you.'

* * *

Ruby began reading as soon as she got on the bus back to Twinford.

Lenny's account was pretty detailed. There was a good description of the lights in the forest, the men standing around as if guarding the site. He had also made a note of everything the dying man had said to him; he had wanted to remember in case he could be of help when the family came to find him or, more likely, to claim his body. Lenny had written:

> The fella was talking about himself as if he had
> already passed, like he knew he was going to die. It
> was the way he answered when I asked him his name,
> he said:

> 'Loveday, it was Morgan... Loveday.'

Ruby stared intently at those four lines.

Could it be a coincidence that both these names were echoed in the Ghost Files?

That would be a pretty *big* coincidence: a kid named Casey Morgan, a kid named Loveday, and a disappearing man named Morgan Loveday – all three connected to strange events.

The name of the suspected would-be assassin merged with the name of the rescuer, making another name for a man who appeared from nowhere and disappeared to nowhere.

What if the injured man had not been the victim of a hit and run, what if the injured guy had fallen from the sky and crawled from the wreckage of his *aircraft*? What if his aircraft had been no ordinary plane or helicopter, but was some kind of space craft connected to the Spectrum Space Programme?

What if the whole thing about the meteorite had been made up and fed to the local newspapers, a cover up? What if the men in black suits were cleaning up the site so no one would be any the wiser about this space activity?

Ruby mumbled the words the injured guy had spoken to Lenny Rivers:

'Loveday, it was Morgan Loveday.'

She repeated them over and over, altering the stress, so that the words became a message. Loveday, it was *Morgan*. Loveday?

What if this guy had not been telling Lenny Rivers his *name* but actually had been trying to tell him something else like, *tell Loveday it was Morgan*?

Loveday, the kid on the river bank, the kid who had saved Baker's life when he was a boy recruit.

Morgan, the kid who had tried to *take* his life.

What if the man on the road was telling this kid from way back that *Morgan* was responsible for his near-drowning, a throwback memory, all confused from a blow to the head.

Or...

What if he had kept in touch with Loveday and he was telling the only person left on this planet who actually remembered what had happened all those years before, that Morgan had come back and he was the one responsible for the explosion?

If that was true then there was only one reasonable conclusion. It seemed more than unlikely, it seemed verging on crazy, but not impossible and, as Sherlock Holmes once said: *'When you have eliminated the impossible, whatever remains,* however improbable, *must be the truth.'*

Everything seemed to be pointing to the fact that the pilot of this craft, the man Lenny Rivers had rescued, must be Bradley Baker.

'I want somebody dead,'
said Casey Morgan...

...The Count shrugged. 'Don't we all.'

'This is different, this boy—'

'A boy!'

'You're not listening...'

The man flashed back a look of steel-cold loathing, pointing his finger so close to Casey Morgan's face that the child stepped back. 'What reason would I have for helping a wretch like you?'

Casey Morgan took a breath and said, 'Because this is no ordinary boy, this boy is Bradley Baker. Take him down and take down Spectrum.'

Chapter 33.
One and the same

HER PARENTS WERE SITTING WATCHING TV when she came home.

'Hey honey, you're back late,' said her father.

'Have you been at Clancy's?' asked Sabina.

'The library,' replied Ruby.

'Rube, you study too hard,' said her father.

'Your father's right,' said her mother. 'You got to start letting your hair down.'

'You know what they say,' said her father, 'all work and no play makes Jack a dull boy.'

'Ruby a dull boy,' corrected her mother.

'Right,' said Ruby, 'I'll bear that in mind.'

She went into the kitchen to fix herself a snack. Bug was asleep under the table, but stirred from his slumbers when he sensed her presence. She scratched the dog behind his ears and pondered what she knew or thought she knew.

The question was, if Bradley Baker *was* alive then why had he not returned to Spectrum?

Because he thinks someone is trying to kill him?

No, this couldn't be the reason. Baker might spend a few months lying low, trying to figure out who he could trust, but not a whole decade.

She needed someone to speak to about this. Not LB, that didn't seem wise.

Blacker? She considered it and then dismissed the idea.

Hitch? Had to be.

She tapped a message into her Spectrum watch

NEED TO SPEAK TO YOU ASAP.

and waited for the message to be received.

It didn't take more than seven seconds.

MONITORING A 678. UNLESS YOU'RE DANGLING BY A FINGER FROM THE SKYLARK BUILDING, I'LL HAVE TO CATCH UP WITH YOU LATER, KID.

'What's a 678 when it's at home?' muttered Ruby.

She reread the notes Rivers had made regarding this Morgan Loveday.

> The doctors told me that apart from his name,
> he can't seem to remember a darned thing about
> himself.

So what if his memory had never come back?

Ruby thought for a moment. *Then why wouldn't he seek help?*

What would Clancy say? she wondered. She could almost hear her friend's voice in her ear; he was saying:

Because Bradley Baker's sixth sense is talking to him.

Because he has a hunch that it's not safe to come back.

Because Casey Morgan is still out there.

When Ruby returned to her room, she found the message light on her answer machine was blinking. She flicked the playback button and listened.

Beep: 'Hey Ruby, this is Red, I'm really sorry but something's happened and well, kinda slightly, actually totally destroyed your guitar, you might not believe this but for once it wasn't my fault, this time it was cos the ceiling collapsed in the kitchen – squashed it flat. Anyway, that's not the point. I'm gonna replace it, but I'm gonna be saving for a while, you know, but hang in there, I got a Saturday job now. Sorry, call me OK, don't be mad, I mean *do* be mad but I'm super sorry, so keep that in mind.'

Beep: 'Hi Ruby, it's Quent. I have this invitation, it's for a bring your dog party and I'm going to take my dog and I'm allowed to bring one person with me and *their* dog and I wondered if –' *oh brother,* muttered Ruby, *here it comes* – 'you and Bug would be my plus twos!'

Beep: 'A message for Ruby Redfort. This is Daily Supplies

up in Little Mountain Side, those hen of the woods mushrooms you were after have finally come in. If you can get in early I'll be there, but later than noon I'm shutting up the store. I got an appointment I can't miss. But don't worry, I'll leave them with Clara in the bookshop, can't risk leaving them at the Little Green Diner – they might eat 'em. So just say Mo Loveday left you a box behind the counter.'

Bang.

Mo Loveday.

Morgan Loveday.

One and the same.

Chapter 34.
I remember nothing

RUBY LEFT EARLY IN THE MORNING on the first bus out of Twinford, the dawn bus. She changed at the city terminal, took the mountain road bus to Maple Falls and the mountain pass bus up through the Sequoias to Little Mountain Side.

She was there waiting for him when he arrived at 7am to unlock the store, sitting on the little wooden bench bundled up against the cold.

He smiled in a puzzled sort of way.

'Ruby?'

She peeped out from the hood of her snow parka.

'Boy, you must want these mushrooms a lot.'

She didn't reply.

He took his key from his pocket and turned the lock. 'I'm telling you, you're not the only one, I've had a lot of orders.'

Silence.

'Are *you* going to be cooking them up or are you going to leave that to somebody else?'

Still she said nothing.

'Hey, kid, I gotta be honest here, you're spooking me a little.'

She took a deep breath. 'There's something I need to tell you.'

He stood on the threshold looking at her, and then, 'Sounds serious. I guess you might want to come inside.' He switched on the lights.

'You look near frozen. You want tea, chocolate, coffee?' he asked.

Ruby nodded. She didn't much mind what the beverage was, so long as it was piping hot.

He lit the wood burner and went into the back room to boil the kettle. Ruby thawed her hands and waited to deliver the news which would erase Morgan Loveday quicker than you could blink.

He returned with tea and a couple of muffins which she was grateful for, having left the house with nothing but a pack of bubblegum – chewing on that only made the hunger grow.

He sat down opposite her and said, 'So what's the big deal, why the early visit?'

'I figured something out,' she said.

'Must be pretty important to have you on the dawn bus from Twinford.'

'It's big,' she said. 'Important.'

'Important to me or important to you?' he asked.

'Important to everyone,' she said.

He nodded. 'OK, so what is it?'

Ruby looked him hard in the eye and said, 'You're not Morgan Loveday.'

The guy smiled. 'I'm not?'

'No,' said Ruby.

He shrugged. 'I'd argue with you, but I don't have much of a memory.'

'And why is that?' asked Ruby.

'I was hit by a truck, got a nasty bang to the head.'

'You *think* you were hit by a truck, but there were no witnesses,' said Ruby.

'OK, there's no proof, but I do have the scars, pretty good ones too.' He rolled up his sleeve. 'Plus there's my leg injury and let's not forget a punctured lung – they had to be caused by something pretty dramatic, right?'

RUBY: *'I agree, but what were you doing walking along that stretch of mountain road?'*

MO: *'Hiking?'*

RUBY: *'Doesn't it strike you as odd that you were out there alone, no backpack, no flashlight, no hat, no gloves in what was it, October?'*

MO: *'So maybe I was driving, maybe I crashed my car and it rolled down into the gully?'*

RUBY: *'Lenny Rivers, the man who found you, went back and he searched, but he didn't find any wrecked vehicle nor was there any sign of tyre marks – I read his whole account.'*

MO: *'Sounds like you've been doing your homework. So what's your take on it? What hit me?'*

RUBY: *'I think there was an aircraft.'*

He furrowed his brow.

MO: *'You're suggesting a plane hit me?'*

RUBY: *'Not* hit *you, of course not hit you. I'm saying you were in an aircraft, and that craft crashed.'*

MO: *'But then wouldn't every TV station in the state have reported it? They would have known who died, who survived.'*

RUBY: *'But you weren't flying a passenger plane.'*

Pause.

MO: *'Wait a minute, you're saying I was* flying *the plane?'*

Ruby nodded.

MO: *'I can fly planes?'*

RUBY: *'You can.'* **Pause**. *'Well, you* could, *you're probably a little rusty now. I mean don't go climbing into a cockpit any time soon.'*

MO: *'So what kind of plane was I flying, a freight plane, a light aircraft?'*

RUBY: *'A Delta V DSO.'*

MO: *'I don't even know what that is.'*

RUBY: *'Well, no one does, at least no one who isn't part of Spectrum's space programme.'*

MO: *'I have no idea what that is either – Spectrum? You've gone all sci-fi on me.'*

RUBY: *'Well, I guess it is a little sci-fi.'*

He cocked his head to one side, trying to understand what she was saying.

RUBY: *'Listen, it's probably gonna blow your mind, but stay with me because it gets weirder.'*

He nodded the way someone who was under hypnosis might nod.

RUBY: *'Spectrum is a Secret Agency.'*

MO: *'And you work for Spectrum?'*

RUBY: *'Yes.'*

MO: *'And you're saying I did too?'*

RUBY: *'Uh huh.'*

MO: *'So are we the good guys or the bad guys?'*

RUBY: *'Excuse me?'*

MO: *'Spectrum.'* **Pause.** *'Are we the good guys or the bad guys?'*

RUBY: *'Oh, we're the good guys.'*

MO: *'Everyone always thinks they're the good guys.'*

Ruby smiled, remembering how she had uttered the exact same words when she had first learned about Spectrum.

RUBY: *'Actually, you have a point, cos to be totally honest I'm no longer sure.'*

MO: *'That doesn't sound good.'*

RUBY: *'No, but I think it's all connected to what happened to you.'*

Pause.

RUBY: *'Someone infiltrated Spectrum. It wasn't an accident, the order to vaporise your aircraft, it came from someone inside the agency... well, the boss actually.'*

MO: *'My boss tried to kill me. We not get along or something?'*

RUBY: *'You got along pretty well.'* **Pause.** *'Actually better than well. To be clear – your boss was your most trusted ally.'*

MO: *'I guess I'm a pretty bad judge of character.'*

RUBY: *'Actually, I think you are a good judge of character.'*

MO: *'So you mean maybe I deserved it?'*

RUBY: *'No, I don't think that's right either. Nothing I read in the files nor anything anyone has ever said about you leads me to believe that you were anything but on the level.'*

MO: *'So...?'*

RUBY: *'So I got it from the horse's mouth, meaning the boss, and it all made sense.'*

MO: *'How so?'*

RUBY: *'You ever heard of the Trolley Problem?'*

MO: *'Maybe, maybe not.'*

RUBY: *'So your boss was given an impossible decision. One life or one thousand and twenty-seven lives. – 1 = + 1027.'*

MO: *'So my boss chose to minus one.'*

RUBY: *'You.'*

MO: *'So he made the right decision.'*

RUBY: 'She – *she made the right decision, if there* is *a right* *decision here.'*

MO: *'OK,* she *made the right decision.'* **Pause.** *'So what's her name? This boss of mine who likes me so much she decided to kill me.'*

Ruby looked at him.

RUBY: *'LB.'*

He blinked several times, like he was trying to conjure some long-dead memory.

RUBY: *'You remember her?'*

MO: *'No.'*

RUBY: *'Do you believe me?'*

MO: *'About what?'*

RUBY: *'Everything.'*

He looked at her then, and nodded. He was sure. It was something to do with the way the girl was staring at him that made him believe; something to do with her green eyes made him trust that what she said was true.

RUBY: *'You see if you are him, it explains why a guy with a not-so-great leg is able to virtually run up a giant redwood and solve cryptic crossword clues without a second thought.'*

He was looking at her, really looking at her. This thirteen-year-old girl had his past, and *understood* what he had struggled for more than a decade to know. This kid held the answer to the most important question he had ever asked himself: who am I?

RUBY: *'All along I just thought, boy, this guy is unusual for a grocer, but I really had no idea who you really were. How could I?'*

'So who am I?' he asked.

Ruby looked him hard in the eye and said:

'You're Bradley Baker.'

Chapter 35.
Who to tell?

RUBY WAS TRYING TO FIGURE OUT what she should do next. It was one thing locating a dead man only to find him alive and in pretty good shape (if you ignored the slight limp and the long-term amnesia), but now she had the problem of who to tell and how to break it to them.

Hitch? Well, of course she should tell Hitch, but hadn't he said 'unless you're dangling by one finger from the Skylark Building, you're gonna have to hold on'?

LB?

Ruby wasn't sure how her boss was going to take this news. How do you tell a person that the man they had shot out of the sky more than a decade ago was actually alive and well and eating a blueberry muffin in the grocery store he now ran in a one-horse town in the Sequoia Mountains? *Oh, and by the way, LB, he has no idea who you are.*

Yes, if anyone was going to deliver this news then it sure as eggs wasn't going to be her.

Of course there *were* other agents of senior rank, but there was no one she felt comfortable broadcasting this news to. For a start, she had a feeling she would spend a whole lot of time trying to convince them that it wasn't some prank.

The other question was, who to trust? Blacker? Of course, she could trust him with her life, but this was bigger than Blacker.

Agent Delaware? She couldn't contact him without going via Hitch or LB. Agent Trent-Kobie, same problem.

In the end, it was Hitch she told. Although she didn't actually *tell* him anything, she just contacted him via the fly-barrette emergency locator, and left it at that. Let him figure out where she was.

She left the barrette in the coffee shop, with a note attached which simply said:

    wait here

because she knew Hitch would need several good cups of coffee when he came face to face with this news and his old colleague, agent Bradley Baker.

When Ruby and Baker walked into the Morning Star coffee shop half an hour later, Hitch was already sitting at a table in the back. He was pouring a heavy dose of sugar into a mug of coffee and stirring it slowly round and round with a teaspoon. While he stirred he gazed out of the window at the view. He was twitchy but he wasn't showing it – only the tiny movement of his jaw muscle betrayed him. He didn't catch sight of Ruby until they were almost at his table and by the look in his eye he was pretty mad.

'You know, you don't look like you're hanging by one finger from the Skylark Building.'

'No,' agreed Ruby, 'but what I have to tell you is a thousand times more dramatic and if by the time I finish telling you you don't agree, then I promise to go directly to the Skylark Building and get climbing.'

'All right, kid,' said Hitch, 'you've got my attention. Why the big mystery? How come you've got me helicoptering out to the back of beyond at...'

He didn't finish his sentence; something to do with the man standing just behind Ruby.

He squinted as if the strangest thought was occurring to him. He dropped the spoon, which fell into the coffee, which splashed onto his suit. He stood up, knocking the cup onto the floor, but he didn't seem to register any of this. All he could see was that the man standing there in the Morning Star might just as well be the man from Mars.

'Bradley?' he said. 'Bradley Baker, is that you?'

'Actually, I have no idea,' said Mo.

'You're not dead?' said Hitch.

'So I'm told,' said Mo.

'So how... why... who...' Hitch wasn't getting his words out.

'I'll let your friend here field the questions,' said Baker. 'I still feel a lot like the guy who runs Daily's Grocery store in Little Mountain Side.'

Ruby explained as much as she could, as much as she had managed to put together, that is.

RUBY: *'I wasn't even trying to find him, I mean why would I? As far as I was concerned he was dead. So the fact that I had actually **met** him never occurred to me.'*

HITCH: *'I can see that.'*

RUBY: *'I've only seen two pictures of Baker and in neither one did he have this whole wild man of the woods deal going on.'*

HITCH: *'You mean the facial hair?'*

BAKER: *'It's just a beard, for crying out loud.'*

HITCH: *'How are you not dead? No one thought it was possible you could have survived.'*

BAKER: *'Did anyone look?'*

HITCH: *'Sure they looked, but when you weren't found, the area was cleared because the mission you were on was top secret, and the explosion and subsequent fire and crater in the mountainside... well, that was all left to the public imagination.'*

RUBY: *'Most people concluded it was a meteor.'*

HITCH: *'So how did you make it out alive? Did you deploy the ejector?'*

BAKER: *'I remember nothing – remember?'*

HITCH: *'I forgot, sorry.'*

RUBY: *'The knock on the noggin erased his past.'*

HITCH: *'All of it?'*

RUBY: *'He retained all the stuff about rescuing cats up two-hundred-foot trees but he can't remember the name of a single person he once called friend.'*

HITCH: *'Really?'*

BAKER: *'Try me.'*

HITCH: *'Did you know me?'*

BAKER: *'I have no idea.'*

HITCH: *'We worked in the same department for about seven years straight.'*

Baker shrugged as if to say, *you see*?

HITCH: *'So where does the name Morgan Loveday come from?'*

RUBY: *'It's what he mumbled to Lenny Rivers, the old guy who found him dying on the road.'*

HITCH: *'So who is the real Morgan Loveday?'*

RUBY: *'There isn't one. I mean of course there is likely to be a Morgan Loveday somewhere in the world, probability and all that, but Bradley didn't acquire the name from an actual person.'*

BAKER: *'You're suggesting they are random names I came up with?'*

RUBY: *'Oh no, not random, not random at all. Just... two people's names, squished together.'*

BAKER: *'So people I know? People I like?'*

RUBY: *'No and yes.'*

BAKER: *'OK. So who was Morgan?'*

Ruby took a deep breath.

RUBY: *'A kid who tried to kill you.'*

BAKER: *'A kid?'*

RUBY: *'Yeah, a kid.'*

BAKER: *'This kid, did he catch me by surprise or something?'*

RUBY: *'Yeah, but if it makes you feel better it happened more than thirty years ago and you were a kid too.'*

BAKER: *'And Loveday?'*

RUBY: *'The kid who saved you.'*

BAKER: *'Where did this happen?'*

RUBY: *'Australia.'*

BAKER: *'How did I come to be in Australia?'*

Ruby looked across at Hitch, expecting him to at least question how she had come by all this confidential information, but he said nothing so she continued.

RUBY: *'You were part of the Junior Space Recruitment Programme, also known as Larvae. In fact you were the first kid ever recruited, therefore older than the others. Larvae got shut down when Casey Morgan, the one who tried to kill you, went rogue.'*

BAKER: *'What did I do to make this kid Morgan so mad?'*

RUBY: *'You made it to Larva level, meaning you became a recruit for the Spectrum Space programme. Morgan's ambition was to be part of the Space Encounter team but from what I read he couldn't even graduate to Larva recruit – he had too much self-interested ego to make it to agent or* astronaut.'

BAKER: 'And this kid who saved me was also from the programme?'

RUBY: 'No.'

BAKER: 'No?'

RUBY: 'This was a kid who just happened to be there, a kid who was fishing or camping out or something and observed the whole thing.'

BAKER: 'So do we know if Loveday is a first name or a surname?'

RUBY: 'Only thing I know is that Loveday is Australian and was around the same age as you .'

HITCH: 'As I understood it you were almost dead when they fished you out of that river, so who says you even got to meet Loveday? Why would this name come to mind when you were found half dead on the road?'

RUBY: 'So perhaps they *did* meet, perhaps Loveday became someone Baker trusted.'

HITCH: 'I don't see how we can ever know the truth if we don't know who the kid is.'

BAKER: 'So the million-dollar question is: who is this Loveday?'

It was only then that they became aware of the woman standing not far from the table.

'Me,' said LB.

Chapter 36.
Loveday

NO ONE HAD NOTICED THE SPECTRUM 8 BOSS enter the Morning Star coffee shop. She had picked up the distress call to Hitch and, wary of recent events, had made the decision to follow up.

She'd stepped quietly in through the door, without a sound, and had been watching them unobserved.

When LB spoke, her voice was steady, not a hint of shock, surprise or emotion, but Ruby couldn't help wondering on what kind of inner reserves she must be drawing, what it was costing her to hold it together instead of collapsing clean to the floor.

Several seconds passed before anyone said anything, and when they did it was Ruby who said it.

'You are Loveday?'

'I am,' said her boss, her eyes trained on the man sitting opposite Hitch.

'L for Loveday, so B for...'

'Byrd,' said LB.

Baker stared back at LB as if he was struggling to pluck

some memory.

'Loveday Byrd?' mused Ruby.

'My parents had questionable taste,' said LB.

'It's very... sorta...' Ruby began.

'Romantic...' suggested Baker.

'Loveday Byrd...' she switched to a whisper, '*Uggerlimb*.'

'Ah,' said Baker.

'Which is why I went with the initials.'

'I can see why you dropped the U,' said Ruby. 'What I don't get is how can no one know your real name?'

'I changed it a long time ago. The only person to know me as Loveday was Baker... and I thought he was dead.'

She sat down. Her face was hard to read.

LB was looking directly at Baker when she said, 'We never found your body, we thought it had been consumed by the flames. There was no sign of you, no sign that you had managed to struggle from the wreck or eject from the craft, no time to go over the area with a fine-tooth comb. We had to erase the evidence before the TV crews and newspapers showed.' She paused, turning to Hitch. 'And by the way, it wasn't an accident.'

'What wasn't an accident?' asked Hitch.

'The crash.'

'The crash was planned?' said Hitch. 'Someone shot down Baker's space craft – who?'

'Her,' said Baker, pointing his thumb in LB's direction.

'How do *you* know? I thought you had amnesia?' said LB.

'*She* told me,' said Baker, now pointing his thumb at Ruby.

'You read *that* in the Ghost Files?' said Hitch, looking at Ruby.

'Run that by me again?' said LB.

'The kid broke into the Ghost Files,' said Hitch.

'She *what*?' said LB.

'How do you know I broke into the Ghost Files?' asked Ruby.

'Someone found your pencil,' said Hitch, producing it from his pocket.

'So why didn't you say?' asked Ruby.

'I had my reasons,' said Hitch.

'I'd love to hear them,' said LB.

'And I'm sort of dying to know why you decided to kill Baker,' said Hitch.

'Reading the Ghost Files won't tell you,' said LB.

'No, that's right,' said Ruby, 'it was the Count who told me.'

'Told you what?' asked Hitch.

'Told me that it was LB who killed Bradley Baker.'

'As everybody is beginning to figure, I'm not actually dead,' said Baker.

'Which is a miracle,' said Hitch.

LB turned to Baker. 'I had to make a choice between one life or more than a thousand. I chose to save the thousand and twenty-seven – I chose to kill you.'

Baker smiled. 'How could you not? It had to be that way.'

And she flashed him a look which told of pain and grief.

There followed a debriefing of sorts where Ruby explained again what had led her to Baker and how she had discovered all she had discovered.

LB was unusually calm about the three break-ins to the Prism Vault. But then again, how could she possibly be angry? Without Ruby's total inability to abide by Spectrum rules, Bradley Baker would still be up in Little Mountain Side standing behind a counter in a grocery store, chatting to customers and filling in the squares in the cryptic crossword. Grateful though she was, LB did make an emergency call to Froghorn and tell him to reconfigure the Prism Vault code.

'And Froghorn,' her voice was stern, 'do better this time.'

Hitch looked at his watch: the weather forecast predicted snow flurries.

'Kid, we should go if we want to get that helicopter back to base.'

They left the Spectrum 8 boss and former agent Baker sitting at the little table in the Morning Star coffee shop, deep in conversation and barely seeming to register their colleagues' departure.

Once outside, Ruby turned and, looking back through the window, what she saw was a couple lit up by the cosy glow of the cafe, snowflakes beginning to drift across the scene. It looked for all the world like a Christmas card.

Chapter 37.
A safe house

BRADLEY BAKER LEFT LITTLE MOUNTAIN SIDE the very next day. It was decided that it would be impractical for him to stay on there. He was reluctant to leave, but he understood that the debriefing would take time – there were a lot of missing memories and no one was sure if they could be recovered. It was LB's feeling that while security was compromised at HQ, Spectrum would not be a safe place for Baker to be. Furthermore, information regarding Baker's survival should be restricted to those agents LB had faith in and could trust with her life; these individuals would have to work outside of the Spectrum headquarters.

So after much discussion and deliberation, it was decided that the safest place for Bradley Baker was Green-Wood House. Baker would be well protected: on the one hand, there was the new state-of-the-art security system, and on the other, living with the Redfort family would provide perfect cover. Since no one was aware Baker was alive, no one was going to come looking for him.

'Not a word of this gets discussed over the airways, are we clear?' said LB. 'Baker's name should not be mentioned in company, nor anywhere in the Spectrum building, and no one but those *authorised* to know should be made aware of his existence.'

So just like that Bradley Baker became a guest of Sabina and Brant, only he would be known as Mo Loveday. Hitch made the call, which went something like this...

'I hope you will understand, Sabina –' (Sabina Redfort had always insisted on informality) – 'if there were any alternative I would certainly take it.'

'Why yes, of course Hitch, but what are you asking exactly?'

'My cousin from out of town?'

'A cousin, how wonderful!' Pause. 'What about him?'

'You didn't get my message?' said Hitch, who hadn't actually left her a message.

'No,' said Sabina. 'I've been so busy with the Christmas shopping I just haven't had time to do another thing, I'm so sorry.'

'Well, I left a note to say, my cousin Mo has just had a spell in the county hospital and I want to keep an eye on him.'

'Oh dear, what happened to him?'

'He had an accident of sorts...'

'Oh my, how awful. What sort of accident?'

'It involved a chicken of the woods.'

'He was attacked by a wood chicken?'

'No, it's an edible mushroom, not to be confused with the hen of the woods, a different fungus altogether. Anyway, he ate a chicken of the woods and suffered a bad reaction, it happens from time to time.'

'How dreadful,' said Sabina; she paused and then said, 'and oh dear!'

'What is it?' said Hitch.

'Oh dear, oh dear, I believe Mrs Digby is preparing a maitake that's hen-of-the-woods mushroom stew for this evening's supper and your poor cousin really won't want to look a mushroom in the face after what he's been through! I mean I should know after that terrible bout of oyster poisoning I contracted.'

'He'll be fine,' said Hitch. 'He's a bit disorientated is all, just don't ask him too many questions. Questions tend to throw him.'

'Oh,' said Sabina, 'I'll be sure to tell Brant, *no* questions.'

'Anyway, the thing is, I don't like the idea of Mo being alone, what with his...'

'Confusion?' said Sabina.

'Exactly,' said Hitch.

'Right,' said Sabina, herself confused. 'Of course you don't, Hitch, neither do I. He must come and stay, we have the guest room and he's welcome to use it.'

The Green-Wood guest room was actually more like a guest *apartment*, which meant if the guest so wished, there was no need for him to venture into any other part of the house. But this was not how the Redforts liked things: they enjoyed company, and they prided themselves on being good hosts.

'I can't wait to meet him,' said Sabina, clasping her hands excitedly. 'I will make such a fuss of him.'

'No fussing,' said Hitch. 'He's not good with fussing.'

'No fussing,' promised Sabina, 'but I really will have to change the menu.'

When Baker arrived that Saturday it was by the city bus, no fanfare, no big welcome party, everything was deliberately low-key. Ruby and Bug met him at the corner of Cedarwood Drive, and they walked casually on towards Green-Wood House.

'Nice to see you out and about. I hear you suffered some kinda toadstool poisoning?'

'I think that's unlikely,' said Baker. 'I kinda know my mushrooms from my toadstools by now, but I'll play along.'

Ruby filled him in on the occupants of Green-Wood House.

'Mrs Digby you'll like, she's a straight-talker, and so long as you appreciate her cooking and never interrupt her when she's playing TV bingo, you'll get along just fine. Though she's furious with you.'

'What, already?' said Baker.

'You're the reason her hen-of-the-woods stew had to be abandoned.'

'But I love hen-of-the-woods stew,' argued Baker.

'Yeah, but you've just suffered a bad case of mushroom

poisoning,' explained Ruby.

'This is a very inconvenient lie,' said Baker.

They crossed the road, and once on the other side Baker stopped and looked around.

'What is it?' asked Ruby.

'I don't know, just a feeling,' said Baker.

'Like you've been here before?'

He shook his head. 'Something else,' he said.

They walked on up the steps and before Ruby could reach for her key, the door was flung open and there was Sabina Redfort smiling her biggest Sabina Redfort smile.

'Hey Mo!' she said. 'Come in come in, how lovely to see you, you must make yourself comfortable, how was your journey? Are you tired? Do you want a tea? A coffee? Oh –' she remembered what Hitch had said about questions, *no questions* – 'just come in, let me help you with your bag, do *whatever* you want, take your boots off, keep them on, if you're cold turn up the heat, if you're hot open the windows, anything goes... oh –' *no fussing,* she remembered, and quickly corrected herself – 'I mean just go right ahead and help yourself and I'll leave you to it.' She walked quickly upstairs and disappeared into the lounge.

Bradley Baker looked confused but Ruby shrugged, 'My mom's a little strange,' she whispered, 'just go along with it.'

Mrs Digby sniffed when she saw him; it was a disapproving sniff and he picked up on it right away.

'I am all apologies Mrs Digby, I don't know what to say, all the efforts you've gone to producing a wonderful supper and I've ruined it all by almost dying of mushroom poisoning – some house guest,' said Bradley.

This did the trick and two minutes later Mrs Digby and 'Mo Loveday' were chatting away while he sliced onions and she boiled potatoes. They talked of foraging and survival and Mrs Digby explained how her old pa had taught her to move without sound when stalking prey.

'I don't often get the chance to use this talent,' she said, 'but I tell you once in a blue moon it comes in very handy indeed.'

By the time Ruby decided to turn in for bed, Sabina, Hitch, Bradley, Brant and Mrs Digby were settled in for a long night of poker.

Chapter 38.
Lost and found

HITCH HAD ARRANGED THINGS WELL: It was Sunday and Brant and Sabina had suddenly found themselves invited to an exciting auction of rare and hitherto unseen works by the artist Pietro Tomassini. This exclusive event was celebrated with a slap-up lunch hosted by Miersons Auction House and held at the Circus Grande. This was to be immediately followed by the opera – Hitch had somehow managed to get his hands on a pair of tickets for *L'Amitié est Aveugle*.

'He must have connections,' said Sabina. 'Tickets to see Flora Steffanelli sing are just about gold dust.'

'He's some butler,' remarked Brant.

'Honey, Hitch is a house-manager,' corrected Sabina. 'He doesn't like to be called butler, he's very particular about that.'

'Well, he's some house-manager,' said Brant.

The point of all this was to get the Redforts out of the house. Mrs Digby, Hitch had dispatched to an all-day, all-night poker session. He'd been tipped off about the game by an acquaintance known as Bunny All Thumbs, and Mrs Digby, needless to say, couldn't get down there fast enough.

Once the coast was clear, it was easy enough for Spectrum to come and go without arousing suspicion.

Dr Harper arrived first. She was there to check Baker's blood pressure, shine a light into his eyes, tap a little hammer on his knee, that sort of thing.

'So you're the great Bradley Baker?' said Dr Harper. 'Everyone does talk a lot about *you*, don't they?'

'I'm afraid I wouldn't know. You gotta remember, I've been dead for eleven years.'

'How could I forget? Someone brings that fact up at least once a week,' said Harper.

'Sounds tedious,' said Baker.

'You get used to it,' said Harper. 'I'm just happy I finally got to meet what all the fuss was about.'

The examination didn't take a great deal of time, but when it was done and doctor and patient walked back into the kitchen, Ruby saw something different in Harper's expression, though she could not pinpoint what it was.

'So doc, can you do anything about the missing pieces?' said Bradley, tapping his finger to his head.

'That's a question for SJ. She's our memory expert.'

'SJ?' said Baker.

'That's me,' said SJ. 'Good to see you again sir.' She stepped forward.

'Glad to see you too SJ,' said Baker, shaking her by the hand. 'Forgive me for not remembering you, let's hope you can put that right.'

'I'll do my best Agent Baker, you can count on it,' said SJ.

Dr Harper handed SJ a file before pulling on her coat. 'A real privilege to meet you, Agent Baker,' she said, picking up her doctor's bag.

'Likewise,' said Baker.

Harper disappeared, LB arrived. It was the weirdest day, seeing the great and good of Spectrum walk in and out of the Green-Wood House front door.

'So what are we thinking,' said LB, sitting down at the Redforts' kitchen table. 'Any chance of restoring the memory?'

'Is it even possible?' asked Baker.

'I think we might be able to gradually restore your memory, piece by piece, but to try and bring it back too swiftly could be damaging,' said SJ. 'I can't say we have ever done anything as radical as restore biographical memories. We have had great success restoring partial memories: how to tie shoelaces, things like that... But what Baker here has is more difficult than that. He remembers how to do things, how to speak... he just doesn't remember his life. When Pinkerton was alive, we spent a lot of hours trying to understand how memories are laid down and recovered, but—'

'You *knew* Pinkerton?' said Ruby. 'Homer Pinkerton?'

'Of course,' said SJ. 'When I first started at Spectrum, I was

Professor Pinkerton's lab technician. He taught me everything I know about memory.'

SJ picked up Baker's file and went to set up whatever it was she needed to set up downstairs in the guest apartment. Not quite forty minutes later, she returned.

'So, we're ready,' she said. She glanced at LB. 'I'll push the treatment as far as I can, but Baker has to take it easy.' She glanced down at the file Harper had given her. 'Anything too stressful, any physical over-exertion could be very dangerous –' again she looked at LB, her expression suddenly very serious – 'fatal even.'

LB just nodded. 'Baker, are you happy to do this?' She reached out and touched his arm, and Baker smiled at her. 'Of course,' he said. 'Without memories, what are we?'

Ruby had never seen LB make any kind of gesture that might suggest actual affection, but with this one small movement Ruby saw the tiniest hint of what Bradley Baker meant to her.

'OK,' LB said, 'so go easy on him. Time's not on our side but let's not go killing him in the process.'

While Baker was having his memory worked on, Ruby went up to her room to continue her trawl through the yellow notebooks.

What she found was not particularly enlightening.

Much of it involved watching the Lemons trying to collapse Archie Lemon's stroller, or get their dog Dudley to fetch a ball. Dudley seemed to spend most of his waking hours howling at squirrels.

A few hours later she came back downstairs to the kitchen to find SJ writing up notes in her file.

'Where's LB?' she asked.

'Back at HQ,' said SJ.

'Where's Baker?' asked Ruby.

'Resting,' said SJ. 'Probably fast asleep; this recall treatment really takes its toll.'

'Want a snack?' asked Ruby.

'What you got?' asked SJ.

'Cookies or crackers,' said Ruby.

'Cookies,' said SJ.

But before they could open the tin, Blacker walked in with five bags of take-out.

'Hitch sent me,' he explained.

'Where is he?' asked Ruby.

'Back at HQ,' said Blacker. 'He's got a lot on his plate. So who's for lunch? I got Chinese, Lebanese, Japanese,' he announced. 'I wasn't sure what you'd prefer, so I kinda ordered everything.'

While they were eating they talked about Baker, his work, his recruitment and how he had been the only kid to actually make the grade, the only one to become a fully qualified Larva junior agent.

'As I guess you already know,' said SJ, turning to Ruby, 'Baker was taken on a few years before the JSRP was set up. He was such a bright kid, and a *good kid* – by which I mean he had a sense of responsibility, strong moral compass, that sort of thing – basically an all-round nice person.'

'Yep, he was one in a million you might say,' agreed Blacker, reaching for a serviette and dabbing at a splash of soy sauce which was never going to come off his shirt. 'But I think his brilliance sorta clouded Spectrum's judgment, made them think it would be easy enough to find a whole troupe of children who could do just what he did.'

'But they only abandoned the Larvae Programme when Casey Morgan went rogue?' said Ruby. 'Morgan was just *one* rotten apple, right?'

'As I understand it, the cracks were beginning to show before that,' said Blacker, reaching for the Singapore noodles. 'I read that there were a lot of senior Spectrum staff who thought bringing kids into this business was a crazy idea, and when LB joined a few years on she absolutely refused to even consider hiring junior recruits.'

Yet, I'm here, thought Ruby, but what she said was, 'OK, so what I don't get is, what happened to these junior recruits once they stopped *being* junior recruits. I mean they were trained up as agents and space recruits and then they were returned to normal life. Wasn't Spectrum worried they might blab?' she asked.

SJ put down her chopsticks and took a gulp of water. 'OK, so after the whole Casey Morgan incident, Spectrum realised the whole thing was a very bad idea. They disbanded the programme immediately, but before they sent the kids home, all memories relating to the JSRP were extracted and replaced with benign childhood memories; only then were the boys sent home to mommy and daddy, no harm done.'

'Specific Memory Extraction?' said Ruby.

'That's right,' said SJ, 'SME.'

'But *Baker* didn't undergo the SME?' said Ruby.

'No,' said SJ, 'because there was no need – Bradley was the only child recruit Spectrum retained from the training programme. He was older than the other boys and had been Larva for a number of years.'

'And Morgan?' asked Ruby.

'Now here's the thing: Casey Morgan ran,' said SJ.

'And Spectrum never caught up with him?' asked Ruby. 'I mean never?'

'According to records he just seemed to disappear without a trace,' said Blacker.

'But how is that possible?' asked Ruby.

'Pinkerton had a theory on that,' said SJ. 'Most in HQ thought it was a little far-fetched, a little paranoid.'

'Why?' asked Ruby.

'He was sure Morgan had sought out the Count, had become one of his apprentices,' said SJ. 'He was sure Morgan had completely reinvented himself – if this were true it would mean his own mother wouldn't recognise him, not even if she shook him by the hand.'

'And what do you think?' asked Ruby.

SJ looked first at Blacker and then back at Ruby. 'I'm beginning to come round to his point of view,' she said.

'So why did the professor quit working for Spectrum?' asked Ruby.

'There was a falling-out,' explained SJ. 'Pinkerton wanted SME used as a cure, that was the point for him. His vision was to research how harmful memories might be isolated and removed, so freeing victims of the trauma of crippling memories. He disagreed with Spectrum using SME on the kids – the youngest ones were ten – and he began to be troubled by the idea his pioneering work might be used unethically. Pinkerton thought this was like dipping a toe into something dangerous, he began to wonder what might happen if SME got into the wrong hands.'

'So did he destroy his work?' asked Ruby.

'He told me that he hid it,' said SJ. 'He split the formula into two parts, one piece he gave to Baker and the other –' she shrugged – 'he never told me.'

'Effectively, he stole the SME code,' said Blacker.

'Stole it?' said Ruby. 'But how could he steal it? He developed it after all.'

'Technically, he developed it with Spectrum resources when he was on the Spectrum payroll, so it belonged to Spectrum,' said SJ.

'So you thought what Pinkerton did was wrong?' asked Ruby.

'*Morally* I am in agreement with him. I think Spectrum's use of SME was questionable,' said SJ. 'But, however you want to look at it, Pinkerton *did* remove something that did not belong to him.'

This discussion over, Ruby and Blacker cleared the table and SJ went down to check on Baker.

'One thing I noticed from the files,' said Ruby. 'There were no girls recruited as Larvae candidates, not a one.'

'Old-fashioned times,' said Blacker. 'There were no female field agents in the whole of HQ, not until LB arrived and shook things up.'

Chapter 39.
Cousin Mo

THE NEXT MORNING Ruby had breakfast with Bradley Baker, chatted about basketball, dogs, record collections, movies, hen of the woods, chicken of the woods, snow sports and breakfast preferences.

'Of course you gotta have maple syrup, what's a pancake without it?' said Bradley.

'That's what I spend my life explaining to my mother,' said Ruby.

'I'll have a word with her,' said Bradley.

It was like a miracle: one week ago Bradley Baker, legendary agent and one-time hero had been dead; today he was alive and well and discussing pancakes in the Redfort family kitchen.

'So who's that guy?' asked Del before Ruby had even had a chance to take her seat on the bus.

'What guy?' said Ruby.

'That guy,' said Mouse, pointing to the man on the sidewalk outside the Redfort house.

'Oh, that guy,' said Ruby.

They watched as Bradley Baker and Bug crossed the road.

'Is he the new dog-walker?' asked Mouse.

'No,' said Ruby, 'that's Hitch's cousin, Mo, he's staying with us for a couple of weeks.'

Ruby watched him from the window, turning her head as the bus passed by. He stopped when he reached Mrs Beesman and she saw him help the old lady manoeuvre her heavily laden shopping cart onto the sidewalk. Ruby wasn't sure, but they actually seemed to be exchanging words. Now that was unusual, super unusual.

'You have Bradley Baker living in your *house*?' whispered Clancy in class. 'Your actual house?'

'Yeah,' said Ruby, her voice hushed, 'and no one's to know, at least, no one's to know his real name. He's called Mo, not Bradley, OK?'

'OK, but he's alive? Bradley Baker's alive?' Clancy was flapping excitedly.

'Would you quit flapping, Clance, he's meant to be just some old cousin of Hitch's.'

'But really?' said Clancy again. 'He's a-l-i-v-e?'

'Well, yeah, Clance,' hissed Ruby, 'he's not some sorta spectre, if that's what you're wondering.'

'But how?' said Clancy.

'I'll tell you later, but all you gotta know right now is that he's called Mo Loveday and he's Hitch's cousin from Little

Mountain Side.'

'OK,' said Clancy, 'got it.' Pause. 'So why's he staying with you?'

'On account of the fungus poisoning,' said Ruby.

'He ate a toadstool? I thought he was some kind of fungus expert?'

'No, not really!' said Ruby.

'He isn't a fungus expert?' said Clancy.

'No, I mean *yes*! He *is* a fungus expert but he *didn't* eat a toadstool, it's just something Hitch told my mom to account for him needing to recuperate at our place.'

'So what kind of toadstool did he not eat?' asked Clancy.

'A chicken of the woods,' said Ruby.

'But that's a mushroom,' said Clancy.

'When did you get to be such an expert?' asked Ruby.

'I've been reading up on them,' said Clancy.

'Well, my mom has decided they are toadstools,' said Ruby.

'Oh,' said Clancy, 'I got it... I think.'

'Good, so long as you don't go around blabbing about Bradley Baker everything should be fine.'

'What do you mean blab? When do I ever blab?'

'Never, OK, don't get your underwear in a bunch.'

'So what happens next?' asked Clancy.

'There's this whole debriefing thing, you know, to find out what Baker knows, or remembers he knows.'

'Has he lost his memory?' asked Clancy.

'Yeah, but LB thinks there might be a way of restoring it, or at least part of it.'

'Like with hypnosis?' asked Clancy.

'No... I mean well... I don't actually know,' said Ruby.

'Do you think they have this kinda time-machine chair like in that film, you know, where the guy gets transported back into all his different memories?' suggested Clancy.

'No, Clance, I don't,' said Ruby. 'Like I said, I don't know how it works but I'm pretty sure there won't be some special chair.'

'So who administers the memory serum?'

'What memory serum?' said Ruby. 'Actually, forget I asked. I have no idea how any of this works but that doesn't matter because SJ does.'

'She's the scientific one?' asked Clancy.

'Well, if you're getting technical then yeah, she's the scientific one.'

It was after school and Ruby was sitting up in her room reading through notebooks 400–450. She had discovered a lot of interesting things, but nothing that could be considered useful to this case.

There was a knock at the door. 'Who is it?' called Ruby.

'It's me,' said Baker.

'Come in,' she said. She forgot about the notebooks spread out across the desk.

'What are *they*?' he asked.

She hesitated a second. 'I make notes,' she replied. 'Jot down things that I see – anything really.'

He nodded. 'Good idea,' he said, 'I mean even the mundane can tell a story, right?'

'Right...' said Ruby slowly.

He looked at her. 'Look Ruby, I know I don't have much in the memory bank but why don't you try and catch me up to speed on things; who knows,' he said, tapping his head, 'something might flicker on in there – worth a try, you think?'

'Uh huh,' said Ruby, 'anything's worth a try.'

'So start at the start,' said Baker. 'How did this all begin?'

'With the Jade Buddha of Khotan,' said Ruby. 'It was missing for a long time, around a thousand years to be approximate, until it was recently rediscovered encased in a block of ice somewhere north of Alaska.'

'I read about that,' said Baker. 'So who found it?'

'Enrico Gonzales, the curator of the City Museum,' said Ruby.

'He found it by accident or was he looking for it?'

'An anonymous donor sponsored the search. It took years to find it.'

'I heard it was quite the artefact, most beautiful thing since sliced bread.'

'You could say that,' said Ruby.

'People do seem to rave about its eyes; gems, aren't they?'

'Rubies,' said Ruby.

'Almost made me want to drive into the city so I could take a look, and I'm telling you, I *never* come to the city, not unless I absolutely have to.'

'Well, you certainly missed something,' said Ruby. 'Not just the Buddha, you missed the explosion at the bank and the museum break-in and quite a few wannabe murderers too.'

'That's exactly why I avoid coming into Twinford,' said Baker.

'Yeah, well, most of the time that doesn't happen,' said Ruby.

'So who was responsible for all this mayhem?' asked Baker.

'They call him the Count,' said Ruby. 'Real name, Victor von Leyden.'

She went to her desk and took out the movie encyclopedia Frederick Lutz had loaned her.

'Here,' she said, 'this is him.'

Bradley Baker leaned forward in his chair. He looked at the picture for three long minutes before announcing, 'I *know* this man. I *remember* him.'

'Of all the people to remember,' said Ruby, 'you remember *him*?'

Baker frowned. 'Yeah, I'm getting that.' He looked at Ruby. 'He's a killer, right?'

'Killer is a nice word for what he is,' said Ruby. 'I believe he tried to murder you one time.'

'Did he?'

'He tried,' said Ruby, 'but you got away. He's just not a nice guy. I mean he attempted to bury me in sand once, and paralysed me with jellyfish venom another, and I'll never forget the giant octopus incident...'

'I'll bet not,' said Baker.

'What I now know for sure,' said Ruby, 'is that that night back at the City Museum wasn't about stealing the Buddha. I'm not saying that wasn't a part of it, but there was a bigger prize.'

'How do you mean?' said Baker.

'Well, if it was all about acquiring the Buddha then why would the Count waste time looking into its eyes?'

'He got distracted, maybe?' suggested Baker. 'The myth of the Buddha is something that has perplexed a lot of people down the centuries. What is it they say about that Buddha? Look into its eyes at midnight and double your wisdom and halve your age.'

'But the thing is, he wasn't just looking into its eyes,' said Ruby, 'he was *really* looking into its eyes, with a little infrared light thing, and he didn't just *happen* to have a *little infrared light* tool on him, he knew what he was doing here.'

'OK, so what was he doing?' asked Baker.

Ruby took a deep breath. 'OK,' she said, 'I think he had been hired, commissioned, instructed, whatever to find something and he was insuring himself against the worst-case scenario that his plan to steal the artefact failed.'

'In other words, the objective of the whole operation was to *read* the eyes,' said Baker. 'That was the prize?'

'Yeah,' said Ruby. 'The icing on the cake would have been to walk away with the Buddha itself.'

'So you concluded the Count is working for someone else?' asked Baker.

'I know that now, but I didn't know it at the time,' said Ruby.

'What does Hitch think about that?' asked Baker.

'That it's perplexing because the Count has always been independent.'

'Not an evil genius for hire, you mean?' said Baker.

'No,' said Ruby. 'Hitch says the Count has always committed crimes purely for the pleasure of it.' She paused. 'Well, that and his weakness for souvenirs.'

'What kind of souvenirs?'

'You know, priceless treasures like eighth-century Buddhas, eighteenth-century ruby necklaces, twentieth-century invisibility skins,' explained Ruby. 'So what I'm thinking is: why is this master villain spending his precious time helping some other villain do their dirty work? He doesn't need money.'

'Sounds like someone has something over him,' said Baker. 'Either this person is blackmailing him – unlikely in the circumstances – or a lot more likely they have something *he* wants and the only way to get it is by doing as he's told.'

'That's the conclusion I came to,' said Ruby. 'Oh, and there's one other thing: Homer Pinkerton used to work with the Count, a long time ago when the Count was in the movie business.'

'Is that so...' pondered Baker. He was quiet for minute before he looked up and said, 'So what else you got?'

And so one by one they went through each and every crime, examining every little piece of evidence. Until they had it all written up and spread out on the floor.

Chapter 40.
On the cards

THREE HOURS LATER, Ruby was vaguely aware of the ring on the doorbell and the footsteps on the stairs, but her mind was focused on the task in front of her and she only really came to when she heard Clancy's voice.

'Rube, it's me.' He stuck his head around the door. 'Can I come in?'

'Of course.'

He stepped into the room, being careful not to stand on the arrangement of coloured cards spread out across the floor.

'I called you about ten million times.'

'I unplugged the phone.'

He looked around her room at the many telephones.

'What, all of them?'

'Yeah, I needed to concentrate.'

'What are you doing?' asked Clancy. He was staring down at all the cards, which he now saw were covered in typewritten notes. As he stood looking, so Ruby continued to move them as if trying to find an order to a puzzle that she did not understand.

'Bradley and I are trying to figure how they connect,' said Ruby. 'I've been talking him through the events of the past ten months. Boy, is he a quick learner.'

'I guess he would be,' said Clancy. 'So are you getting anywhere?' he asked.

'Yes and no,' said Ruby. 'You see, there has to be a connection between the Jade Buddha and the truth serum and the cyan scent and the key-tag and the snake lady, but so far we can't see what it might be.'

'So what did Bradley say about the key-tag?'

'That's one of the many memories that hasn't drifted back yet,' said Ruby. 'But I asked LB about it and she told me the reason she held on to that tag all these years is because it was found not so far from the crash site by one of the clearance crew. Baker's fingerprints were all over it.'

'Had she ever seen it before?' he asked.

'Uh uh, turns out you were right about that – it wasn't that she was sentimental about it, because it had belonged to Baker. It was important because it was the last thing he'd touched.'

'But no one knows what it is?' asked Clancy.

'No,' said Ruby, 'no one knows.'

Clancy looked around. 'So where *is* Bradley?'

'He's gone to Penny's Books,' said Ruby. She was still looking down at the cards. 'The truth serum, I understand. It's like we discussed. It's useful: you can get a very unblabby person to talk with a truth serum.'

1 SHOWS LOCATION OF...?

THE JADE BUDDHA

THE MARS MUSHROOMS

3 WORKED TOGETHER

DISCOVERED BY

2

PROFESSOR HOMER PINKERTON

5 KILLED BY

CLAUDE FONTAINE (TIGHTROPE WALKER)

7 WORKS FOR

LORELEI VON LEYDEN

10 STOLEN BY

THE LUCITE KEY TAG

11

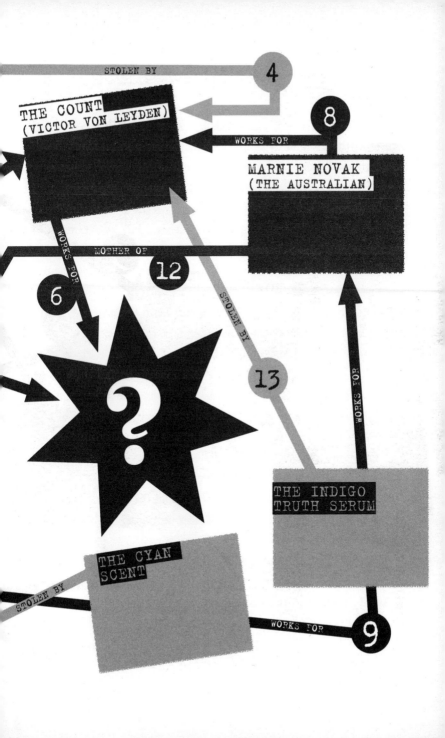

'An unblabby person... like an agent, you mean?' said Clancy.

'Yes, like an agent,' agreed Ruby. 'Maybe the plan is to, I don't know, kidnap someone from Spectrum and make them talk, but since no one seems to have a clue as to what any of this is about it's hard to imagine what useful thing they would say.' She picked up a second card. 'And as far as we know, the cyan scent would also come in handy. Used correctly, it could draw a person out of hiding, same as luring prey to the wolf. You could lure your victim or bait to a location without them really understanding they're being lured.'

'I don't think it would work on me,' said Clancy. 'I *know* the scent, I know what to smell out for.'

'Same here,' said Ruby. 'I think I might be cyan-scent-proof.'

Clancy picked up one of the cards, the one which had the word 'Oidov' printed on it.

'Still drawing a blank on Amarjargel Oidov?'

Ruby sighed. 'Why try to kill her? Why not just *steal* the snakes if it was the snakes this creep was after?'

'Because maybe it wasn't about the snakes,' said a voice.

Neither of them had heard Baker come in.

'Boy, you move quietly,' said Clancy.

'Must be the training,' said Bradley, stepping carefully over the cards. 'These snakes are rare and ancient and amazing to look at, but I don't think the attempted murder of Oidov has much to do with reptiles.'

'So what *does* it have to do with?' said Ruby.

'So there's a few thoughts I've been mulling over,' said Bradley. 'Two weeks ago you came into my store asking if I had ever read anything about so-called 'Mars Mushrooms', which I'd never heard of but later discover you read about in those confidential Spectrum files – a discovery of this Pinkerton guy, right?'

Ruby nodded.

'So I asked SJ and she filled me in on Pinkerton's findings, told me how these 'Mars Mushrooms' enhance your memory – by a pretty big factor by the way; they also extend your life by quite a number of years, but you know all this, right?'

Ruby nodded.

'So what did you conclude?'

'That if anyone got their hands on these mushrooms they could pretty much name their price.'

Baker nodded. 'Which brings me to these rare and ancient mushroom-eating snakes. Have you noticed how everything keeps coming up mushrooms?'

Ruby and Clancy were staring at him.

'So I went to meet Consuela...'

'Consuela Cruz?' said Clancy.

'Yeah,' said Bradley, 'we're old friends.'

'When?' said Ruby. 'I mean when did you meet her?'

'Just now,' said Baker.

'You said you were going to Penny's Books.'

'That's where I met her,' said Baker.

'Oh,' said Ruby.

'What's Consuela got to do with anything?' asked Clancy.

'She's researching the snake mushrooms,' said Ruby slowly.

'Yeah, she's been analysing the mushrooms that the yellow snakes feed on, so we cross-checked her findings with Pinkerton's Mars Mushrooms and guess what?'

Ruby looked at him, suddenly knowing what he was going to say. 'They're the same,' she said.

'Precisely,' said Baker. 'So I took it a little further and I began to wonder why a person would want Oidov dead when she appears to be the only one who knows where these snakes who eat mushrooms live, or rather where these mushrooms the snakes feed on grow.' He looked at her. 'And then I thought to myself...'

'Maybe someone wanted Oidov dead because she *wasn't* the *only* person to know where these mushrooms grow,' said Ruby.

'My thoughts exactly,' said Baker. 'So what if... I mean think about it before you fall about laughing, what if the Jade Buddha has something to do with all this? What if whatever's embedded in those eyes, written there, encoded or what have you, what if it's a location? Coordinates telling you where to find the Mars Mushrooms?'

'That makes a lot of sense,' said Ruby. 'The legend... look into the eyes of the Buddha at midnight and *double your wisdom and halve your age.'*

'That's what I thought,' said Baker. 'It's telling you where to go if you want to discover the secret to immortality – or something approaching it.'

'Ah,' said Clancy, 'so the looking into the eyes bit doesn't automatically make you either smart or youthful...'

'That would account for my dad's unchanged state,' said Ruby.

It felt like a breakthrough, and as Ruby rearranged her clue cards she saw that the puzzle was fitting together.

Bradley Baker excused himself. 'I might take a nap. This memory recall stuff really knocks it out of you.'

They had been working flat out for several hours and it really was time for a snack.

'You want to go ask Mrs Digby if we could have one of her Digby Clubs?' said Clancy.

'You got legs, why don't you go ask?' suggested Ruby.

'I'm totally wiped,' said Clancy, 'I can't even move.'

'Well, tough, I'm busy.'

'I know,' said Clancy, 'I'll get Bug to ask, I'll get him to do the "Go find" trick.'

'Good luck with that,' said Ruby. 'He only does it when he's in the mood.'

Clancy looked at Bug asleep on the floor and tried to discern if the husky was in the right frame of mind to perform this most useful of tricks. He wrote Mrs Digby a sandwich order and tucked it in Bug's collar then he said,

'Go find Mrs Digby.'

But the dog just stared up at him.

'Go find Mrs Digby,' he repeated.

And the dog lay down and closed his eyes.

'Why won't he do it?' moaned Clancy.

'Because you're saying it all wrong,' said Ruby. 'You have to say it with energy. 'Bug, go find Mrs Digby!'

Immediately, the dog got to his feet and pushed his way through the door and downstairs to the kitchen.

Seven minutes later Bug returned carrying a basket of clementines in his mouth.

'This isn't what we ordered,' complained Clancy.

'You'll have to go make them yourself,' said Ruby. But before anyone could do anything Mrs Digby arrived with a plate of Digby Clubs.

'I got your message,' she said, 'and it's your lucky day that I happen to be feeling so generous-spirited. Tomorrow you can fetch your own darned sandwiches.'

An hour later, once Clancy had gone, Ruby went to find Baker. She felt she had better say what had to be said.

'Look, you're probably wondering how come I'm discussing all this confidential stuff with Clancy. I mean this is strictly not allowed. Spectrum's rule number one being *keep it zipped.*'

'Is that so?' said Baker.

'Yeah,' said Ruby. 'I mean I would most definitely get kicked out of Spectrum if they knew I was discussing cases with a civilian.'

'So why do you?' he asked. 'Discuss this stuff with Clancy, I mean.'

'Because I can't not,' said Ruby. 'I can't lie to him, he knows everything. Don't ask me how, he just has a sorta sixth sense – he looks at me and he can just tell if I'm lying, like he can see into my head.'

Bradley Baker nodded. 'Yeah, I think I used to know someone like that.' He gave her a sideways look. 'So anyone else in on your Clancy Crew secret?'

'Just Hitch,' said Ruby. 'Him, me and Clance – that makes three of us.'

'So now it's the four of us,' said Baker, 'and it's your lucky day because I'm good at keeping secrets.'

Chapter 41.
What we know

WHEN RUBY GOT HOME FROM SCHOOL THE NEXT DAY she found the Spectrum 8 boss standing on the stoop.

'Have you come to see Bradley?' asked Ruby.

'Well, I'm not here to see your mom and dad,' said LB, 'charming as I'm sure they are.'

The door was opened before Ruby could reach for her key.

'Howdie mam, do come in, let me take your coat.' Mrs Digby performed the coat-taking with such speed and vigour that LB was yanked sideways.

'Don't worry, one of my arms is still attached,' said LB, steadying herself. 'Thank you.'

The housekeeper turned to Ruby and said, 'I've baked, I've toiled, I've put snacks on a plate and drinks on a tray. I trust you can manage the rest yourself.'

Then she turned back to LB. 'Delighted to meet you mam. Relax, enjoy, use the facilities.'

With that the housekeeper disappeared down to her apartment.

'Does she have some peculiar condition?' asked LB.

'It's TV bingo night,' said Ruby.

'I have no idea what that is, but it obviously isn't good for the soul,' said LB.

They walked upstairs to the kitchen, where they found Hitch cutting sandwiches.

LB looked at him. 'Is this really what Spectrum pays you for?'

'I can assure you it's money well spent. I make a pretty good Digby club sandwich by now.'

'Well, I'm glad the job seems to be challenging you,' said LB. 'And where's Baker, vacuuming the lounge?'

'Watching *Crazy Cops*,' said Hitch.

'I sincerely hope that's not true,' said LB.

'*Crazy Cops* is actually a pretty good show,' said Ruby.

'I'll take your word for it,' said her boss.

LB and Hitch went up to the top of the house to find Bradley, Hitch balancing the various plates on his arm, waiter-style. Ruby fetched the drinks prepared by Mrs Digby and followed.

When she teetered in with the tray it struck her how surreal it was to have the three most important members of Spectrum 8 sitting there amongst her records, books, phone collection, assorted objects and – rather mortifyingly – strewn laundry.

Baker, of course, was not watching *Crazy Cops*. He was working on the case and had been for a straight twelve hours – no breaks.

'So what do we know?' asked LB.

Ruby gave her a quick breakdown of where they were:

'The Australian was an actress who went by the name of Marnie Novak; she was the protégée of the Count and she was and *is* loyal to him and him alone. She had a child named Lorelei who became the Count's apprentice, learning the art of disguise to an extraordinary level. Lorelei is still out there giving everyone *including* the Count a big headache.'

LB: *'But you don't think Lorelei's part of this?'*

RUBY: *'No, she's just a disrupter – a dangerous one.'*

LB: *'And the Count's motivation – are we any clearer on this?'*

BAKER: *'We have theories. It could be the promise of* Hypocrea asteroidi.*'*

LB: *'Pardon me?'*

BAKER: *'Mars Mushrooms.'*

LB: *'Ah yes, the professor's discovery.'*

BAKER: *'Homer Pinkerton was once a friend of the Count's and it's conceivable that Pinkerton told him about the life-giving properties of the mushrooms, and now the Count can't think about anything else. Problem is, he is unable to get them without enlisting the help of this other character, the evil genius who seems to be pulling the strings.'*

HITCH: *'But we can't know any of this for a fact?'*

BAKER: *'That's right. It's just a theory.'*

LB: *'So any theories on who might be pulling the strings?'*

'I think it's the child from the rapids.' said Ruby.

'Casey Morgan?' said LB.

'Why?' asked Hitch.

Ruby told them about the chalk message. 'It fits,' she said. 'It all makes sense.'

LB: *'But no one knows who Morgan is?'*

HITCH: *'Not a clue.'*

RUBY: *'Other than it's someone in Spectrum.'*

LB: *'Hardly narrows it down.'*

HITCH: *'And this Larva badge, we still don't know how it came to be outside Pinkerton's house?'*

'It couldn't have been Baker,' said LB. 'He lost that badge over thirty years ago when he almost drowned at the rapids.'

'I don't think it was lost,' said Ruby, 'I think the kid Morgan stole it, which means the adult Morgan dropped it.'

BAKER: *'Maybe.'*

HITCH: *'So if the Larva badge was dropped by Morgan then it's more than possible that Pinkerton's dog was stolen by Morgan.'*

BAKER: *'That would seem logical.'*

LB: *'And the point of stealing his dog would be?*

RUBY: *'To hold Pinkerton to ransom, I guess.'*

LB: *'So what did Casey Morgan want?'*

HITCH: *'It could be many things. Pinkerton knew a lot of Spectrum secrets?'*

BAKER: *'Whatever it was we know he didn't get it; we know*

this because the Count told Ruby that he's still looking.'

LB: *'OK, so I have another question. Why make a second attempt on Baker's life so many years after the first?'*

RUBY: *'Two reasons: the first was a grand plan to bring down Spectrum.'*

HITCH: *'Have LB shoot down Baker, thus killing Spectrum's finest agent. LB is finished, Spectrum destroyed.'*

BAKER: *'A neat plan that didn't pan out.'*

LB: *'And secondly?'*

HITCH: *'The second was purely emotional. Baker had everything Casey Morgan wanted: he was a successful agent, he had made Larva, and now he had just fully enrolled in the Spectrum Space Encounter programme – qualified the month he was shot down.'*

'You know,' said Baker, 'I think there's one other reason.'

'What's that?' asked Hitch.

'I think maybe I knew who he was,' said Baker.

'You remember him?' asked LB.

'No,' he said, 'but if I was trying to get a message to you, when that guy found me dying on the road, then I must have figured it was Morgan who was behind it all.' He looked at her.

'So let's start looking for Morgan,' said LB. 'Begin by finding out where he sprang from, where he was born, where he grew up.' She looked at Hitch. 'We don't have time to sit back and wait for him to come to us.'

'Understood,' he said.

Chapter 42.
Chasing a shadow

HITCH DID AS HE HAD PROMISED: a talk with an elderly retired agent was how he found it, a lucky chance. The agent had remembered the boy talking about Colwin City and how much he loathed it there and, as it happened, the agent agreed, he had grown up there too and knew exactly the district, the street, the house in which Casey Morgan had lived.

A day later, Hitch and Ruby were flying down to Colwin City with Agent Zuko, Hitch's pilot friend. They'd been lucky to catch a ride; he was officially off-duty. The plane was a tiny single-engine craft: an uncomfortable flight, but a thrilling way to travel.

'Take all the time you like,' said Zuko. 'I've got nowhere to be – I'll just twiddle my thumbs until you get back.'

They picked up a car at the aerodrome and drove on to the City, a grey industrial town with sprawling suburbs which seemed to stretch for mile upon mile across the flat landscape. There was nothing inspiring about the place, just a lot of ugly pylons marching towards infinity.

The trip was unrewarding. There was no sign of the Morgan house, nor the street where the building had once stood. The whole suburb had been bulldozed long ago to make room for a highway intersection. If the Morgans were still alive after all these years then no one seemed to know about it, and all record of them seemed to have disappeared.

Hitch stared up at the concrete mass of flyovers and shrugged. 'Looks like we're back to square one.'

They got into the car and contacted Blacker back at HQ and told him the news.

'So what did you dig up?' asked Blacker.

'Squat,' said Hitch.

'Huh?'

'Not a darned thing,' said Hitch. 'Not one person can give us any kind of description, not one person can remember ever meeting the boy Morgan. It's like he never existed. We're chasing a shadow here.'

'So what's your next move?' asked Blacker.

'We're coming back,' said Hitch. 'Over and out.'

A message beeped up.

ZUKO REQUIRED ELSEWHERE: ALTERNATIVE TRANSPORT PROVIDED. SPECTRUM X NOW STANDING BY AT COLWIN AERODROME, DUE TO TAKE OFF IN TWENTY-ONE MINUTES, HASTE IS APPRECIATED.

'What's Spectrum X?' said Ruby.

'You're going to love it kid.'

They arrived at the aerodrome with forty-nine seconds to spare, no time to go greet the pilots or do anything more than buckle up before they were airborne.

'This is quite a plane,' said Ruby. 'A lot of closet space.'

'There's a lot of kit,' said Hitch. 'Equipped for nearly every eventuality.'

'Is that so,' said Ruby.

'Talking of kit,' said Hitch, 'LB wanted you to have this.' He reached into a bag and took out the little white fur parachute cape.

'You're kidding?' said Ruby.

Hitch shook his head. 'As far as LB's concerned, you found lost gold; and for that remarkable feat you get this.'

Ruby had only ever seen the cape displayed inside a cabinet in the Spectrum gadget room. Now, holding it in her hands, she realised what an incredible thing it was: super light and super warm, and totally discreet. It was impossible to see where the chute was hidden.

'I might try it on,' said Ruby.

'Be my guest,' said Hitch. 'In fact, take a look around, kid, you might as well enjoy the ride, get something out of this whole bust of a trip.'

It wasn't often – actually it wasn't *ever* – that a Spectrum senior agent suggest that a thirteen-year-old trainee have a good rootle through the hi-tech gadgetry.

It didn't take Ruby long to discover the Flight Kit Room: a narrow tube of a space that contained parachutes, survival gear and flying suits suitable for sub-zero conditions. The suit which particularly appealed to Ruby was gold, gold as in the colour *of*, but actually glimmering as if made from gold leaf. It was the same exact suit she had seen in the photograph on LB's wall, only perhaps a little smaller. Over the top? Sure it was, but when did one ever get to dress like an old-fashioned superhero in an outfit that actually could make you become super? *Might as well try it on*, she thought, *you can't miss this opportunity Rube.*

Unlike the Superskin, the flying suit was easy to get into and what was more, it felt pretty comfortable.

She caught her reflection in the polished aluminium door. The effect was dazzling. It must be even more so when one was diving to earth at great speed. She took the little parachute cape and clipped the harness to the suit.

'Hey kid,' called Hitch, 'you better not be trying on any of that gear.'

'Why would I do that?' called Ruby.

She pulled her snow parka on and stuck her head around the door.

'See!' she said.

'I believe you, kid, plenty wouldn't.' Yawning, he stretched his arms and stood up. 'Fix yourself a snack if you want, the kitchen's back there. I'm just going to check in with the pilot.

The weather conditions aren't looking so good.'

Ruby thought a snack might be a very good idea. She had a feeling that Mrs Digby's chicken surprise was going to get eaten without them.

Hitch stepped into the cockpit, and was surprised not to recognise any of the crew.

'What happened to Sasnik?' asked Hitch. 'Doesn't he usually fly Spectrum X?'

'Oh, they didn't tell you? They switched us, don't ask me why. I'm Matthews, by the way.'

'Good to meet you Matthews,' said Hitch.

'Could you take over for a tick, I just have to make a stop at the restroom.'

'Where's your co-pilot?' asked Hitch.

'She's just checking something in back.'

They were flying over the snow-capped mountains of the northern peaks when something altogether unexpected occurred.

A hand reached around Hitch's throat, and before he could consider his next move, a voice which did not belong to the hand said, 'Stay right where you are sweetie.'

The voice belonged to a woman, an Australian. She stepped forward so she was standing next to him and he felt the sensation of something cold and metal on his temple. It suggested she had a gun.

'Apologies sweetie, this flight is being diverted. I hope you won't decide to make a fuss about it or Mr Matthews will have to eject you from the plane.' She made a show of glancing out of the window. 'And I'm sure I don't have to tell you, without a parachute, it's a long way down.'

HITCH: 'Is Mr Matthews here planning on strangling me? And if not then could I trouble you to ask him if he might loosen his grip? It's interfering with my ability to keep breathing.'

THE AUSTRALIAN: 'Of course. But try to refrain from doing anything stupid.'

HITCH: 'What would add up to stupid?'

THE AUSTRALIAN: 'Any sudden movements; that wouldn't be smart sweetie.'

HITCH: 'I'll try to keep my nervous twitch under control.'

THE AUSTRALIAN: 'I'm impressed by your common sense.'

HITCH: 'I'm impressed by your gun.'

THE AUSTRALIAN: 'Good. It sounds like we're going to get along just fine.'

HITCH: 'So how can I help you?'

THE AUSTRALIAN: 'Just keep flying the plane.'

HITCH: 'So what's all this about?'

THE AUSTRALIAN: 'I want the girl.'

HITCH: 'Why, what good is the girl to you?'

THE AUSTRALIAN: 'That's my business.'

HITCH: 'No, I'm afraid that's my business. You see, I'm here *to make sure nothing happens to her and forgive me, but I don't think you have an exemplary track record when it comes to keeping people alive.'*

THE AUSTRALIAN: *'Oh, I think you've misunderstood my motives, I'm not about to do her harm, far from it. My associate wants her alive and kicking.'*

HITCH: *'Your associate, would that be the man who models himself on Count Dracula?'*

THE AUSTRALIAN: *'I wasn't aware you'd met.'*

HITCH: *'We haven't formally. Who's he working for these days?'*

THE AUSTRALIAN: *'Someone who goes by the name of Casey Morgan. Are you familiar?'*

HITCH: *'I've not had the pleasure, at least I don't think I have, but I'm getting the impression that old Casey keeps a low profile. I had hoped to have the chance to look him in the eyes before handing him over to the FBI.'*

THE AUSTRALIAN: *'A voice down a telephone wire is the closest you'll get.'*

HITCH: *'What a pity, you just can't beat seeing the whites of a person's eyes.'*

THE AUSTRALIAN: *'I'll leave you in the capable hands of Mr Matthews while I fetch your precious Ruby.'*

Ruby was unaware of this high-stakes conversation, busy as she was fixing herself a cream cheese bagel while attempting to tune the radio to something approaching music. Mr Matthews had his eyes firmly trained on Hitch and Hitch was intent on flying the plane – the weather was getting unsettled and the mountains closer. No one at all was aware of the figure, clad, ninja-style, in a black body suit and mask emerging from one of the equipment crates. By the time they did, the shadowy form had karate-chopped Matthews and left him unconscious. Hitch ducked three well-aimed kicks and the plane began to dive.

'Lorelei! Is that you?' snarled the Australian.

Ruby, still in the cabin kitchen, stumbled, her face making contact with something hard. She staggered out, nose bleeding.

The ninja and the Australian were furiously throwing things at each other, whatever they could grab and fling.

'Back off Lorelei, the girl's useless to me dead!' shouted the Australian.

'Ruby, get your parachute on and get out of here!' shouted Hitch from the cockpit.

'What about you?' yelled Ruby, her nose now pouring blood.

'Grab a parachute!' he yelled. 'I got this under control.'

Doof!

'That's not what it looks like from where I'm bleeding,' shouted Ruby, but she did as she was told.

'You have to get out of here kid. Switch on your locator,' he bellowed, 'that way I'll find you.' He ducked a second unidentified object.

Ruby looked at him. *You're gonna be dead*, is what she was

thinking.

'Trust me kid.'

Doof! Another blow as a flight box made contact with his shoulder, followed by a kick to his leg.

'No!' shouted Ruby.

'Jump! Redfort, that's an order!'

Ruby wrenched open the plane door.

But too late. For *there* was the ninja blocking her way.

'Don't mind me bubblegum girl – you go ahead and jump,' said Lorelei von Leyden. Yanking off her ski mask, she smiled. 'Jump? What am I saying? Fall is what I mean.' She tore the parachute pack from Ruby's back. 'Oh, take this instead,' she laughed, throwing her the first aid case. 'A good girl scout always travels with her survival kit – I'll bet there's a band-aid in there for when you go splat!' Lorelei was laughing so hard now she appeared quite demented. 'Oh, don't forget your little snurferboard – you can use it to mark your grave. So long bubble-gum girl.'

Lorelei grabbed one of the hand grips on the ceiling, swung her body forward and kicked Ruby into the air. Her laugh followed Ruby as she tumbled into the sky, the snurferboard twirling behind her.

Ruby counted as she fell: 1,000, 2,000, 3,000.

What to do if you find yourself falling through the air at 53 miles per second without a parachute?

Answer: close your eyes and hope for a miracle.

Ruby did neither of these things, nor did she panic.

For what Lorelei von Leyden didn't know was that Ruby had a plan B.

She tore off the snow parka and watched as it was snatched up by the wind and whirled away. The golden suit twinkled glitterball-like as she plummeted. Around her shoulders was the white fur parachute cape. There was no backup – if the cord snapped or the chute tangled then it would be goodbye Ruby. She looked beneath her at the snow-capped mountain moving fast towards her, and yanked the parachute release.

She felt the amazing jolt as her body stopped hurtling towards the ground and instead began to float, a little gold canopy above her which she was able to steer until her toes touched the mountaintop. Her landing was good. Wasting no time, she detached the chute. The plane had already disappeared from view, but when she looked to the sky she saw one small figure zig-zagging to earth. One survivor... friend or foe? What were the odds that this skydiver was Hitch? One in four? No, the odds were not as good as that. Three maniacs trying to kill one agent. He had a chance but it was small.

First retrieve your pack and the snurferboard. She had kept an eye on them, had watched them spinning to earth, and she found both easily. She wasted no time wedging her feet into position and tightening the board straps. Snow had begun to fall, large sticky pieces making it hard to keep an eye on the parachutist.

She flipped up the viewing lens on the wrist binoculars

attached to the cuff of her suit and scanned the horizon until her eyes locked on the figure in black. Whoever it was seemed to be orientating, looking for someone. Her?

Hitch, is that you? She checked the locator for his signal, but there was none.

She aimed the search-and-find locator directly at the figure, but nothing came back, no signal. No blink of a light. Was the responder not functioning or was the skydiver not Hitch?

The figure was motionless for a moment, and then it seemed to sight her, and then slowly, very slowly began to move towards her.

Spectrum devices are 99.999 per cent reliable, isn't that what Hal had said?

Go with instinct.

Not Hitch, she thought.

Get out of here fast.

She took off at speed, heading down the mountain, taking the fastest route.

RULE 43: IF YOU'VE GOT THE ADVANTAGE – MAKE SURE YOU KEEP IT.

Lose whoever was tailing her.

If Hitch was still on the plane then...

Would he make it back alive?

She didn't need to wait long for her answer.

The explosion boomed across the mountains, the sky lit up red with the flames of a huge fireball.

The plane and whoever it still carried – all gone.

She stood for a minute staring up at the sky, mesmerised, until she suddenly became aware of a rumbling sound and turned to see a huge slab of snow break away from the mountain and begin to cascade towards her. Her fear of this likely *human* killer was completely subsumed by her fear of *nature's* killer. She needed to move diagonally out of the avalanche's path, and get herself across to the pines if she was to have any chance of survival; so long as she didn't smash directly into a tree, of course.

Go!

She was ahead of it, she was fast, she was making it out of there, she was going to beat it, out-run it... but then a second rumble, a second slab of snow began to slide and there was nowhere to go.

Swim Ruby, swim.

She worked her arms as fast as she could, breathing snow and losing direction; she was caught, tumbling, falling like a piece of debris. She pulled her hands in to make an air pocket around her face, no point raising her arm, no point trying to be seen, no one to see her.

The world went entirely white and then just as suddenly, entirely black.

Chapter 43.
WHAT TO DO IF YOU ARE CAUGHT IN AN AVALANCHE

1. Let go of your heavy equipment. *You want your body to be as lightweight as possible, so let go of your backpack and other heavy equipment you may be carrying. This raises the chances that you'll be able to stay toward the surface of the snow. It goes without saying that you should not let go of survival equipment, such as a transceiver and probe or snow shovel; you'll need these if you get buried.*

I have no survival equipment, thought Ruby. She had let go of the first aid case.

People searching for you later may be able to find you if they see some pieces of equipment on the surface of the snow, so you could let go of a glove or something else that's light to increase the chances they'll find you.

Who thought up these rules? If she had had the chance to pull a glove from her hand then maybe she would have, but as it was she was mainly concentrating on not breaking her neck. Plus it had to be considered that the person most likely to find her was the person who had least interest in keeping her alive.

2. Start swimming. *This is essential to helping you stay near the surface of the snow. The human body is much denser than snow, so you'll tend to sink as you get carried downhill. Try to stay afloat by kicking your feet and thrashing your arms in a swimming motion.*

a) *Swim on your back. This way your face is turned toward the surface, giving you a better chance of getting oxygen more quickly if you get buried.*

b) *Swim uphill. Swimming up will get you closer to the surface of the snow.*

This she did attempt. Whether it would make a jot of difference to her final resting place, she had no idea, but rules is rules and when one is in dire circumstances you might as well grab for them.

3. Conserve air and energy. *Try to move once the snow settles, but don't jeopardise your air pocket.*

Make an air pocket, make an air pocket, get air, you need air.

If you're very near the surface, you may be able to dig your way out, but otherwise you aren't going anywhere.

You aren't going anywhere.

Don't waste precious breath by struggling against the snow. Remain calm and wait to be rescued. If you hear people nearby, try to call them, but don't keep it up if they don't seem to hear you. You can probably hear them better than they can hear you, and shouting just wastes your limited air supply.

Try to remain calm and wait to be rescued.

Try to remain calm and wait to be rescued.

Try to remain calm

Try to remain

Try to

Try

Chapter 44.
Buried alive

AS THE SNOW PACKED TIGHTLY AROUND HER, so the dawning realisation that following the rules didn't make the slightest bit of difference when it came to facts.

And just because one raised one's arms above one's head as the snow cascaded down, or threw off heavy equipment, swam one's arms, yelled and screamed, that didn't change the fact that she was buried alive under about a ton of snow – maybe it was eight tonnes, who was there to weigh it? Who was there to care? Hitch was almost certainly dead, Bradley Baker was about one hundred miles away, no doubt chatting to Mrs Digby and eating fresh-out-of-the-oven gingerbread. Everyone else was having a good time playing in the snow, except for maybe Clancy, who wherever he was, was too far away to even have a hunch that anything might be wrong.

And another thing – what was the point of the sub-zero survival training when she wasn't even going to get the chance to try survival? How many people had rescued themselves from avalanches – a handful? She was going to die.

These were all the thoughts Ruby would have been thinking, had her head not been buzzing with white noise, the sound of panic, white cold panic.

I'm buried alive, *I'm going to die,*
I'm buried alive, *I'm going to die,*
I'm buried alive
I'm going to die...
I'm going to die.

Perhaps she passed out for a few seconds, because something changed and her breathing slowed and she could see the faces of her mom and dad: they were smiling, really smiling. And then a voice, Mrs Digby's voice in her head, crystal clear: 'You don't want to be scared of this, child, this is nothing. *This* you can deal with.' It was almost a memory, the way the voice talked to her. 'I'm here and I'll dig you out, sure as eggs is eggs, I'll hatch you out of there. No one buries my little Ruby alive.'

I must be delirious. But just the vision of her parents, the thought of Mrs Digby, the remembered sound of her voice was enough to calm her and when she was calm she was able to think.

She slowed her heart right down, focused her mind on surviving.

RULE 20: NINETY PER CENT OF SURVIVAL IS ABOUT BELIEVING YOU WILL SURVIVE.

So no one's coming to rescue me.
Think.
So I have to rescue myself.

What do I have with *me that might help me get out of here? Think.*

She felt for her wrist – and then hope welled up within.

She hadn't lost it, it was still there: the Bradley Baker Escape Watch.

You have the watch, you have a chance.

Now it was a matter of figuring out which of its functions might best serve her predicament.

How long have I got? she wondered.

She had created an air pocket around her face and she figured that she had maybe fifteen minutes. Pressing the winder so the dial now glowed, she tapped the rescue button. Two words flashed up on the screen:

STATE PREDICAMENT.

She clicked through the numerous options until she reached:

SNOW BURIAL

She clicked **YES.**

The watch began calculating the depth.

APPROX SIX FEET, it read.

'Perfect,' muttered Ruby, 'I'm in a snow grave.'

```
CALCULATING AIR SUPPLY - 22 MINUTES.
```

```
ORIENTATING > VERTICAL
SUGGESTED TOOL > THE SNOW DRIVER.
```

'OK.' She took a breath.

```
GO.
```

The folded blades opened inches from her eyes, and formed a perfect propeller. With an efficient and comforting whirr, the Snow Driver began to tunnel above her, forcing a path upward through the dense and heavy snow. Within two minutes she became aware of air and light. She heaved herself from the Ruby-sized hole, spluttering and spitting snow. She was alive and hardly able to believe it.

Chapter 45.
Cold comfort

RUBY ALLOWED HERSELF A MOMENT, lying there on the cold surface. The soft, fat, sticky flakes were coming down fast and it was pretty much impossible to determine where the sky began and the earth ended. It was like looking into nothing.

She supposed that whoever had been tailing her had either been caught in the same avalanche and was now buried and dead, *or* had witnessed *Ruby's* burial, presumed she was dead, and returned back to their cave of evil or wherever it was these villains hung out. Either way, the human factor was no longer a problem. It was *nature* that might finish her.

She needed to get off the mountain as quick as she could. She was free but she would soon be frozen if she didn't find some shelter. She used the wrist binoculars, setting them to blizzard conditions. They allowed her to see through the blur of snow and make sense of the landscape. Head for the trees.

It was tough going but she made it, and once there, she set about fixing herself some makeshift snowshoes. She made a mental note to thank Sam Colt for the hours of misery he had put her through teaching her these 'dumb tasks'. Boy, was she ever wrong.

The snowshoes worked pretty well and she trekked as far as she could, heading through the fir trees to the west. The forest already provided her with a certain degree of cover, but she needed to make camp, gather wood, build a fire.

She was lucky. She found a partially fallen tree which created a perfect angle to clad in fronds of fir and there was plenty of fuel for a fire.

For now, all her energy and reserves were devoted to this one task. And what's more, Colt was right, it was good to be alive: enjoy the here and now.

RULE 24: STAY ALIVE LONG ENOUGH TO FIGURE OUT YOUR NEXT MOVE. She pulled the hood down over her face, closed her eyes and slept as well as she had slept in a long time.

Ruby's very next move was to wake up. *Not bad*, she thought, especially considering what had happened the previous day. The sky was clear and, despite the minus 10 temperature, the day looked like it might be a good one. She set about the task of rebuilding the fire and making sure she had enough fuel to keep it alive, even if a blizzard hit. She tried not to think about Hitch.

RULE 21: DON'T THINK BACK, DON'T THINK AHEAD, JUST THINK NOW.

That meant keeping warm, finding food and figuring out a plan. She had learned a lot about survival from her spring training camp. She had put herself in grave danger by striving to reach base camp as quickly as possible, rather than assess the situation and keep herself healthy. Once the tasks aimed at keeping her alive were completed, she had time to think. She needed to get help, needed to alert LB to what had happened. Only then did it occur to her that LB would already know the fate of the Spectrum X. No doubt her team was searching for the plane wreckage right now.

But they wouldn't know about her; they wouldn't have any idea that she was still alive and holed up alone in the middle of the Northern Mountains.

She sat staring at the Escape Watch for a full ten minutes, her finger hovering over the FIND ME button before she came to the inevitable conclusion that this was not a smart move. Someone back at HQ was rotten, and though she could send a message direct to Blacker or LB, there was no way she could be certain that this message wouldn't be intercepted. Someone, or some kind of device, had tipped off Marnie Novak. Somehow, Novak had known that Hitch and Ruby would be flying from Colwin City – who had tipped her off? Who had sent Zuko off on another errand? Who had arranged for Spectrum X to fly them home? What had happened to the Spectrum crew? Someone was pulling the strings here. So if it wasn't LB or Blacker then who? Froghorn? Ruby doubted that. He disliked her, sure he did, but he didn't *hate* her, at least not enough to lose his mind.

Hitch? Of course not Hitch, because Hitch was...

Don't think about Hitch. Gotta stay focused, Redfort.

She cooked up what food she'd managed to forage and when she'd eaten she decided to turn in early.

Get some sleep, and head off at dawn.

She stoked the fire, making sure there were enough red-hot embers to see her through the night, then she lay down on her makeshift bed and felt the warmth beneath her. She was almost comfortable. She tucked the parachute cape around her and, with the fir fronds on top, she thought she might just stay warm.

She had slept for no more than an hour when something woke her.

She felt hot breath in her ear, an animal sound, snuffling, a lick to her face.

She shrieked, leapt to her feet, grabbing a stick and...

'Bug?' She stood there breathing hard.

The dog barked.

'How did you get here?' She dropped to her knees and pushed her face into his fur. 'Dog of mine, is it really you?'

She looked past him to see the figure of a man trudging towards her, his hand raised in greeting.

'Found you!' he said.

'Bradley Baker?'

'So I'm told.'

'What are you, some kind of tracking genius?'

'I am pretty good,' he said, 'but actually I cheated.'

'How?' asked Ruby.

'I attached a transmitter to your pack.'

'You did?'

He picked up the backpack, unzipped the pocket and took out the Larva badge.

'That's a transmitter?' said Ruby. 'But you said...'

'It didn't used to be. I just added that feature myself.' He tapped his head. 'You know, peace of mind and all that. Turns out I worry. It must be the Mo Loveday part of me.'

'So why didn't you let me in on this transmitter secret?'

'I didn't want you to rely on it. I wasn't sure it was going to work, I'm kinda rusty on all this secret agent stuff. It's been a while.'

'I guess it has,' agreed Ruby. 'Even so, that bump on the head obviously didn't do as much damage as everyone thought.'

'It's all coming back to me, slowly but surely.' He looked around. 'You built this?' said Baker. 'I'm impressed.'

Ruby followed his gaze. 'Me too, actually. Hard to believe I flunked survival training, huh.'

'You must have paid better attention than you thought,' said Baker. 'Look, I don't mean to undermine your efforts or anything, but I'm pretty sure there's a cabin down in the valley above the lake and it might be a tad more comfortable.'

'You have to be kidding me,' said Ruby. 'You're saying I could be sitting fireside in a snow cabin?'

Baker extinguished the fire while Ruby gathered her things then, hoisting her backpack onto her shoulders, they set off.

'So Spectrum found the pilot,' said Baker. 'He's alive but

pretty shaken – he was tied up back at the aerodrome, he was unable to identify the hijackers.'

'Marnie Novak,' said Ruby. 'Lorelei was also on board but she wasn't part of the plan.'

'OK,' he said.

Ruby looked at him, 'No word from Hitch?'

He shook his head. 'No word,' he said. 'But don't give up hoping, there's none better than Hitch, some almost as good but none better – that's what I'm told. So until we know otherwise then he's alive.' He looked Ruby, square in the eye. 'Agreed?'

She nodded. 'Agreed.'

He handed her a pair of skis and a couple of poles and they were soon off at some speed – Bug chasing behind them.

The cabin wasn't exactly the Grand Twin Hotel, but there were dry logs in the wood stack and once the fire was lit, at least it was something approaching warm.

'You must be pretty hungry,' said Baker.

'Ah, you forget I got my girl scout foraging badge.'

'So not hungry?'

'No,' said Ruby, 'I'm starving.'

Once she'd eaten and thawed right through, Ruby realised how cold she had been before.

'So tell me what's been going on?' said Baker.

'Well, it's been eventful,' said Ruby. 'I got kicked out of a plane, buried alive and almost froze to death, but at least I didn't end up dead like you.'

'I didn't do so badly being dead; look, I started my own grocery business, became an expert in edible fungi and, I have to say, I ended up with some pretty nice friends – quite a few of them too.'

'From what I hear you were never short of them in your previous life either.'

'That's good to know.'

'So does anyone actually have any idea that you're here?' asked Ruby.

'Just LB.'

'Are you sure?'

'Could we have been bugged, is that what you're asking?'

Ruby shrugged. 'It feels like there are ears everywhere.'

'LB and I met face to face and in a mole-free zone. I can assure you, no one was listening in. I'll meet her tomorrow at the rendezvous just a half-mile to the east, bring her back here.'

'There's something I'm curious about,' said Ruby, 'and there's not a chance that LB's gonna fill me in so I wondered if you would?'

He shrugged. 'Try me.'

'OK, so I mean I get that LB rescued you from crocodile-infested waters and all, but how did she end up here? How did she go from the northern territories of Australia to Twinford USA? How did...' She stopped mid question. 'I forgot, you probably don't remember, right?'

'Actually,' said Baker, 'turns out, that recall of SJ's does indeed *restore* the memory – and I *do* happen to know the answer to your question.'

'So are you allowed to tell me?' asked Ruby.

He shrugged again. 'It's not such a secret, it's just LB's not particularly talkative. You may have noticed this.' He smiled. 'I doubt that there are more than a handful of people who know anything much about her.'

He stared into the fire for a minute. 'It seems she was quite a kid, that Loveday Byrd; saved my life more than once actually. But on that first occasion at the rapids I had three ways I could have died. If the rocks didn't kill me and the river didn't drown me then I guess Casey hoped the crocodiles would make a meal of me.'

'But you were saved.'

'Loveday was there, she was a local kid, knew the area inside out and saw the whole thing unfold.'

'She's Australian?' said Ruby. 'She doesn't sound Australian.'

'I guess she lost the accent over the years. She's been living over here a long time,' he said. 'Anyway, she did this incredible thing, I mean I watched her, this tall skinny girl, jump down about twenty feet, land on a shelf of rock no bigger than my two hands and then she leapt across the boulders until she reached me. I can't tell you how she pulled me from the water because the last thing I remember is meeting a pretty big rock head on, but if it weren't for her I'd have sailed right over that waterfall and I doubt if they'd ever have found my body – the crocs would have seen to that.'

'I'm guessing you have no idea what the kid version of Casey looked like?'

Baker shook his head. 'No memory of that, and I heard there is no filed record in the Prism Vault, is that true? I mean you've been in there.'

'The only mention of Casey is in that account of your almost demise. LB never met him and Samuel Colt said he wouldn't be able to pick Morgan out in a line-up.'

'Not forgetting that he's gonna have changed quite a bit by now, it's a lot of years ago,' said Baker.

'And if SJ's right about her theory and Casey Morgan *did* seek out the Count then it's quite possible that Morgan's learned the technique of complete transformation.'

'Which would explain why not a soul knows who he is,' said Baker.

'Except perhaps,' said Ruby, looking at him, 'you?'

Chapter 46.
Run

RUBY HAD NO IDEA AT WHAT POINT SHE FELL ASLEEP, whether it was while *she* was talking or *Baker* was talking, but when she woke up he was gone.

It was the sound of the door closing that woke her. Ruby looked around but there was no sign of anyone, just a note pinned to the cabin door.

```
Gone to meet LB, stay put, back soon.
```

Ruby yawned, stretched her limbs, pulled on her boots and went outside to greet the day. Bug was lying warming himself in the sun, but got to his feet when he saw her.

He followed close by while Ruby gathered some wood and built the fire. She was thinking of boiling up some water for tea when she noticed a light flash in the corner of the cabin. It was shining through the pocket of her backpack. She picked up the bag and searched through it until her hand closed around the mini locator. Its signal was flashing violet.

Hitch, is that you? Are you actually alive?

What to do next, she wondered.

Should I go and find him right now? Or should she wait for Baker and LB to arrive?

She thought for a minute. If he was in bad shape, maybe he wouldn't last another hour... She should go.

She left a note telling them where she was headed and, since she had no way of contacting him directly, she pinned the Larva badge transmitter to her suit so he could track her that way. She did not send a message to LB – the watch transmitter she was wary of.

She wasted no time, grabbing just the essentials: gloves, hat, goggles and first aid kit. Once her skis were on, she checked the locator – it was telling her to head north-west. She whistled for Bug but he stood his ground.

'Oh, come on!' she said. 'Hitch could be dying.'

But Bug just barked.

'OK, have it your own way, Bug, but I have to go.'

She had gone no more than fifty yards when the husky caught up with her.

'I knew you'd come round,' she said.

LB climbed out of the chopper and set about snapping on her skis. Due to weather conditions, she had touched down a mile east of the meeting point, but it would take her no time to ski the final stretch. She held the binoculars to her eyes and searched the horizon. Baker was a good way there already. She was about to set off when her eye was caught by another figure, smaller and clad in gold... and what was that following behind?

'Is that a dog?' she muttered. 'Redfort, where are you off to?'

LB watched as Ruby and Bug headed towards a low ridge not so far from the frozen lake.

Where is she going? thought LB.

She panned across the landscape to see what might be drawing Ruby that way. She counted three figures, crouching low in the trees. She focused in closer and saw a fourth, a woman, sitting on a sled. *Marnie Novak?*

It didn't take LB long to figure what was going down here.

She radioed. 'Bradley, we got a situation; the kid is headed due north-west and about to hit trouble.'

'How many?'

'Four.'

'I'll be there.'

But it was LB who reached the ridge first.

Ruby was still a way off when a shot rang out. The surprise of it caused Ruby to lose her balance and she fell awkwardly, losing her ski.

More shots.

Through the trees Ruby could see movement, blurred figures zig-zagging in the woodland. Then a distant voice.

'Run!' shouted LB. She yelled from far across the valley, and

Ruby began to run, harder than she had ever run. Bug at her side, they ran through the dense woodland where the snow was less deep. They ran downhill towards the frozen lake and they didn't look back.

Baker arrived at the ridge to find three guys unconscious on the ground, and LB searching the trees for the woman.

'Where did she go? I didn't see her go.' LB's own blood drip-dripped onto the pristine white snow.

'You're hit,' said Baker, placing his hand on her bloodied leg.

'I'm alive,' she said. 'Just save the kid.'

He looked into her eyes, pressing his hand to hers. 'You can count on it,' he said.

He kissed her and then he began to run.

'Don't die!' shouted LB.

He turned, just for a split second. 'I never do!'

And he was lost in the trees.

'I'll make it back,' he called.

'I know it,' she said. But her face said something quite different, and her eyes turned glassy. Her sixth sense was telling her something and she tried to blot it out.

'Don't die!' she whispered.

But the voice told her he was not coming back.

Chapter 47.
On thin ice

GIRL AND DOG STUMBLED OUT OF THE FOREST and tumbled down the makeshift path slick with frozen snow. Ruby part-fell, part-slid down to where the lake met the rock shore. From the corner of her eye, Ruby saw a dog-pulled sled swiftly gliding across the flat snowscape to the edge of the trees. She got to her feet. She was standing on the lake now. Several inches of ice separated her from the death-cold water beneath. Nowhere to go but across the expanse of frozen lake, vast and exposed. All she could do was keep going. So she ran, across the iron water, skidding and falling and scrambling and running, and all the time Marnie Novak in her six-dog sled was gaining on her.

'I see you sweetie, you've got nowhere to run, you can't hide in plain sight.'

Ruby turned, tripped and fell; all hope seeped away.

'Even your dog has deserted you.'

She looked around. It was true. *Where is Bug?* She had been running so hard she hadn't noticed him fall. Then she saw him in the distance limping towards them.

Marnie Novak, dressed in fur, stepped from the sled, casting a shadow which fell over Ruby and trapped her where she lay.

'I believe you have something for me?' said the woman.

'I have nothing,' said Ruby. 'What do you think I could tell you, what do you think I know?'

'More than you realise,' said the woman. 'It's time for you to come with me. Casey Morgan would like to look you in the eye and find out what you know.'

'Why don't you look *me* in the eye instead?' said a voice.

The woman spun around, a face of fury and next, sheer puzzlement.

'Who... what are you... how...' she stammered.

'Hello, Marnie,' he said. 'Long time no see.'

Slowly, she smiled. 'Back from the dead, Bradley? How original.'

'It's easy to pull off if you keep breathing.'

'I guess that's true sweetie, but for how long will that continue?'

She fired shots at his feet and there was a cracking as ice split, and a crash as Baker fell into the lake below.

'No!' Ruby screamed.

And then there was Bug. From nowhere he appeared, leaping into the air, knocking into the woman, who lost her footing and went skidding towards the black abyss.

Almost travelling in slow motion to where the water lapped up through the ice.

Her eyes wide with terror, her mouth a silent scream as she disappeared in.

She would not be found until spring.

Ruby began to yell Baker's name.

'Bradley! Bradley! You can't do this!' She only left off when Bug began to bark and she saw him pounding at the ice beneath her feet.

She knew what to do.

The laser function on the Bradley Baker Escape Watch made easy work of the ice, and in under thirty seconds Ruby and Bug were pulling at him, heaving his exhausted body from the oil-dark water. Ruby's strength came from that superhuman place of life and death. As he emerged from this underworld, she let go his hand and sank to her knees. She had saved Bradley Baker as he had saved her, and the Australian? She was gone.

'You gotta get warm,' Ruby said, and she began peeling off his coat. 'It will kill you, you have to get warm.' She snatched the reindeer furs from the dog sled. 'You gotta wrap yourself in these.'

He didn't move.

'You have to,' she said, her face so earnest he smiled.

'It's not funny,' she said, 'you'll die.'

'I know,' he said.

He didn't look so good. He really didn't.

'This is my fault,' said Ruby. 'If I hadn't tried to find Hitch, you would not be here now.'

'Oh, that's baloney, Ruby, that's not how it is, you know that, right? Tell me you know that?'

She was silent.

'My dying has been a long time coming, so if my last breath was taken saving you then it was worth dying for.'

Ruby began to speak but Bradley Baker stopped her.

'Listen, Ruby,' he said, 'these people, well, they aren't people at all, they're monsters and they will track you down until they have what they want, and what they want above all else is you.'

She looked at him like she didn't understand.

And she didn't understand.

He grabbed her arm and closed his fingers hard around her wrist.

'Wake up, Ruby, you gotta see, open your eyes, you start blaming yourself for any of this then you can't win. LB did what she had to do, and she was right. I would have done the same.'

He seemed to catch sight of something way above him, his eyes tracking this imaginary thing as if there might be something floating across the blue. She followed his gaze, but there was nothing there.

'*You have* the answer. You're the only one who can make sense of it.'

He looked very pale, the blood gone from his face. He was dying, she could see that.

'You're not making any sense,' said Ruby. 'Tell me what you mean!' She was shaking him now, this man almost gone, this agent of old, the only one who could unlock the past and cast up the future.

'What are we without memory?' he said. 'Lose memory and lose ourselves.'

'What are you saying?' she pleaded.

'It's in you,' was all he said.

'*I* have the answer? Me? Ruby Redfort? Is that what you mean? Stop dying, and tell me!' She shook him. 'What answer?'

'You,' he said. '*You* are the answer.'

She looked at him, the breath leaving him now, the life almost ebbed away.

'You can't die, LB will never forgive me if you die.'

'Yes,' he said, 'she will.'

'I will never forgive me if you die.'

'There is nothing to forgive.' He smiled. 'Ruby Redfort, you made my life better than it *was*,' he whispered. 'Close your eyes and see the truth.' He closed his own and was gone. And Ruby laid her head on his heart and sobbed.

Chapter 48.
Sorrow

THEY SAT TOGETHER ON THE ICE, the child, the woman and the dog. They sat there because their grief would not allow them to move.

The woman held his hand in hers and pulled it to her cheek and felt his touch for the last and final time. A single tear fell from her eye and landed near his own, and they shared the sorrow, one dead, one living, both loves cut short.

And when she *did* speak she turned to the girl and said,

'I must thank you, Ruby Redfort. I must thank you twice, once for bringing Baker back to me, and once for freeing me of my guilt.'

And Ruby put her arms around her and hugged her tight.

Chapter 49.
We wish you a merry Christmas

RUBY HAD FELT ADMIRATION FOR MANY PEOPLE in her lifetime, but none perhaps so great as the admiration she felt for LB that day. LB had lost him twice, this friend, this colleague and treasured soul, but she did not cast around for someone to blame. Instead she did what had to be done, made the calls, gave instructions and flew him home. But the more remarkable thing was the way she took Ruby in hand. Two days after the tragedy at the lake, Ruby and LB met.

LB, dressed in a white hooded coat, was sitting on the bench under the oak on Amster Green. The sun was setting and a delicate snow had just started to fall. She had contacted Ruby and asked if she would meet her *here*, 'not in Spectrum,' she had said.

LB looked up as Ruby approached, and raising a hand, she smiled.

'How *are* you?' asked Ruby.

'Full of sorrow,' said LB.

They sat watching the snow until LB spoke.

'I will always be in your debt,' she said. 'You found Bradley Baker.'

He's dead, thought Ruby, *and that's down to me.*

'It's not your fault,' said LB, as if she could read her mind. 'Baker came to find you in the Northern Mountains because you were part of his team; it's what any agent would do. His death is down to Novak. We know Novak's instructions came from the Count and the Count has been working for Morgan. So if you want to direct your loathing at anyone, let it be those three, and more specifically the two who are still out there. Do not waste valuable energy beating yourself up, it's no good to Baker and he wouldn't like it.'

Her face was set firm: nothing to be negotiated.

On the issue of Hitch, the Spectrum 8 boss was equally clear. 'Until we know otherwise, Hitch is considered missing, not dead, and we will concentrate on what needs to be done.'

What needed to be done was the partial shut-down of Spectrum 8. Only a skeleton staff was kept in situ and there was no question of Ruby walking into the subterranean headquarters any time soon.

But Ruby also had other things to occupy her mind, concerns *outside* of Spectrum and the drama of Casey Morgan and the Count and whoever or whatever might be lurking in the shadows. The most immediate being: would arriving back home having been so long away spark a series of impossible questions? Would her parents wonder where she had been all this time? Would Mrs Digby have called in Sheriff Bridges and filed a missing person report? And Principal Levine? What would he make of this three-day absence? Would she return to Twinford Junior High only to be faced with a series of detentions?

But she needn't have worried. It was quite clear when she walked into the house that Hitch had done his job; he'd had it all covered. Ruby was supposedly on some snurferboarding trip which her parents had clean forgot about. All excuses made ahead of time, no need for explanations. He had even made provision for himself, explained his own absence in a brief letter to her parents.

'An unforeseen personal situation has called me away, and I have organised for someone to cover for me while I am gone. In the unlikely event that I am unable to return to my post as house-manager, I will have the agency make provision for a permanent replacement. I apologise for the doubtless inconvenience caused, and I deeply regret the short notice.'

There was a short list of things to pass on to Mrs Digby, a long list for Sabina, a message about the new alarm system, and a word of assurance in the form of a P.S. –

You will find my replacement supremely capable.

He was some house-manager, some secret agent, and one very remarkable man.

The Bug injury was harder to explain since Hitch had not been aware that the dog would play a part in any mountain rescue, but Ruby was a quick thinker and she came up with a more than adequate story.

When Ruby walked into Green-Wood House and upstairs to the living room, she found her mother standing in front of the huge picture window, looking out at the snowflakes which were dropping lazily from the sky. The fire was lit, the tree trimmed, Christmas cards decked the piano, and all in all it was a very pretty sight.

Maybe it was looking upon this cosy scene, or maybe it was the fact that Ruby had looked into the eyes of a legend as he had faded away. Maybe it was LB's ability to survive his death, maybe it was something to do with being buried alive, maybe it was because it had been her parents' faces she saw when the snow packed in around her. Maybe it was because it was Mrs Digby's voice that had reached her in her most desperate hour, maybe it was all of these things, but when Sabina Redfort held out her hand and said, 'Rube, how about you and I grab ourselves a nice chicken dinner at Pollo's?' Ruby found herself saying, 'I'd like nothing better,' and she meant it.

Pollo's was the perfect place to be on a pre-Christmas night. A lot of people had had the same idea and the restaurant was busy. They had left Bug sleeping downstairs in Mrs Digby's apartment, his leg now encased in plaster. It was a bad break, but it would mend just fine.

'So did Bug *really* save your life?' asked Sabina.

'Uh huh,' said Ruby. 'My snurferboard landed me in a hole and if he hadn't pulled me out then I would have died for sure.' She looked at her mother. 'I feel just dreadful about his leg, it was on account of me he broke it.'

'I knew those snurferboards were a bad idea,' said her mother. 'Why anyone would want to tie a plank to their shoes and head full tilt down a mountain I will never know.'

They talked of school and Mrs Drisco's annoyance at Del for proving her wrong about the corridor rules. Principal Levine had conceded that since roller-skating was not mentioned on the long list of prohibited corridor activities, Del Lasco could not be punished with litter-picking duty. That said, she had better not do it again or she would be on litter-picking duty for the rest of her days.

'I'm glad Principal Levine saw sense – that Mrs Drisco should think about retiring,' said Sabina sympathetically. Also discussed were: Vapona Begwell's decision to sing in the carol concert, *'one can only imagine the sound that kid's voice is likely to honk out,'* and Clancy's struggles with his French exam, *'I guess I could help him,* said Sabina, *'my French has gotten pretty good now. Est-ce-que vous avez la taille en dessous?'*

'Yes,' agreed Ruby, 'I am sure Clancy will find phrases like that very handy.'

And then Ruby's father arrived.

And so they talked of the approaching holiday and the big New Year's Eve party to be held at the old Eye Hospital.

'I've got some incredible news for you, Rube,' her father said, ruffling her hair. Ruby put her hand up to straighten her locks and realised something was missing – the fly-barrette was gone. With all that had happened, she simply had not noticed. She was sure she'd had it when she'd returned from the lake, *yes definitely*, she remembered Clancy asking her if Hitch had tried to contact her on the tiny transmitter. So where was it?

'Are you OK, Ruby honey?' asked her father.

'Yeah, sure, I just lost my barrette is all,' said Ruby. 'What were you going to say?'

The news was that Brant Redfort, who was owed more than a few favours by party hosts Mr and Mrs Hassensack, had acquired a few extra invitations.

'This means you and Clancy can cheer in the New Year with everyone – Mouse, Elliot, Red *and* Del – you're going to have a blast,' said Brant.

'They'll need to start thinking about costumes,' said Sabina.

'Your mother and I want you and your pals to have the greatest time,' said her father. 'You really deserve it. I took a look at your grades and you are just about acing every class.'

'I don't know where she gets her brains from,' said Sabina, 'but it's more likely to be you than me.'

'Nonsense, honey,' said Brant, 'you're smart as a whippet.'

'Whip,' corrected Ruby. What she didn't say was that all she really wanted to do was stay home, turn the locks in the doors, hunker down and pull the covers up over her head. But instead she just said, 'Geez, thanks Dad!'

When dinner was just about finished Sabina sighed and said, 'Boy, do I ever wish Hitch was here.'

'We all do,' said Brant. 'But he'll be back.'

'What's more,' said Sabina, 'I miss Mo too. There was just something about that man that made you want him to stick around.'

'I agree,' said Brant. 'You couldn't meet a nicer fellow.'

'I had hoped he might want to spend the holiday with us,' said Sabina. 'Do you think there's a chance?'

Ruby shook her head. 'I don't think he's coming back this way.'

'A pity,' said her father.

'But I know for a fact that he would have liked to,' added Ruby.

'Shame,' said her mother, 'but he left me just the nicest note.'

'A note?' said Ruby.

'Yes,' said Sabina, taking it from her purse. 'See?'

Dear Redforts,
Thank you for your warm hospitality. I loved every minute of the time I spent with you. I am only sorry it couldn't have

been a lot longer. Please forgive me for not saying farewell in person, but where I had to be just couldn't wait.
Yours with affection, Mo
P.S. look after that kid of yours, she's one in a million.

'And you know what?' said her mother. 'He's right, Rube, you really are the most incredible kid.'

'So say all of us,' agreed her father.

Hitch was being missed for a whole lot of reasons. Though he *had* provided more than adequate cover, house-manager Luke Philips (or to those in the know, *Agent* Philips from Spectrum 1) was indeed *supremely* capable. Things moved like clockwork in the Redfort home, every household issue was attended to, and though no one was aware of it, their security was monitored and every safety procedure followed. But life seemed dull without Hitch. His replacement had little interest in engaging with Sabina's whims and fancies, Brant gave up attempting to chat to him about his day at the office, and Mrs Digby felt a little affronted that this man never ate seconds of her home-cooked nourishment. Ruby crossed her fingers, and then her toes for good measure, and hoped that Hitch would surprise them all and walk through the door before Christmas.

But the only surprise that walked in that Christmas came through the doors of Twinford Junior High. No one believed she would turn up, no one imagined she would actually climb onto the stage and stand there in front of the entire school, but she did. Vapona Begwell not only got up on stage but she sang a solo *and* – biggest surprise of all – she had a voice which left her audience teary-eyed for all the right reasons.

'Simply looking at the kid could just about scare the pants off a person,' commented Sabina, 'but when she hits the high notes, I mean who could care less about pants?'

And then came Christmas and Mrs Digby cooked her goose and five different vegetables and served eggnog and biscuits and cake and ham and so on, and *still* Hitch did not walk through the door.

And Ruby, she began to give up hope that he ever would.

Chapter 50.
Even the mundane can tell a story

IT WAS ONE DAY DURING THE WEEK between Christmas and New Year that Ruby stumbled across something very small and not particularly thrilling. It was as she was pulling notebook 114 from the stack that the whole pile of yellow books toppled and slid untidily between the joists.

'Darn it,' Ruby muttered. She didn't want to have to waste time getting them all back in order; she lifted them out, a few at a go, and stacked them there on the floor, as far as possible keeping them in their correct position. She did this by turning them face down so the most recent books were on the bottom of the piles and the earliest on the top. As she picked the last remaining notebook from the hole in the floor, so she revealed something she had no memory of at all. She reached in and pulled it out. It was yet another little notebook, but this one was not yellow. Instead it was blue and had an illustration of a little fluffy dog on the cover, a cartoony thing with big eyes, the sort of image Ruby might once have considered cute. She opened it, flicking through the pages, only a little curious to see what they held.

There was a date, November 1962, though it was spelled Novmember 1962, written in her own little-girl handwriting, which wasn't bad considering she had still been a few months shy of three. She remembered *studying* handwriting from a calligraphy book she'd found in the library, and the first few pages were just filled top to bottom with the alphabet as she practised her joined-up letters. But as they went on little sentences appeared.

```
'we have a new white couch, mom says no
 eating food any wher near it'
```

```
'misses Beesman has 50 cats and 3 mor new
 ones.'
```

```
'mom took me to see misses Humberts new baby
 it is named Quent he looks very pink and
 makes a bad noise'
```

```
'mom and dad said we can not have a dog you
 are to yung.'
```

```
'misses digby made pancakes I ate 12.'
```

It was pretty riveting stuff and it continued in that vein.

```
'spilled banana milk on the couch it would
```

```
not rubb off but I moved cushons on top so
it is gon'
```

But then it got more interesting.

```
'mr pinkoton has left he did not say
goodbye.'
```

OK, so her three-year-old self *had* noticed the old man's departure.

But it was this line which really grabbed her.

```
'misses Beesman has a dog in her yard I herd
it barking.'
```

```
'the dog has been barking for one hole week
and one day.'
```

The eccentric lady who kept all those cats in her yard now had a dog? That was strange; strange because Mrs Beesman didn't like dogs, strange because as far as anyone knew she had only ever kept cats. Ruby turned the page to see what else she had noted.

```
'mom moved the cushons she got very mad when
she saw the banana milk sploge.'
```

There was nothing more.

Ruby was called down to eat her supper and while she was chewing on her slightly over-cooked lamb chop, she asked Mrs Digby if she could remember Mrs Beesman owning a dog.

'A long time ago,' said Ruby, 'like maybe when I was about two and three-quarters, going on three?'

'Are you out of your mind, child? That old lady can't abide hounds, never could; she sees a hound, she crosses the road.'

'She doesn't cross the road when she sees Bug,' countered Ruby, 'she doesn't seem to dislike *him*.'

'That's different,' said Mrs Digby. 'No one dislikes Bug. He's more than a dog.'

But the note about the barking lodged there in Ruby's brain; it might seem of little consequence, a barking dog in the cat woman's yard, but **EVEN THE MUNDANE CAN TELL A STORY**. It was **RULE 16.** So what story was *this* mundane piece of information trying to tell her?

By the next day, Ruby decided that she really, really needed to know. In fact, she thought she might creep into the old lady's yard if that's what it took, and in the end that's exactly what she did.

The yard gate had long since been secured with nails and screws to prevent any unwanted visitors, which actually meant *anyone,* but there *was* a way in if you knew exactly where to look, and Ruby *did*, because for many years she had watched cats come and go this way. A couple of the fence slats were secured by just one nail and so could be pushed to one side to create a gap big enough for a medium-sized animal to crawl through, or a particularly small thirteen-year-old girl. Once inside, the problem became about finding whatever it was she was looking for, and to be honest she had no idea what that might be.

Ruby had stood in Mrs Beesman's yard only once before. It was back in April when she and Clancy had helped to clear the junk which was piled up so high it was getting to be a health hazard. They had shifted quite a lot of it, but had only worked to clear the area nearest to the house where it was at its most precarious.

The junk seemed to be growing again and it wouldn't be long before it would be back to how it had once been. Ruby looked around her. *What a dump*, she thought, *and where exactly do her cats hang out? Poor creatures.* Ruby couldn't see any of the 74 felines Mrs Beesman was rumoured to have. Then as she poked around she noticed a narrow channel between stacked-up crates and she edged her way through, expecting to find another wall of garbage. But what she actually found was another gate, this one unlocked, and when she levered it open she found herself in a garden. Not a formal garden, or even a well-weeded or maintained garden, but it was certainly a garden. A garden with coloured bottles suspended from trees and tin-can sculptures and a broken-crockery mosaic path; a beautiful garden, even in winter. So struck by it was she that Ruby began to walk along the twisting mosaic walkway which snaked around the trees and plants. The land to the back of the house was a lot bigger than she'd ever realised; she had just never seen beyond the junk.

At the far end, Ruby saw another little work of art in the form of tiny rows of coloured boards all decorated with words and numbers, all sticking out of the ground. She moved closer and read: Fred, Billy, Giggles, Fluff, Bertrude, Rolly, Puddle...

Cat graves! thought Ruby. *Here lie Mrs Beesman's cats...*

And the names went on. Hubert, Flip, Fester, Kimble, Mnemosyne...

Ruby stopped. The same name as Mr Pinkerton's dog. A coincidence?

But Ruby didn't believe in coincidences, not when they were as big as this.

She looked at the name again. This *had* to be Mr Pinkerton's dog. There were hardly likely to be two animals called Mnemosyne, not on the same street, probably not even in the same city.

The date said November 1962. It made sense, this had to be the dog whose barking she had heard, the date fitted. But why had it arrived here, and why had Mr Pinkerton never come back to find it?

Ruby did not hear the footsteps as they neared, she only became aware of the hunched figure behind her when she felt a hand on her arm.

'I see you got your coat back,'

Ruby shrieked. 'Jeepers, Mrs Beesman!'

'I found it in that alley, you ran off pretty quick,' said Mrs Beesman. 'Looked like you had taken fright.'

Ruby had never heard the old lady say so many words all at once. And her voice was not the voice Ruby had imagined, not gruff as Ruby had expected, but softly spoken and perfectly clear.

'It looked warm,' said Mrs Beesman. 'Too good to lose.'

'*You* returned it?' said Ruby. 'It was *you* who left it on the stoop?'

The old lady didn't seem to hear. 'So you're the child,' she said.

'Uh, well, yeah,' said Ruby, 'I'm the Redfort girl.' She pointed unnecessarily towards her house across the street, as if the old lady hadn't observed her day in day out for the past thirteen years. But Mrs Beesman just nodded.

'Thank you,' said Ruby, '...for the coat.' She hesitated. 'You're probably wondering what I'm doing here?'

'You're looking for Homer Pinkerton.'

Ruby nodded, 'Well, yes,' she said, 'I guess I am.'

'He hid for a long time, years and years he hid and then one day they found him – came and took his dog,' said the old lady.

'Who?'

'I don't know,' said the old lady.

'Why did they want his dog?' asked Ruby.

'They knew he would do anything to get her back,' said Mrs Beesman, 'and what they *wanted*, he *had*.'

'What was it?' said Ruby.

The old lady shrugged. 'He told me one day someone might come.'

'He did?' asked Ruby.

'He said he had something that people wanted and when they figured out he still had it, they would find him and make him give it to them.'

'So he did?'

'I don't know, he never came back,' said Mrs Beesman.

'But his dog did. Mnemosyne came to you – why?' asked Ruby.

'Mr Pinkerton trained her to find people – a smart dog, that mutt. He called it the 'go find trick'. If he told her where to go then she would go.'

Ruby thought of Bug. Bug could do that trick, but only when he was in the mood.

'Were all his dogs as smart as Mnemosyne?'

'He only had one,' said Mrs Beesman. 'He lived for her – had her for forty years, you know.'

'What?' said Ruby. 'That isn't possible. A dog's lifespan is twelve years, fifteen maybe.'

Mrs Beesman shrugged again. 'All I know is what I know – that dog lived forty years. He said he kept her healthy but I think it was something to do with those mushrooms he fed her.'

'Mushrooms,' mouthed Ruby.

'Mushrooms,' nodded Mrs Beesman.

'What kind of mushrooms?' asked Ruby.

'He said they came from Mars,' said the old lady, 'but I don't know about that. The dog died two weeks after Homer Pinkerton went missing, call it a broken heart, call it what you will but that dog couldn't do without him.'

And then without word or warning, Mrs Beesman picked up a spade and began digging in her yard, pulling up a rose bush with her gnarled old hands.

Was that it? Conversation over? Ruby was unsure if she should stick around, so she turned, walked towards the gate and headed back towards the fence.

She was halfway through the gap, one leg out on the sidewalk, when she felt a tap on her shoulder. She looked up to see Mrs Beesman, her hands muddy. In her grip was a dog's chew toy, a bone made of blue rubber all covered in earth. She pushed it into Ruby's hand and looked at her with an expression that Ruby had never seen before and would never see again.

'He said you might come,' she said. Then she tottered away and seemed to disappear into the pile of junk.

Ruby walked slowly back towards her house, clutching the bone in her hand.

She went up to the kitchen, poured herself a banana milk, sat down at the table and wrote down everything Mrs Beesman had said. She looked up when she heard Mrs Digby open the door.

'Where did that come from?' asked the housekeeper, her eyes

trained on the muddy chew toy.

'You won't believe me,' said Ruby.

'Well, that's more than likely,' said Mrs Digby, 'but I'm willing to take a chance.'

'Mrs Beesman gave it to me,' said Ruby.

Mrs Digby picked up the dog bone. 'That poor old soul, she really has lost the plot.'

But Ruby was beginning to wonder if Mrs Beesman was the only one to have any sense of what the plot might actually be.

Chapter 51.
The fly barrette

BACK IN HER ROOM, Ruby sat at her desk and stared at the bone.

What did it mean? Was it a clue? And if it was then what exactly was it trying to tell her?

The telephone began to ring and Ruby reached for the lobster.

'Hey,' she said.

'Rube, where are you?'

It was Del.

'What do you mean, where am I? You just called *me* – I'm at home, bozo.'

'You're the bozo, bozo.'

'How do you figure that?'

'Cos you're meant to be at Red's place checking out space costumes for the Eye Ball, *remember*?'

This had completely slipped her mind.

'Oh,' said Ruby.

'Yeah, you got that right,' said Del.

'I completely forgot,' said Ruby.

'I figured,' said Del. 'You did this last time, Halloween remember?'

'Sorry,' said Ruby.

'Everyone's here waiting for you.'

'Sorry again,' said Ruby.

'So are you coming over?' asked Del.

'Sure,' said Ruby, 'give me five minutes and I'll be there.'

'Redfort, there's no way you're going to be here in five minutes,' said Del.

'OK, so maybe six,' said Ruby. She put down the phone, picked up the blue dog bone and stuffed it in her laundry basket. It was as good a place as any to hide it. Then she pulled on her boots, grabbed her coat and ran out of the door.

Once on her bike, she rode as fast as she could down Cedarwood onto Amster and when she met Dry River Road she hit the hyperspeed-boost button and the bike suddenly accelerated and Ruby tore down the road.

She arrived at Red's house exactly as she had predicted, six minutes later.

Red's mom Sadie had brought home a selection of space-themed costumes, pretty good ones too, so it took a while for everyone to pick and choose, but once they had, Sadie pinned them on and made alterations where alterations were required. They were just waiting for the pizza delivery guy to arrive when Clancy yelped, checked his watch and began to flap his arms.

'Six seventeen! I gotta split,' he said. 'I promised my mom I'd be back to watch Olive.'

He was pulling on his coat and already halfway out the door. 'I'm going to be late,' he said, sounding more than a little panicky.

'I'd drive you there, Clancy,' said Sadie, 'but the car's got a flat. Let me order you a cab at least.'

'It's OK,' said Ruby, 'I'll take him. Jump on the back of my bike, Clance, you'll be home in four minutes, I swear.'

When they reached Ambassador Row, some three minutes thirty-nine seconds later, Clancy was clearly impressed.

'Boy, that's some bike,' he said. He looked both impressed and relieved. His mother was very committed to punctuality.

'Yeah, I mean I could almost forgive it for being red,' said Ruby, 'but I'm going to respray it as soon as I have a minute.'

Ruby was about to head off when Clancy remembered something.

'Oh, I forgot, I found your scarf, the striped one,' he said. 'Come in for a minute, I'll fetch it.'

They stepped into the house and immediately a voice called down from the first floor.

'Clancy? Is that you?'

'Just a minute, Mom!' he called.

'Now!' called his mother.

Clancy gave Ruby an exasperated look.

'Don't worry, Clance, I'll fetch it,' said Ruby.

'It's down the hall corridor,' he said. 'Just coming!' he yelled, as he made for the stairs. 'I'll see you tomorrow, Rube, OK?'

'Sure,' said Ruby.

She found the scarf draped over a chair at the far end of the corridor, and was just turning to leave when she was confronted by Olive, who was coming the other way. She was pushing Buttercup in a tiny stroller and talking to her as she went.

'Now, Buttercup, I don't want to hear another peep out of you or you will have to go right to bed without any tomatoes.'

Olive was dressed in her mother's (no doubt very expensive) pink blouse which trailed down past her knees. On her feet were a pair of Lulu's high-heeled shoes and she made for a strange sight as she shuffled along. What made her look even odder was that she had pinned one of her mother's hairpieces to her own curly head and it was secured in place with approximately thirty assorted barrettes. Some of them looked to be Minny's since they were printed with words like 'puke' or decorated with skulls and other gothic images. Others, Ruby suspected, were Lulu's, since they twinkled quite a lot and Lulu was a fan of things which twinkled.

'Nice look,' said Ruby as she approached Olive. 'They your sister's barrettes?'

'They're not barrettes,' said Olive, 'they are wig *j-e-w-e-l-s*.'

'Right,' said Ruby, trying to step past the little girl.

'This one's an emerald and this one's a diamond probably,'

said Olive, pointing first at a snot-green hairclip, and then at one covered in gold sequins.

'Well,' said Ruby, 'don't look now but you have a fly in your hair.'

'That's not a fly,' said Olive, 'it's a spider.'

'Wait a minute,' said Ruby, moving in to take a closer look, 'that's *my* barrette.'

It was too.

'Olive, I'm gonna need that barrette back.'

'It's not a barrette, it's a wig jewel,' said Olive.

'Whatever,' said Ruby.

'You'll have to pay me,' said Olive.

'Why should I pay you for something that's already mine?'

'Finders keepers,' explained Olive.

'Olive, do you have many friends?' It wasn't really a question.

'Buttercup's my friend,' said Olive.

Ruby sighed. 'How much d'ya want for it?'

'Five hundred dollars,' said Olive.

'I'm not giving you five hundred dollars,' said Ruby.

Olive frowned. 'Twenty-five...'

Ruby gave the kid a hard stare.

'Cents?' suggested Olive.

Ruby reached into her pocket and pulled out a quarter. 'You drive a hard bargain, Olive Crew.'

Olive smiled and as she tugged the barrette from the hairpiece, so she took a chunk of the fake hair with it. Olive would have trouble combing her way when Mrs Crew made it downstairs.

Ruby slipped the fly-barrette into her hair and walked off down the corridor and out of the front door.

Ruby was attempting to cycle while also winding her scarf around her neck. It wasn't easy because the breeze kept catching it and whipping it away and the bag with the space costume in kept banging against her side. Eventually, she saw sense and came to a halt on Everglade, leaned the bike against the wall and attempted to untangle it. Suddenly she felt a hand grab her and pull her away from the streetlight's glow and into black.

She would have certainly yelped had it not been for the palm pressed over her mouth.

'Don't scream,' hissed a voice, 'I am not in the mood for screaming.'

The hand let go.

'Don't look so alarmed, Ms Redfort, I am not the Grim Reaper, not today at least.'

'S-so...' stammered Ruby, stepping back a pace, 'what *do* you want?'

'I want the key-tag,' said the Count.

'The key-tag?' said Ruby. 'But you already have it. You took it when we were on the roof of the Hotel Circus Grande, you must remember?' Her heart was pounding.

'I gave it away,' he said bitterly. 'A mistake, as it turns out.'

'Who did you give it to?'

He didn't quite answer, instead he said, 'Someone who started off as a little fly in the ointment but over the years seems to have grown into a spider. I had this apprentice once you see, but he has got quite above himself, and now I find I am rather at his mercy.'

'It must be very embarrassing for you,' said Ruby.

'It *is* irksome,' said the Count, with a wave of his arm. 'Little Casey Morgan sought me out when just a tiny rat of a boy, begging me to teach him the dark art of disguise, real disguise you understand, transformation of face and voice so convincing that if you mastered it your own mother wouldn't know you.'

'Homer Pinkerton taught you...' said Ruby.

'Oh, so you know about dear Homer. Such a friend until he became an enemy.'

'An enemy you killed?'

'No, no, why would I do that when he held such a secret? No, Casey Morgan killed him – the fool.'

'Doesn't that make you the fool?' said Ruby. 'You trusted him.'

'I'll admit it was poor judgement on my part,' he said. 'I trusted him to find me the one thing I had been seeking for so many years.'

'A soul?' suggested Ruby.

The Count clapped his hands. 'Very witty Ms Redfort... no, I'm not interested in souls; they are ten a penny. No, it's long life and wisdom I am after.'

'The Mars Mushrooms?'

'*Hypocrea asteroidi,* exactly so,' said the Count. 'I set little Casey Morgan the task of finding where they grew and thirty-three years later he did indeed find what I so desired. Encased in an iceberg north of Alaska.'

'In the eyes of the Jade Buddha of Khotan...' said Ruby.

'Oh, congratulations, you figured it out, or was that dear dead Bradley? My what an agent he was, what a shame he had to die all over again.' The Count made a sad face before continuing with his tale.

'Morgan betrayed me, reneged on the deal, which is why I find myself doing his bidding.' He tutted to himself. 'A word to the wise... *if* you ever make it that far – which of course you won't – never impart knowledge which might bring about your own downfall.'

'But it was you who looked into the Jade Buddha's eyes,' said Ruby. 'Why give what you saw there to Casey Morgan?'

'Alas,' said the Count, 'I do not have your talent for deciphering code and the eyes held a code which only Morgan could undo.' He looked at her sadly. 'It seems I am now the prisoner of my protégé.'

'Don't expect me to feel bad for you,' said Ruby. 'This problem is yours.'

He gave her a pitying look.

'I don't think you are seeing the big picture here,' said the

Count. 'Such blinkered vision – the reason you *should* feel bad, very bad indeed is because, Ms Redfort, Casey Morgan is very much *your* spider too and he's creeping closer and closer across his web and, forgive me for noticing, but you seem to have your wings all tangled.'

'Then tell me who Morgan is,' said Ruby.

He gazed down at her with a puzzled expression. 'You really don't understand do you, little Ms Redfort?'

There was brittle anger in his voice and her heart began to thud. 'Understand what?' she asked. 'Understand what?'

'That I have no idea who Casey Morgan might be.'

In her surprise, Ruby began to laugh, an involuntary reaction not of her choosing.

'While you delight in my misfortune you might want to think of your own.' He peered into her eyes and said, 'Remember, Morgan is coming for *you. The spider is getting ever closer.'*

And he turned on his heel and disappeared into the dark, his footsteps accompanied by his final words:

'My advice: look closer to home, very close to home.'

Chapter 52.
Instinct

IT WAS ONLY AS SHE WAS PARKING HER BIKE to the side of the house that Ruby realised she no longer had her space costume. At some point she and it had parted company and who knew where it now was. She had no desire to go back out there, no desire to leave home ever again. She climbed the steps and before she could reach the front door it swung open and there was Hitch.

'Hey kid, it's been a while.'

She looked at him, really looked at him.

'You're not dead?' she said. 'I thought you were.'

'If I was then I seem to have made a full recovery,' said Hitch.

'But the plane crash?'

'I jumped.'

'But where have you been all this time?'

'I've been busy,' he said.

'But that's good,' said Ruby, 'that you're not dead. Great, I mean.'

'Why ever would he be dead?' said her mother, appearing from her room. She shook her head and kissed Ruby on the cheek, and she and Hitch walked upstairs and into the living room.

'It's swell to have you back,' said Brant, raising a champagne glass. 'Mrs Digby has cooked a delicious chicken surprise in your honour – you completely missed the last one.'

Hitch turned to Mrs Digby. 'So what makes this chicken such a surprise, Mrs Digby?'

'The fact that you actually bothered to show up and eat it,' said the housekeeper. She gave him an irritable look and he gave her a kiss on the cheek and she immediately forgot her grievance.

The dinner that followed was indeed delicious. It was also full of meal-time chatter, and Sabina and Brant spent the evening firing questions at Hitch.

SABINA: *'Where did you get that suit?'*

HITCH: *'London.'*

SABINA: *'How chic.'*

BRANT: *'Why London?'*

HITCH: *'I have a tailor there; he makes very hardwearing suits and I need my suits to be hardwearing.'*

SABINA: *'Of course, I see, butlering must play fast and loose with one's clothing.'*

HITCH: *'You'd be surprised.'*

SABINA: *'I'm sure I would.'*

HITCH: *'The last thing one needs is for a suit to rip at the seams.'*

BRANT: *'You must give me the name of your tailor.'*

And when they were done quizzing him, they filled him in on the latest Twinford gossip.

SABINA: *'The Eye Ball is going to be magnificent, you will come, won't you?'*

HITCH: *'I'll think about it.'*

BRANT: *'What's to think about? It's the only party in town.'*

SABINA: *'No, honey, it's not the only party in town, it's just the best party in town.'*

BRANT: *'That's what I meant, darling, the best party!'*

There was little chance to talk to Hitch alone, and though of course Ruby should have told him about the Count encounter there and then, the evening was so perfect and everyone seemed so happy that she just couldn't bear to spoil it.

I'll tell him tomorrow. Tomorrow I can face it, but not now.

She climbed into bed and switched off the light.

She lay for a while just thinking about things. The best thing had happened, almost a *miracle*: Hitch had returned. When she thought of Marnie Novak and Lorelei, the plane crash, it made her shudder. The odds of Hitch surviving all that seemed so slim, so unlikely. It really was *something* that he had survived.

She stared at the tree shadows as they waved their spindly arms. What was it that was gnawing away at her, because *something* was. Something ugly was lurking in the very darkest part of her mind and every time she tried to drag it into the light, another thought blocked it.

At exactly 3.33am Ruby woke up. She was drenched with sweat and finding it hard to breathe. She sat up, reached for the bedside light and knocked over a glass of water and stumbled out of bed. Bug woke too, his eyes fixed on hers as he got awkwardly to his feet, his plaster-cast leg tap-tapping as he followed her to the bathroom.

Ruby ran the faucet and splashed her face with water. Bug was standing next to her, his ears alert for danger.

Ruby was muttering.

How did Hitch survive that plane crash?

Who booked that plane? Well, Spectrum had. *Who told her to jump?* Hitch. So had he actually wanted her to plummet to earth? She thought about it. Without the parachute cape, then she would be splatted over the mountain-top.

He had given her the parachute cape, a gift from LB, so he *hadn't wanted her to die.*

She thought again, no, he hadn't wanted her to die *falling from the plane,* but had he set her up for what came later?

What if Hitch had been the one to call in that request to Zuko, what if he had scheduled the Spectrum jet – tipping off the Australian, allowing her to get on board, bringing with her, her own henchman?

No, this is stupid, thought Ruby. *Hitch was punched by those guys, he was all beaten up.* She pondered on this, and another horrible thought spread. *But what if that was staged?* All part of the plan, right up until Lorelei appeared, then things had gone wrong. *Lorelei wasn't meant to be there,* thought Ruby, *Lorelei wanted me dead and Marnie for some reason needed me alive.*

Was *that* why Hitch had told her to jump? He knew she had a chute, knew that she could make it out of there in one piece. *The plane was meant to land safe and sound, but it didn't, couldn't.*

I got down to earth, but I might have died afterwards. No one could have known she would survive. *Not only that,* she thought, *but no one could have known they would find me.* In fact they *hadn't* found her, *she'd* found them, so there it was, an accident, a cruel twist of fate, *if I hadn't picked up that signal on Hitch's locator, if Marnie Novak hadn't taken Hitch's locator then I would never have followed the signal... Oh...* another bad thought. What if Hitch had handed his locator to the Australian knowing that this would be the way to lure Ruby, knowing that if Ruby got Hitch's signal then she would come and find him? What if he'd planned all this, faked his own death and then disappeared for a while so he could do whatever he needed to do without anyone asking tricky questions?

Ruby slept fitfully, as you might expect someone to sleep if they had a probable murderer sleeping three floors below them.

But by the time the light began to creep into her room so her suspicions faded and the very notion that Hitch might in some way be implicated in her capture seemed ridiculous.

When Ruby came down for breakfast she found her parents dunking croissants into bowls of coffee while they perused *Paris Match*. There was no sign of Hitch.

'He might be in his room,' suggested her mother, 'though he said he was going out for the day so you may have missed him.'

Ruby went down the two flights of stairs to the ground-floor apartment and knocked on his door. There was no answer so she tried again, a little harder this time. When she knocked the second time, the door sort of drifted open. She peered in. She knew she shouldn't, but she couldn't seem to help herself.

'Hitch?' she called.

No answer.

She stepped into the room; it was tidy as always, but today there was a file on the desk. It was very unlike Hitch to leave anything like that lying around; his desk was always clear, save for a glass paperweight, a black fountain pen and a pad of white paper. She walked over to see what this file might be. As it turned out it related only to the house, the new alarm system and security devices, nothing of any consequence. As she slid the file back to the centre of the desk so she noticed his document case. It must have slipped off the chair, because it was lying on its side and some of its contents had spilled out onto the floor. She picked up a little metal card. It was a Spectrum swipe key, with his name, date of birth and his agent code.

'Child! Where are you?'

Ruby ran to the door, slipped out into the hall and up the stairs.

'Here!' she said. 'I'm here!'

Mrs Digby gave her a look. 'I'm not gonna ask what mischief you've been getting into because I know I won't like the answer.' She handed Ruby a stack of envelopes. 'You can mail these on your way out.'

Chapter 53.
Nothing is completely safe

SHE MET CLANCY AT THE DONUT, just as they had planned.

Once they were seated she told him about Hitch's return, how she'd arrived home and there he was.

'But that's great,' said Clancy.

'I know,' said Ruby.

'So why do you look like someone stole your sneakers?'

'That's it Clance, I don't know.'

Then she told him of her spiralling paranoia.

'It's understandable,' said Clancy.

'Yeah, but you haven't heard the worst,' said Ruby.

'What?' asked Clancy.

'I actually went into his room.'

'When he wasn't there?' whispered Clancy.

'I know,' said Ruby, 'it's bad, isn't it?'

'You're lucky he's not Minny,' he said, 'she'd kill you if you stepped inside her room.'

'Maybe he will,' said Ruby. 'He's bound to have some little tripwire system.'

'So what did you see?' asked Clancy. 'A dirty teacup, biscuit crumbs on the floor?'

'Nothing that extreme,' said Ruby, 'just his Spectrum identity card.'

'So what was on it?'

'Just "Hitch", his agent code and his date of birth,' said Ruby.

'So how old is he?' asked Clancy.

'Forty-two, like he said,' said Ruby.

'So what's the big deal here?'

'Nothing, other than I have his ID and I need to get it back into his room before he realises it's missing.'

'You're kidding!'

'I know, it's bad, I'm losing it, super losing it.'

'You're not *losing* it Rube, you're just trying to fit a puzzle together, trying the pieces, some of them fit, some of them don't,' said Clancy.

'You're right,' said Ruby.

'And some of the pieces are missing,' he added.

'That's certainly true,' sighed Ruby.

'And maybe some of the pieces belong to a different puzzle,' he said.

'OK, stop with the puzzle metaphor, you're over-doing it, Clance.'

'The point is,' said Clancy, 'there's a lot to juggle.'

'You got that right,' said Ruby. 'But what am I *doing* putting

Hitch in the frame? He's saved me from a forest fire, he rescued me from Baby Face Marshall, Nine Lives Capaldi. Jeepers, he's saved my bacon more than a *few* times, so it seems a little unfair to even *imagine* he might be trying to kill me,' she said. 'I mean if I were him I would want to clonk me on the head just for being so darned ungrateful.'

Clancy shrugged. 'I think Hitch would understand. Like I said, sometimes you have to allow yourself to think the worst...' he paused, 'and, let's face it, the thing is, well, lately...' Again he stopped as if not wanting to finish the thought.

'What?' said Ruby.

'Well,' Clancy said, 'he *has* been acting kinda odd. I mean where has he been all this time, why didn't he try to contact you? Put your mind at rest, and...'

'What?' asked Ruby.

He looked at her. 'You're in danger and he hasn't been there for you.' His eyes were round and scared as they looked into hers.

'It's OK Clance, really it is.' She could not tell him about the Count, not now.

'But you're worried,' said Clancy. 'You're wondering if you can trust the person you need to trust most.'

She stared across at him,

'And what's your instinct Clance?'

He said nothing for a long moment, but when he finally did, he looked Ruby straight in the eye and said, 'You have to go with *your* gut feeling. You have to trust in your own sixth sense because deep down you know the answer.'

When she arrived home there was still no sign of Hitch, which was good because it meant she had an opportunity to slip back down to his apartment and replace the identity card on the floor where she had found it. She was busy trying to position it exactly where she'd picked it up from when she saw the corner of something almost hidden but not quite. It was just poking out from under a low sideboard and when she slid it out she saw it was a passport.

Curious, she opened it. As one would expect, there was a photograph of Hitch, recently taken, and his date of birth, which corresponded with his ID card. It was his name which troubled her: Art Hitchen Zachery, the boy from the rapids.

Her mind began to process this information.

So he had *been in the Larvae Programme.*

But he'd told her he hadn't.

But he would have undergone SME, *so how would he know?*

That's right, SJ had told her so, the Junior Space Recruits had all undergone Specific Memory Extraction – '*some of them as young as ten years old.*'

She looked at his date of birth... *now that doesn't seem right.*

Forty-two in 1973 meant he was...

s*even,* when he was in the Larvae Programme.

No memory-zapping for Hitch.

So why would he not be able to remember being a Junior Space recruit?

Because he was lying, that's why.

She quickly slid the passport under the sideboard, slipped through the door and closed it quietly behind her, but as she turned to climb the stairs she heard a voice.

'Why were you in my apartment?'

But she found herself unable to speak.

'*Come* on kid, I'm sure you can come up with some explanation – *some* plausible reason for snooping.'

Still she couldn't find a single word.

'No?' he said. 'Should I be worrying about what team you're rooting for?'

'I saw your passport,' said Ruby, 'you're Art Hitchen Zachery, you were in the Larvae Programme. You told me you weren't, but you *were.*'

'I had no memory of it. I told you the truth as I knew it.'

'*Really*? That's weird because you didn't undergo SME – the only kids who did were ten or older – SJ told me.'

'And did SJ tell you *why*?'

'You were too young?' said Ruby.

'I went into shock – getting chomped by a crocodile will do that to you. I remember nothing about it – nothing about that training week, which by the way is when I joined, I only know any of what I'm telling you because last night I took a look at my file and it didn't make for pleasant reading – turns out Casey

Morgan threw me to the crocodiles; apparently I caught him launching Baker into the rapids.'

'*Oh*,' said Ruby.

'Yes,' said Hitch, '*oh*, is right.'

'Sorry,' said Ruby, 'it's been a tough week.'

'It certainly has,' said Hitch.

She looked at him, her face full of regret. 'I'm sorry,' she repeated.

He sighed. 'It's OK.' And he extended his hand.

'Do you forgive me?' she asked.

'Nothing to forgive,' he said.

They shook on it.

'Will you be coming to the Eye Ball thing tonight?' she asked.

'I'm not sure kid, depends where I need to be.'

'I thought it was your night off,' she said.

'Butlers don't have nights off, don't you know that?'

'So you *are* a butler, and there was me thinking you were a secret agent.' She smiled.

'Secret agents definitely don't take nights off – they'd wind up dead if they did.'

She paused. 'I'm not sure I want to go,' she said.

'Did something happen?' he asked.

'The Count. Last night I met the Count, he was waiting for me.'

'You didn't think to *tell* me this?' Hitch looked bemused.

'I'm telling you *now*,' she said. 'He said all the usual Count stuff, it was creepy like always but nothing was so creepy as what he said when I asked him who Morgan was.'

'What did he say?' asked Hitch; there was something different in his voice, less even perhaps, unlike himself somehow.

Ruby looked up at him. 'He said "I have no idea who Casey Morgan might be".'

Hitch held her gaze for several seconds. He said nothing and then,

'You can't stay here, you have to go. You'll be safer surrounded by all those people, you *all* will.'

'Wouldn't I be safer here?' suggested Ruby. 'With all these alarms and security features? It's completely safe, you said so.'

'Nothing is completely safe, kid. Go to the Eye Ball with your folks, try to have a good time and forget about spiders just for one night.'

Some chance, thought Ruby.

'I'll be there,' said Hitch.

She smiled. 'You will?'

'Sure I will, you can count on it,' he said.

Ruby went up to find her mother, who was talking to her father about the car and the driver and her outfit and a whole lot more.

She caught sight of Ruby, standing in the doorway. 'You'd better get changed, honey, we have to leave in a half hour.'

Ruby ran upstairs to her room and was surprised to see her

laundry strewn across the floor.

What's going on? she wondered. There was a strange gnawing sound coming from the bathroom. She found Bug chewing on something.

'What have you got there?'

She peered at him and then she saw it.

'Bug! Drop it, will you drop it!'

He let go and the blue rubber bone fell to the floor.

'Jeepers Bug, what's got into you?' She picked it up and saw that the husky had chewed right through it.

There was something inside: a piece of paper.

What's that? she wondered. She found some tweezers and pulled it free.

Chapter 54.
All systems are down

The piece of paper was a note written in a wobbly hand. It said:

Dear Ruby Redfort,

    I chose you because you are the smartest child I ever knew and I predicted that one day you would grow up and achieve great things.

    Many years ago I developed a way of extracting memories, an invention intended for good but lately I have begun to fear it will be used for ill. For this reason I encoded the formula, split it in half and hid it in two places. The first is a Lucite rectangle, disguised as a key-tag. If the Lucite reaches freezing point it will reveal the image of two eyes.

    The second part of the formula is hidden in the pattern of your irises. I don't need to explain to you how all eyes are unique, much like a fingerprint. If these Lucite eyes are placed directly over your own what's imbedded in the tag can be perfectly read.

It is essential that if the code tag gets into the wrong hands you deactivate the code — this you can do by wearing the contact lenses hidden in this container.

Once in place these lenses will ensure that whoever looks through the tag into your eyes will be given a scrambled reading, though they will believe it to be accurate. I cannot stress how vital it is that you use the lenses if you fear the tag is stolen.

Ruby picked up the blue rubber bone and peered inside. There was no contact lens blister or jar or tube or pouch, nothing.

She looked at the husky and rightly concluded that Bug had eaten them.

'Great, just great Bug.'

Hearing his name, he pottered over to where she sat, a little piece of paper hanging from his mouth. She took it, and unfolding it, saw that it was another note. This one said:

In case of emergency and these lenses fail you or become lost there is a second pair. I asked SJ to put them in the Ghost Files, in a folder marked 'Blink'.

Ruby turned and ran, right down to the apartment at the bottom of the house, as quickly as her legs would carry her, but when she got there, there was no sign of her protector.

'If you're looking for Hitch, he left ten minutes ago,' shouted her mother. 'He said he'd received an urgent message and he had to go – he didn't say why.'

Ruby's heart began to race. 'He just left us?' she said.

'It's a shame, I know,' said her mother, 'but it won't spoil your evening – you're going to have a high old time,'

Ruby couldn't believe it. What kind of bodyguard did this, what kind of agent was he? She was alone.

Don't panic, she told herself. What she needed to do was act quickly, make contact with someone at Spectrum. She ran up to her room and clicked on the Escape Watch and set it to transmit – maybe she could bring him back. But when she clicked "contact" nothing happened, it just wouldn't connect.

She tried SJ too but it was the same story.

This can't be happening.

It was the same with LB, and Blacker and Gill. She began randomly pressing buttons, but to no avail.

Finally, in utter despair, Ruby triggered the emergency bluebottle SOS symbol – still nothing. Her agent locator had been deactivated. She felt for the fly-barrette and pulled it from her hair and clicked the radio transmit switch, but found it wouldn't engage, and when she took a closer look she saw why: it had got bent out of shape, probably due to Olive's manhandling.

That kid is nothing but one big pain in the derièrre, she cursed.

And then she had an idea. She wasn't sure if it was brilliant or totally stupid, but it was the only one she had – and good ideas were getting hard to come by. She pressed the HQ call button, held her breath and waited.

 Would the call go through?

'Yes,' said a voice.

'It's me,' said Ruby.

'Yes,' came the reply.

'I need your help,' said Ruby.

'Why?'

'Because I can't reach anyone else,' said Ruby.

'All systems are down.'

'I figured that,' said Ruby, 'which is why I'm calling you – you're the only one who can help me.'

 Silence.

'Look, I mean I know we've never actually really gotten along or anything... OK, so you probably don't actually like me, I mean do you *like* anyone? But could we just let bygones be bygones? OK, how about just for today, just this one day, try to be interested in what I have to say, after that you can go back to being totally bored.'

 Silence.

'Look, I'm begging you, I need your help, OK, simple as that. What I need to know is in a file called "Blink" – it's hidden in the Prism Vault.' Ruby paused before continuing. 'Only the thing is, I can't get inside the Vault because I can't make contact with anyone, but you can.'

'I don't have the authority to enter. I need a written request or good reason.'

'I have good reason!' said Ruby. 'The reason is, if we don't figure out how to obscure the code which I hold then it has a good chance of getting into the wrong hands. If you want an instruction in writing then I'll gladly write it down. Could you at least try to be helpful?'

She was getting desperate now, pleading, almost begging.

'You gotta see, this isn't only about me, it's about you, it's about Spectrum and Twinford and maybe *everything*. If Casey Morgan gets his hands on this code then...'

'Who is Casey Morgan?'

'That's the thing,' said Ruby, 'I don't know, no one knows, how can you avoid someone if you don't know what they look like?'

Silence.

'Are you there? Will you help me?'

Pause. 'All right,' came the reply, 'I will look for this file. When I find it I'll contact you – where will you be?'

'The Eye Ball,' said Ruby.

'I'll come find you.'

'Thank you,' she said. 'Thank you, Buzz.'

She was no longer alone.

Chapter 55.
Make like bananas

HER MOTHER WAS CALLING.

'Ruby! Are you changed? We're about ready to go. Mouse and Elliot are already here.'

Ruby looked at herself, standing there in her jeans and T-shirt, the word *swat* printed across it.

Her space costume, lost somewhere between Everglade and Cedarwood – she would have to come up with an alternative or her mom would be on her tail. She pulled out the black jumpsuit and correctly predicted her mother's reaction.

When she arrived downstairs Sabina looked at her and said, 'Ruby, what on earth are you wearing?'

'Don't you mean, what *in space* are you wearing?' said Elliot.

'Well, if I do then I can't imagine what she is meant to be,' said Sabina, looking at Ruby's all-black clothes.

'I'm infinite space,' said Ruby, 'isn't that obvious?'

'Not to me,' said her mother. 'So I'm wondering: a) are you actually infinite space or b) is infinite space just an excuse to wear that black jumpsuit I told you I didn't like?'

'Quite a heavy question,' said Ruby, 'but I swear it's option a.' Ruby really didn't want this conversation; wearing the right party outfit was way down her priority list. Tonight pleasing her mother came a long way behind moles and madmen and mushrooms.

Mrs Digby was all dolled-up and wearing one of Cousin Emily's hair ornaments. It looked a little dangerous, precariously sticking out of her bun at a troubling angle: a long, jewelled, silver chopstick.

'So what are you dressed as, Mrs D?' asked Brant.

'I'm an earthling,' said Mrs Digby. 'An earthling who works all the hours God sends and doesn't have time to waste trying to cobble together some crazy costume.' She turned to fetch her coat, almost taking Ruby's left eye with her.

'Yeeks! Careful with that, Mrs Digby, you almost got me with your killer chopstick.' But Mrs Digby wasn't hearing; she was checking the rouge on her cheeks.

'You'd be safer wearing your glasses,' said Mouse. 'That way she wouldn't be able to prong you in the eye.'

'I'm trying to make my mom happy,' said Ruby. 'She's not a fan of my glasses.'

'It's because you have such beautiful green eyes,' said her mother. 'A girl needs beautiful eyes and it's such a shame to keep them behind those big black frames.'

'What are you, some kind of Victorian?' exclaimed Ruby.

'You do know we are on the cusp of 1974? What happened to all your feminist talk?'

Sabina looked torn. Ruby had a point. She sighed. 'You're probably right, wear whatever you like.'

'Actually, Mrs Redfort, I really like Ruby's glasses,' said Elliot. 'I think they are kinda cool. They give her an edge, you know what I'm saying? They make her eyes look big – like when you look at fish in a tank.'

'Thanks,' said Ruby, 'you're quite the smooth talker. Maybe I'll stick with the lenses.'

Mr Redfort clapped his hands. 'So are we all ready to go, folks?'

'Where are Red and Del?' asked Sabina.

'We're picking them up on the way,' said Mouse.

'OK, so let's make like bananas and split,' said Brant.

Sabina looked concerned. 'Bananas?'

'Let's get out of here, let's go!' explained Brant.

'Wait a minute,' said Ruby, 'I just have to fetch Bug.'

'For the last and final time, we are not bringing Bug. Mrs Hassensack is allergic,' said Sabina.

'I'm not leaving him on his own,' said Ruby. 'The vet said he needs to be reassured; she said don't let him get anxious.'

'Why would he get anxious?' asked Brant.

'New Year's Eve,' said Ruby, 'and you know what that means?'

'Champagne and caviar?' said her mother.

'Fireworks,' said Ruby. 'Bug *hates* fireworks. We can't leave him alone, he'll totally freak out.'

'But he's been alone before,' said Sabina.

'Yes, but he's suffered a trauma,' argued Ruby. 'He's vulnerable and if he freaks out with this injury then he could really do himself some damage.'

'I know Bug broke his leg,' said her mother. 'That's awful of course, but I don't see what that has to do with fireworks.' She looked confused. 'Bug has never liked loud noises, but he'll just lie under the table like always, won't he?'

Ruby would have liked to have explained, make her mom really understand what Bug had been through, but that would mean telling her about the incident in the Northern Mountains on the edge of the frozen lake, and how could she do that? So instead she just looked at her mom with her most pleading expression and said, 'You do know Bug saved my life?'

She knew her mother would be unable to say no to *that*.

'Brant, what do *you* think? Ruby's concerned about leaving Bug and maybe she's right, that poor hound has been through the wringer.'

'I'll square it with the Hassensacks,' said Brant. 'Bring him along, Ruby, one condition – don't let that dog leave your side. Got it?'

'I swear on my life,' said Ruby.

**Meanwhile,
eleven years earlier...**

...he could only hear the voice; his blindfold prevented him from seeing his captor, but he knew who it was, he knew without a single word being spoken – his sixth sense told him.

'You?' he said. 'Of all Spectrum, it's you?'

'You are surprised?'

'Who would have thought you capable?' said the old man.

'Of murder?' said the voice.

The old man shook his head. 'No, of deception. I saw you many times in Spectrum, but never once did I ever consider you a risk. What a clever disguise.'

'You have no imagination,' said the voice.

'Perhaps you are right,' said the Professor, 'or perhaps I saw someone I could trust.'

'People see what they want to see.'

'That's true,' said the old man. 'Sometimes you have to close your eyes to see the truth.'

'And sometimes you have to look beyond the face to see the man – you disguised yourself well,' said the voice. 'It took me years to find you.'

'And was it Victor von Leyden who sent you searching?'

'The Count – yes, it was his idea to seek you out, but the dog-napping, that idea was all mine.'

'Where is she – where is Mnemosyne?' asked the old man, anxiety in his voice.

'Oh, so that's its name, how wry – you named your dog after your life's work. How old is the mutt, by the way – thirty, forty? Such a long

time to own a dog, you must be very attached to her, very attached indeed.'

The professor felt a pang to his heart.

'Is this what it's all about? You want the location of the Hypocrea asteroidi?' I'm afraid I no longer know, plucked out that memory, but you'll find the answer you're looking for in the eyes of the Jade Buddha of Khotan.'

'It's Victor who wants to prolong life and stave off senility; my only interest in the so-called Mars Mushrooms is to see him beg. His time is marked, he's greedy for life.'

'So what do you want?' asked the old man.

'I want the power to wipe memories,' said the voice, 'to destroy the only things we humans can truly hold.'

'For without memories, what are we...?' mused the old man.

'Nothing,' replied the voice. 'Without memories we are no one, we are lost.'

'Poor little Casey Morgan, did life deal you an unfair hand?'

'Just tell me what I want to know, and save your little dog's life,' hissed the voice. 'I'm afraid I will not be able to promise you yours.'

'I will tell you what you ask, but first you must free Mnemosyne.'

His captor laughed. 'Your wish is my command, old man. What use have I for some wretched hound?'

The dog was fetched and the old man reached to stroke her head and then bent to whisper something in her ear.

'Go find Mrs Beesman,' he said.

And the dog licked the tears from the old man's cheek and, with *one last lingering look, turned and ran.*

'How touching,' said the voice. 'Now tell me where it is, this SME coder.'

'You'll find it in two parts: the first is in a Lucite tag. The second is hidden in the eyes of a child.'

'And how do I find this child?' asked the voice.

'You need to find the man who holds the tag.'

'And who is this man?' said the voice.

'The man you killed,' said Professor Pinkerton. 'Your nemesis – Bradley Baker.'

Chapter 56.
The Eye Ball

THERE WERE MAYBE TWO HUNDRED CARS inching along in double rows down 3rd Avenue, all waiting to pull up in front of the City Eye Hospital. It had been billed as 'an exclusive event' but it looked to Ruby as if the entire city had been invited. It felt like the Eye Ball really was the only party in town. The gowns were phenomenal and the costumes suitably out of this world. Some guests had taken the space theme on whole-heartedly: Freddie and Marjorie Humbert, for example, who had come as the constellation Gemini. They were dressed elegantly in black. Freddie's suit and Marjorie's gown were threaded with fibre optics so when they stood against a dark backdrop what you saw were the little white points of light denoting the arrangement of stars. Other guests just nodded to the theme, with a subtle hair decoration or patterned tie or item of jewellery.

Brant and Sabina had opted for glamour, Brant sporting a silver tux, Sabina stunning in a gown embroidered with silver sequins – when the light caught her she beamed so brightly that it was possible to imagine that, were she floating in outer space, she might just outshine the planet Venus.

'I swear there are more people dressed as stars than there are stars in the whole galaxy,' said Sabina.

'That would be somewhat impossible,' said Ruby dryly, 'I mean considering there are more stars in the sky than grains of sand on the beach.'

But her mother wasn't listening, she was too busy taking in the scene.

'How do you even *know* that?' asked Elliot.

'She reads stuff,' said Mouse.

'Yeah, but how do the people who write stuff *down* know this stuff. I mean, has anyone actually gone into space and counted *every* star?'

Ruby rolled her eyes. 'It's an estimate,' she said. 'There are approximately 100 to 400 billion stars in a galaxy. There are estimated to be around 100 billion galaxies in our universe, which means that there are approximately 10 sextillion stars in our universe. Maybe around 8,000 grains of sand can be packed into one cubic centimetre, 10 sextillion grains of sand could create a sphere with a radius of 10.6 kilometres. Some say there are give or take 700 trillion cubic metres of beach on our planet, which could hold approximately 5 sextillion grains of sand. So basically it means there are twice the number of stars in the sky as there are grains of sand on the beach – give or take.'

They all stood looking at her like she had just beamed down from the planet Zuton.

'Anyway,' said Mouse, 'the point is, your mom's got a point. There are an awful lot of stars at this party.'

The group made their way up to the 33rd floor, taking one of the eight elevators.

When the doors opened they were greeted by a woman in a gold dress and elaborate hairdo, a tiny satellite sticking up out of her brunette curls. She checked their names against her list and directed them to the cloakroom where they shed their coats and wraps before moving into the main ballroom. The ballroom opened into a whole series of other rooms, which in turn opened out onto balconies and terraces. It was 'some party', as Brant Redfort correctly remarked.

Ruby was not surprised that the first person she ran into was not exactly the kid she was looking to spend the evening with, but that of course was the whole thing about parties – they were unpredictable.

'Hi, Ruby!'

Ruby looked round to see a slice of Emmenthal smiling at her.

'It's me! Quent! I'm moon cheese.'

'You can say that again,' said Ruby.

'Is that your dog?' asked Quent.

'Well, it's not my grandmother,' said Ruby.

'He's got a broken leg,' said Quent.

'Yeah, I noticed that too,' said Ruby.

'I wanted to bring *my* dog, Dorothy, but my mom said it was strictly humans only, which is a shame because I was going to dress her up as Laika, the first dog in space.'

'Well, that's *tragic*,' said Ruby.

'Why?' asked Quent.

'Because Laika never made it back to earth.'

Quent's face fell. 'No one told me that.'

'Sorry to burst your bubble, Quent, but it was no fairy-tale ending for that poor dog. Laika just went round and round in space until...'

Ruby stopped mid-sentence when she saw that Quent's lip was beginning to tremble.

'You know, Quent, maybe I got that wrong. Maybe I'm thinking of something else... you know what, it was probably that film *Moon Mutt*, or *Space Spaniel* or something space-dog related.'

Quent dabbed his eyes with his cheese sleeves, and smiled. 'Well, that's a relief.' He took a closer look at Bug. 'So what has your dog come as?' he asked.

'I don't know,' replied Ruby. She glanced down at the husky. 'Pluto, I guess.'

'Doesn't Pluto have big droopy ears?' said Quent.

'OK, the dog star,' said Ruby.

'But then shouldn't he be silver – like a star,' suggested Quent.

Ruby shrugged. 'So he's a Martian.'

'He doesn't look like a Martian,' said Quent.

'How would you even *know*?' said Ruby. 'Have you ever been to Mars?'

'Uh uh, but I'm pretty sure Martians are green.'

'Why? Why are you pretty sure they're green?' asked Ruby.

'Because that's what people say,' said Quent.

'Do you listen to *everything* that people say?' asked Ruby.

'Not *everything*,' said Quent, 'but a *lot* of people seem to think Martians are green.'

The conversation was going nowhere and Ruby was relieved when Red joined them. She was dressed head to toe in green with a radio antenna waving about on her head.

'So what are you?' asked Quent.

'I'm a Martian,' said Red. She tried to catch a look at herself in one of the many mirrors. 'Don't I look like a Martian?'

'You look *exactly* like a Martian,' said Quent.

'I should do,' said Red. 'This is the original costume from the film *The Missing Martian of Manhattan.*'

Quent looked at Ruby. 'You *see*! I *told* you they were green.'

'Oh brother! Look, talking of Missing Martians, has anyone seen Clancy?'

'*I* saw him,' said Quent. 'He arrived the same time as me, and all these gazillion girls were with him.'

'His sisters,' said Ruby.

'They looked kinda grumpy,' said Quent.

'His sisters,' said Ruby.

'Hey, look, that's them.' He was pointing at the Crew family, who had a whole bunch of cameras pointed at them, and photographers were rattling off shots while the ambassador's family attempted to say 'cheese' and look like they meant it. The only people who seemed truly happy about it were Ambassador and Mrs Crew. Amy had pulled the fakest smile it was possible to pull, Nancy was looking weird, Minny looked cross and Lulu looked bored, while Olive had her cardigan over her head – there was no sign at all of Clancy.

'Excuse me, Quent, I'll leave you to orbit on your own for a light year. I just need to check in with ground control.'

Ruby weaved her way through the crowd to where the Crew girls stood. 'Hey Minny, is Clancy around?'

'He was,' said Minny, 'but Olive dropped her stupid Buttercup doll when she got out of the car and Clancy volunteered to go down and fetch it.'

'That's cos he's nice,' said Amy.

'He's not being *nice*,' argued Nancy, 'he just didn't want his picture taken is all.'

'Who can blame him,' said Lulu.

'I don't see why *he* should get out of it,' said Minny.

'I'll bet he's gone looking for that astronaut guy, what's his name?' said Lulu.

'Dave Scott Mackintosh,' said Ruby.

'Yeah, that's it,' said Lulu, 'he's kinda obsessed with this whole space thing. I'm telling you, he can be quite a bore about it.'

'Well, he's come to the right party,' said Ruby. She could see Del waving at her. 'So Lulu, when your brother finally decides to make it back to the 33rd floor, can you tell him to come find me? I'll probably be over by the chocolate fountain.'

'There's a fountain of chocolate?' said Lulu.

'Yeah,' said Ruby.

'Don't tell Nancy,' said Lulu, 'she'll stick her face right in it.'

Clancy was beginning to wonder if he wouldn't prefer to be smiling for the cameras *after all*. This whole Buttercup errand was taking him a lot longer than he had anticipated, and he was keen to get back to the party – it looked like fun. Plus he wanted to see Ruby, and if he was honest more than anything he wanted to see Dave Scott Mackintosh. He had specially brought along his silver indelible pen, the one that worked on pretty much any surface or any fabric. Clancy was going to ask Dave Scott Mackintosh to write something on his shirt. He had decided against his Jupiter costume and instead worn black: black shirt, black suit, black everything – it felt more spacey. It was a most un-Clancy-like thing to do to have his shirt signed, but this *was* Dave Scott Mackintosh, and having him sign one's actual shirt was the best space-themed outfit one could wish for. His mom would naturally be livid, but how often do you find yourself in the same room as a real-life spaceman? Actually, for Clancy that would be twice.

Rats, he thought, *I'm wasting valuable minutes.*

He just hadn't foreseen that he'd have such a hard time locating his father's limousine, but it wasn't an easy task: the underground parking lot was crammed with limousines, and one limousine really looked pretty much like another. When at last Clancy found the Crew car and the doll lying on the tarmac next to it, he grabbed it up, stuffed it in his jacket pocket and lost no time wending his way through the lot towards the elevators. He was a few yards away when he got the funniest feeling, like there might be someone else lurking in this underground place, some*one* or some*thing*. He got down low and crouched behind one of the shiny black vehicles, holding his breath and trying to determine what this thing he sensed might be. There was a sound of a car door opening just a couple of rows over, and then the sharp *tap tap tap* of good-quality shoes walking purposefully across the lot. What *was* it about that sound that suggested something bad? What was it about the waft of cologne that caused goosebumps to appear on his arms? Clancy kept very, very still. He didn't twitch so much as an eyelash until he heard the elevator's *ping* as the doors opened and then the soft *thunk* as they closed. He watched the numbers light up as the elevator car reached level 1, 2, 3, and kept on going, 14, 15, 16 and on until it reached 34.

The next thoughts that went through Clancy's mind were very conflicted.

Get out of here Clancy, get out of here right now, go home...
You have to follow him...
You know what, it probably wasn't actually him...

Are you crazy? Of course it was him...

Let someone else deal with the problem, I'm just a boy...

Don't be a coward, Clancy Crew, you have to find out what he's up to, just follow him, would you!

Oh brother, I hate myself...

Clancy of course had a sixth sense for this kind of stuff, he'd always had it.

And now a voice told him: *Something bad is going to happen and it's Ruby that it's going happen* to.

Sometimes he really wished he didn't get these hunches; it would save him a whole lot of grief if he was more like Del, no intuition and no sensitivity... If you were Del, you saw trouble, you met it head on, and you punched its lights out. But unfortunately for Clancy, he wasn't Del, so instead he hurried over to the elevator and stepped inside, thumped the button for floor 34 and when the doors closed he leant back breathing hard.

What to do, what to do?

He watched as the numbers blinked up: 30, 31, 32, 33...

34.

Ping.

Chapter 57.
A man about a dog

SABINA AND BRANT WERE SIPPING GREEN MARTIANTINIS
and chatting with the Humberts.

'I only wish they had managed to finish the roof garden in
time; the view's spectacular from the top of the building.'

'They won't let you up there,' said Freddie.

'Never mind,' said Marjorie.

Sabina looked longingly at Brant. 'Oh, but I had my heart
set on popping a few corks while we sipped champagne in the
light of that giant eye.'

'I know you did sweetheart,' said Brant.

'Why the roof of the eye hospital?' asked Marjorie.

'It's where we got engaged,' said Sabina. 'We sat on that
eyeball and knew we were for keeps.'

'How did that come about?' asked Freddie.

'It's a long story,' said Brant.

Clancy was standing face to face with Victor von Leyden, Count
of all darkness.

'How sweet of you to make it all so easy, Master Crew. I must confess I thought it was going to be so much more difficult, but now I can enlist your help to bring Ms Redfort to me, most of my work is done.'

'What do you mean?' stammered Clancy. 'What's Ruby to *you*?'

'What is she to me?' mused the Count. 'She's bait, a little fly tangled in a web. She will bring the spider out of its lair; if I dangle her from the roof it will come,' he smiled. 'You see, she holds a secret right there in her eyes and I know someone who wants it.'

'What someone?' asked Clancy.

'I must say, he had me guessing,' said the Count, 'but once I saw it, I knew it had to be true, it's so wickedly perfect.'

'Who?' whispered Clancy, fearing the answer.

'Her so-called guardian angel,' said the Count. 'Trust makes you vulnerable, leads you into trouble, the same sort of trouble *you* have just walked into, but at least *you* have a way out – bring Ruby Redfort to me and I will spare your life.'

'Never,' said Clancy. 'I would never do that! You can throw me to a pack of wolves or feed my toes one by one to a bunch of crocodiles, but I will never do that!'

The Count fixed him with his black shark eyes. 'It would be my pleasure, if only *wolves* or crocodiles were to hand, but alas there are none, so please know that I *will* without qualm drop you from this rooftop, if you refuse me.'

'Then that is what you'll do,' said Clancy, looking back at him. Without a blink or a tremble, he held the man's gaze. 'But I will not betray Ruby Redfort.'

The Count smiled at that.

'I do believe you speak the truth.' He circled the boy, stepping round him, his eyes fixed firm on Clancy's. 'You know, it is *rare* that I admire another human soul – you *almost* move me. What loyalty, what a *friend*, what a *waste*.'

And from his black coat he took a vial of indigo, exquisitely inky blue, and unscrewing the top he took the dropper and squeezed it full.

'Do you recognise this?' he asked, holding it to the light.

Clancy kept his mouth firmly shut because he *did* know what it was and it frightened him *more* than crocodiles, more than wolves.

'The serum of honesty,' announced the Count. 'It will *make* you talk, and whatever you say will be the truth, the whole truth and nothing but the truth so help you, wretch.'

'Open wide,' he said, his hand pressed hard on Clancy's windpipe, forcing him to gasp for breath, and when he did the Count dropped six pretty tears of indigo-blue on Clancy's tongue. He slid his gold watch from his pocket and waited for the hand to tick round once and then he sighed.

'Now, you tell me how I bring your *pal*, your *friend*, your *kindred spirit* to *my* little party.' The words were hissed out, full of hate. 'You'll tell me now because you have no choice.'

Clancy shook his head and the Count laughed.

'Get ready to blab.' He made a snapping motion with his hand. 'And look,' he said, 'not a crocodile in sight and all your toes intact.'

The party was going very well, and it seemed everyone was having the time of their lives, except for Ruby who was anxious. Where was Clancy? He couldn't still be down in the parking lot. She and Bug did a quick circuit of the main room and then went back to ask the coat check girl if she had seen him, and then the party greeter, but they shook their heads.

Ruby and her husky circled back and rejoined the friends by the chocolate fountain, Elliot transfixed by the bubbling gloop.

'No sign of him?' Ruby asked.

'No,' said Mouse, 'but I just saw Hitch.'

'When?' said Ruby. 'Where is he?'

'He said he was going to see a man about a dog,' said Red.

'I have no idea what that means,' said Del.

'It's English for *mind your own business*,' said Elliot.

'I thought the English were meant to be so polite?' said Mouse.

'It's a myth,' said Elliot.

'Is Hitch English?' asked Red.

'Where did he go?' said Ruby. 'Can anyone tell me?'

'Hey, look there he is,' said Mouse.

He was making his way through the party people, his face

serious and his stride purposeful.

Where are you going? thought Ruby.

She called out to him but he didn't hear her, and continued snaking his way through the crowd.

She hurried after him, but he seemed to evaporate into the mass and she was left zigzagging this way and that in an effort to spot him.

'Darn it!' she muttered. 'I need you.' And then she had an idea.

'Bug! Go find Hitch.' She reached to stroke the husky's neck, but found he wasn't there. 'What? You gotta be kidding me.'

The Count pointed to a telephone. 'All I'm asking you to do is make a call to the front desk, and tell the greeter that you urgently need to speak to Ms Redfort, that she must come to the phone, and when she does and she asks you where you are, you say, 'I'm dangling out of a window on the 34th floor, please come to my assistance as fast as your little legs will carry you.'

'But I'm not dangling out of a window on the 34th floor.'

'Give me a minute, it's easy to arrange,' said the Count, and he smiled. 'So what do you say?'

'OK,' said Clancy.

'OK, what?' asked the Count.

'OK, I'd be happy to,' said Clancy.

'Why?' said the Count, furrowing his brow. 'Why would you be *happy* to tell her that?'

'Because,' said Clancy *truthfully*, for there was no other way for him to tell it, 'she'll know right away that something is up. She'd know I'd never put her life in jeopardy like that; she won't believe me not for a second, she'll assume I'm kidding around.'

The Count frowned as he considered this hiccup in his plan and then he said, 'So Master Crew, tell me, what *will* bring Ms Redfort running? Tell me what is her so-called *Achilles' heel* when it comes to the tugging of her little heartstrings?'

'Bug,' said Clancy without hesitation.

'Bug?' said the Count. 'Who is Bug?'

'Her dog,' said Clancy. 'If Ruby's here tonight then Bug's sure to be here too; she wouldn't leave him home on New Year's Eve, and if Bug wanders off, she'll go find him.'

'And why should she care about a dog, pathetic creatures that they are?'

'Bug is not pathetic. Ruby is crazy about that dog, she would do anything for him, plus he's injured, so she's feeling very protective, won't let him leave her side.'

The Count clapped his hands together. 'Music to my ears! So let's get that hound to come to us.'

'If we do, she's sure to follow,' said Clancy.

Ruby had hoped that the dog would have moseyed back to the group, but there was no sign of him.

'Mouse, have you seen that dog of mine?'

'I thought he was with you,' said Mouse. 'He's probably

sniffed out the buffet room.'

'You better not let Mrs Hassensack see him,' said Elliot. 'She's not so crazy about canines.'

'It's because she has allergies,' said Quent. 'I have allergies, but I love dogs so much I don't care.'

'Actually, she is phobic about dogs,' said Red.

'Is there such a thing as a phobia of dogs?' asked Elliot.

'Cynophobia,' said Quent.

'That's a big word for a small kid,' said Del.

'I know everything about dogs,' said Quent.

'So how do you know that Mrs Hassensack has cyno-whatever?' asked Mouse.

'My mom designed her costume,' said Red, 'and they got chatting. Turns out Mrs Hassensack has issues.'

Suddenly, bringing Bug to this crazy party seemed like a very bad idea. There would be a scene, her parents would be mortified, Ruby would be in the dog house, and all in all it would be a very bad start to 1974.

'I better go fetch him before we both get sent to the pound,' Ruby sighed. 'Look, if you see that Crew boy, tell him he's royally late.'

'Where shall I say you are?' asked Elliot.

'I don't know, tell him I'll be on planet Mars – which is where I wish I was, by the way.'

'Sure,' said Elliot.

'You want me to come with you?' asked Mouse.

'Nah, I won't be a minute. I'll bet he's gone to find Consuela. She's a soft touch when it comes to Bug.'

Ruby began to weave her way through the party, making sure to avoid her parents, who were in the middle of a highly animated conversation with the planet Neptune and a flying saucer, or *some* unidentified flying object, it was hard to say.

'Bug!' hissed Ruby. 'Where are you, you horrible husky?' She looked in the rooms either side of the grand corridor. There were people everywhere, elegant gatherings clustered here and there, some sitting, others standing, all of them chatting, but no Bug.

'Hey, anyone seen a husky?' she called.

Barbara Bartholomew turned around when she heard Ruby's voice. 'Oh, hey Ruby, I *did* see Bug and you better catch hold of him before Mrs Hassensack sees him. She's not a fan, if you know what I mean. She has allergies, and that thing, what's it called?'

'Cynophobia,' said Ruby.

'That's the one.'

'Thanks Barbara. Could you grab a hold of him if he comes this way?'

'You can count on it, honey.'

Ruby lingered a second. 'Would you maybe not mention it to my mother?'

Barbara gave a theatrical wink. 'I'll keep it zipped, no reason to ruin her evening.'

'I appreciate it,' said Ruby.

She continued on until she reached the staircase. She wasn't certain why, but if she had to guess, instinct told her to go up rather than down. As she climbed the stairs, so the chatter and laughter receded, and once on the 34th floor it was just a gentle hum and burble. She cocked her head and listened, and then she thought she heard the sound of Bug's plaster cast tapping along the marble floor. She quickened her pace, rounded the next corner and then there she saw him.

'Bug! What in jeepers are you doing?' The dog stopped, turned to look at her, paused for just a moment and then walked on.

'Bug, you come back here!' But he wasn't listening. This was odd, super odd. Bug was one very well-behaved dog – at least he *was* on just about *any* other day.

'Hey, what's got into you? Geez, Bug, you choose *this* moment to give up on the whole command thing?'

It was then that she became aware of the air. It wasn't the smell of candles, perfume and food that she now breathed. It was something far richer. It was different from the other delicious smells which were coming at her from *all directions* and *everywhere*. This scent was intoxicating. More exotic than jasmine, more heady than roses, more...

Cyan, she thought.

She knew that scent. The last time she had smelled it, she was on top of Wolf Paw Mountain, nose to nose with its fearsome creator, the Blue Alaskan wolf. Cyan. The rarest perfume in the world, a scent designed to lure prey.

'Bug, come back here!' she hissed. But the dog wouldn't be called.

When she turned the next corner, she saw him standing there at the far end of the hallway. He paused just a moment and then he was gone.

Her instinct was to follow, but she knew this was a trap. Whoever was luring Bug was actually luring her. *Don't follow. If you do whoever is round that corner will kill* you *and then* they will kill your dog. *You live, Bug lives.*

She could hear footsteps coming her way. She backtracked, slipping in through a half-open door. The room was dark. The footsteps moved quickly.

A man? And then she heard a voice. It was hushed, but there was no mistaking who it belonged to: *Hitch*? She was about to step out from her hiding place, when his words caught her. He was speaking into some kind of radio device.

'I'll find her,' he whispered. 'She's here in the building. I saw her come up, she'll be lurking somewhere in the shadows. She's smart but I can outsmart her.' He stopped almost directly in front of the door behind which she hid. 'I know we want her alive,' he said, 'but that all depends on whether I reach her before our friend the Count does.' He sniffed the air. 'I smell cyan – he's here already and he'll kill her if he gets the chance.' The way he spoke was matter-of-fact, urgent but without emotion. 'At least with her gone, it would bring everything to a close.'

He began to walk, his footsteps heading off down the

passageway.

Ruby didn't move. *Stay still until you are absolutely sure the coast is clear.* Was that a rule? She couldn't remember.

It was while she stood there as still as the walls, that the Escape Watch flashed red.

A message from HQ.

YOU ARE IN DANGER!

This word message was followed by a picture message. A black-and-white photograph appeared on the screen, a boy of about six, maybe seven.

She stepped backwards as if the small white teeth of the boy might take a bite. For the eyes which stared back at her were the eyes of the Redforts' very own house-manager, the eyes of Spectrum Agent 192.

The image dissolved and the following words appeared:

THE FACE OF
CASEY MORGAN.

Chapter 58.
No Rule 81

THE MESSAGE WAS FROM BUZZ and was followed by the words:

> I AM COMING TO FIND YOU, STAY WHERE YOU
> ARE, KEEP AWAY FROM HIM.

It was hard to be exactly reassured by this.

It was good to know that someone was on the way to rescue her from mortal danger, but if Ruby could have picked anyone to come to her aid then it would not have been the woman who sat, mushroom-like, surrounded by telephones, picking up messages and passing on instructions. Of all the people in Spectrum 8, Buzz seemed the least likely to be capable of saving her. But it was turning out to be that kind of day, since Ruby had to admit that of all the people she had worked with, Hitch seemed the least likely to be the one to try and kill her.

RULE 81: WHAT TO DO WHEN YOUR MOST TRUSTED ALLY TURNS OUT TO BE A PHONEY?

The answer was not in Ruby's little magenta rule book, because for most of her life, Clancy Crew had been her most trusted ally and so she had never once had to contemplate the thought.

Clancy Crew, meanwhile, was trying to recall any one of Ruby's rules in the vague hope that it might perhaps give him even the faintest clue as to what he should do next. Bug had been shut behind a door, the Count obviously didn't trust this injured husky not to take a bite, and so Clancy alone stood staring into the eyes of Count von Viscount, unsure of what his next move should be.

'So Master Crew, we have managed to acquire a dumb animal but failed to lure the smart girl.'

'Yes,' agreed Clancy.

'Why is that?' asked the Count.

'She didn't follow,' said Clancy.

The Count looked at him with cold disgust. 'She did not.'

Clancy said nothing.

'You lied to me,' said the Count. '*You lied.*'

Clancy looked back at the man. 'How could I? You gave me a truth serum and I told you the truth.'

The Count's eyes were boring into him; he could almost feel their stare. 'What do you think I am, some kind of fool? An imbecile?'

'A bear,' said Clancy.

The Count looked puzzled.

'Do you know what I'm capable of?' he hissed.

'Anything,' whispered Clancy. 'You're capable of anything.'

But the Count didn't hear. His attention was caught by another sound – footsteps moving fast, two people, but not together. He let go of Clancy, who stumbled, his head hitting the edge of the sill, a nasty thud.

'I'll catch up with you later,' said the Count. 'You might as well stay where you are. No one can save you now.'

I think that might be true, thought Clancy as he watched the man walk away, his shoes *tap tap tapping* on the cold marble floor.

WHAT TO DO IF YOU MEET A BEAR – WISH YOU HADN'T!

As Clancy lay there, he thought about the unsolvable problem, the problem which had no answer – bears. The only thing he and Ruby had always agreed on was who in all the world might save you should you have the misfortune to meet one.

'*Mrs Digby,*' he whispered, before passing out.

As Ruby turned the corner she saw him and, more to the point, he saw her.

'Ruby!' called Hitch.

She turned and ran.

'Kid, where are you going?'

But she didn't reply. She just tore down the passageway as fast as ever she could. She made it to the back staircase and quickly sprinted down the zigzag stairs to the 33rd floor. She was relieved to be back where the party was, where all the people were. She ran along the deserted east corridor until she reached the big wooden doors which led to the grand hall. She could hear the hubbub on the other side. She reached for the handle and pushed down hard, expecting the doors to swing open, but they didn't – they were bolted shut. She hammered hard with her fists, but no one was going to hear her, not with the racket of the music and the dancing and the laughing and happy chatter.

Where is Buzz? Darn it, where is Buzz! She pulled at her hair and slapped her hand to her head several times. *Keep calm,* she told herself. *Focus Ruby, stop freaking out and focus.*

She closed her eyes, took a breath. And just like that an idea popped into her head. She remembered that overheard conversation – her mother talking about the party, the little catering lift, a sort of updated dumbwaiter that was going to be installed to carry food and dishes from the newly built kitchens all the way to the grand dining room on the 33rd floor. If Ruby could find that then she could climb inside, she was certainly small enough, and once in the lift she would be able to travel to the basement level and grab a cop or a passer-by. She really wasn't feeling choosy.

If only she had paid attention to her mother's chatter, if only she had, she would have known why this plan was simply not going to work. Two minutes later she found out. The room was an empty shell of a space, a building site. There was no dumbwaiter, just one desperate girl.

She could hear Hitch, his footsteps clicking along the marble corridor. How had he known she would come this way? Could he read her mind? Was it some Spectrum intuition? And as she lifted her hand to her head she found the answer: the fly-barrette, she must have triggered the locator. It was not broken, just jammed. Hitch knew exactly where she was because *she* had told him. She began barricading the door with ladders and construction workers' tools and anything that might possibly buy her one more second of time.

RULE 44: WHEN IN A TIGHT SPOT, BUY YOURSELF SOME TIME: ONE MINUTE COULD CHANGE YOUR FATE.

Now what? Wait for help to arrive? *Buzz, you walking mushroom, where are you?*

She could hear him outside, trying the handle.

'Kid, I don't know who's spooking you, but you've got this all backwards.'

She kept quiet, as if silence was a good way to fool him, make him think she wasn't there.

Not a chance.

Clancy came round and realised he was very uncomfortable sprawled there on the floor. Something rock-like was digging into his hip. He reached a hand under his side.

'Buttercup?' he said, pulling the doll from his jacket pocket. 'Oh boy, I forgot about you. Olive's going to be mad at me, Mom and Dad are going to be mad at me, and where am I? Flat on my back doing nothing about nothing.' He looked sadly at the doll. 'Why don't you go get help, Buttercup? I'll try crawling off to find Ruby, while you find someone to save us.' And then he remembered the last thought he'd had before he'd slipped into unconsciousness. It had been about Mrs Digby and bears and he wondered, *was it possible that* she *could save Ruby?*

He groped for his indelible pen, he still had it in his back pocket, and he scrawled a silver message on the doll's face.

It said:

`Follow me back to Clancy`

Then he sort of half-walked, half-staggered to the door that held Bug.

The dog wagged its tail, pleased to be released, pleased the frightening man in the long black coat had gone. Clancy stroked the husky's head.

'OK Bug, you gotta do this one thing, think you can?'

The dog wagged its tail some more.

Clancy held the doll out to him. 'Go find Mrs Digby?'

The dog's ears pricked up when he heard her name.

'Here, go find Mrs Digby.' But Bug just stood looking at Clancy and the trickle of blood running down his cheek. 'Bug, go, you have to go, OK?'

But the husky did not move.

'Bug, you know this game, you're really good at it.' Clancy threw the doll, and said in his most commanding voice, 'Bug, go find Mrs Digby!'

The dog stood still.

Clancy was getting desperate, his voice losing hope. 'Bug, for jeeper's sake, you have to go get Mrs Digby, you have to or Ruby will die, you understand? I need your help.'

And the dog *did* seem to understand. He picked up Buttercup and he turned and he ran back down the corridor towards the staircase.

'Kid, open the door, you've *got* to open the door.'

'I don't gotta do anything, I'm not listening to you, listening to you is how Bradley Baker wound up dead.'

'I don't know what you're talking about, Ruby.'

'Your *picture* is what I'm talking about. It was found buried in the files, the files you tried to hide.'

'Kid, you're not making any sense.'

'You've been lying to me!' she shouted. 'But you're good at that, aren't you? Because that's what you are, just one big lie.'

'You're all mixed up kid – open the door and we can talk.'

'If you think I'm gonna open this door to you, you must be crazy – oh, I forgot – you *are*!'

'You *have* to let me in, Ruby!'

'Never!'

The noise that followed was of Hitch's shoulder thumping into the door. The barricade was beginning to give. There was no way out. Except via the window. She was a long way up; what was this, the 33rd floor? Another storey and then the roof.

She went to the window – a broken latch, no way to open it. 'Ruby?' A small voice came from the watch. 'Ruby? Are you there?'

'Buzz, is that you? – where are you?'

'I tracked you, I'm on the other side of the wall; can you make it to me?'

'How?' said Ruby. She was feeling straight-up panic now.

'There's a ledge. Do you think you could get yourself to me?'

'Maybe if I can get out of the window.' She looked around, there was a fire extinguisher in the corner. She heaved it from the wall and ran at the window, smashing it into the glass, tiny fragments exploding into the air.

Jeepers Rube, is this how you want to die?

Ruby peered out and looked to the sidewalk below.

Oh brother, she thought.

'It's a long way down.'

'I see that,' said Buzz, 'but you can make it, I'm right here.'

She saw Buzz's hand beckoning her. Six yards, maybe eight, and she would be safe.

'You can do it, Ruby.'

Buzz was right, she could do this; she'd done so before. It was just back then, a few months ago, when she'd taken a walk along the outside of the Sandwich Building, there had been no ice-cold wind, no ice, and more to the point – no psychopath trying to pluck her from the ledge.

Don't think about that.

She stepped through the window and out onto the narrow stone shelf.

Behind her, there was a crashing sound as the door finally gave and Hitch sort of tumbled into the room. He righted himself, looked around, wondered where she'd gone, ran to the shattered window and then he saw her.

'No!' he shouted. 'Don't do that!'

'Get away from me!' she yelled. 'I know who you are, don't you see?'

'Whatever you think you know, you got it wrong,' said Hitch, his voice steady.

'I know what you did, I know who you are.'

'And who's that?' asked Hitch.

'You're Casey Morgan,' said Ruby.

Chapter 59.
Follow me

MRS DIGBY FELT A NUDGE to her leg and looked down to see Bug.

'Well, where in the dickens did you come from?' said Mrs Digby. 'You're meant to be with Ruby.'

The dog nudged her again, and the old lady's drink, a precarious sort of red cocktail, splashed from its glass onto her dress. 'Well, now look what you've gone and done,' she said, tottering to the nearest table and wiping at her skirts with the edge of the elegant white tablecloth. The dog followed her, butting her leg with his head. 'Stop it, would you, you're making a scene.' She bent down to grab his collar and for the first time registered what Bug had in his mouth.

'What is that horrible thing?' She reached for Buttercup. 'Where did you get this?' The dog looked at the old lady and *she* looked more closely at the big round face of the baby doll, and the silver words scrawled across its face.

```
Follow me back to Clancy
```

Mrs Digby looked at Buttercup's round green eyes staring unblinking back at her, and then she looked at Bug.

'You got something you want to tell me, dog of mine?'

Bug wagged his tail, sensing she had finally understood.

'Come on then,' she said. 'You take me to Clancy.'

Ruby was losing her nerve. Safety was too far away. She was still several icy steps from the window where Buzz stood calling to her.

'Be careful. Don't slip Ruby, just focus,' Buzz urged. 'LB is on her way.'

Ruby tried not to think about what would happen if LB didn't show.

'Kid, you're making a big mistake, the biggest of your life. Who fed you this information?'

'It doesn't matter who told me, because I just heard you talking to your accomplice not ten minutes ago. I know you want me dead! As soon as you have the code, I'll be toast!'

Her fingers searched for something to grip, to hold on to.

'Kid, that wasn't *you* I was talking about! – that was—'

'He'll kill you Ruby!' Buzz warned. 'Just like he tried to kill Bradley Baker, that day at the rapids, just like he tried to kill little Art Zachery.'

'Not true!' yelled Hitch. 'The boy who almost got *chomped* by a crocodile was me.'

'Well, forgive me if I don't take your word for it.'

'Wanna see the bite? It's ugly, took an awful lot of stitches to put me back together.'

Ruby felt her foot slip on ice and she barely managed to steady herself.

'Ruby!' cried Buzz. 'Hold on, keep moving – focus on me.'

'Focus on her and you'll wind up dead,' shouted Hitch.

'Don't listen to him Ruby! He stole someone's name and plotted murder.'

'Talking of names,' shouted Hitch, 'do you know what *Buzz* stands for kid?'

'Of course I know,' cried Ruby, 'Brenda Ulla Zane. What's that got to do with anything?'

'Nothing,' shouted Hitch. 'Not until you know what those initials *really* represent: **B**aker, **U**ggerlimb, **Z**achery, all the agents Buzz wants dead. Baker, the boy who was better than her, and the two who tried to save him – oh, and you can add *your* name to that list – once she has obtained that code, you really *will be* toast. You can stake your life on it.'

'You're actually trying to tell me that an HQ *administrator* is part of this?'

'Not *part* of this – the whole deal, the one who's been pulling the strings all this time.'

'*Buzz* is Casey Morgan? You're out of your mind if you think I'm going to believe that!' yelled Ruby.

She was looking at a piece of jutting stonework, trying to figure out how to get past it.

'He's a liar and deep down you know it Ruby,' yelled Buzz. 'Ask him where he's been all this time, where was he this evening, for instance – why didn't he answer your call?'

'Want to know where I was? I was on a wild goose chase, that's where – and someone cut my line.'

'It was you who shut down transmission, you!' yelled Buzz.

'Why would you do that?' shouted Ruby.

'You're missing the big picture here kid.'

'That's funny, the last time I heard those words they came out of the Count's mouth – friend of yours, is he?'

She was grappling to find handholds, her feet kept slipping on the ledge.

'The Count's a friend of no one, you know that. Ask Buzz, she used to be his apprentice, didn't you Buzz?'

'You're the assassin!' shouted Buzz. 'After all it was *you* who took her up in that plane! *You* who handed her to Marnie Novak! *You* who went missing without contact! Abandoning her to all that danger! It was you!'

'I was left for dead in the back of beyond!' yelled Hitch.

'Don't listen to him! He's trying to save his own skin.'

'Believe me, Ruby, you're about to grab the hand of Casey Morgan!'

'How could Buzz be Casey Morgan? Casey Morgan was a boy!' yelled Ruby.

'No kid, Casey Morgan was a girl who *disguised* herself as a boy in order to become Larva – no women in Spectrum, not back then, that made little Casey mad, it wasn't fair and it *wasn't*, was it Casey? It was most definitely *not* fair – but instead of proving herself, little Casey here decides to take out the competition.'

'If I'm so smart that I can outwit all you brilliant agents with all your training, then how come I'm sitting surrounded by phones taking calls and passing on messages?'

'It's true,' shouted Ruby. 'How could a mushroom like Buzz be some evil genius!'

'Because she's not a mushroom, she's a toadstool, sitting there attracting flies.'

'He'll say anything to make you believe his lies.'

Who's lying, who's lying, who's lying?

RULE 29: JUST BECAUSE A LION SAYS IT'S A MOUSE, DOESN'T MAKE IT A MOUSE.

Just because an agent says he's a butler doesn't make him a butler.

Just because an agent says he's one of the good guys, doesn't make it true.

Just because a toadstool looks like a mushroom doesn't make it any less dangerous.

Who's lying?

She was stuck halfway between Hitch and Buzz, her back to the building, the snow gently falling, with no idea which way to go.

'He's playing you, Ruby,' said Buzz. 'You've been working for him, feeding him information.'

'All this time,' said Hitch, 'it's been Buzz sitting right there in the corner of the room, so obvious we didn't see her, like a spider spinning a web, catching flies, catching agents.'

It was Ruby's mind which was beginning to spin...

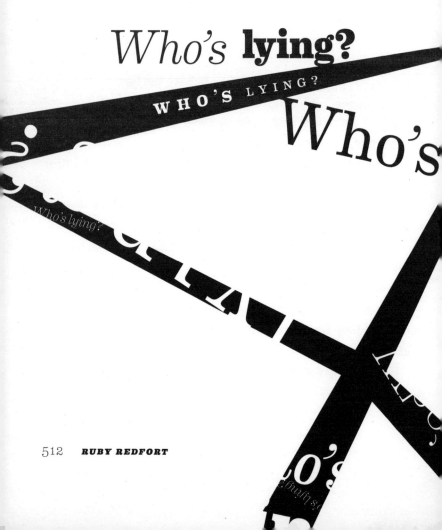

She looked up and saw the great blinking eye at the top of the old City Eye Hospital.

Who's lying?

Who's lying?

How to know?

Who would know?

Clancy would know...

She closed her eyes. 'Clancy, where are you?' she yelled. And to her great surprise a voice came back to her.

'I'm here, Rube! Up here!'

Ruby looked above her to see Clancy's small face looking down from the roof of the building.

'Climb up to the sign,' said Clancy. 'Get up on the roof! I'll be here for you!'

Get up on the roof!

And Ruby began to climb, away from Buzz, away from Hitch and up to safety. She looked down; she could no longer see Buzz but out of the corner of her eye she could see Hitch. He was at the far edge of the building and climbing.

'Keep going Rube,' urged Clancy, 'just keep going.'

She was moving fast. Though the snow was falling and the ironwork was slippery she was already halfway up the sign.

'You've nearly made it,' said Clancy. 'Just grab the eye and you're almost there.'

'I can't, I'm caught on something,' she screamed. 'My shoe is caught!'

'Don't panic Rube, take it easy, just try and wriggle free.'

'I don't know who to trust Clance,' she cried.

'Rube, what do you do when you meet a bear?'

'Wish you hadn't,' whispered Ruby.

'No,' shouted Clancy. 'You go with your gut instinct, tune into your sixth sense.'

'I don't have one!'

'*Everyone* has one! Who is it telling you to trust?'

Ruby closed her eyes.

'Hitch,' she said.

Chapter 60.
Hanging on by an eyelash

IT WAS HITCH WHO REACHED THE ROOF FIRST. He looked around for Ruby and saw a figure crouching near the parapet, just caught by the light.

'Clancy, is that you?'

Clancy got to his feet. 'Yeah, it's me.'

'Where is she?' asked Hitch.

'On the sign!' said Clancy. 'Her shoe is caught.'

Hitch ran to the edge. 'Stay there kid, I'll get you.'

'You gotta save her,' said Clancy. 'The Count – once he figures she's up here he'll follow – you have to save her!'

'You can bet on it kid, but you have to hide, no heroics, do you hear me?'

Clancy nodded.

'So go hide in the shadows; no one will see you in that black suit.'

Clancy did as he was told and Hitch began to lower himself over the parapet.

Too late he heard the *tap tap tap* of Italian shoes.

Too late he turned to see the silhouette of Victor von Leyden.

And he was too late to save himself from what was to come.

The Count didn't hesitate. He aimed and fired – not a bullet, but a dart of paralysing parasol poison, and Hitch felt its sting as he reeled backwards, arms flailing as he grappled air.

The Count picked his way carefully to the roof's edge and peered down to see Hitch hanging on by an eyelash, quite literally clinging to one of the giant iron eyelashes which surrounded the vast neon eyeball.

'Let's hope it doesn't blink,' said the Count, looking at his watch. 'Five minutes to go,' he laughed. 'It blinks and you die.'

Hitch was trying to grab on with his other hand, but it wouldn't move, the venom having already taken hold.

'Want to strike a bargain Casey dear fellow?' called the Count. 'I'll give you the girl – if you give me the location of those Mars Mushrooms.'

'I'm afraid I can't help you with that,' shouted Hitch.

'You don't have long,' warned the Count. 'Once that paralysing poison takes hold, *you* will no longer be able to – those parasol fish really are quite deadly.'

'Like I said, I can tell you nothing,' yelled Hitch.

'They'll be no use to you once you fall, and you *will* fall.'

'I don't have the location,' yelled Hitch.

'Don't lie to me. You betrayed me, Casey Morgan, and I want what's mine.'

'Oh, I'm not Casey,' called Hitch, 'you've got the wrong guy.'

'Of course you're Casey,' hissed the Count.

'No, Casey would be the woman standing right behind you.'

As the Count turned, so Buzz kicked him hard in the back of the knees, the Count lost his balance, pitched forward and fell headlong into the sky.

And at the very same moment Hitch lost his grip; the poison took hold, but as his hand let go of the lash so his jacket caught it. The dark grey fabric of his Savile Row suit was the only thing between him and the great abyss.

And next they heard Clancy's voice, yelling from the darkness. 'Over here, I'm over here!'

The distraction bought them time. Buzz ran to the shadows, but could not see the boy; his dark suit blended with the night.

'Ruby!' yelled Hitch. 'Kick off your shoe and climb! Get out of here!'

'What about you! She'll kill you!'

'Get out of here! That's an order!' he yelled.

She yanked her foot and the shoe came away and she began to move, hand over hand, reaching for the top. She stretched out her arm and felt for the stone but instead of stone it found...

'Buzz!'

'Call me Casey,' she said.

Chapter 61.
Blink and you die

THE WOMAN FORMERLY KNOWN AS BUZZ was much stronger than Ruby would have ever guessed. Her grip so strong Ruby was held there, struggle was futile.

Casey Morgan pressed the 8-key key-tag that had once belonged to Bradley Baker into the snow and slowly the etched eyes appeared. Then, very carefully, Casey Morgan held the Lucite eyes over Ruby's own.

'Blink and you die,' she hissed.

She peered into green, trying to align the pattern in the Lucite over the pattern in Ruby's irises. But something was wrong, she couldn't get a reading, and then she realised why.

'You're wearing lenses,' she hissed. 'Pluck them out or I'll kill your friend.'

In the darkness Ruby could see Clancy creeping up. All he had to do was push.

Suddenly Buzz flung out her arm and Clancy went sprawling across the roof.

'I don't think he'll be getting up from that,' she snarled. 'Lose the lenses or I'll pick them out myself.'

And so Ruby did.

Buy yourself some time: one minute could change your fate.

And while she waited for Casey Morgan to read the code, through the blur Ruby thought she could see a figure, two figures, one human and the other animal... a dog.

The human figure crept slowly and quite silently.

Casey Morgan heard not a footstep until the figure drew something from its hair; it glinted in the moonlight.

And then with one sudden move the figure jabbed it into the rump of Casey Morgan. The shock caused her to let go of Ruby and as she twisted around to face her attacker so Casey lost her footing, and tumbled away into darkness.

Her scream could not be heard because at the very moment of her falling so the bells began to ring, announcing the arrival of 1974.

Chapter 62.
1974

THE FIGURE LEANED DOWN to help Ruby up, and Ruby saw the silver chopstick glinting in her hand.

'Mrs Digby?' said Ruby. 'What are you doing here?'

'Just looking out for what's mine.' said the old lady.

'You know you saved my life?'

'All part of the service,' said Mrs Digby. 'No one messes with my Ruby.'

Then she hurried over to tend to Clancy, who was lying flat on his back while being licked vigorously on the face by the husky.

A searchlight panned across the rooftop and suddenly there shone the brightest silver light, brighter than the Venus star, so bright it seemed it could almost blind.

Ruby watched as the silver thing moved quickly towards her.

'Ruby?' came a voice. 'Look Brant, it's Ruby!'

Sabina's dress had become a mirrorball and as it moved so the light danced around it.

'Honey, you're much too close to the edge, you could fall,' said Brant.

'Yes, that occurred to me too,' said Ruby, taking her father's hand.

'Oh, and Mrs Digby!' said Sabina.

'Howdie,' said the old lady.

Clancy opened his eyes. 'Happy new year, Mrs Redfort,' he groaned.

'Are you OK son?' asked Brant.

'How jolly!' cried Sabina. 'How tout à fait joyeux! Our own little party! What a way to welcome in 1974.'

'I don't suppose you could give me a hand?' The call came from somewhere not quite on the roof.

Mr and Mrs Redfort peered over the edge of the building to see their house-manager dangling precariously, hooked on a single eyelash of the giant eyeball.

'Hitch, whatever are you doing?' asked Sabina.

'I lost a cufflink – I was just reaching for it when this happened.'

'Cufflinks,' said Brant. 'They're a terrible liability.'

'Thank goodness for a good suit,' said Sabina.

'You can always rely on Guy & Hills,' said Hitch.

'I think you should unhook him,' suggested Ruby.

'Yes,' said Hitch, 'I'm afraid my arms have gone rather numb.'

'It will be the cold,' said Sabina. 'Help him up Brant, darling, his seams might go.'

And just as Hitch was hauled back onto the roof so a helicopter hovered overhead and two figures began to descend, a woman and a man.

'At last,' said Hitch, and they all watched as Loveday Byrd and Agent Blacker touched down.

'Have we missed anything?' yelled LB.

'No,' shouted Ruby, 'I'd say you're just in time.'

'Gee, how exciting,' exclaimed Sabina.

'What a show!' said Brant.

'Is it a show?' asked Sabina.

'It's hard to say,' said Ruby.

'Well, *something* just happened,' said Sabina. 'What do *you* think, Mrs Digby?'

'You know what, Mrs R,' she said, looking up at the glittering figure with a placid expression. 'It's like I always say: ask me no questions and I'll tell you no lies.'

Two lucky escapes

It would seem Casey Morgan had been attempting to track down the child with the code in her eyes for the past eleven years. She had set elaborate traps hoping to draw the girl to her, though only two of these plots had come close to succeeding.

The first was printed on the back of a Choco Puffles packet and although Ruby had spotted it, solved it and even filled in the coupon with her name and address, the information had never reached its destination. This was due to her father's forgetfulness: he had neglected to mail his daughter's envelope and in so doing had undoubtedly saved her life.

The second lure was a yellow balloon printed with a smiley face and tied to a long pink ribbon attached to a brown parcel tag. Had Ruby thought to look, she would have seen that there was something contained inside that smiling yellow sphere, but she missed it, finding the brown label more desirable than the balloon. She had carefully detached it from the ribbon and then let go, watching as it climbed high into the fall sky before completely disappearing.

Heroics

From the Twinford Hound...

NEAR FALL AT THE EYE BALL

It was high-rise mayhem last night at the Eye Ball. The New Year extravaganza, dubbed "the only party in town", hosted by Twinford millionaires Mr and Mrs Gerald Hassensack, was brought to an early close when an intruder was spotted climbing up the side of the building.

Detectives suspect that the woman, Brenda Ulla Zane, was there to rob guests of their jewels and valuables. She was challenged by plucky thirteen-year-old Ruby Redfort, who in a hair-raising turn of events had to climb for her life in a daring effort to escape the robber.

Art 'Hitch' Zachery, house-manager to the

Redfort family, came to the teenager's rescue but was pushed from the rooftop by an as yet unidentified man. Mr Zachery was saved when his suit jacket became hooked on the Eye building's landmark giant blinking eye. When asked to comment on his heroics he said, "I would just like to thank my tailor at Guy & Hills".

The incident was brought to a close when housekeeper and senior citizen Mrs Myrtle Digby bravely confronted Zane, who in an attempt to evade the law, leapt, slipped and plummeted 34 floors to her death.

Brant and Sabina Redfort, parents to Ruby and employers of both Mr Zachery and Mrs Digby, said they were "relieved to have everyone home in three pieces".

The oak on
Amster Green

The six friends had spent the afternoon sitting in the Donut Diner, eating pancakes and catching up on the previous night's events, but it was now time to head on home.

'Rube, are you sure that butler of yours is actually a butler?' asked Elliot, as he pulled on his hat.

'He's a house manager,' said Red.

'Yeah, but he behaves like some sorta secret agent,' said Del Lasco.

Mouse turned to Ruby. 'Hey, maybe you should become a secret agent, you might be good at that stuff.'

'What, with my eyesight?' said Ruby.

When the others had gone, Clancy and Ruby climbed up the old oak on Amster green and sat for a while looking at the passing traffic and chatting about all sorts.

'So how did Olive react to you scribbling on her doll's head?' asked Ruby.

'Surprisingly well,' said Clancy. 'She was very excited about it, she thinks Buttercup is trying to communicate with her.'

'Because she has the words, "follow me back to Clancy", scrawled all over her face?'

'Exactly,' said Clancy.

'People will believe anything,' said Ruby.

'Tell me about it,' sighed Clancy. 'Now she's following me around like I'm some kind of superhero.'

'You're welcome to come and stay with us any time you like,' offered Ruby.

'Great,' said Clancy. 'I'll get the removal company to bring over my stuff.'

They sat there until the stars came out and it was time to say goodbye.

'Hey, Clance,' called Ruby, 'thanks for saving my life!'

'Any time!' shouted Clancy.

'And I forgive you for blabbing!' she yelled.

'I never blabbed!' shouted Clancy. 'I was truth-serumed!'

'I know it! Don't get your underwear in a bunch – I was kidding.'

'You could dangle me over a pit of wolves...'

'Feed your toes to crocodiles,' added Ruby.

'And I still wouldn't blab,' shouted Clancy.

'And you know why?' yelled Ruby. 'Because you're some friend!'

'It takes one to know one,' shouted Clancy.

A badge of approval

When Ruby walked into Spectrum 8 she was greeted by a friendly wave from the young man sitting in the middle of the round telephone desk.

'Go on in, Ruby,' he said, 'LB's expecting you.'

Ruby entered the office to find her boss sitting there in white, her feet shoeless. The only colour in the entire space: the red of her nail polish.

LB took no time getting to the point.

'Spectrum is very appreciative that you didn't give up the code.'

'That wasn't really down to me,' admitted Ruby. 'It's thanks to our housekeeper.'

'Yes, and how exactly did she come to be there at precisely the right moment?'

'You'd have to ask Bug,' said Ruby.

'You're suggesting I talk to your dog?'

Ruby shrugged.

'So this housekeeper of yours, can we trust her?'

'I think you can trust her with your life,' said Ruby.

'She won't blab?' asked LB.

'Not a chance,' said Ruby. 'But if you want to keep her sweet, then send her a subscription for *Poker Chips Quarterly*.'

They discussed the case, the events, the outcome.

The Lucite tag had been recovered but it was now nothing more than a key-tag; its fall from the rooftop had damaged it beyond readability. As for the Count, there was no sign of him at all. He had quite simply vanished.

'Is he alive, is he dead?' mused LB. 'I guess we'll just have to wait and see.'

And just as Ruby thought the debrief was coming to a close, LB threw her a curve ball.

'You seem to have a hard time managing rule number one. Why is that, Redfort?'

Ruby was caught off guard. 'Are you talking about Clancy?'

'I am indeed talking about Mr Crew.'

'The thing is,' Ruby began to explain. 'The thing about Clancy is he knows things without knowing things; he has this sixth sense.' She looked up at LB. 'Do you know what I mean?'

'Yes,' said LB, 'as a matter of fact I do.'

'You're saying you knew about him,' said Ruby. 'That I talk to him? How come you never said anything?'

LB held her gaze, unblinking. 'I had a best friend too, I know how it is.'

'But you stuck to the rules,' said Ruby.

'Quit looking at me like a dog who's lost a bone, Redfort.' She reached into the drawer of her desk and pulled out a circle of white tin. 'Here, it's yours, you deserve it.'

'Deserve what?' asked Ruby.

LB held out her hand. 'You made Larva, kid, the second child to ever make the grade.'

'But I thought I just broke rule number one.'

'Let's not be dramatic, Redfort. After all, rules are just rules and I think we all know, rules are made to be broken.'

Team players

Hitch was waiting for her when she exited the ice rink on Bowery.

'How did it go?' he asked.

'I got a badge,' said Ruby.

'For good behaviour?' he said.

'Something like that,' said Ruby. 'By the way, sorry for mistaking you for a psycho.'

'Perhaps it was my cologne that was throwing you off.'

Hitch was surprised that she had not figured out the part he had played in getting her into the Prism Vault. The access to Froghorn's code maps, the scytale cylinder, the clues he had given to her.

'What do you think that trip to the planetarium was all about?' he asked.

She shrugged. 'I thought you just liked it there.'

'Kid, I'm beginning to think you might be losing your edge.'

Ruby wondered why he hadn't just told her. 'Why be so cloak and dagger about it?'

But he only replied, 'I had to keep it all under the radar. I kept an eye on you though.'

'I felt like someone was watching me,' said Ruby.

The other surprise was how Hitch had come to realize that Buzz was Morgan.

'You know it was Froghorn who figured it all out, if he hadn't gone into the files that night and put two and two together, then you would have been toast.'

'I underestimated him,' said Ruby. 'I guess I owe him one.'

'I guess you do,' said Hitch. 'Give him a break why don't you, buy him a donut or something.'

'I might just do that,' said Ruby. 'I might even give him the whole box.'

'That's the spirit,' said Hitch.

And as they pulled up in front of Green-Wood House, Ruby said, 'You know, Hitch, you're some agent.'

And he gave her one of his winning smiles and said:

'Right back at you, kid.'

Crime pays

From the Twinford Hound...

Mrs Myrtle Digby and Ms Ruby Redfort are all the richer for appearing on hit quiz show, Thirty Minutes of Murder. The pair achieved an unprecedented perfect score when they answered every single question correctly.

'I was raised on horror movies,' said thirteen-year-old Ruby, by way of explanation, 'and I was watching TV Crime Night before I could run.'

The big cheque was presented by the show's producer Jovis Van Straubenzee in front of an excited studio audience. Myrtle commented, 'like my old Pa always said, crime does pay.'

A note on the Prism Vault codes

by Marcus du Sautoy, supergeek consultant to Ruby Redfort

Ruby has to break several codes in order to gain entry to the Prism Vault, all of them set by her arch-nemesis at Spectrum, Miles Froghorn.

The grid

Ruby is faced with two 10x10 grids of black and white dots. So how does she figure out that the grids encode a four-digit code number? Here they are:

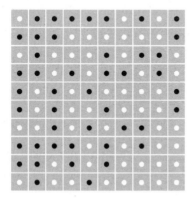 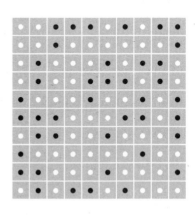

What she spots is that the grids have a rather interesting property, which reminds her of a book she saw in Froghorn's office about error correction codes. Ruby notices that if there is an odd number of black dots in the first nine boxes of each row then the last dot is black. If there is an even number, then the last dot is white.

The same is true of the columns. If there is an odd number of black dots in the first nine boxes going down a column, then the last dot is black. If it is even then it is white.

For example, there is an odd number of black dots in the first nine boxes of the first row so the last box in that row contains a black dot. But there is an *even* number of black dots in the first nine boxes of the first column so that last box at the bottom of the column has a white dot.

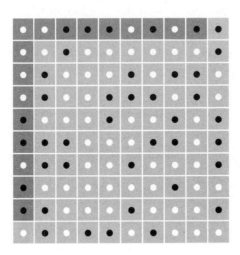

This type of code is called a *parity bit code*. It belongs to a family of codes known as error-correcting codes, which are used by computers to detect errors that might have crept in when they are sending messages via the internet or beamed between satellites. Error correcting codes like this are used in everything from encoding digital photographs to helping you talk to your friends on the internet.

You've probably experienced, when trying to talk to someone on a phone, that you can't always make out everything the other person says. When computers talk to each other, they have the same problem, but using clever mathematics we've managed to come up with ways to encode data that can get rid of this interference.

In real life, due to its simplicity, the parity bit code in particular is used extensively in computer-to-computer communication where large amounts of data are being transmitted.

This is because computers send most information in the form of binary data – a sequence of 1s and 0s. Parity bit codes are attached to these streams of data, telling the receiving computer whether there should be an odd or even number of 1s or 0s in the message. If the parity bit says odd but there is actually an even number, or vice versa, then the receiving computer knows that something has gone wrong.

That property of the parity bit code is key to how Ruby cracks it. Like a computer receiving a transmission, she notices that there seem to be mistakes in the grid: in one of the rows and one of the columns. Can you spot which row is wrong?

Look at the fourth row. It has an odd number of black dots in the first nine boxes but the last box has a white dot. It should be black! Also, the ninth column is wrong because there are an odd number of black dots and again the last box has a white dot.

Ruby realizes the mistakes are deliberate are are telling her that the first two digits of the four-digit code are 4 and 9.

Can you work out the other two digits from the second grid? Which row and which column are wrong?

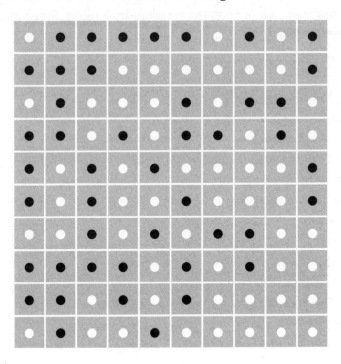

The chromatic code

Later, Ruby is faced with a code that involves listening to a sequence of musical notes, then playing a response on a keyboard.

The input device she sees looks like this:

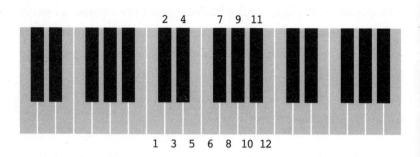

This code relies on the fact that there are twelve notes in a chromatic scale: a sequence of 12 white and black notes on the piano that are repeated.

If you number them from 1 to 12 then what Ruby hears are the notes:

6   7   5   8   4   9   3   10

She realises that the four missing notes are:

2   11   1   12

Which she has to play on the keyboard in order to access the files.

But how does Ruby know which notes to play? Well, in this case, she has noticed that the notes she heard belong to a famous mathematical sequence, and that the last four are missing.

The permutation of numbers is in fact a well-known card shuffle called the Mongian shuffle. If you have a pack of twelve cards numbered 1 to 12 in your right hand, then by continually taking top and bottom cards and placing them on top of a *new* pile of cards in your left hand you get this sequence:

6   7   5   8   4   9   3   10   **2**   **11**   **1**   **12**

Having identified what she is hearing, all Ruby has to do is play the four missing notes, shown here in bold.

This sequence of notes was used by French composer Olivier Messiaen in his piano piece 'Ile de Feu 2'. Interestingly, Messiaen, like Froghorn, was synaesthetic: he experienced musical notes and chords as particular colours, and used this in composing his music. Perhaps this is why Froghorn thought of him when setting his chromatic code.

PICTURE THIS...

Here are some ideas of mine about what the characters look like. I could be right, I could be wrong, and what is more, they keep changing. If you've read this far, you'll have your own images in your mind. There's very little description of the characters' appearances in the books because I wanted you to be able to form your own impression of them.

Lauren Child

...But Clancy I have always seen many different ways. He could be any one of these three (opposite and below). He looks a bit too young in this one (below right)...

RUBY

CLANCY

CLANCY

Mouse

...definitely looks like this. She's cool, she's quiet and she's a great observer of the world.

Elliot

...I did have other pictures, but I think this is him.

RED

...is one of the few who really can't change much: the long red hair, the freckles.

Del ...she's tall, tough, sporty and doesn't spend much time with a hairbrush in her hand.

Hitch

In my mind he was Cary Grant, but on paper he turned out square-jawed and tougher looking, more Gregory Peck (two old-school film stars, look them up).

Sabina & Brant

Elegant, charming Sabina, and handsome, affable Brant in his tennis gear. (Sabina looks rather serious here, but I'll let you in to a secret: it's much harder to draw people smiling. Teeth are tricky.)

Consuela

Si, Consuela. Now you understand why she attracted so much attention. It wasn't just the vegetable smoothies.

Mrs Digby

*...if you asked her how old
she was, she'd just say,
'Sixty, seventy, eighty?
Who's counting?'*

LB

...is another
chameleon. She
was inspired by
Lauren Bacall,
but I never
managed to settle
on a name for her,
which is why she
ended up as 'LB'.
By book four I
had decided she
looked more like
Pam Grier.

Lorelei
von Leyden

And Lorelei
disguised as Nine
Lives – who knew
she had such a nose?
You cannot find the
mind's construction
in the face, but if
you could...

Acknowledgments

I have been working on the Ruby series for the past seven years and have been extremely lucky to be surrounded by so many generous and inspiring people throughout. First I would like to thank some of those who worked directly with me to create the books and to produce, promote and sell them:

AD, Ruth Alltimes, Carla Alonzi, Martin Brown, Mary Byrne, Kate Clarke, Emily Faccini, Rachel Folder, Thomas Gardner, Nick Lake, David Mackintosh, Kerrie McIlloney, Lily Morgan, Phil Perry, Tanya Brennand-Roper, Alice Lee and the ID Audio team, Alison Ruane, Sandro Sodano, Marcus du Sautoy, Rachael Stirling, Geraldine Stroud, Sam Swinnerton, Nicola Way, Danny Webb, Sam White and all the HarperCollins team.

I would also like to thank the many booksellers, librarians, teachers and reviewers who have been so supportive.

Many friends contributed ideas, gave me feedback or generally helped me to get on with things. There are more than I can thank here, but in no particular order, thank you Marcia, Natalka, Neyla, Ilona, Aneta, Abi, Cress, Maisie, Jo, Quincy, Pete, Trisha, Simon, Ben, Richard, Conrad and Enzo.

Special thanks to the following for being readers: Lucy Grosvenor, Lucy Lardle, Georgie, John, Molly, Delfina, Bay, Louis, Lorelei, Matilda, Alice, Peps, Inaara, Isaac, Sarah, Stanley, Claudia, Albie, Vincent, Hal, Sasha, Beatrice, Josey, Sophia, Nell, Rachel W, Jenny, Cousin Lucy, Cousin Phoebe, my father, my mother, and, especially, Tuesday, who although too young to read or listen to the stories, still tells me she enjoys them.

Most of all, thanks to you for reading the books. I am very touched and grateful that you do. I have had some lovely letters about Ruby and seen some inspired Ruby T-shirts, drawings, phrases, and further adventures, so thank you.

Finally, huge thanks to my publisher, AJM, the LB of HC.